Inside the Video Game Industry

Inside the Video Game Industry offers a provocative look into one of today's most dynamic and creative businesses. Through in-depth structured interviews, industry professionals discuss their roles, providing invaluable insight into game programming, art, animation, design, production, quality assurance, audio, and business professions. From hiring and firing conventions, attitudes about gender disparity, goals for work–life balance, and a span of legal, psychological, and communal intellectual property protection mechanisms, the book's combination of accessible industry talk and incisive thematic overviews is ideal for anyone interested in games as a global industry, a site of cultural study, or a prospective career path. Designed for researchers, educators, and students, this book provides a critical perspective on an often opaque business and its highly mobile workforce.

Additional teaching materials, including activities and study questions, can be found at https://www.routledge.com/9780415828284.

Inside the Video Game Industry

Game Developers Talk About the Business of Play

Judd Ethan Ruggill, Ken S. McAllister, Randy Nichols, and Ryan Kaufman

Routledge
Taylor & Francis Group

NEW YORK AND LONDON

First published 2017
by Routledge
711 Third Avenue, New York, NY 10017

and by Routledge
2 Park Square, Milton Park, Abingdon, Oxon OX14 4RN

Routledge is an imprint of the Taylor & Francis Group, an Informa business

Library of Congress Cataloging in Publication Data
Names: Ruggill, Judd Ethan, editor. | McAllister, Ken S., 1966– editor. |
    Nichols, Randall K., editor. | Kaufman, Ryan, editor.
Title: Inside the video game industry : game developers talk about
    the business of play / edited by Judd Ethan Ruggill, Ken S. McAllister,
    Randy Nichols, and Ryan Kaufman.
Description: New York : Routledge is an imprint of the Taylor & Francis Group,
    an Informa Business, [2017] | Includes index.
Identifiers: LCCN 2016023991 | ISBN 9780415828277 (hardback) |
    ISBN 9780415828284 (pbk.) | ISBN 9780203521588 (ebk)
Subjects: LCSH: Video games industry. | Video games—Design. | Video games—
    Marketing.
Classification: LCC HD9993.E452 I67 2017 | DDC 338.4/77948—dc23
LC record available at https://lccn.loc.gov/2016023991

ISBN: 978-0-415-82827-7 (hbk)
ISBN: 978-0-415-82828-4 (pbk)
ISBN: 978-0-203-52158-8 (ebk)

Typeset in Warnock Pro
by Apex CoVantage, LLC

Contents

Acknowledgments

We are very grateful to the following people and groups for their interest in, assistance with, and/or support of this project:

Suellen Adams, Toni Alexander, Derek Bambauer, Matthew Beale, Megan Boeshart, Maury Brown, Mike Bruck, Bill Carroll, Bryan Carter, Kate Chaterdon, Tobias Conradi, Steven Conway, José Cortez, Zuleima Cota, Adam Crowley, Michael DeAnda, Jennifer deWinter, Jason Dewland, Gwen Downey, Javier Duran, Lyn Duran, Alain-Philippe Durand, Richard Edmiston, James Fleury, Sarah Elizabeth Fredericks, Jeremy Frumkin, Cynthia Gaffney, Ron and Elizabeth Gard, Angelia Giannone, Jason Gill, Harrison Gish, Daniel Griffin, Diane Gruber, Alexander Halavais, Chris Hanson, Bryan Hartzheim, Kati Heljakka, Gina Hernandez, Justine Hernandez, Zachary Hill, Nina Huntemann, Antonnet Johnson, Kim Jones, Jeffrey Kassing, Douglas Kelley, Barbara Kienzle, Carly Kocurek, Aynne Kokus, Kyounghee Kwon, Owen Leach, Jamie Lee, Adela Licona, Jonathan Madog, Megan McKittrick, Lindsey Mean, Marijel Maggie Melo, Kevin Moberly, Ryan Moeller, Mia Moran, Majia Nadesan, Jennifer Nichols, Jude Nicholson, Rolf Nohr, Dean O'Donnell, David O'Grady, Marc Ouellette, Jessica Paxton, Matt Payne, Anushka Peres, Ramsey Eric Ramsey, Roberto Reyes, Reneé Helen Reynolds, Quentin Rezin, Dave Rick, Theo Rohle, Lorenia Romero, Jane Ruggill, Robert Ruggill, Marjorie Sanders, Chris Schlerf, Ron Scott, Charles Watkins Scruggs III, Alice Srubas, Rachel Srubas, Deborah Spargur, Jason Thompson, Sam Tobin, Celeste Leigh Helen Trimble, Marlene Tromp, the fine folks at the University of Arizona James E. Rogers College of Law Intellectual Property and Entrepreneurship Clinic, Stephanie Vie, Jeremiah Webb, Bonnie Wentzel, Erica Wetter, Mary Wildner-Bassett, Karen Williams, Greg Wise, Women in Games—Boston, and Josh Zimmerman.

Author Bios

Judd Ethan Ruggill is an Associate Professor of Computational Media at the University of Arizona and co-founder and co-director of the Learning Games Initiative. He researches computer game technologies, play, and cultures, and is the co-author of *Tempest: Geometries of Play* and *Gaming Matters: Art, Science, Magic, and the Computer Game Medium.*

Ken S. McAllister is a Professor of Rhetoric and Associate Dean of Research and Program Innovation for the College of Humanities at the University of Arizona. A co-founder and co-director of the Learning Games Initiative, McAllister is the author or co-author of numerous books and articles on topics ranging from game preservation to critical technology studies.

Randy Nichols is an Assistant Professor in the School of Interdisciplinary Arts and Sciences at the University of Washington Tacoma. His research has focused on understanding the political economy of the video game industry and its intersections with other cultural industries.

Ryan Kaufman began his career at LucasArts Entertainment, and for ten years worked as a tester, designer, and content supervisor on games such as *Full Throttle, Star Wars: Rogue Squadron N64,* and *Star Wars: Republic Commando.* He is currently Director of Design at Telltale Games, contributing to titles including *The Walking Dead, The Wolf Among Us,* and *Game of Thrones.*

Introduction

When it comes to its inner workings, the normally voluble video game industry is remarkably silent. Like in a hot dog factory, the finished product is everything, while the creative process leading to that product is nothing—or at least nothing to be shared openly with the public. As a result, there is precious little information available to those interested in the business and labor of electronic play. This is not to say, however, that there is a paucity of information about getting a job in game development. On the contrary, seemingly dozens of books are produced each year that purport to proffer insider secrets and commonsense career advice about how to break into the industry, whether one is a programmer, musician, artist, or designer. Almost all of these guides include short interviews, extended pull quotes, or short anecdotes by well-known professionals, and they all directly or indirectly characterize the nature of making games for a living.

Such books rarely, however, convey much information about the actual day-to-day work of game development, and they say almost nothing at all about how that work is secured, funded, organized, outsourced, iterated, and ultimately either shipped or shut down. Rather, they tend to explain how to gain employment, not what it is like to stay employed. As a result, potential workers—and people who study games and the creative and corporate environments from which they emerge—have an exceptionally narrow view of this world, with glimpses of its inner workings only when stories such as "EA Spouse" or "Gamergate" hit the mainstream press.

The view is obscured further still by the fact that the game industry is supremely competitive. Even the largest companies may have slender profit margins, making intellectual property protection and its attendant self-imposed silences more doctrine than custom. Readers of this book will almost certainly come to wonder about the necessity of such secrecy. To us, it remains an open question; not only is the game market rapidly expanding globally—meaning that the zero-sum assumption driving much of this profit competition is suspect—but there are also significant marketplaces where a hyper-competitive stance is discouraged. Among these more open peers, game developers tend to be quite free in the ways they share corporate resources and information. They compare notes on how quality of life and team structure differ from company to company, and they exchange ideas and production techniques in ways that would almost certainly trouble their respective public relations and legal department counterparts working in more litigious countries.

What is particularly curious—perhaps even concerning—is that such information exchange is actually vitally important everywhere. The game industry is one in which job migrations are commonplace, whether due to greener pastures, personal needs, or professional necessity. Factors such as these routinely trump even the most terrifying pre-hire and severance contracts, creating a kind of dark network in which dialogue about changes in the industry emerges according to an unwritten code that guides insiders' career decisions not through published books but through barroom conversations and private messages. In addition to discussions about career options, game developers are also justifiably proud of what they do, so discussing their latest breakthrough with industry colleagues is understood to be a mutually beneficial activity, an opportunity for inspiration to fuel innovation. Such conversations happen casually most of the time, but there are also occasions for more formal collaborations and revelations, through presentations and postmortems at industry events such as the Penny Arcade Exposition (PAX) and the Game Developers Conference (GDC), as well as in trade-oriented websites like *Gamasutra*. Thus, access to intelligence about the game industry unfolds along a continuum, from the most public of social media exposés to the most covert late-night rendezvous.

One consequence of this protectionism, at least in the markets where workplace secrecy approaches the acuteness of national security, is that the game industry's immense public relations apparatuses must work hard to fill the resulting silence with shameless and excessive PR and point-of-sale promotion. Efforts like these effectively crowd out the possibility of candid insights into how the industry actually operates. It is also frustrating that the spirit of sharing so often valued by individuals in the game industry is commonly bracketed off from curious outsiders. A common anecdotal notion within the industry holds that this attitude stems from game development's roots in hacker culture, where insider bragging and sharing is encouraged, but outsider involvement is highly suspect and to be avoided. In our experience, most developers think deeply about what they do and how they do it, even though it can be difficult to observe this intellectual, critical, and creative work when one peers through the cracks between the fence boards surrounding the general game development project.

This book aims to pry at least a few of these fence boards loose so as to allow a wider view of how the game industry works on a daily basis for a relatively wide range of personnel. In general, we seek to clarify for our colleagues and ourselves the contemporary experience of game work. Our specific goal is to illuminate the industrial labor of the proverbial factory floor, and in the process relate some of the notable ways in which game workers conceptualize their jobs. Accordingly, we have gone straight to the source: this book contains eighteen critical interviews with professionals from across the industrial spectrum and with a wide variety of experience. All of the major game development disciplines are represented (programming, art, design, producing, quality assurance, audio, and business), as are the major market segments (individual contractor, independent studio, midsize studio, AAA studio) and geographies (North America, Europe, Australia). One notable exception to our investigations was Japanese studios, which, as we indicate below, proved uniquely difficult to coordinate with.

In terms of gender diversity, the interviewees roughly reflect the industry's demographics (Weststar and Legault), though we would have preferred a more proactive balance had we been able to arrange it. The interviews are broad in scope but narrow in focus, concentrating on labor issues and how they elucidate industrial economics, corporate/company structures, gender topographies, hiring and firing practices, marketing strategies, workplace practices, and other integral but often mystified mechanisms of game development.

Each interview is preceded by a biographical sketch of the interviewee, and the interviews are grouped according to development discipline. Each discipline is introduced with an explication of the job type, contains at minimum two interviews—generally one from a staffer and one from the game industry's equivalent of an executive from that type—and concludes with a discussion of the interviews and what they mean for understanding industrial game production. Disciplines with notable subdisciplines (e.g., animation tends to fall under the broader umbrella of art) or with deep leadership structures (e.g., programming) contain additional interviews to attend to that breadth.

Importantly, this book is intended for readers interested in the critical study of video games. It is not designed to entertain game aficionados or instruct students on how to navigate the job market successfully—by far the two most common rationales for giving game industry insiders a venue for their professional reflections and observations. That said, we would hope that both groups will find elements of interest and import in these interviews and analyses. We expressly downplay—and even reject, to a certain extent—the apprenticeship and fan approaches to labor that the game industry promotes. We did not produce this book to celebrate the industry but to explore it, and we believe that even potential new employees within the industry may well benefit from becoming more familiar with what their professional future might look like.

We also want to emphasize that this is not an ethnography, at least not in any comprehensive sense. To be sure, there are a number of features reminiscent of ethnographic research here: interviews, emic (i.e., insider) descriptions of local practices, historical investigation, critical cultural analysis, and a set of co-created workplace narratives that emerged through our iterative interview process. We even had direct access to an industrial worksite through our co-author Ryan Kaufman, a longtime game developer. Despite these similarities, however, *Inside the Video Game Industry* is what might be more fairly called a proto-ethnography. Assembled here are relatively detailed stories of life in the game industry offered by the people who live them, as well as a series of critical and interpretive reflections on those stories and their multivalent interconnections. What we do not provide is a detailed interpretation of the "webs of significance" (as Clifford Geertz would say) that these stories present, and which would be a hallmark of a fully formed ethnographic study. What we hope is that the work in this book will present some points of traction for readers who may be considering an ethnographic study of the game industry but are perhaps uncertain about where to begin or what significant industrial issues might be best investigated through the use of such a research method.

In light of these limitations, we make no pretense toward plenitude with this volume. In fact, two outstanding lacunae are publication and distribution. Publishers and distributors—who are sometimes one and the same entity (e.g., Valve Corporation)—are arguably the most important agents in the game industry, controlling as they do the means of production (i.e., money) and distribution. And yet, publishers and distributors are not typically considered game developers, at least not to industry information outlets such as *Gamasutra*, which accords neither group a distinctive category in its annual salary survey ("Transitions"). While there is excellent academic research on game production and distribution generally, it orbits primarily at the macro level, detailing an entrenched and highly concentrated market structure consisting of hardware production, software development, software publication, and retail sales (De Prato et al.; Kerr; McCrea; Nichols; Peréz Fernández; Portnow et al.; Sandqvist; Šisler; Williams; Zackariasson and Wilson). Just as with programming, art, design, producing, quality assurance, audio, and business—all covered in the present volume—the labor of game publication and distribution demands a close examination, but they are beyond scope of this book.

Another important clarification about this project is that it is not free from industrial influence. On the contrary, the interviews were sanctioned and vetted by the interviewees and their corporate higher-ups (and/or legal representatives) prior to publication. Such approval was necessary for both the interviews and their attribution; without it, even the most willing and loquacious of developers would have been difficult (if not impossible) to engage, and in fact we had a number of potential interviewees who were unable to participate in the project for precisely this reason. We also had interviewees and/or their companies pull interviews during the review stage for reasons (that seem to us) alternately reasonable and ridiculous. The truth of the matter is that the game industry and many of its laborers are simply too careful with their ideas and reputations to chance unwanted exposure, even when that exposure is for public benefit and guided by university professors who are legally and ethically bound by copious, detailed, and inviolable institutional review board requirements. For the industry, however, the risks are too high, the margins too slim, and the future too uncertain to gamble.

To an extent, we understand this concern, in spite of our personal interest in and professional obligation to the acts of discovery and knowledge production. And because we very much wanted attributable data, we accepted the recommendations of our industrial advisors and developed a data collection strategy that integrated a measure of corporate control over the content of our primary material while preserving full autonomy over the critical and editorial elements of the project. In our estimation, such primary data, though stamped with their respective corporate imprimaturs, ultimately feel more credible than anonymized or pseudonymized information, if only because in the context of video games one can actually play the games the interviewees worked on instead of just imagining what they might be like or gazing at them through the prescribed lens of a company's marketing machine. With attributed interviews, readers can peer into the game medium itself and see the tool marks of specific makers—makers who readers have come to know through these extended critical interviews. Attribution, in other words, allows for a more intimate understanding of the human face of game production, a face often obscured by industrial practice and predilection.

Attribution is also important for trust. If the game industry is to open up to researchers in ways other media industries have—and we hope that it will, to the benefit of scholars and developers both—it needs to be able to trust its interlocutors. Allowing the industry to have input on its image seemed to us a reasonable accommodation in the service of facilitating that trust. This is not to say that we abdicated our scholarly responsibilities and became corporate shills during the course of this project; one need only read the interviews and our analyses to see that our critical priorities are wholly intact and well in the foreground. Rather, we felt that corporate review was a price we were willing to pay for access and attribution.

Along this same line, it is important to remember that this book is the product of an academic/industry partnership. While three of us are university professors (Ruggill, McAllister, and Nichols), the fourth (Kaufman) is a game developer. He has worked in the industry since the mid-1990s and is now Director of Design for one of the most critically and commercially acclaimed game companies in North America, Telltale Games. Consequently, this book is a hybrid of academic and industry epistemologies, interests, communications, and concerns. It occupies neither sphere completely nor comfortably, a quality we see as a strength. Indeed, we are excited about the possibilities of future academic/industry knowledge making of this kind and the insights it might bring, and we view this book as a small but important first step (for us) in that direction.

Before concluding, a few words about our process of data collection are in order. The interviews contained in this book are semi-structured and draw from both written and oral interactions. Based on our research and on interviews we had conducted previously (Nichols; McAllister and Ruggill; Ruggill and McAllister), we expected certain motifs to pepper the interactions: staffing structures, collaboration, unionization, ownership dynamics, project workflow, outsourcing, career trajectories, and recruitment and retention. Therefore, while we approached each interview as unique and organic, allowing the conversation to evolve according to the interests and orientation of the interviewees, there were certain questions we asked of everyone based on our expectations and on our desire to establish a distinctive and shared foundation to our inquiries and the book in general. The stock questions we asked were:

1. What are the most significant internal and external challenges you face in your job?

2. What sorts of workplace changes would you implement if given the opportunity?

3. How is the work you do in the game industry different from the work you have done elsewhere?

4. Are there model companies or ways of working (both within and outside of the game industry) that you look to for inspiration?

5. What are the dominant challenges facing the industry over the next decade?

6. How would you describe the management structure and workflow in your company?

7. How does the workflow differ when working on different types of games (e.g., different genres, AAA versus casual games, etc.)?

8. What are some of your notable quality of life issues and career progression issues (if any)?

Not every interview includes answers to these questions. In some instances, the interviewees elected not to answer them; in others, the answers were redacted by the interviewee (or the interviewee's corporate/legal counsel) due to non-disclosure issues or public relations optics. In still other instances, we exercised our editorial authority to expurgate indelicate responses for the sake of the interviewee's job security, career opportunities, and public image. After all, this book is not meant to be a whistle-blowing tell-all about corporate intrigue, horrible bosses, and insufferable coworkers—though such topics did crop up. Rather, it is intended to be an inside look into an industry that from the outside looks nubilous.

On the subject of redaction, it is important to understand that all of the interviews are heavily redacted in one way or another, occasionally due to content but always due to length. There just was not enough space to include everything, even if we had wanted to and the press would have allowed it. With that in mind, we have endeavored to preserve the flavor of the interviews as much as possible in our editing, even when that meant including sometimes less-than-juicy material. Our goal was to preserve the argot and authenticity—with all of the freight these terms carry—with which the developers spoke.

Also, given the care with which we orchestrated the interviews ahead of time, we were surprised to discover that the process of securing final approval to publish the interviews sometimes proved more than a little challenging. One company, for instance, invoked a standing policy whereby the company name is not to be used by employees in interviews. However, this same company also has a policy requiring employees to self-identify as such when doing any kind of public relations, creating a confusing brand identity paradox and obliging us to work with the interviewee and company to suss out exactly what would constitute compliance (both, as it turned out, were to be enforced). There were other curious interactions surrounding the "need for appropriate messaging," as one interviewee described it, including several interviews that were so heavily redacted upon review as to be completely unusable. In these instances we were reminded of Captain John Yossarian's censoring of military letters in Joseph Heller's *Catch-22*, where only the salutations were left unexpurgated. In less drastic cases, our back-and-forth exchanges took more than a year to finally gain corporate approval to publish. We can only caution researchers interested in pursuing similar kinds of industrial relationships that patience, a sense of humor, and a decent command of the law as it pertains to defamation are helpful.

Additionally, the challenge of finding interviewees willing to go on record was not always only complicated because of brand management and employment concerns; sometimes it was also due to the general industrial workload that virtually everyone making video games experiences. Many of the developers we approached were interested in participating but were too busy, with some apologetically dropping out in the midst of the interview process because of project deadlines, changes in employer, or other workplace issues. Even the interviewees who were able to make it through to the end of the process often required creative and patient scheduling on our part. Game developers, we discovered, are busy regardless of the country or size of the studio in which they work.

As we noted earlier, the challenge of the game industry's many languages and cultures also shaped this book, most notably in the conspicuous absence of interviews with Japanese game developers. This was not for lack of trying on our part. Unlike our colleagues Aki Nakamura (Ritsumeikan University) and Bryan Hikari Hartzheim (Reitaku University), for example, whose institutional affiliations and knowledge of the Japanese language and customs have given them considerable access to that country's game industry, we were unable to move any Japanese developers or their companies through the entire interview process.

The effects of these various challenges can be seen most clearly in the resultant interviews considered as a set. Not every position or studio is represented, clearly, though there is considerable diversity and coverage in the collective work history of the interviewees. Game developers are itinerant and their professional relationships incestuous, largely by industrial mandate. As almost every biography in this collection chronicles, to work in games means to move, sometimes leaving colleagues in one company to (re)join others at a different one. Again, however, this book is not meant to provide a detailed accounting of the industry, nor a comprehensive critical analysis of its inner workings. To do either would require volumes, and even to try would be, to some degree, disingenuous. The game industry is neither monolithic nor standardized; its positions, practices, and practitioners vary widely depending on studio size, corporate vision, personal ambition, target market, business strategy, geography, management style, and more. To suggest otherwise would be to give the lie to a surprising truth: the game industry is in many ways quite diverse (and in other ways, not so much). There are, however, certain themes that cut across this diversity, and are capturable only in a collection such as this one. The issues of workload, quality of life, aging, and the importance of interdisciplinary communication, for example—themes that appear in virtually all of the interviews, and that together depict an industry that is both invigorating and enervating—all emerge particularly strongly here, no matter how established the company or how long in the tooth the employee.

Rather than comprehensive, then, this book is suggestive, an aerial snapshot of the industry's workforce and its labor relations. It is intended to enable developers' voices to be heard, not in the paradoxical isolation of a barely read personal blog, nor slicked back with frictionless Madison Avenue pomade, nor (we hope) inscrutably entombed in the discourse of academic researchers. Instead, we mean to hand the microphone to a wider variety of industry experts than is ordinarily assembled, to hear their voices, and to attend to the remarkable candor and insight that their talk reveals about the work they do every day.

▶ WORKS CITED

De Prato, Giuditta, Sven Lindmark, and Jean-Paul Simon. "The Evolving European Video Game Software Ecosystem." *The Video Game Industry: Formation, Present State, and Future*. Ed. Peter Zackariasson and Timothy L. Wilson. New York: Routledge, 2012. 221–43. Print.

Fernández, Agustín Pérez. "Snapshot 2: Video Game Development in Argentina." *Gaming Globally: Production, Play, and Place*. Ed. Nina B. Huntemann and Ben Aslinger. New York: Palgrave Macmillan, 2013. 79–81. Print.

Geertz, Clifford. *The Interpretation of Cultures*. New York: Basic Books, 1973. Print.

Heller, Joseph. *Catch-22*. New York: Alfred A. Knopf, 1995. Print.

Kerr, Aphra. *The Business and Culture of Video Games: Gamework/Gameplay*. London: Sage, 2006. Print.

———. "The UK and Irish Game Industries." *The Video Game Industry: Formation, Present State, and Future*. Ed. Peter Zackariasson and Timothy L. Wilson. New York: Routledge, 2012. 116–33. Print.

McAllister, Ken S., and Judd Ethan Ruggill. "On the Practice of Contemporary Computer Game Development: An Interview with Ryan Kaufman." *Journal of Media Practice* 12.1 (2011): 89–93. Print.

McCrea, Christian. "Snapshot 4: Australian Video Games: The Collapse and Reconstruction of an Industry." *Gaming Globally: Production, Play, and Place*. Ed. Nina B. Huntemann and Ben Aslinger. New York: Palgrave Macmillan, 2013. 203–07. Print.

Nichols, Randy. "Ancillary Markets—Video Games: Promises and Challenges of an Emerging Industry." *The Contemporary Hollywood Film Industry*. Ed. Paul McDonald and Janet Wasko. Malden: Blackwell, 2008. 132–42. Print.

———. "Who Plays, Who Pays? Mapping Video Game Production and Consumption Globally." *Gaming Globally: Production, Play, and Place*. Ed. Nina B. Huntemann and Ben Aslinger. New York: Palgrave Macmillan, 2013. 19–39. Print.

———. *The Video Game Business*. London: British Film Institute, 2014. Print.

Portnow, James, Arthur Protasio, and Kate Donaldson. "Snapshot 1: Brazil: Tomorrow's Market." *Gaming Globally: Production, Play, and Place*. Ed. Nina B. Huntemann and Ben Aslinger. New York: Palgrave Macmillan, 2013. 75–77. Print.

Ruggill, Judd Ethan, and Ken S. McAllister. "Testing, Testing, One, Two, Three: Quality Assurance and Game Development." *Journal of Gaming and Virtual Worlds* 4.3 (2012): 289–95. Print.

Sandqvist, Ulf. "The Development of the Swedish Game Industry: A True Success Story?" *The Video Game Industry: Formation, Present State, and Future*. Ed. Peter Zackariasson and Timothy L. Wilson. New York: Routledge, 2012. 134–53. Print.

Šisler, Vit. "Video Game Development in the Middle East: Iran, the Arab World, and Beyond." *Gaming Globally: Production, Play, and Place*. Ed. Nina B. Huntemann and Ben Aslinger. New York: Palgrave Macmillan, 2013. 251–71. Print.

"Transitions: Gamasutra Salary Survey 2014." *Gamasutra: The Art & Business of Making Games*. UBM Tech. 22 Jul. 2014. Web. 10 Oct. 2015. <http://www.gamesetwatch.com/2014/09/05/GAMA14_ACG_SalarySurvey_F.pdf>

Weststar, Johanna, and Marie-Josée Legault. "Developer Satisfaction Survey 2015: Summary Report." *International Game Developers Association*, 2 Sept. 2015. Web. 1 Feb. 2016. <http://c.ymcdn.com/sites/www.igda.org/resource/collection/CB31CE86-F8EE-4AE3-B46A-148490336605/IGDA%20DSS%202015-SummaryReport_Final_Sept15.pdf>

Williams, Dmitri. "Structure and Competition in the U.S. Home Video Game Industry." *JMM—The International Journal on Media Management* 4.1 (2002): 41–54. Print.

Zackariasson, Peter, and Timothy L. Wilson. "Marketing of Video Games." *The Video Game Industry: Formation, Present State, and Future*. Ed. Peter Zackariasson and Timothy L. Wilson. New York: Routledge, 2012. 57–75. Print.

1

Programming

▶ INTRODUCTION

Programmers—also known as engineers, or more colloquially, coders—develop and modify the software environments, apparatuses, and technical assets that enable games to be built, compiled, executed, and played. This work may occur within a commercially available game development suite (e.g., *Unreal Engine*; *Unity 3D*), a proprietary development environment, or a combination of the two, and can involve scripting as well as programming. Additionally, programmers are tasked with optimizing the software's process performance—including the development of patches and hotfixes—as well as additional post-release content.

Programming personnel typically occupy one of three primary position classes—programmer, lead, and technical director—with the lead and technical director serving in a broad supervisory or administrative capacity that usually involves interfacing with other development disciplines and the public. Depending on the game type or studio size, programmers may take on specialty roles, focusing on engine, tools, artificial intelligence (AI), or network development, for example.

As a result of specialization, programmers often work closely with one or more other development disciplines. A graphics engineer, for example, may work with the art department to create new visual effects, simulating camera lens flare or optimizing the number of characters or particles on screen at a given time. Similarly, AI programmers may collaborate with game designers to create specific non-player character behaviors and movement patterns in order to greater challenge players.

Because programming typically requires a high level of technical proficiency, programmers have often earned at least an undergraduate degree in computer science/engineering prior to entering the programming discipline. Like other software engineers, programmers tend to use common programming languages such as Java or C++ in their work, though they sometimes adapt these languages to the needs of a particular game or software application. As a given piece of game code can be used for many purposes, from displaying graphics on-screen to simulating artificial intelligence in creatures and enemies (all of which must be integrated and work well with many other pieces of code), using a common codebase is highly desirable among programmers, especially those working in large teams.

According to the 2014 Gamasutra Salary Survey, programmers earn an average annual salary of $93,251 in the aggregate ("Transitions" 2). Programmers with fewer than three years of experience earn an average of $71,855 annually, while programmers with six or more years of experience earn an average of $103,789 per year (Ibid.). By comparison, lead programmers and technical directors with six or more years of experience earn an average of $116,151 and $135,781 annually, respectively (Ibid.). Additionally, US-based programmers earn approximately 12% more on average than their Canadian counterparts, and 50% more on average than European programmers (Ibid.). Finally, male programming personnel average $93,977 per year, while female employees average $79,318 annually (Ibid.).

John Sietsma
Programmer

John Sietsma is a programmer and educator. He is currently on the faculty of the Academy of Interactive Entertainment, and previously worked for Many Monkeys Development, Chocolate Liberation Front, League of Geeks, Dekko Experiences, Big Ant Studios, Transmission Games, Arterial Software, 80–20 Software, Spinifex Computing, and Victoria University in a variety of capacities, including as lead programmer, senior programmer, programmer, technical director, games developer and designer, and creative developer. He has also worked as a freelance developer. He holds a master of technology degree in intelligent systems from the Royal Melbourne Institute of Technology and a Certificate IV in Training and Assessment from Selmar Education Institute. His shipped titles include *Armello, Wollongong University Kinect Experience, Oscura: Lost Light, Oscura: Second Shadow, Table Top Speed, Dekko Monkey, ACO Virtual Orchestra, Jewel Collector, Rugby League Live, Heroes Over Europe,* and *Ashes Cricket 2009.*

* * * * *

How did you come to work in the game industry?

I was a professional software developer for seven years before I joined the game industry. At one point during that time, I was working on a search engine that had some intelligent features and I was also playing a lot of games. That combination got me thinking about non-player characters and how they behave, which in turn made me want to study that stuff further. So, I enrolled in a graduate program to study intelligent systems, and my research focused on modeling emotions in non-player characters. I then got a job as a tools programmer in a game studio and soon became lead of the internal technology team. After that, I moved into making augmented reality games. During this period of my career, I worked independently for companies that weren't primarily games companies but tech and venture-oriented organizations. After that, I got involved in starting a game studio, and now I'm a game programming teacher.

Is AI still of interest to you?

Believe it or not, I've never done any AI in games, even though that was the reason I entered the industry. I suppose the psychological aspect of AI remains interesting to me, but the technical stuff has dropped away. As I've progressed through my career, I've become more interested in game design, and this was particularly so when I was doing augmented reality work. That sort of work is really about how people experience a new technology. What affordances are there? What experiences can people get that are unique to this particular combination? I still keep up on stuff related to the psychology of game playing, and I read regularly about how to design for the different emotional states players go through during play.

How do you apply this knowledge to your development process?

I apply it all the way through development, but especially at the beginning because that's the danger place in terms of purely functional design. You actually see this a lot in indie games, where the design revolves around a particular mechanic or functionality. I think programmers often naturally fall into the engineering role, where they think, "I'm going to make this game, I'm going to take this mechanic and put this twist on it, and that's what's going to make the game really great."

I try to focus more on the player experience really early on and adopt it as an essential decision-making tool. I ask, "What am I feeling here? What's the goal?" and I use my answers as a reference for design decisions. If the game is about a sense of wonder and surprise, for example, then I'll use that sense as a reference when I'm thinking about the mechanics, aesthetics, and what I'm going to add to the game. Doing this enables me to fact-check the design against the player experience or emotional state I'm shooting for.

What are the principal job tasks of a lead programmer?

Communication with the other departments is a big one. There's also some task scheduling typically, but the job is mostly about having a knowledge of everything that's being built, managing the team of programmers that's doing the building, and providing technical design advice. Another way of thinking about the job is that it involves a lot of talking to people when they're building different systems, making sure those systems are being built in a good way, and ensuring that the builders are getting lots of feedback. Additionally, being a lead programmer means managing team spirit, and making sure people are pulling together. It also means writing code yourself. If there are any gaps in the development process, you fill them. You take on jobs that others haven't gotten to, and you write systems.

The great thing about game development is that you have all these disciplines working together, and it's really enjoyable to be a part of the group. But you have to be careful to make sure that you're communicating well and understanding what other departments need. Being the lead programmer means thinking beyond programming and staying connected to all the work being done in the other development areas. That's true for all the disciplines in game development, and part of what makes development so challenging and rewarding.

What are some of the workplace similarities and differences in the companies you have worked for?

When I worked for Dekko, the augmented reality start-up, development was very much focused on getting funding. Everything we did was short term by necessity. You had goals to attain over the span of a few weeks that were vital, which were then replaced by a new set of vital short-term goals after the first ones were achieved. This is different from typical game development, where you have just the one major goal of seeing a game completed at the end. There are short-term goals in typical game development too, of course. There might be a festival coming up or a publisher coming in and a certain feature needs to be ready. But those goals are in the context of a much longer development cycle, which is the main focus. With Dekko— and really any start-up—our focus and efforts were much shorter. We might need a thirty-second grab to show investors, or a brief demo to get into the news somehow. Everything was much smaller scale, including the timelines.

The augmented reality technology and experience in general was also new when I was at Dekko. As a result, there was a lot more cycling around ideas, a lot more rebuilding things and re-doing parts of a given game over and over again based on testing or just trying out new ideas as we were feeling our way around. That kind of work is also different from more conventional game development because the process really involves looking for something you can put into an investor's hands that they'll immediately understand and can have a great experience with even if they aren't interested in games. The target market for the products with Dekko was the investor, not the consumer, which makes you think about the processes and goals of game design and development differently.

When you're making a game for an investor who has no games experience, you want something that may not necessarily be challenge- or progress-based like a more conventional game. That's because you need to be able to put the person at the start of the experience and have them immediately enter a very small loop that's instantly enjoyable. This is especially important with a new technology or an inexperienced audience. If someone isn't used to games or how to control them—particularly with something new like augmented reality, where most of the mental battle is getting used to how things work—then the game itself has to be a very light experience. It needs to not be frustrating at all, because you don't want someone to pick up the game and immediately die or fail to fulfill its challenge. So a lot of game building for an investor involves going for other senses such as wonder, excitement, or perhaps even an entirely different emotional register than you'd find in traditional games, which tend to focus on challenge and mastery.

As far as conventional game development, I've worked at two large studios: Transmission Games and Big Ant Studios. Both were about 100–150 people. Transmission was interesting because it was my first large studio, and we went through a big structural change while I was there. When I started, there was an engine team and an art team, and the engine team would spend months making something and then throw it over the wall to the art team. Often, what we made would be wrong, and so the company structure was reconfigured into strike teams. These strike teams worked really well. Depending on the game, there'd be a cinematography team or a terrain team, and each would have a producer, designer, artist, and programmer. It'd be a mix of people, and they'd concentrate on a particular aspect of development. This removed a lot of the communication barriers that had plagued the company previously. Programmers were less prone to making stuff that they thought was fun or might be needed at some time in the future and instead were able to focus on solving specific problems to get a game feature done.

It's important to mention that neither Transmission nor Big Ant were highly structured at that time. In fact, they seemed chaotic compared to the ordinary IT programming world I'd been in. It was interesting coming from outside the game industry, because there was a lot more process around what we did there than what you typically find in games. In non-game-oriented software development, there are lots of procedures related to schedules, risk management, how to code, how a feature gets implemented and checked off, and so forth. It makes a huge difference in terms of delivery. Take the game *Heroes Over Europe*, for example. It was scheduled to be in development for a year to a year and a half, but it ended up going for over four years. Software schedule overruns are common in any industry, however I think that with *Heroes Over Europe* it was a symptom of the lack of process. The finished product in those large game studios was always six months away, or two months away; it was never ready. I don't think they'd learned to use the techniques developed in the enterprise software world that allow leaders to sit down and really schedule something to make sure it'll be delivered on time.

There was a lot of work that was thrown away too, a lot of stuff that didn't quite work. For example, the PlayStation 3 has a different architecture than the PlayStation 2, and so we needed a new job system for *Heroes Over*

Europe. We spent three or four months writing that system only to find out that it wasn't suitable and didn't fit in with the rest of how the game worked. There was a lack of communication or lack of checking beforehand, which resulted in a big chunk of work being thrown in the garbage.

Likewise, I worked on a city generation tool meant to recreate some of the great European cities during World War II. The idea was to be able to generate Berlin or London as a fully destructible environment. We worked on that tool for about six months, and when we showed it to the artists they said, "That's not the look we're going for. The inside of the blocks is all wrong. We're just going to do it by hand." Again, work wasted and the timeline extended.

It was these kinds of things that fueled the transition to strike teams. Instead of having the engine team just make stuff—which might not have been vetted by people outside the team—strike teams made it much easier to show programming work immediately to artists, designers, and producers to see if it was on the right track. Before the restructuring, programmers ended up wasting a lot of time and then artists didn't necessarily have the tools they wanted to do their work.

How was it possible for the development of Heroes Over Europe *to continue over such a long a period and with so many fits and starts?*

I think there was probably a bit of a gambler's fallacy going on. In fact, our publisher actually went bankrupt during that time. It must have always seemed to the publisher that the finished game was only six months away, and they weren't prepared to throw away the huge investment they'd already made if the game was so close to completion. But the completion date kept stretching and stretching, and we were working on other games at the same time, some of which were in pre-production but never went into full production.

At that time in game development, maybe 80% of the technical work was engine-related or systems-related as opposed to gameplay-related. That's a big difference from what you might see today, especially on an indie team, where almost all of the work has to do with building and refining gameplay. Back then, some of the internal technology we needed to create as part of the development process was to build systems designed to enable a fast turnaround. The goal was to make it so that if an artist was working on a model, she could make a change in the model and have the least amount of friction getting it seen in the game environment. That meant being able to process the asset, convert it, and transfer it—to rebuild the game, transfer it to the target console, and then see it on the screen. We actually spent a lot of our development time just on facilitating this kind of workflow.

Some systems we worked on were performance-related. The games needed to be able to render particles or do some sort of calculation, and there was the whole technical challenge of how to do that efficiently. And in the case of the PlayStation 3, the challenge was how to spread that work across multiple processing cores where before it had just been done on one. So there was a lot of effort spent on performance-related stuff, which, as you can imagine, also took a lot of time.

How is the work you have done in the game industry different from the work you have done elsewhere?

First of all, the game industry pays less. I took a major pay cut when I moved to games, and I continue to get paid far less than I would working as a software developer elsewhere. Also, there's less career growth in the game industry. Because there aren't a lot of large studios here in Australia, there aren't many career options beyond starting your own studio.

On the other hand, the game industry is more creative than other parts of the software industry. I get to work with people with really diverse skill sets, and we often go outside the technical brief. The game industry also has a strong internal culture. People making games tend to come from a distinct subculture, which can make the environment more community oriented and fun than other parts of the software industry.

The thing about games is that it's a creative industry, and so they do the pay scale differently. There are a lot more people who'd like to get into games and there's much more competition for game jobs, which affects salaries. It's a supply and demand thing. Again, I took a hit when I moved into games; I think that's the nature of the industry. I took a pay cut of about a third—maybe a little more—when I did my first games job, and that relative difference has remained throughout the course of my career in games.

It's definitely a little tough to accept the fact that you're getting underpaid, but I also think you need to do things you find interesting. I've certainly enjoyed my time making games, and there's an important quality of life question to address if you're doing work you don't really find interesting, even if it pays well.

What are the fundamental skills required in game programming?

There's the learning of a programming language or languages, obviously, and there's a mind shift that happens when you do that. There are things that click into place where you understand something according to a programming way of thought. Once you have a language down, you need to be able to think on a larger scale, so again there are design patterns and ways of organizing things. Using a given programming language to do something can involve a lot of complicated problem solving, and with games it's good to know about how various systems like the rendering engine work. It's also good to know about game trees, spatial partitioning, and other game-specific techniques, even if you're using a game engine. It's really helpful to know what goes on under the hood. Then there's all the teamwork and softer skills that are important for programmers to learn. Things like good communication skills, asking the right questions, and an ability to work effectively with people in other disciplines all make for a better programmer.

What does the game programming workflow typically look like?

The first stage is pre-production. We prototype unknown or risky gameplay areas, write documents that give the central vision of the game design and make important technical decisions, and evaluate the scope and budget of the project. Pre-production is essentially focused on reducing risks. If you're unsure about your gameplay, then you spend your pre-production time making sure you know your gameplay is right. By the time you go into production, your unknowns should be reduced so you can then really just start cranking things out and making adjustments on the fly as timelines shift. And if you're a lead programmer, it's your job to communicate what it all means. If someone says, "We want to change this to that," you have to say, "Well, that means X in terms of time or Y in terms of risk." As a programmer, regardless of rank, you have to give feedback so that people can make informed decisions.

The next stage is production. Here you break down game design into tasks. You regularly check your progress against your goals, and use tasks completed to estimate forward progress and risks. Ideally, you're also able to change the scope or budget as you come to better understand the project.

The production stage can be more or less iterative depending on budget and time pressures. I like to track progress closely so that I can accurately estimate what we can get done in the future. I emphasize knowing the risks and rate of progress as early as possible so that good business and design decisions can be made in response. It's perfectly valid to spend more time perfecting a mechanic or starting again with something new, but I want that to be a decision that's consciously made rather than something that just happens.

The last stage is post-production, which includes delivery, support, and so forth.

With augmented reality and other new technological arenas, the work is pretty much all pre-production. You're just looking for ideas. You're looking for hooks and ways you can do things in a studio. With more conventional development, programming pretty much all happens during production. The design is settled fairly early on and so a lot of the work left to do is just getting the jobs done. You make a lot of lists in terms of the final goal and try to figure out how to break things down, measure progress, and that kind of stuff. I suppose my take on project management is always that most software engineering projects are going to be late by some degree, and trying to make sure that doesn't happen isn't always within your control. So, the role of the lead programmer is to identify problems with the timeline as early as possible and to make the best decisions going forward. When I worked for Chocolate Liberation Front, we had a fixed budget. There was no more money for things beyond what was in the bank, so if we were late, we didn't get paid. That meant that every week we measured. We looked at what we did the last week, we looked at our complete progress through the game, and then I made decisions: "Okay, we're running late on levels. Let's cut the levels and we'll get some extra help."

How does the workflow differ when working on different types of games (e.g., different genres, AAA versus casual games, etc.)?

New genres and technologies require more pre-production to validate ideas. When I worked in augmented reality, for example, most of my time was devoted to solving interaction issues or iterating game mechanics. With the freelance work that I do now, the budget tends to be fixed and the mechanics better known. Most of these projects are all about production, that is, getting tasks done and managing risk and scope.

What is interdisciplinary communication like from the programming side?

I personally haven't had any drama between the disciplines, but I've noticed that there are big differences between the disciplines' outlook, character, and how they approach work. That can often be a point of contention, and it's not unusual to hear snide comments and to have eye rolling between the disciplines. The disciplines do tend to segregate, and I don't know whether that's a programming culture thing, an art culture thing, or just because they often sit separately.

The programmer's job is to go and ask questions, to find out what's going on. Programmers often do things because they enjoy programming; they see a system they want to build and get excited about it. They then build it but it winds up not being useful to the given project. For me, I really try to connect with people and find out what needs to be built, and I do this by going and asking questions. Regular communication is really important. The thing is, programmers don't always naturally go and talk to people about what they need. A generalization is that programmers tend to be introverted. In my experience, the strike team model works really well because when you actually get people to sit next to each other, there's more natural and productive communication.

What are the most significant internal challenges you face in your job?

I've worked at a few companies that have been in financial trouble. This has meant a lot of stress and long hours trying to meet deadlines, which has had negative impacts on me and my family. Most game companies have younger employees who don't have children, and the corporate culture often equates life sacrifices with dedication and passion. After a number of years of overtime, I started to put limits around the amount of overtime I'd do, and this caused issues with my employers and coworkers. Needless to say, I find the academic side of things to have a much better family environment.

There's another challenge related to age, too. We made a lot of *Armello* without any funding, and therefore the company had a revenue share model . . . which I found very difficult. I came into the games world quite late, and a revenue share model works best for young people, who have a greater percentage of disposable income. I have three children, and so a remuneration model based on sweat equity for a later payoff is tough. After two and a half years of putting my own money and time into the project and then trying to work around the needs of my family, it was just too much. Keep in mind, too, that the development time on that project was close to five years. So, that's a big ask when you're doing it without getting paid, when it's all sweat equity. Obviously, I had another job at the time, and so I'd often work four days a week at that job and then spend a day working on *Armello* or just do things on the weekends and nights, fitting them in whichever way I could. I was able to do the work, but at the expense of my personal life.

What are the external challenges you face in your job?

The big one is a lack of development opportunities in Australia. There are few big companies still around, and there are few small companies with the money to hire experienced developers. The big challenge of being an individual game developer is that it's difficult to be self-sustaining. There are a lot of games being released, but that actually makes it hard to make a full-time living on the independent side—there's just a lot of competition.

Which companies or ways of working (both within and outside of the game industry) do you look to for inspiration?

As far as ways of working go, I use an Agile methodology in my development work. I've found that it helps me get accurate estimates on things and allows me to work with low production risk. In terms of companies that inspire me, I like Valve's way of working, although I'm wary of informal power structures replacing formal ones. I like the worker-centered ethos and the creativity that comes out of what they do. They have a flat management structure, and you work on what you find interesting. In my experience, people often get stale or burned out when there's no room outside of their specific role to explore. It's nice to have a studio environment with fuzzier boundaries between disciplines and what you work on. At Valve, you can decide to work on things that interest you, and that really helps you develop as a person as well as be more useful to the company. I suppose that's a little more human-centered rather than process-centered in terms of the end result.

How has game programming changed over the course of your career?

The biggest shift recently has been the move away from individual engine development. When I worked in large studios, the work often centered around building a custom engine or modifying one built in-house. These days, the work in a lot of studios has shifted to working within existing engines rather than building custom ones. A lot of the game development principles have stayed the same; it's just the engine emphasis that's changed on the programming side.

What are some of your notable quality of life issues, both routine and exceptional?

As I mentioned, working long hours is often seen as a sign of commitment, which clashes with my family time and has led to issues for me. Likewise, the mental effort and intensity of the work has often meant that I spend non-working hours in recovery mode. And of course, a career of lower pay has meant that I have less retirement savings than I would if I worked in another industry.

It was interesting coming into the game industry as an adult without having been part of a game subculture. It was a big culture shock walking into the studio for the first time and seeing toy figurines everywhere and people dressed unconventionally. People who get into game development are often part of a game subculture, and I think that really shapes which sorts of games get made and how developers think about their jobs. It keeps some of the less desirable parts of the game development cycle going sometimes, and that's something I'd like to see change. I think the industry needs to get more people from different backgrounds interested in making games. That would open up things a lot more.

Also, most of the large Australian studios are gone, and a lot of the work they used to do is now done in Canada and elsewhere. It's hard to find work here, which creates a tough situation, quality of life–wise: Do you stay and try to make something happen, or do you move to another country?

I've definitely gotten a lot better as I've gotten older in terms of knowing where my personal and work boundaries are. I've realized how ineffective crunch is, and that if you want to make and ship a game, it's a lot more about your development practices than the number of hours you put in. Putting up boundaries around your time, though, can be a problem because people often see this as not having enough passion or not being willing to support the team. The game industry can be a really strong, supportive place to be. It can also be alienating.

What are some of your notable career progression issues?

As I've said, there aren't a lot of game development jobs in Australia. I've been making games for nine years and programming for nineteen, but I apply for the same jobs that new university graduates do. Unfortunately, a lot of development roles don't require the experience I've gathered outside of programming, such as game and interaction design.

Can you see yourself returning to the game industry full-time?

If I went back full-time, I probably wouldn't want to work for a studio. I left the industry due to quality of life issues, and I wouldn't really want to go back if those structures hadn't changed. At the moment, I enjoy teaching and the interaction with students. I'm learning new skills and I still have time to work on games. When I make games now, the process is much more about self-expression or things I find interesting.

Do you teach with the strike team model in mind?

In my program, our teams are already strike teams because there are only six to eight students on a team. So, they're all blended anyway—there aren't enough people in the class for students to go and sit in their disciplines. That said, there's definitely still an issue in the sense that all of a sudden students from different disciplines are making projects together, and that means a lot of cultural differences. The students don't know each other, and there's definitely an effort that needs to be made to get their communication working well. So, we try to get them working on projects as early as possible, even if those projects are just game jams or little things. The goal is to get the students used to working with other people, which is fundamental to game development.

Has the growth of the mobile sector influenced how you teach design and development?

In some ways the growth in the mobile market has made it very hard to know what to teach. I try to teach fundamentals that are platform agnostic and then get the students to apply those fundamentals to a particular project so that they have skills that are transferable. The idea is that they have the ability to find their feet quickly, regardless of the size of the studio they wind up in. The technical barrier is lower in mobile development than in console development, and you can teach someone how to use *Unity 3D* fairly easily and get them to make a game. But they wouldn't be equipped to go work in a larger studio or on a larger project. So I try to teach base-level skills that can be applied anywhere.

In development today, there are definitely two systems with two different skill sets. I think it's great because now anyone can make a game. As a result, there are a lot more people who can make mobile games or simpler games but don't necessarily have the complete skill set for working in a big shop.

What is the logical conclusion to this divergence in skills and game types?

I think what it means for development going forward is that there are going to be fewer specialist roles. Certain types of positions—graphics, for example—will continue to hire, because graphics are such a big thing. There'll continue to be graphics programmers and graphics-specific work in larger studios because those places have their own specialized teams. But because it's getting easier to make games across the board, a lot of other specialist roles will disappear. People will just become more focused on game making in general, rather than on a particular facet of it.

How do you broach these challenges with your students?

I'm quite honest with them about the challenges of the industry. Game education courses in Australia have boomed in recent years, and we're now producing all these people who are going to find it difficult to get work. I think the top students in my classes will find employment because there are new studios forming. Most of my students won't find work in games locally, though, and will have to transfer to another industry or go overseas.

What other challenges are facing the industry over the next decade?

Shifts in game player demographics and interests will be difficult for some developers. There's also the problem of the popularity cycle. Most industries and platforms go through a boom and then consolidation phase. Even though there are a lot of indie studios starting up here in Australia, games will become dominated by big players again, which will squeeze out some of the smaller developers. Concomitantly, finding niches, especially outside of traditional gaming genres, will be a necessity, not just an opportunity.

Gender diversity is another major issue. I've worked with very few female programmers and I think this is one of the reasons games can be so myopic and repetitive. I really hope we get more diversity in the industry and some more ideas brought to the medium. Importantly, there's a lot more openness in the indie community to the issue of diversity. There are already specific events around women and gaming, for example, and there are a lot more people who make games as personal expression. For some people, game development doesn't necessarily have to be their career, so I think that'll open things up. I think we're going to start seeing more diversity in the business structures and motivations of the game industry generally, with the indie community leading the way.

It may take a while for these changes to happen, though. Lots of the small studios here in Australia aren't actually employing people yet. Many of them consist of just the founders, or maybe two or three people working on a game. These people are often doing the work for sweat equity or very little money, and so it's not a stable employment environment. I think that'll change over time. As some indies get established, they'll become larger companies, employ more people, and provide more stability. So, right now, it's very exciting and people are making interesting games, but they're working away for years without a stable income, which isn't sustainable over the long term.

John Alvarado
Lead Programmer

As the former senior software engineer and now technical director at inXile Entertainment, John Alvarado is an industry veteran. In addition to his thirteen years at inXile, Alvarado has logged many additional years with companies such as Designer Software, MicroProse, LIVE Studios, Virgin Interactive Entertainment, Seven, Big Grub, Shiny Entertainment, and Interplay Entertainment, and in positions ranging from president (Big Grub) to artist (*Spec Ops: Airborne Commando*) to voice-over cast (*Choplifter HD*) to tech support (*Super Caesars Palace*). His earliest credit runs back to an Atari *Centipede* conversion for the Commodore 64 in the 1980s, and since then he has shipped more than thirty titles on virtually every major platform of the last three decades. From his 3DO Interactive Multiplayer version of *Demolition Man* to the recent *Wasteland 2*, Alvarado's games represent the widest possible range of genres, styles, studio sizes, and project complexity. Alvarado holds a bachelor's degree in linguistics and computer science from the University of California, Los Angeles.

* * * * *

How did you come to work in the game industry?

I began making games with friends in high school for the Apple II, Atari 800, and Commodore 64 (C64), just for fun. We loved playing arcade games and wanted to make our own. Our experience led to a contract job with Designer Software to port *Centipede* for Atarisoft from the Atari 800 to the C64. It went from there.

What is the day-to-day rhythm of your job now?

These days, I'm mostly on one project, which is pretty cool. In the past, I've been overseeing multiple projects, but we're at the tail end of *Wasteland 2* and trying to get started on our next project, *Bard's Tale IV*. When I first get to work, I usually check my email. There are always people sending me email who need an answer sooner rather than later. We're dealing with a lot of localization tasks at the moment, so that's a big source of questions. Localization is what we call the process of adapting the game content for other countries (making it work for the locality in which it's played, hence the term "localization"). In addition to translating the language (text and voice-over), localization may require adapting other game content for the sensibilities and/or requirements of non-US cultures. For example, in Germany they don't allow blood and gore for games below a certain age rating, so you have to put switches in the code to turn off those effects for the German release. At the moment, we're trying to get the last-minute localization fixes in for a *Wasteland 2* patch that's coming out. As a result, I'm in constant communication with the localization teams. We did crowdsourcing localization for this project, which was cool because it was like free localization, but not really free because it took a lot of my time to work with these different groups. It was a fun process, but a lot of work.

After I've dealt with the most important things, what I do next depends on what phase of the project we're in. Right now, since we're in a patching and fixing phase and using bug-tracking software, I'll look at the list of current bugs to see what I need to work on. Even though I'm the technical director,

I'm still a day-to-day programmer as well. I try to get in as much programming as possible. Usually the best time for me to program is early in the morning or in the evening when everyone's gone, because there are fewer interruptions. During the day, there are lots of meetings and people asking questions about the code or localization. I try to do as much coding in the middle of all that as possible, but it's not easy. That's a typical day.

In terms of the general structure of a workday, it's flexible, but we're responsible for getting in eight hours of work. We also have what are called "core hours" during which we have to be at the office. That's between the hours of 10:00 a.m. and 5:00 p.m. so that we overlap with each other for a certain amount of time. If you just come in from 10:00 a.m. to 5:00 p.m., that's obviously not eight hours, so people either have to work later or come in earlier to get in their eight hours. If someone is coming in late—past the 10:00 a.m. core hours time—they have to call or email a supervisor and the human resources manager. We also use an internal social media app called *Yammer* that lets people post to their colleagues that they'll be late. If you forget to do this, someone from human resources or your boss will come over to remind you to let people know when you're going to be late. Other than that, no one's really tracking our hours; people just notice whether or not you get stuff done. If you get stuff done and the project is meeting its goals, then no one complains. I think it's like this at most places. The industry is goal-oriented and companies just want to make sure that people are on track with their milestones.

Personally, I haven't needed to stay late or work a lot of crazy hours for the last few years, which is really good. This seems to coincide with the moment we started crowdsourcing our projects, which allowed us to have better time and goal management. It's definitely nice to not be under the thumb of a publisher. We still have crunch periods here and there when we're trying to push something like our first alpha or beta to Steam, or when we're close to actually publishing and trying to get in all the polish we can to make it the best game possible. For the last few projects, crunch has really been self-imposed by the employees rather than by the company saying that everybody has to work twelve hours to get the project done. Everyone knows what needs to be done and people work hard because they want to make the game great.

I'm not saying that crunches are totally avoidable though. The fact is that if you're passionate about the product you're making, you're going to encounter a crisis point when the product needs to be finalized but you still want more time to iterate on it and improve it. So as the end approaches, even though the game is all there and is pretty good, you still want to make it better. You end up spending every little bit of available time to get in those last little details, those last little bits of polish that you've had on your list for a long time but haven't been able to get to. I'd call this a good kind of crunch, where it's self-imposed because you're excited about the product and you're wanting to make it shine as brightly as possible. This is different from the kind of crunch where you're doing the death march just to meet your milestones so that you get paid or don't get canceled by your publisher. That's a very different sort of crunch.

How do you balance being both an administrator and a programmer, two very different roles in the industry?

The most important part of this balancing act for me is to not bite off more than I can chew on the programming side. We typically have some other lead programmer on whatever project we're working on; I'm just supposed to be helping out as necessary when there's a particularly technical challenge or there's something that I have a lot of experience with (like localization). "Balance," then, happens simply by not saying "yes" to too many things. When I say "yes" to too many things, that's when I end up with self-imposed long hours to do the jobs I said I would. As I said, when I'm at the office, there are lots of people, design decisions, and various other interruptions to contend with, so it's hard to get programming done. Basically, I try to divide up the day and create chunks of programming time when I can work uninterrupted for a while.

This is pretty common for people who have dual roles like this. I've known people at other studios working in similar positions, and they have the same challenge: how do you balance your time between getting your hands dirty in the code, managing a team, and watching the schedules to ensure that all the mundane tasks of game development are getting assigned out to the appropriate people and completed? You just have to divide up your time so that you spend part of the day doing management, and other parts of the day doing coding.

Is it professionally precarious to be a boss during one part of the day and a worker in the trenches later?

I think that one of the things about most workplaces is that there are regular formal reviews to tell you how you're doing from the boss's perspective. These can be good because they help you understand where you are professionally, but they can also make you feel a little precarious, especially when you're doing more than one job. It's hard to do two jobs well simultaneously. Interestingly, though, I haven't had many formal reviews in my career, so I haven't felt that precariousness very often. In the beginning, of course, there were more formal reviews, but at a certain point I took on more responsibilities, and my bosses really just wanted to know that things were getting done. If they were, then the bosses were happy, and I got raises, and there wasn't a lot of formal reviewing going on. Occasionally, I ask for a raise, and I usually get it.

In the long term—that is, over the life of a project—how this balance between project management and programming unfolds depends on which phase we're in. Toward the end of a project, the balance tips toward programming and away from the organizational role. This is because at that point, you're at beta and basically done with the game, but there are still a lot of bugs. The administrative work in this phase is really just assigning out all the bugs to the people in charge of the relevant areas of the code. Once that's done, you just go to work on the bugs, troubleshooting the ones assigned to you. There's also a middle period, too, which emerges once production is really underway and the big tasks have been handed out. At this point, the big systems have to be implemented and tested, and people know where they're headed. They've got big chunks of work to do, so there are fewer meetings and more programming going on.

How would you describe the management structure in your company?

There's a hierarchy consisting of top management (CEO, president), middle management (directors and producers), and developers (programmers, designers, artists). Despite this hierarchy, it feels fairly flat because the upper levels delve into production (design mostly), and they listen to feedback from the developers, so it feels much more collaborative than hierarchical.

How would you describe the workflow in your company?

Development goes through phases over the course of developing the game: high concept (defining the sensibilities and goals), pre-production (specific design), production (design implementation), iteration (making it fun), and finalizing (making it "bug free"). The edges of these phases can be a little blurry or overlapping, especially between pre-production, production, and iteration.

How does the workflow differ with different types of games (e.g., different genres, AAA versus casual games, etc.)?

For games that have a small scope—for example, mobile games—the process is similar to more complex ones, but less time is spent in the high concept and pre-production phases, and more time is spent in production and iteration. Nevertheless, all the parts are still there.

What are some of your notable quality of life issues, both routine and exceptional?

At the most basic level, proper nutrition is a challenge, as companies tend to stock up on processed snack foods and drinks to keep developers going during late nights. My company has been pretty good about providing healthier options like fruit, instant oatmeal, and granola bars. The fact of late nights is another challenge for those of us with a spouse and children.

But even when work hours are normal, it's easy to neglect exercise and good nutrition. For years, I've taken advantage of our proximity to the beach to run along the shore at lunchtime a few days a week. More recently, I've switched to running daily in the early morning to train with some hard-core runner friends for races. I find that having athletic performance goals helps motivate me to exercise and eat healthy. This year, I finally achieved a big goal of running a marathon in under three hours. Back in May, I ran the OC Marathon in a time of 2:51. I proudly hang my marathon medals over my desk at work, including a Boston Marathon medal from 2011. There's a story behind that one. I'd qualified in a local marathon but didn't plan to run Boston because I didn't want to take time away from work to travel just for a race. But when I mentioned it to my boss, Matthew Findley, he said something like, "Are you kidding? Not many people get that opportunity. You'd be crazy not to take it. You gotta do it!" So we scheduled the vacation time, and I took my wife and three sons to Boston for a week to tour the city and run the race. It was a great time, and I'm grateful to inXile for that kind of encouragement and for the flexibility in work hours that makes it possible, even in the face of the many challenges of game development.

We're pretty good at inXile about acknowledging and addressing these challenges, including being realistic in our design phase about what can really be accomplished without requiring a death march from the developers. We also plan out how to cut parts of the design if it becomes necessary. But there are inevitably periods during the project (especially at the end) where we demand more of ourselves in order to put out the best product possible. When this happens, we invariably neglect other parts of our lives. This is just part of being passionate in a creative career.

What are some of your notable career progression issues?

I started my own company (Big Grub) with some partners at one point and did more management and design, even as I was still programming. The company lasted seven years, but I really spread myself too thin and my family suffered the most, financially and emotionally. I've been much more successful focusing on one role (technical), but have inevitably been pulled into management as a senior developer because I have a lot of experience. At three different companies, I've been tasked with taking over technical management of a project after the previous lead left or was asked to leave. Balancing those roles is challenging, but still not as bad as when I ran my own company.

I admit that I still think about striking out on my own again. I know my wife wouldn't like that idea. When I did it the first time, we lived pretty lean for a number of years. I was able to pay my employees but wasn't necessarily paying myself all the time, so it was a burden on my family. The thing is, once I decided to come to inXile, I found that I really enjoyed the work here and enjoyed the fact that there are actually people assigned to the different roles I had to do myself when I ran my own company. At this point, I think that if I were to start another company, it wouldn't be in the games business. I've been pretty happy here and I really like the people I work with, so that do-it-myself itch hasn't come up again in any serious way.

Another part of what makes striking out alone less than appealing is that inXile started out with a philosophy that was intentional about improving quality of life issues. Even the location where they chose to locate the business, right next to the beach in Newport Beach, speaks to this. The founders wanted to be able to go out surfing in the morning, and today we have a whole bunch of surfboards lined up on the wall here. Even though there are now just a couple of surfers in the company, in the early days a lot of people surfed. In fact, when I came here, it was my boss who taught me to surf. I ended my surfing career shortly after it began when I got stitches in my head from the board hitting me, but we still go out and play beach volleyball and soccer on the soccer field nearby. The founders wanted to have a company culture where getting outdoors and playing in nature was part of the daily routine. It was their sense that sometimes the best thing for game development is actually getting your mind out of the code. And it can be really helpful. Going for a run on the beach and getting my mind off a problem I'm struggling with can be the perfect way to find a solution.

In any case, they made the decision early on to try to strike a balance among work, play, and private life. In the early days of a start-up, of course, you end up having to work hard just to survive and to meet your milestones. But over time, the company has gotten better at not biting off too much at the start of a project and at realizing when we need to cut things so that we don't have to do a death march of work to get it done. It's also been my own decision to not stay too late or sacrifice myself too much. I need to be willing to make those difficult decisions, to cut things or do things in simpler ways—I can't only depend on the company to make those decisions for me. Each developer has their own set of ambitions and goals, and they need to make their own decisions about whether or not it's right for them to push themselves to work long hours to achieve what they're hoping to achieve. As I've gotten older, I've learned that I'm better off not overdoing things and instead being smarter about planning. I've also realized that what really ends up making a better game is when people don't overcommit and don't work themselves to death.

You have been in the industry a long time, which is unusual. Even more unusual, however, is that you tend to stay in the same job for a long time. What is it about you and your skill set that allows for such longevity?

Part of it, I think, is that I'm very good at what I do. As a result, companies usually want to keep me around. On top of that, I approach my job such that I don't see my employer as an adversary. Instead, I see myself as being part of the company, and given that the company's success is important to me, I align my interests with the company's so that we're working together. The times I've left a company—for example, when I left Virgin Interactive to start my own company—I did so not because I didn't like it there anymore, but because starting my own company was an ambition I'd long had. So I did it. And then I got to find out how hard it is to run your own small development company. Even then, though, I stuck with it for about seven years.

Another reason is because I'm generally a pretty loyal person. I've often found that my commitment is rewarded with more responsibilities. This was true at Virgin, then at Shiny Entertainment, and now here at inXile. During the Big Grub days we contracted at Shiny because I knew David Perry (founder of Shiny Entertainment) from my days at Virgin. He needed some help on *Wild 9* and *R/C Stunt Copter*, and we were between game projects and needed work. At one point on *R/C Stunt Copter*, the producer from Interplay, Matthew Findley, asked me if I could take over and ship the product without the lead programmer. I said yes, and the lead was gone the next day. I took over and we shipped the game. A similar thing happened when I joined Matt at inXile a few years later, and that's how I went from senior software engineer to technical director. These additional responsibilities I take on mean that I'm more valuable to the company. It also usually means that I enjoy my work more—so I stay.

I also think I'm easy to work with, so that helps the company want to keep me. Working well with others is the most valuable skill after your primary professional skill. Everyone has opinions on game design and even on implementation methodology. This leads to conflict. What I've found to be the most important part of turning conflict into consensus is demonstrating that you value other people's ideas. You do this by listening to them and truly understanding, and then repeating back what they're saying before offering alternatives or pointing out problems. Also, giving credit to people for their ideas and their work when talking to others is huge. For example, if a designer comes to me with an idea for a feature that I begin to think isn't worth the amount of work it would require to implement, I don't immediately say that. I first ask questions to understand what they think this feature adds to the game—what feeling they're trying to create in the player, or what problem it solves for the player's interaction with the game. Then I make sure I understand the details of the feature enough to be able to implement it. Then I discuss what I think it would take to implement the feature, including time and art/audio resources. Sometimes, along the way I've changed my mind about the value of the feature, or about how much work it'll take (having better understood its details and scope), and I'm happy to carry it forward. Sometimes they begin to see that the cost is too much, and then we brainstorm other ways to achieve the same thing, but now we're on the same side and they're ready to listen to any ideas I have. I guess that's the crux of it—getting people to feel that you're on their side so you can work together toward mutually agreeable solutions. Active listening and giving credit where it's due are two ways to do that. To do this effectively requires cultivating in yourself a true desire for your teammates to succeed, which may seem obvious, but some people fall into the trap of competing with their teammates for approval and attention of their bosses and other coworkers. That's bad for the team and the project.

Here at inXile, we went through a really rough period a while back. We had, at one point, an entire mobile division plus a major AAA console title in development. We had around eighty people here in our small space in Newport Beach. Then things got tight and the economy went bad; publishers weren't wanting to do deals anymore, and we couldn't find a big console project for the company. We had to lay people off, including a bunch from our mobile division. We actually got down to twelve people at the lowest point, and I was one of them. I really wanted to see us come back from that and succeed because I really love the people I work with. We started looking at some creative funding ideas, including starting a new studio in Southeast Asia. I made a trip to Singapore with my boss to seriously explore that possibility and to talk to the government there about their incentives for game companies.

But this was also right when the whole Kickstarter trend blew up because of Tim Schafer's project. I'd previously talked to my bosses about Kickstarter and wanted to try it for some of our smaller "passion projects" that we wanted to do but that no publisher was going to pay for. At first, they didn't believe that people would pay a company (versus a small indie developer) to develop a game. They thought we'd look bad, as an established company, asking for donations. That was early in the Kickstarter phenomenon, of course. When I saw Schafer's project go big, though, I immediately contacted my bosses and they were already on it. That's when we did our Kickstarter for *Wasteland 2* instead of trying to open a Southeast Asia studio. So, yes, I've been willing to stick through the lean times and keep being creative, which makes me valuable to my employers and keeps a seat open for me.

I think my longevity in both the industry and in particular jobs also emerges from the fact that I've developed a diverse skill set over the years. I was fortunate to have gotten into the industry early, which has meant that I've been able to grow with it. Like I said, I started small with just a couple guys in a room and got to do some art, and then I started learning programming. And even though that project was small, it still had a deadline and a budget, so from the very beginning I was also being made sensitive to business elements like money and deadlines. I also got to experience early on what it feels like to ship a product. It's surprisingly difficult to do this, actually, and some people aren't very realistic about what they can get done in a certain amount of time. Having started small, though, I think I learned early on what my limits are and how to be realistic. Just knowing when you have to cut stuff, or when to not overdesign, or even when to bite off a little bit too much then be willing to work hard to get the project done and get it out the door, are great skills to have. Not to know your limits means canceled projects, which I've also had one or two of here and there, mostly for reasons out of my control. With experience—working on lots of projects, starting my own projects, building up to bigger projects with more people—my skill set has expanded, which makes me pretty versatile.

Is it this versatility that makes for a good technical director or lead programmer?

Yes, I think so. As a lead programmer, you have to keep your eye on the big picture. Part of the lead programmer's job is to aim for making the best game possible, even while pushing back on the designers when they start asking for cool new features that are going to require too many programming resources. Part of the production management side of things is recognizing (as a programmer) how much work will be required to add new systems to the game. You have to try to strike a balance between passion for the game and understanding that there's a limited amount of time and resources to make it. This requires someone who's not only smart about programming and time management, but also about leadership of people other than programmers. This is really important for the lead programmer.

One of the things that'll sink a project is committing to too much—art, music, technical systems, levels, whatever. When you throw too many features into a game, you never get to the point where you can really polish them all. It's really important early on, therefore, to limit the scope of what you're attempting to do given the budget and deadlines you have so that you can get to the iteration point of game development when you're crafting all those aspects that make the game fun. You only get to polish a game that's basically finished; that's when you start improving and tweaking all those details that make it really fun. If you put in too much stuff at the start, you'll never get to this iteration phase, and at some point you'll realize that you'll either have a bunch of poorly implemented features in your game or you have to cut stuff like crazy, which will then likely mean that the parts aren't cohesive anymore. Having discipline early on, not trying to do too much, having a plan—these all require versatile and experienced leads. As long as everyone has the same basic vision and knows all the signposts, cool new ideas that come up can be assessed accordingly. Metrics are part of this and will tell you when you need to pull back and, for example, go to plan B because you're not as far along as you'd intended, which means not enough time for polish. A good plan actually includes moments when you can decide to cut certain things.

Versatility is also important for technical leads because sometimes there are heated discussions between designers and programmers. Some programmers are fairly conservative in terms of game development; that is, they're risk averse. They aren't willing to try to reach for something great because they're afraid that it's going to be too much work for something that can't succeed. As a result, they'll overestimate how long it'll take to do something. Because I've worked with all kinds of different people, I can usually recognize when this is happening and make a decision based on my own experience. Sometimes this takes a little bit of pushing and helping people to become better problem solvers and collaborators. In some cases, their estimate would be realistic if they were working by themselves with lots of unknown quantities, but that's not usually the case in an established game company. There are lots of resources available to help keep things moving forward. Sometimes I can just sit with programmers and show them a different approach from the worst-case scenario they were imagining, and they'll realize that the change isn't too bad.

Part of your versatility, then, involves good communication skills?

Absolutely. One of the industry's big challenges is that designers aren't necessarily programmers, so it's hard for them to look at a feature on the surface of the game and understand what's going to have to happen under the hood to support that façade. But without that kind of technical understanding, it'll be hard to assess whether or not that feature will be worth the time spent generating it. On the other hand, designers get tired of hearing from programmers that every new feature is going to take a long time to implement; as a result, they often don't trust programmers' assessments, and come up with ways to convince a boss to add the feature so that the boss will tell the programmers to go figure it out. Technical leads need to understand these dynamics and find ways to explain to everyone involved what's realistically required for each new feature in terms of data structures, programming, assets, and so on. Without doubt, the most successful designers and producers are the ones who have some technical experience, because then they can communicate with programmers better.

By the way, just to add to the importance of good communication skills, it's important to know that there's another side to how programmers estimate the length of time it'll take to add a new feature. Rather than overestimating, they'll underestimate, sometimes by as much as 20%. It's a tough job that producers and designers have wrangling programmers.

As an industry veteran, do you have opportunities to mentor people coming up through the ranks?

Usually the mentoring I'm able to do is more on the programming rather than management side. I've had a number of occasions to bring in new people fresh from college. I've even gotten some high school interns, who are great to mentor in a real-world context. I remember a kid when I was at Big Grub, a high school student who had sent me his résumé and a sample game he'd made. He was just looking to do some work with any game company that would have him. I saw his passion for making games, and I really loved that he was already making games on his own and that he wanted to get involved in a company. I called him back and interviewed him, then brought him in as an intern. He told me that he'd sent his stuff out to game companies all over the place, and I was the only one who responded. That kid was Bryan Perfetto, who now works in Amazon's gaming division. After working for me as an intern, he went to college, and then I hired him back afterward. Later, when I started working at inXile, I hired him here in the mobile division. I really enjoy helping people who have a passion for developing games and giving them opportunities to grow.

Over the years, as I've looked at résumés and interviewed people, it's always been more impressive to me to see someone already trying to make games on their own than someone who has a computer science degree but has never worked on a game. I'll usually take self-taught people because I think their passion is crucial for being in the industry. To stay here, you have to really want to make great games, be willing to work hard on them, and be able to enjoy them even though you also make them. This passion also makes for good teammates.

When I see passion for the industry in others it reminds me of my own, which I've had from the very start. I remember being in high school and playing games at the arcade, which then inspired me to make games with my buddies. We started by cracking open the manuals and figuring out how to program an Atari. I learned that I really enjoyed all aspects of the game development process, from design to programming to all the management that goes into creating a finished product. Having passion for the industry helps you avoid burnout because it helps you see how many ways there are to work within it. As a result, you have a chance to exert more influence over the work you do and are less likely to feel like a cog in the machine (which is where a lot of burnout comes from). When things keep changing—the technology, the projects—it stays interesting.

In your experience, are more people being hired into the industry because they were specifically trained to be game developers in school, or because they are passionate autodidacts?

I'm not sure about the industry as a whole, but we've done all of the above. We've hired people straight out of computer science programs, from game schools like Full Sail University and similar game development–oriented institutions, and from university-based game programs like the one at the University of Southern California. We've also hired people with no college degree, people who are just passionate and self-taught. One of the guys we hired for our mobile division was like that. He'd done a lot of work modding *World of Warcraft* user interfaces and stuff like that, all self-taught. It got him in, and he worked out great.

How big are the teams you usually manage? Does their size and disciplinary diversity vary from project to project?

They definitely vary. We've done mobile games as well as console and PC games. The mobile teams are really small—maybe one programmer and a couple of artists. Console games, on the other hand, may have half a dozen programmers and maybe a dozen artists. That said, it's common for there to be multiple mobile projects in development at the same time, so multiple people still have to be managed, even though they're working on several different games. I don't think I've ever had to program on mobile and console game development at the same time. Or program on mobile and PC games at the same time. However, I have simultaneously managed multiple teams working on separate mobile, console, and PC games. Modern game engines, such as *Unity 3D* and *Unreal Engine*, enable the simultaneous development of console/PC/mobile versions of the same game, but I have yet to work on a project where we develop them all simultaneously. Usually we lead on PC and then implement console or mobile versions later. For example, we developed *Wasteland 2* for PC with the *Unity 3D* engine, but we didn't give any consideration to the console versions until after the PC version shipped. Doing so would have drained some resources from the PC version, and we didn't want to shortchange our backers on the PC game we promised to deliver.

How has the industry changed from a technical perspective in your experience?

It's changed quite a bit from the very first paid project I worked on, where it was just me and my best friend, Gregg Tavares, doing everything. On *Centipede*, I was doing the art, and he was doing the programming. Later, I started doing some programming as well, but at first it was just a couple of guys in a room coding and making art until we'd ported the entire game. With that game, we started with the Atari 800 code and ported it to the Commodore 64. It took us six weeks and we were paid 3000 dollars, which we split. But we hardly cared about the money. I was so excited about that game when it actually made it into stores—it was an incredible feeling, as I was just out of high school.

Our next project was to recreate the *Mario Bros.* arcade game on the C64 just based on looking at how it worked on the original arcade machine. We didn't have the code or any art assets at all. Fortunately it was a favorite game of ours, and we had already spent many hours (and quarters) playing the game in two-player mode. We were very familiar with it, but I still spent a lot of afternoons at the local arcade observing the attract mode and making sketches on paper of the level layouts and character animations so I could recreate them faithfully on the C64. I worried that the owner would kick me out for loitering because I wasn't dropping any quarters in the machine, but fortunately that didn't happen. This was the first professional game where I did a little programming—I programmed the collision-resolution code that made Mario and Luigi bounce off of each other. It was all in 6502 Assembly. We actually finished that game, but it was right at the time when the game industry crashed, so Atari never published it. I found out many years later, when I was working at Virgin Interactive, that it had gotten leaked into the pirate circuit. A couple of my coworkers at Virgin Interactive, Gary Priest and Doug Hare, were from the UK and said it was one of their favorite games. It was funny how this came up. We were talking about old games and the C64 became the topic. They said *Mario Bros.* was one of their favorites. I said, "What? I made that game, but it was never released!" That's when they told me about it being on the pirate circuit, which made me really happy. I was glad to know it had gotten out there and that people had played it.

Anyway, at first it was just me and my buddy, Gregg, working by ourselves in his bedroom. After I graduated from college, I did some contract work with my programmer buddies—Tavares, Greg Marquez, Ron Nakada, and Dan Chang—living and working out of a house in Mission Viejo. I was close friends with Tavares, Marquez, and Nakada, as we had come up through junior high and high school together. Chang, whom Tavares had befriended while at MicroProse, fit right into our group. It was still just a couple of programmers on each game, but now we had some artists who had been contracted by the guys we were working for. Still pretty small teams. We didn't have version control software or any of the fancy stuff we have now. We had a system of 3" × 5" cards that had the names of all the C source files on them, and you couldn't touch the code unless you held the card. That's how we managed to keep people from stomping on each other's work. We'd grab the card from them and get the latest version. It's pretty funny, looking back on it, but it worked.

When I went to Virgin Interactive, the teams started getting bigger, mostly on the art side. The consoles and PCs were getting more powerful, so we were able to display better graphics—which meant that we needed more and better art. On my first couple of projects at Virgin Interactive, I was still the only programmer, but there were a bunch of artists. When the 3DO Interactive Multiplayer came out, that was the first big project at Virgin where I had a couple other programmers working with me. That's pretty much the way it's gone. As the consoles have become more powerful, you need more people to create the content.

The 3DO project stands out for me because it was my first movie license: *Demolition Man*, which starred Sylvester Stallone and Wesley Snipes. The 3DO was notable for its cutting-edge graphics, which allowed us to recognizably portray the movie stars in gameplay. *Demolition Man* was the first movie-license game in which Hollywood stars shot extra footage exclusively for use in the game, and which was in production during the shooting of the film. It also led to my first appearance on national television. *Entertainment Tonight* broadcast a segment on the *Demolition Man* movie/game production and came to Virgin to get shots of the studio and some quotes from the team. I appeared for a few seconds commenting about what it was like working with Sylvester Stallone. I got to meet him at the green-screen shoot for the game, and he was super nice. He took pictures with the team, and he even play-boxed with sound designer Tommy Tallarico, who jokingly challenged "Rocky" to a fight. Stallone was also very helpful. We had a long list of action shots scheduled (shooting, fighting, walking, running), but he took time between shots to look at how we were going to use the material and what we were trying to do overall with the game. He then suggested adding some reaction shots that he said we could use to connect scenes together. They proved invaluable when the video editors were composing the transition movies that played between gameplay segments. Trip Hawkins actually visited us to see the game toward the end of development, and we ended up winning the 3DO Best Design Award that year. The trophy sits on my desk today. I share that award with Brandon Humphreys, who later joined me in starting our own companies (Seven and Big Grub) and who works with me to this day at inXile. I think he just wants to keep that design award in sight.

Making the *Demolition Man* game was in many ways like a movie production, right down to the Hollywood stars. As game hardware has accelerated, the games have gotten bigger and making them is even more like movies in terms of cost and complexity. You've got a bunch of permanent programmers, artists, and designers, plus a bunch of contracted people (individuals and companies) who do the writing, music, and make the intro movies and other tasks that can be well defined and contracted out. And it takes multiple producers to keep everyone organized and moving in the same direction.

People outside the industry are usually surprised to learn that it's an artist-heavy world, but it makes sense when you think about all the environments, models, prop objects, and animations required to make a big, detailed game. Making games is so much bigger now than it used to be, and what has become especially important is the whole production management side of things. Managing all these people, scheduling all the tasks, handling all the pre-production and design work that has to happen before anyone can actually start working on code and art—these are all huge undertakings. We do a pretty big pre-production phase where we really plan out the whole game. Things always change as you go along, of course, but you try to work out the major design ideas.

What makes a game great from a technical perspective?

I don't know if that's a good way to think about games, actually. You can certainly look at a game and see that it's pushing tons of polygons. When you look at Naughty Dog and Insomniac Games, for example, you see studios that have great technical talent and have been able to push game systems to their limits. Their games have really great-looking graphics and lag-free streaming worlds. I can look at technical things like this and admire them. I might also notice when a studio has solved some technical challenge, maybe in terms of getting content moving right away, having low load times, or having lush environments with high frame rates. But those things alone don't make a great game. It has to be fun.

The fact is that people really don't notice the technical stuff unless it breaks down. Mostly, they just want to get immersed in the story or gameplay. We definitely don't want to have the game suddenly slow down and the controls get sluggish and that sort of thing, but we don't necessarily need to be pushing the most polygons of any game on the market in order to create an immersive experience for players. Here at inXile, founder Brian Fargo said from the very beginning that we weren't going to be a company where we developed our own game engine and be heavily into the technology side of development. Instead, we license engines and focus on making great gameplay and content. This has sometimes been a challenge, because every time we switch engines, there's a learning curve. But the idea is to focus on the gameplay and immersion. My job here as technical director is to make sure that the player isn't distracted by the technology. We're not trying to set a high bar for technical achievement. We want the player to experience the game without technology getting in the way.

I think part of the reason game engines in particular come up when talking about what makes a game great, technically speaking, is that engines are really hard to make. I think Brian had some bad experiences when he was at Interplay Entertainment with programmers going off into a room to create an engine and coming back a year later with nothing usable. It was experiences like this that made him realize that for him, at least, a better approach would be to take a working engine and build a new game with great content around it.

With this development principle established, all we have to do for each project is to choose the best engine for the job at hand. We start by looking at what engines are available and what kind of game we want to make. We consider our design goals, especially graphically and in terms of game design, as well as the user experience we're trying to create. After that, it's just a matter of examining the available engines' features to see how well they'll support our vision and at what price. Early on, we were using *Unreal Engine*, then we switched over to *Unity 3D* for *Wasteland 2*, and now we're going back to *Unreal* for *Bard's Tale IV*. Engines change, pricing structures change, our goals for the games vary—it's an iterative process of reviewing what's available and reevaluating what we're trying to do.

One of the challenges of this kind of approach, of course, is staying on top of all the field's technical innovations so that when it's time to choose an engine, you really know what your options are. If a decision isn't pressing, then this sort of continuing education happens for me mostly in my spare time. If we're in the engine evaluation phase of a project, then I'm definitely spending time at work downloading engines, running examples, looking at specs, and that sort of thing. But on a daily basis when we're going through the different standard development phases, technology is advancing even as we're working on a particular project. New products and techniques are being announced, and it's my responsibility to keep abreast of those things, which I usually do on my own time, maybe while I'm eating lunch at my desk. I read industry and technical articles, go through the news, hunt down technical announcements, and things like that. So there's a formal phase where I spend work time researching technical information, and then there's an informal and ongoing learning process for keeping abreast of what's happening technology-wise.

How has the process of making games out of licensed properties changed over the course of your career?

Well, one of the things about the early console makers like Nintendo and Sega was their emphasis on the proprietary nature of their systems. You had to be signed up as a developer, and not just anyone could make games for those systems. They had to vet your company and agree that you could be a developer, and the hardware you got from them was under license and you couldn't move it around; it had to stay at the location where you said it was going to be. So from fairly early on, companies have been pretty serious about protecting their platforms and controlling what gets published on them. The driving force behind this was maintaining a certain level of quality and, of course, to ensure that they'd get their cut of software sales. Things haven't changed much. If you want to develop for the iPhone, their logistics are well guarded, and you have to go through Apple to publish anything.

Working with different licensed intellectual property (IP) isn't always the same. Disney is notoriously difficult to work with because they're very strict about how you use their IP. When I worked at Virgin, the company did the

Aladdin game and Disney was really happy with it. I didn't work on the game directly, but I did work on some tools for it and heard through some of my colleagues that Disney really wanted to control everything that was going on in development. But really, this is just the nature of the business. Everyone's trying to control their IP so that they can make the most money from it.

You mentioned that the proprietary console development systems that you have used are effectively locked down in the studio. What happens to those machines when the platforms for which they create builds become obsolete?

Well, sometimes the company takes everything back. I know we've had to send some systems back to Sony. I don't remember doing this for Microsoft, but maybe. More often than not, studios end up holding onto them, and they eventually get piled up in a closet somewhere. When the next generation console comes out, the previous one is no longer useful. If they don't ask for them back, and we're not allowed to get rid of them, then they just pile up.

What are the most significant internal challenges you face in your job?

Balancing my desire to develop a game to my utmost ability in terms of quality against the relatively fixed constraints dictated by the development process and my personal life. As part of the design and engineering team, I have to make difficult choices about what design features and implementation strategies to commit to, all of which impact the player's experience, the work environment, and various quality of life issues.

What are the external challenges you face in your job?

The demands of publishers—the external parties who pay for development— can be difficult to work with and sometimes seem fickle. It's hard enough to complete a project without an external party changing the goals or adding new requirements along the way. There can also be difficulty meeting the expectations of the publisher on the milestones to which payments are tied. In the game industry, "milestone" is a fairly ambiguous term. Imagine a game about bank robbery. A milestone in that game's development might be "You're able to go into a bank and rob it." That's a milestone. But there are a lot of aspects to that experience that might or might not be there when you're implementing the game: Do you have to case different banks before robbing them? Do you have to hire a safecracker and bring a getaway car?

How you determine whether or not the milestone of being able to go in and rob a bank has been reached is open to debate if it's not designed and agreed upon in detail ahead of time. Without these kinds of understandings, you might reach a point in the development process when the developer says, "Okay, you can go into the bank and rob it," but when you send it to the publisher, they say, "Yeah, but we were expecting that you'd have to deal with bank customers coming in and out. That's what makes robbing the bank challenging." The producers are imagining what the game is going to be like and have pinned milestones to those fantasies. If the developer doesn't share that vision, then the ambiguous milestones will probably result in some missed payments.

Some companies ensure that everyone's on the same page by putting together a detailed design plan during pre-production. Once that's done—and this is sometimes written into the contract—then everyone agrees to specific, well-defined milestones. It doesn't always go this way, unfortunately, so you do end up in situations sometimes where the milestones are open to interpretation and the publisher becomes a stickler. That's when it can get difficult.

When this happens, upper-level management gets involved—the CEO and president talking to the publishers and producers who are assigned to the project. Ambiguous milestones can really mess with a project, because if a publisher decides to stick to their guns and withhold payment until *their* expectations for a particular milestone are met, then you end up having to meet the letter of that milestone as quickly as possible so that you can get paid and continue the project. This might mean implementing things out of an optimal order or even implementing things in a way that's not going to be valid for the finished game. This latter case is called "programming to the milestone," a pejorative industry term that means you're just trying to get paid and not really doing things in the project's overall best interest. As you might expect, when you program to the milestone, you usually end up having to make up for it later with crunch hours because at some point everything that was supposedly finished earlier has to be redone in order for the game in its later stages to work. But by that time, there's no more time left on the schedule, so you end up having to do the late nights to fix the system.

I've experienced this in some of the projects I've worked on with big publishers. It's unfortunate that it happens, but it does. And even though publishers know it happens, I don't think they really want developers to be taking shortcuts to milestones that are likely going to be detrimental to the finished product's quality. No one wants pieces of the project to have to be done twice. Basically, I think producers—especially inexperienced ones—believe that their only means of control is to rule with an iron fist: this milestone, then that one, then that one. What they don't realize, though, is that this kind of inflexible control, combined with ambiguous milestones, ultimately really hurts a project.

How does the industry's increasing dependence on contract labor impact these kinds of development dynamics?

We use contractors quite a bit and it's always tricky. I say this having worked as a contractor for Interplay and others, as well as having hired contractors. The best relationships I've had with contractors is when they have a stake in the final product—for example, when part of their pay is in the form of royalties. We've had some really good working experiences with a company in Canada called Square One Games. They did the ports of *The Bard's Tale*, which was inXile's first game, to the mobile and Mac platforms. They were cut in on the back end, so they really cared about making a good product. If, on the other hand, you just have someone you're paying as work-for-hire (lump sum)—even with milestones—to do a certain job, and they're trying to do the least amount of work possible to get their money, then you're probably not going to get great results. Even good contractors don't usually want to end up spending tons of hours to get something perfect; it's just not worth their time. If they work for a lump sum, the more hours they put in, the less they make per hour. As a result, they do the best job they can in order to meet the milestones they're given for a rate they're happy with. They're not going to be endlessly iterating to get something just right. You have a tough time contracting something out and getting good results unless you know exactly what you want and can be very specific about it ahead of time. Developers want the most bang for the buck, and contractors want the most buck for the bang; that's the fundamental tension when working with contractors, whether it's for code, art, music, or whatever. This problem more or less dissolves when you cut a contractor in on the back end.

What sorts of workplace changes would you implement if given the opportunity?

One of the challenges of a collaborative effort is to balance the need for individual quiet (especially for programmers) with the need for dynamic and spontaneous collaboration. I'd prefer individual offices arranged around central meeting areas. The offices would provide the ability to close out noise for concentrated periods of work, but opening the door would allow people to hear and participate with others in the central meeting area.

How is the work you do in the game industry different from the work you have done elsewhere?

I've worked in landscaping (digging ditches, laying down sod, etc.) and in a cafeteria. Software development involves very little manual labor but a lot more collaboration and creativity. As a programmer, it can also be difficult to share and explain the challenges and triumphs of programming with people who aren't familiar with its practices.

Another challenge in the game industry is getting enough exercise. It's mostly a sedentary job, so I use a stand-up desk, and I run and practice yoga to maintain my health.

Which companies or ways of working (both within and outside of the game industry) do you look to for inspiration?

In the movie industry, Pixar has a development methodology, as described in the book *Creativity, Inc.* by Ed Catmull, that has been very inspirational. And although it's based on second-hand knowledge, in the game industry, I admire Blizzard Entertainment for its quality-first commitment to development. I know a lot of people who work at Blizzard. Somehow, early on in the development of their company and corporate culture, they were able to get away with not shipping a game until it was really done, even when it would cost them a lot more money than was originally anticipated. Brian Fargo, who knows Allen Adham, one of the founders of Blizzard, has shared stories about that. He tells how Allen would lie on his office floor agonizing over missed deadlines and being over budget, but allowing the producers to decide when the game was done. He had a commitment to quality and knew that if you finish a game on time but it's not fun, then it won't make any money. If it's not great, it's not going to be a hit—and he was committed to making hit games. I don't know if he was putting in his own money or where his funding was coming from, but once that standard was established, it became the way the company always operated. Now they make games that sell in the millions, and publishers and investors trust them because they know what they're doing. Consequently, publishers are willing to let Blizzard spend more money on a project, because they know it's going to be great when it comes out, which means it'll make tons of money. Somehow Blizzard was able to establish this philosophy and stick with it, and now they have a reputation for prioritizing quality—and they've made a lot of money doing things that way.

I don't mean to suggest that only an elite franchise or studio can operate according to the quality-first philosophy, but it's definitely challenging if your starting point is less ideal. Again, the key is working out as many details as you can during pre-production, and not overdesigning a game such that there's no time left to iterate it into a well-polished title. Of course, a lot also depends on marketing so that you get good visibility for your game. A good game can go out and not do well because it doesn't have an adequate marketing budget. A lot of things have to come together to make a hit game, but a huge part of it happens in the early stages of vision setting, design, and pre-production. This is where a lot of studios fall down: they think a great game has a lot of stuff in it, so they overdesign it, end up with too many features and not enough time, and ultimately have to ship (or cancel) an unpolished product.

What are the challenges facing the industry over the next decade?

The main challenge has always been meeting the rising expectations of players as the technology races forward in terms of computing power, display density, and input systems. Developers are constantly pushing the edge of what's possible with new systems. In the next decade, we'll see the development of virtual and augmented reality follow a similar curve of advancement and evolution. Adapting to these changes in order to stay relevant is the premier ongoing challenge.

Richard Sun
Technical Director

Richard Sun is the co-founder and managing partner of Rogue Rocket Games, a company he launched in 2011 to develop unique properties for digital download marketplaces. Prior to forming Rogue Rocket Games, he worked for LucasArts from 1999–2004, and for Planet Moon Studios from 2004–2010. He joined LucasArts after earning his BA in computer science from the University of California, Berkeley, and over the course of his career he has held the positions of junior programmer, programmer, senior programmer, and lead programmer. Mr. Sun has developed games for consoles, personal computers, and mobile devices, and to date has shipped fourteen titles including *Escape from Monkey Island*, *Star Wars: Republic Commando*, *Infected*, *SushiChop*, and *Gunpowder*.

* * * * *

How did you come to work in the game industry?

I cold-mailed a résumé to LucasArts, but didn't expect much. I did get one of those lovely cards back that said something like "Sorry, we're not going to hire you, but we'll keep your application on file." I always thought those cards meant "Résumé inserted into shredder," but as it turns out, that's not always true. I got a call from them a little while later—they'd seen my website and were impressed by my creative writing skills. They wanted to interview me based on those skills. The fact that I had graduated from Berkeley with a computer science degree meant to them that I was able to program in the capacity that they needed at the time, and they were more interested in the fact that I seemed to show a bit of creativity.

What are the duties of the position(s) you have held?

Being a co-founder of a studio as small as ours—five full-time employees— opens you up to a great deal of responsibility compared to a role in a larger company. In a general sense, my co-founder Nick Bruty and I divide up the classic roles of making a game into him being in charge of art and design, and me being in charge of programming and production/team leadership (though we do share the responsibility of design fairly often). In practice, I wind up doing a great deal more of the business end of things such as finance, operations, legal, human resources, business development, and so forth. We have a stable of external professional services people to help with several of those things: a lawyer, accountant, human resources specialists, etc. These are what every small business uses—it's not different for the game industry. We also utilize a variety of contractors: artists, animators, testers, designers. These are people we bring in and out depending on what it is we need on any given project at any given time.

Is there a clearinghouse or service that helps you identify contractors and external services personnel?

We largely rely on our previous contacts and connections. It's a lot easier. We haven't really used Craigslist or other job posting sites too much because it's a lot of effort. You have to wade through a lot more BS. There are a lot of people in those forums who are trying to make themselves sound better than they are. We're lucky that Nick and I have been around for a while and have a lot of different contacts.

Now, there are places you can go to try to get good professional help, like recruiting services. There are also game development service companies— you ask them to generate some art and they assign your project to a specific artist or team they have. When I worked at LucasArts, there wasn't much need to rely on outside services because the company was so large. At Planet Moon Studios—which at its peak was about forty to sixty full-time employees—we sometimes still had to rely on outsourced staff. And we used the same mechanics to find those people—in the game industry, everyone pretty much has their own contact lists.

Recently, we tried out a few new-economy recruiting online resources, such as Workable and Internships.com. These turned out to be effective in reducing the administrative headaches of locating and screening candidates, and I'd recommend them to interested hiring managers.

In your experience, to what extent is the game industry comprised or structured around informal relationships (e.g., people's contact lists)?

Based on anecdotal evidence, referrals from people you know are still very important because it's costly to assess someone's value. It's really hard to identify a person's skill set without actually trying her/him out for a while, and that's a costly exercise. Having someone you trust tell you that somebody's good is incredibly valuable.

Is it fair to say, then, that unless a company is quite large, reliance on external professional services is a common practice in the business of making games?

Unless you're making something exceedingly simple, I'm not sure how you can get away from relying on these kinds of services. For example, in one of the games we made—*Gunpowder*—we needed some 2D animated characters. There's just no cost-effective way to keep a guy like that on staff, a guy who does 2D cartoon animation. That's too specific a skill for our small company unless you're making 2D animated characters all the time in every game. So almost certainly, if you want someone to do that kind of work with a high level of quality, you're going to have to rely on someone from outside. We just happened to know someone Nick had worked with in the past who had that particular skill set and was highly sought after. He's very good, but he has his own company. They're a service company that builds art for people, as well as building their own products.

Are there downsides to having to rely on contract services?

Yes, they're the same risks any kind of company would be exposed to. They're particularly stark in California because labor laws are so complicated and messed up. There's also the normal human stuff that arises when there's no implied commitment in either direction. Generally, a contract is for the length of a project or the completion of a specific task, and therefore when a contractor is done, s/he could just disappear. Or in worse cases, the contractor could disappear before they're even done. You might wind up with a very good resource that you have no real hold on, and the next time around you've got to start from scratch again . . . which is actually both a strength and a weakness of that relationship. The strength—from my side of things—is that I'm not promising I'm going to keep paying a contractor after the job is done, and I actually may not be able to. So it's a fair exchange in the sense that they're free to go wherever they want afterward.

In California, in particular, the rules about how you qualify a person as a contractor are tricky waters to navigate, and that's where you've really got to be careful. It's dodgy. The rules are more important and become more of an issue the longer you work with somebody. Many California companies have really complex setups to try to avoid potentially troubling scenarios. And it's not remotely a game industry problem—it's just California labor laws, and it makes running a business in California challenging.

In setting up your own game company, what were your priorities in terms of jobs and functions that you needed to have in-house?

In the case of Rogue Rocket Games, we weren't given the luxury of having a lot of time to plan the company. It arose quickly as a result of Planet Moon Studios imploding. At the time, Nick and I both had families, mortgages, and all that stuff. We couldn't sit around not taking in any money for all that long. So, we just started building stuff, a few of us. The nice thing about the partnership that Nick and I have is that our natural skill sets fall across what's commonly thought of as the four major verticals of making a game: team leadership/production and programming, which I handle, and art and design, which Nick oversees (although as I said, I contribute a lot to the design as well). If a game is small enough, the two of us together can build it on our own. What we wound up doing was building a prototype to shop around for our first deal. And once we got that deal, we focused on who we'd hire as a function of what we needed to build the game we'd prototyped. This isn't exactly what you'd want to do if you're trying to create a long-term strategy for a fresh company, where you're supposed to have a clear business plan. I did, however, decide that we should keep as many people in contract status as possible to reduce risk—there's all sorts of things that come with taking on full-time employees, and risks come with them. We did that as long as possible, and we ended up converting several people to full-time when the time was right. We sort of naturally landed at our current personnel makeup as a function of who we were working with, how they fit in, and, more organically, how the whole team fit together.

How is the work you do in the game industry different from the work you have done elsewhere?

It's hard for me to answer this question because my first real job out of college was making *Escape from Monkey Island* for LucasArts. Before that, I worked as a summer intern in a couple of other companies that had nothing to do with games. Keeping that caveat in mind, working in the game industry for me is much more rewarding than other kinds of work in terms of both the type of work involved as well as the pride I feel in the final product. Aside from that, the actual experience of working in the games business is entirely different. It moves faster, giving you little chance to get bored. It rewards creative thinking more directly in many roles. And the game industry is constantly changing. A successful development environment is much more dynamic and collaborative than other sorts of work environments. Game industry people are generally more colorful and varied too.

The game industry isn't without its relative costs, though. It's fraught with peril in comparison to other types of work. Planning to generate "fun" is extremely difficult at best, and planning to make a profit even if you succeed at generating fun is even harder. Knowing exactly what you're trying to make ahead of time is nearly impossible. But it's all part of the nature of the beast if you're in a business that demands constant evolution. Being in the games business, unless you're in the top 5% or so of successful companies, means that you're likely to be significantly less compensated, particularly as an engineer. Segueing engineering skills in the game industry to something more mundane like building enterprise software would commonly result in a 50%–100% increase in overall compensation. This is less true in the highly competitive hiring environment of the last two years for mobile/social, but I predict this may change for the worse. Anyway, the game industry's lower general compensation is to be expected because the industry allows people to do things they really want to do. As a result, people tend to be willing to do these jobs for less than if they were doing things they'd rather leave at the office at the end of the day.

What challenges—if any—exist within your company that hinder you from performing your duties at an optimal level?

Time, time, time, time, time. Running a small business is hard. It's rewarding, but hard. Money is a huge factor as well, but in most important cases, money is interchangeable with time. At Rogue Rocket, we're bootstrapped with no investment, so resources and cash flow are always something on my mind. Keeping up with what I need to know to stay competitive is really a lot of work, a lot of parsing of information. Doing that, on top of running a company and a team—and doing hands-on development—is quite a lot.

What challenges—if any—exist external to Rogue Rocket that hinder you from performing your duties at an optimal level?

The current business environment for games is at a major interchange, and while there are more channels than ever before with mobile, tablets, consoles, and PCs, there's also more competition for players' money. One article I read aptly described the industry as having become so competitive that it's driven the price for a game down to zero dollars. Because of that, discovery and communication channels have become the number one concern. Finding a way to reach your audience has never been harder or more expensive, unless you already own a major franchise or have a ton of money for conducting marketing campaigns. This is the number one thing that needs to be solved to create more stability in the business environment. It's driven the resource needs for products higher in new areas, such as business intelligence, live operations, and user acquisition. Making a fun game that people like isn't good enough anymore.

What sorts of workplace changes would you implement if given the opportunity?

I'd like to pay my people more, and I'd like health-care costs to stop sky-rocketing. Obviously, this isn't specific to games, but still impacts the business nonetheless. I'd also like to have more resources (i.e., people) to whom I could delegate responsibilities, and a more aesthetically pleasing office, decorated more intentionally and thoughtfully. In addition, I'd like to have a better balance of men and women, which is more about the general supply of women developers than anything specific about my current team. The most important benefit of a more balanced team would be having the perspective of both women and men to contribute to discussions about the games we make and how they relate to different market segments. What the men and/or women actually do (i.e., their job responsibilities) beyond that is less important.

Other changes I'd like to see include some new, more modern servers and a spectacular view from the office. More seriously, though, I'd like better (but more reasonably priced) Internet connections. This week, for an upcoming move to a new office, I got a hilarious email from Comcast. They'd done a site survey and said that if I want to continue to have connections installed, I need to pay them $240,000 to do street-level construction. What the hell, man!

How would you describe the management structure and workflow at Rogue Rocket Games?

It's very flat. My business partner and I are the final authorities in various realms, but generally we're extremely collaborative and everybody is empowered to drive decision making. Fortunately, a team of five doesn't require a great deal of management overhead. We use a simplified version of Scrum that we honed while at Planet Moon Studios to do task tracking and planning.

In your experience, how does the process of game development differ when working on different types of games (e.g., different genres, AAA versus smaller games, etc.)?

The process changes as much with the people involved as it does with the type of product. The main thing driving AAA process overhead is the simple fact that it requires an outrageous number of resources to even finish the product, much less make it good. Wrangling hundreds of people working on an infinite spectrum of small nuggets of the overall whole is a massively difficult undertaking. It takes people with strong personalities, willpower, insight, and perseverance to drive a group like that to success.

Small games generally benefit from high efficiency, assuming the team consists of functional members. If you have some dysfunctional members in a small team, though, their negative impact is vastly more devastating since they represent a high percentage of the overall resources. Of course, different genres will dictate the details of how you wind up making the game, but that's only in the details of what you're making specifically and how. The bigger factor is how much experience your team has building that type of thing versus how ambitious and evolutionary/revolutionary you're trying to be. And then, of course, there's the overall scope of the game in terms of "units of content." An RPG will likely be harder to build than a single-player FPS on the axis of generating content, but that's just because the expectations of a decent RPG involve a great deal more choice, exposition, characters, locations, etc. It's less about the genre in that case and more about how much content and how many features the game itself necessitates.

Are there model companies or ways of doing your particular work (both within and outside of the game industry) that you look to for inspiration?

Yes and no—it's actually difficult to answer. I say "yes" because there are many companies I respect and whose success I hope to be inspired by. They "have their shit down," so to speak. They're leaders in innovation, quality, financial success—all of the important stuff. Companies like Supercell, Naughty Dog, BioWare, Big Fish Games, and inXile Entertainment come to mind. They're really different companies that succeed in very different ways and for very different costs.

I say "no" because trying to emulate another company that's successful just means you're chasing, not innovating. What works for them may not work for you. Making what they made isn't a surefire path to success. Instead, I try to take individual lessons from what they're doing and adjust and apply them to our team in a way that makes sense for what we're trying to do and with the people we have. That's a different thing than modeling ourselves after another company.

From your description, you spend a great deal of your time working on finance rather than development. What was the appeal of starting a game development company if development takes a back seat to finance?

It's the same answer anybody would give who has started a small business—and it's actually an intensely personal question. It has more to do with what an individual person wants out of life than it does with games in my case. Some people start a small business because they're trying to be the "start-up guy," and they have to start small and raise money. For other people, it's a lifestyle company, and for others it's something in between. For me specifically, I like to build things, and I like the product to be a reflection of whatever it is I'm trying to do. And the truth of the matter is that if you're working for a large company, your individual contribution to a game—even at a high level—is really diluted. Beyond that, the business of running a large game company isn't necessarily a safer bet, because you're making a game for tens or hundreds of millions of dollars. It's a very large financial risk.

As far as the business side of things in my job goes, that came with the territory. I didn't actually know if I was going to like it or hate it, or if I was going to be any good at it. I had no idea. It was just something I wanted to try. It turns out that I like doing that stuff. It's rewarding to discover that I'm not terrible at those things. I kind of enjoy the business development part of making games for a living.

You have been working in the game industry since 1999. Why embark on building your own company in 2011? What made the timing right?

In general, I think people tend to find a lot of inertia in their place in the world. They just continue doing what they've been doing because they don't want to fight the inertia. A lot of times what happens—and this happened to me—is that a major event causes you to have to make a choice. In my case, the previous studio I worked for—Planet Moon Studios—suffered what I would call a "devastating business event," which is to say it shut down due to unforeseen misfortune. I had to decide what I was going to do. I could've gone out to find another job, or I could've changed industries, or I could've started a company. It happened to be that my partner and I were working on some stuff, and everyone I talked to thought I should go out and do my own thing. That really helped—having other people believe in my ability to actually pull it off, or at least have a good go at making something happen.

Also, the notion of working with a small team and being close to the product was/is appealing to me. I don't like the politics of a large company (with large being a relative term)—the general difficulty of the logistics of managing that many people is a pain. I comfortably managed seven direct reports at Planet Moon Studios, all programmers. It was fine, but at some point you just start losing efficiency with the logistics. That's fine too, but I enjoy a tight-knit group more.

With the collapse of Planet Moon Studios, did the employees move into other, perhaps more stable or lucrative industries?

Not that many people left the game industry—maybe two out of the thirty or forty people who were displaced. It was an unusual scenario because the owners of the company were really good people. They went out of their way to figure out how to minimize the number of people who were left without a job over the holidays. The owners actually managed to discover and make a deal with a German game development company—Bigpoint—that was trying to staff up a branch office in San Francisco. And Bigpoint basically offered jobs to 90% of the displaced staff, myself included. I didn't end up taking that job, but the majority of the people from Planet Moon did go there. The unfortunate end of that story is that things didn't go that well there and the San Francisco branch wound up closing. So, pretty much everyone had to go find a job again after about a year and a half.

Given the development budgets at large companies, do employees there have good access to professional continuing education in order to keep up with technological developments?

That isn't nearly as prevalent as you might think. It's something I believe is really important, especially at a large company. Large companies tend to be places where people accidentally stagnate. I heard that EA offers (or once offered) EA University, where knowledgeable types come in and give lectures that employees can sign up for. These are voluntary classes on things that employees might want to learn. I thought it was a really cool idea, and at Planet Moon Studios I had the opportunity to implement Planet Moon University (PMU). We'd invite different people at the company to give a talk on something they felt that they could reasonably dispense information about. An artist could talk about how to use a specific tool, the philosophy behind art—whatever they thought would be useful to people at the company. People could sign up for these talks if they wanted, and we'd provide lunch. It was really good while we could keep it going. It was just hard to get people to do the talks, as the preparation could be pretty time-consuming. It's hard to find time to do other things when you're under the gun to produce a game.

At a small company, however, there just aren't resources to do this kind of thing. So, you rely on people learning on the job. It's common knowledge that hiring is the one thing you need to be most careful about. The people you hire are the most important resource. That's particularly true for a small team because employees have so many responsibilities. I tend to only keep people who can do that, who can learn on the job and be aware of the world around them. Staying abreast of new developments is hard, but as technology moves so quickly, things that used to be the common topics of education (e.g., How do I make the fur on this creature look super awesome?) are being solved by the subset of the game industry that makes game engines . . . at least for small companies. Big companies still have in-house folks who do nitty-gritty, hardcore, crazy graphics stuff. As a result, we can focus more effort on building the actual game and less time than in the old days on getting the game engine to work. There's a lot of going to conferences and talking to peers, of trying to be aware of what's not in the marketplace, and then finding ways to hedge the fact that you have limited resources. You try to do things like make partnerships with external groups and work with other people who are really smart. For example, we use this analytics package called *Swrve*—it's a premium service, but we got to know the company behind it when they were under the radar and we were able to create an informal partnership with them. We learn a lot from them. We also work with larger publishers, and they fund the development of some of our games. Sometimes they have resources that we can go to if we have questions. It's very organic.

How has your work changed as you have moved from a large company, to a mid-sized company, to founding your own small company?

The game business in general has changed. When I first started, game development and publishing was "fire and forget": games were released into the wild and the first month or two worth of sales defined success, after which the games were somewhat forgotten. The industry was hit driven, with one or two hits making up for a publisher's many misses. It was all about guessing what the marketplace would sustain. There wasn't a good path for updating games, or patching them, or changing them over time without creating a sequel product.

Now, everybody's connected. Their devices are online all the time, and game development has moved from fire and forget to being more service oriented and more direct sale. Developers and publishers are now constantly connected to the consumer, and business intelligence has become super important. Business intelligence has been a thing in non-gaming industries for quite some time, and now it's made its way into games thanks to Zynga, who claim that they don't make games but analytics engines that optimize players' behaviors in order to extract money. However, Zynga has also proven that emphasizing data over the art and design of games is unsustainable, and evolution must continue. At this point, people in the game industry are trying to figure out this transition; that's where a lot of activity is.

How has the formation of game-specific higher education programs and degrees affected the game industry?

It's actually been really good. There's a clearer starting point for future game developers. When I graduated in 1999, there was nothing: 0% college-accredited, game-focused anything. By 2006 or so, we started seeing applicants who came out of trade schools and subprograms. They were on legitimately better footing than someone who just had a degree in computer science. One of my senior programmers who has since left to join a larger company—I worked with him at Planet Moon Studios—came out of one of those programs. Another member of my team was in a game development-focused program in San Francisco, and he's really good. I think what game-focused programs do is give people the opportunity to concentrate on games if that's what they're interested in, and gives them a better understanding of how to use concepts required for building games. So, in my opinion, the establishment of game-specific programs has been really good, even though it's only been in the past few years that those programs are starting to know how to train their students correctly. Early on it was really wild and you didn't quite know what kind of person you were going to get. But now I've come across a lot of people who've come out of those programs, and in general they've been very good.

Before, if you hired someone like me—some guy with a computer science degree fresh out of college—you had no idea if they'd be competent. You really didn't. It came down to the hiring manager's intuition on whether or not the person could do the job. Hiring was much harder. Because employers didn't know what they were getting, they'd tend toward people who had tried to do small, personal projects on the side just to prove that they had a creative bone in their body and were self-motivated. Employers would take a half-chance on these folks, saying things like "I can't give you a programming job, but if you want to work your way up from the bottom you can start out as a tester and see where things go from there." There are now many more prepared people available.

Can you describe the process of signing a deal for an original game?

There are so many ways in which deals get made in this business, but signing original games in particular is really difficult to pull off. The fact that Rogue Rocket has managed to do it several times is kind of amazing. I don't quite know how we've been able to do it, actually, but I think part of it comes down to the fact that the team members have a lot of previous experience and we have a reputation for not bullshitting people. We enjoy some good street cred. I think we've also just happened to talk to the right people at the right time. For example, we built a game with Microsoft and they really liked us, which led to another deal.

There are work-for-hire deals, where there's a game idea—yours or the publisher's—and you get paid for an agreed-upon amount of work. When that work is done, so is the deal. There are also royalty-based, dev-funded deals—we've gotten these a few times. With these kinds of deals, the publisher fronts money for the development of the game, and the developer gets some share of the royalties on the back end after a somewhat complex arrangement involving different recoupment rates. The net result is generally that the publisher sees a profit before the developer. It makes sense because the publisher is taking all the financial risk.

And there's the whole question of who owns the IP. There's no fixed way this happens—it's totally a deal-by-deal scenario. The publisher might take the IP, they might let the developer keep it, the publisher might buy the IP from the developer—it's all just a bunch of wiggly pieces.

Finally, there's also some of what I call "lazy publishing," which is when the developer builds the game and then starts distributing it online. The developer then uses the analytics of the game's performance (i.e., how well the game is doing in the marketplace) to approach a publisher about promoting the game. The publisher then takes a part of the profits to promote the game via the publisher's already established channels, and with a theoretically larger marketing budget. It sounds mercenary, but you follow the money. If someone's willing to put ten million dollars down to push your game, you're probably going to wind up with something that you couldn't have done on your own. So, as a developer, you take a smaller cut than you would've, but you wouldn't have gotten there anyway unless you could find that ten million dollars' worth of marketing. I call it "lazy publishing" because the publisher basically doesn't spend any money until they see something that they already know is going to make them money. That's a newer type of deal because of the availability of real-time data. People have gotten sophisticated enough that they know exactly how much it costs them to acquire users given the channels they have available. And so they just do really simple math. It's totally insane: people pay from one to eight dollars or more to acquire a single mobile iOS user for a free game. So, if that's the case, then you know that over the lifetime of the average user you have to make more money than you're spending to acquire that user. People just do the math, and if the math works out, they go, "Sure, I'll put money into this."

As far as pitches go, that's something you have to decide to do and do with a concerted effort. You go to everybody you know, because cold-calling people with pitches is really hard. People just get bombarded by pitches; there are all kinds of people who just sit in their rooms drawing on paper and then send that as a pitch to publishers. Unless you know somebody who knows somebody, it's hard to get a publisher to pay attention. So, you go and blanket the world with whatever you're trying to pitch.

In the case of *Gunpowder*, for example, I played an iPad game I thought was pretty cool, and it was published by a division of Bungie. I thought we had some game ideas that might thematically and play-wise be similarly interesting to the folks at Bungie, so I went to my friend who worked there and asked if he could put me in touch with whoever was in charge of publishing that game. I talked with the publisher and showed him some stuff. He thought it was cool and introduced me to his former contact at Microsoft, as he thought they might be interested. The Game Developers Conference (GDC) happened to be coming up, so we met with the Microsoft folks there. We pitched them a couple of things, and they were a little lukewarm on all of them. We sensed that they were looking for something different, and we had an idea in our back pocket that hadn't been that well developed yet, but we pitched it. They told us, "That one sounds pretty interesting," so then we went through a full pitch process with them. They decided they liked the pitch, we made a deal, and made the game. The folks at Microsoft really enjoyed working with us and liked the game, so we still get to talk to them.[1]

Of course, if you're a well-known developer, getting a deal is a lot easier. If you can tell a random gamer your name and they know who you are, that's going to get you a deal much more easily.

What is the importance of community management in terms of the games you design in your studio?

We're trying to do community management and not doing it very well. Community management is hard to get right, in my opinion, and I don't really know how to do it right. If I think about the successful community management scenarios that are out there, they're largely idiosyncratic. Certain games just develop a cult following, and once they do, the community management is easy in the sense that you just have to hire someone who's good at managing that. Our problem is that nobody is really interested in talking about our company much, so there's not much to manage. We have a forum, a Facebook page, and a Twitter feed. There's not a ton of people looking at any of that stuff. How do you get in there? It's really hard unless you already have something that people are interested in. Currently, community-type stuff has become very important as we head toward an attempt at a Kickstarter campaign to fund a new game. Community and social outreach is essential to that. We have a game—*SushiChop*—that got four or five million downloads, so at least that many people have seen the game at one time or another. But the game is so simple and casual that the players don't seem to become followers of our brand. Our current strategy is to try to leverage some of our previous known games into public interest, and work with some external partners to help us gain additional awareness, such as a part-time community manager and a PR specialist.

There are companies out there whose entire business is community management. I suspect that a lot of companies, even large ones, will actually contract out to these specialized companies if their community requirements become large enough. One example is Lithium; that company is focused entirely on community management for large brands and it's been around for quite some time. I believe Lithium spun off from another Web company called Gamers.com, which was a site dedicated to game press. That company was founded by a guy named Dennis Fong, and he was well known—world famous even—for being the reigning *Quake* champion. Nobody could beat the guy. Anyway, Lithium does community management for all kinds of things, but they have games-related roots.

What are the challenges facing the industry in the next decade?

Consumer transition and too much competition. People are going to wash out, both out of the industry and out of games in general. It has to happen. The industry has to figure out a way to make its distribution channels cater to more than the top 1% of companies that have money or already own brand channels. The industry also has to figure out how to stay ahead of the curve to find new markets and not get left behind. We also need to figure out how to not let the "democratization" of game development devalue the people who make games. I'm not saying that democratization is bad, but those of us who have more experience need to push ourselves to stay ahead of the curve. Finally, the industry needs to keep its relationship with players fresh and constantly adjust to consumers' habits and comforts.

▶ DISCUSSION

In many ways, programming-related jobs within the game industry are the most challenging because they are, by necessity of the medium, the most interdisciplinary. Programmers, technical leads, and similar positions routinely require people trained in computer science and software engineering not just to occasionally interact with the likes of animators, illustrators, writers, designers, musicians, and business personnel, but to collaborate closely with them. As a result, coders in the game industry almost always work under decidedly non-technical conditions, and thus must develop ways of listening to and implementing concepts described to them in forms ranging from dramatic dialogues, watercolors, and poetic character descriptions, to business memos, musical subjects, and stick figure animations. It is hardly surprising, then, that a major theme that emerges in this set of interviews is that exemplary communication skills are highly desirable for the game industry's most technical people. As the interviewees describe here, such skills are not limited to the ability to write clear progress reports or document code well. Repeatedly, Sietsma, Alvarado, and Sun imply that good games are built by coders who can understand the perspectives and priorities of all the other people on the development team, whether at a small independent studio or a giant AAA-producing empire.

Such communication skills, note the interviewees, are often most needed by people predisposed to keep to themselves, a situation that can be deadly for the production process if those skills are underdeveloped. Because technical people serve as the primary interface between the idea and execution of a game, when they are unable to connect with the wide variety of other contributors to the project, the project itself suffers. Consequently, numerous team management styles pervade the industry, from formal ones such as Scrum, Agile, and strike team development processes, to informal ones such as open office space designs, free time for company athletics, and the creation of workplace environments that complement rather than constrain the game industry's tendency to attract highly creative and versatile people.

One downside to this sort of creative salmagundi is that it contributes to the industry's propensity to require long hours and an obsessive commitment to the work. By being subject to the ever-changing needs of designers, artists, and other creatives on a development team, programmers and their ilk must constantly adapt both their code and their social skills in order to keep the project moving forward. Such efforts are not only internally oriented within a studio; increasingly, technical personnel are tasked with finding software solutions specifically designed to accommodate and expand distribution channels and audiences, tasks that regularly require coders to also think like marketers, managers, and social media mavens. As the number of hats that technical personnel must wear grows, so too does the amount of work they do, a fact signaled by the ubiquity of crunch time in the industry. Notably, ubiquitous crunch has itself led to a number of countervailing—and often controversial—industrial practices, from the extensive use of contract labor, to the close surveillance of work time and productivity, to unwritten workplace mores that link overwork with corporate commitment. Overall, Sietsma, Alvarado, and Sun suggest that the dynamics of a creative industry built around a core of highly technical people tends to create workplaces that can be, at turns, professionally supportive and personally alienating, and ultimately leads to many of the industry's other distinctive qualities.

From a programming perspective, for example, game development can be very different from other kinds of software development, particularly enterprise software development. The organizational procedures in game programming are often more fluid than in other domains, ostensibly to accommodate the ebb and flow of creativity and problem solving associated with a multidisciplinary production like a game. There is also the matter of compensation to consider; in Sietsma and Sun's experience, game programmers earn significantly less than other software developers. This pay gap may be offset somewhat by job satisfaction—interviewees throughout this book describe the passion many game developers have for their jobs, and how this passion enables developers to thrive under crunch, survive other workplace challenges that game making can present, and (in Sietsma's and Sun's cases) make peace with a less-than-competitive salary—but the method of remuneration may not. Revenue share models, for instance—particularly those associated with long project development timelines—may be untenable for employees with families or those in other asset-dependent situations. Thus, there are distinct and downward structural pressures in games that prioritize single and risk-tolerant employees (i.e., youth) over more experienced workers, something Sietsma and other interviewees in this book highlight. This phenomenon is not simply a matter of companies wanting to keep development costs in check, but a demand imposed by the current economics and production practices of game development.

Another significant difference between technical positions in the game industry versus similar positions in non-game development contexts is that despite the high degree of specialization in job types, it is not uncommon for game programmers to occupy multiple positions at the same time (e.g., programmer and technical director), even at medium-sized and large studios. Thus, while there is still the need for specialization (e.g., art, quality assurance, design) in game labor, there is also a need for multi-specialists, that is, employees who can function at both the production and management levels beyond the scope of lead and that position class's responsibilities. The workload balance between a multi-specialist's given areas of expertise can change depending on the development timeline, and can also complicate annual reviews and other assessment procedures. That is, it can be hard to evaluate performance across disciplines and time-lines. By the same token, multi-specialization can be key to a long career in the industry, despite the toll it can take on worker well-being. As both Sietsma and Alvarado explain, it is often up to the individual to decide when enough is enough—a company may not be aware of, interested in, or able to recognize specific instances of overwork or burnout—even though such experiences may have significant consequences for workplace inter-personal dynamics.

Such skill diversity issues also raise questions about employment preparation. While in Chapter Three (Design) Andrew Rubino speaks plainly about game education from the perspective of a trade school graduate, here Sun paints a rosier picture of game-specific higher education from the perspective of an employer. For Sun, game development education programs now reliably produce predictable levels of quality preparation, and in the process eliminate some of the uncertainty in hiring that has historically plagued the game industry. This is no doubt a relief to many employers and helps optimize their talent acquisition pipelines; however, we cannot help but wonder about the long-term effects of the sedimentation of game development education. Specifically, is there an innovation cost to vocationalizing game development training? That is, what are the design, process, and product implications of moving from a hiring model based on possibility (in Sun's words, "You just didn't know what you were going to get") to one based on probability (again, in Sun's words, "There's a clearer starting point for future game developers")?

Concomitant with—though not necessarily related to—the emergence of vocational game development education has been a shift from what Sun terms "fire and forget" development to development as sustained customer service. Game production no longer simply means product development, but now includes product maintenance, service offerings, and community management as well. The process has expanded in scope alongside the mobile game boom, the proliferation of distribution outlets, and rising production costs for premium titles. Thus, even though low-cost development tools and accessible publication platforms now abound, the obligations—and therefore the resource commitment—associated with game production have expanded. In other words, and ironically, game development has gotten more expensive and therefore less accessible even though in some ways it has gotten cheaper and more practicable.

Finally, it is clear that the growing number of platforms for games—from high-end consoles to mobile devices to Web delivery to virtual and augmented reality hardware—is only exacerbating many of the industry's most complex labor issues among its technical personnel. Increasingly, the coding-based details of game development are being integrated with—not just subject to—the business details of game development. As profit margins shrink, development costs rise, and user bases become ever more niche, programmers are being tasked with projects designed not around fun but around intelligence gathering. Where once gamers were the primary audience for clever programmers' graphics advancements and gameplay optimizations, in many studios today it is for the investors and producers that programmers design and deploy their most original code. Curiously, such rational systems seem most necessary for smaller rather than larger studios, where one's livelihood quite literally depends on a set of interoperable systems that produce enjoyment and user analytics in equal measure. If there is an upside to this development, it may well be that it will force the industry to earnestly address issues of workplace diversity—especially in the context of gender, ethnicity, and sexual orientation. As games are increasingly designed from inception to analyze the people who are playing them—both to optimize the play experience and to commodify the user—a broader audience for games will need to be developed. User analytics, along with more effective methods of localization, are bound to direct astute developers, then, to recognize that the most diverse development teams will most likely be the best equipped to reach either a larger general audience or a wider array of profitable niche markets.

▶ NOTE

1   For a more detailed postmortem of *Gunpowder*, see Sun's blog post "Gunpowder: How We Brought a High Quality Premium Game to iPad and Steam."

▶ WORKS CITED

Bibliography

Catmull, Ed. *Creativity, Inc.: Overcoming the Unseen Forces That Stand in the Way of True Inspiration.* New York: Random House, 2014. Print.

Sun, Richard. "Gunpowder: How We Brought a High Quality Premium Game to iPad and Steam." *Gamasutra: The Art & Business of Making Games.* UBM Tech. 21 May 2015. Web. 10 Oct. 2015. <http://www.gamasutra.com/blogs/RichardSun/20150521/243952/Gunpowder_How_We_Brought_a_High_Quality_Premium_Game_to_iPad_and_Steam.php>

"Transitions: Gamasutra Salary Survey 2014." *Gamasutra: The Art & Business of Making Games.* UBM Tech. 22 Jul. 2014: 1–8. Web. 10 Oct. 2015. <http://www.gamesetwatch.com/2014/09/05/GAMA14_ACG_SalarySurvey_F.pdf>

Filmography

Demolition Man. Dir. Marco Brambilla. Perf. Sylvester Stallone, Wesley Snipes, and Sandra Bullock. Warner Bros., 1993. Film.

Gameography

ACO Virtual Orchestra. John Sietsma. John Sietsma, 2011. Mobile.

Afterburner: Black Falcon. Planet Moon Studios. Sega, 2007. Sony PlayStation Portable.

Armello. League of Geeks. League of Geeks, 2015. Multiple platforms.

Ashes Cricket 2009. Transmission Games. Codemasters, 2009. Multiple platforms.

The Bard's Tale. inXile Entertainment. Vivendi Universal Games, 2004. Multiple platforms.

Centipede. Atari, Inc. Atarisoft, 1983. Commodore 64.

Choplifter HD. inXile Entertainment. inXile Entertainment, 2012. Multiple platforms.

Dekko Monkey. Dekko Experiences. Dekko Experiences, 2012. Personal computer.

Demolition Man. Virgin Interactive Entertainment. Virgin Interactive Entertainment, 1994. 3DO Interactive Multiplayer.

Disney's Aladdin. Virgin Games USA/Disney Software. Sega, 1993. Multiple platforms.

Escape from Monkey Island. LucasArts. LucasArts, 2000. Multiple platforms.

Gunpowder. Rogue Rocket Games. Rogue Rocket Games, 2013. Personal computer.

Heroes Over Europe. Transmission Games. Ubisoft, 2009. Multiple platforms.

Infected. Planet Moon Studios. Majesco Entertainment, 2005. Sony PlayStation Portable.

Jewel Collector. John Sietsma. John Sietsma, 2010. Mobile.

Mario Bros. Nintendo Research and Development 1. Nintendo, 1983. Coin-operated.

Oscura: Lost Light. Chocolate Liberation Front. Surprise Attack, 2015. Personal computer.

Oscura: Second Shadow. Chocolate Liberation Front. Surprise Attack, 2014. Personal computer.

Quake. id Software. GT Interactive, 1996. Personal computer.

R/C Stunt Copter. Big Grub/Shiny Entertainment. Interplay Entertainment, 1999. Sony PlayStation.

Rugby League Live. Big Ant Studios. Tru Blu Entertainment, 2010. Multiple platforms.

Spec Ops: Airborne Commando. Big Grub. Gotham Games, 2002. Multiple platforms.

Star Wars: Republic Commando. LucasArts. LucasArts, 2005. Multiple platforms.

Super Caesars Palace. The Illusions Gaming Company. Virgin Games, Inc., 1993. Sega Genesis.

SushiChop. Rogue Rocket Games. Rogue Rocket Games, 2011. Multiple platforms.

Table Top Speed. Dekko Experiences. Dekko Experiences, 2013. Personal computer.

Wasteland 2. inXile Entertainment. inXile Entertainment, 2014. Multiple platforms.

Wild 9. Shiny Entertainment. Interplay Entertainment, 1998. Sony PlayStation.

Wollongong University Kinect Experience. Many Monkeys Development. Wollongong University, 2014. Personal computer.

World of Warcraft. Blizzard Entertainment. Blizzard Entertainment, 2004. Multiple platforms.

Softography

Swrve (https://www.swrve.com)

Unity 3D (https://unity3d.com)

Unreal Engine (https://www.unrealengine.com/what-is-unreal-engine-4)

Yammer (https://www.yammer.com)

Videography

Entertainment Tonight. Paramount Domestic Television/CBS Paramount Domestic Television/CBS Television Distribution. 1981–2016. Television.

2
Art

▶ **INTRODUCTION**

The art discipline is responsible for producing a video game's visual assets, including concept and in-game art, animations and visual effects, the user interface (UI), and graphics used in packaging, promotion, and other para-textual materials. Certain artists (e.g., technical artists, animators) also work to ensure the smooth functioning of art assets within the game environment itself, and their jobs incorporate scripting, light programming, and other technical design tasks. Art production tools consist of a variety of commercial image creation and editing applications (e.g., *Maya, ZBrush 4R7*), specialized design peripherals (e.g., Wacom pen tablets), and even physical media such as sketchpads and paints on occasion.

Typically, artists hold one of three general position classes—artist, lead, or director—though the first two classes are often specialized by area emphasis (e.g., environmental artist, visual effects artist, lead animator). Whereas artists and leads both focus on asset creation and refinement, leads also assume supervisory and administrative duties. Art directors, by contrast, are principally supervisory and administrative in their job function, overseeing artists and leads as well as interfacing with the leads of other development disciplines.

Animation is a distinct subcategory of art and focuses on the creation of animations for characters, objects, and UI elements. Animators are also integral to the production of promotional materials and in-game cinematics (aka cutscenes), though these may be created independently from the larger game development process. Animations applied to in-game characters or objects, however, must be carefully crafted to achieve not only specific visual qualities but also to support the gameplay pacing or feedback required by the game's design. Consequently, many animators work more closely with the design and programming disciplines than do other artists.

Because of the high degree of specialization found in art, it is worth briefly noting the range among the most common disciplinary specializations. Concept artists, for example, are charged with developing the initial aesthetic of a game's characters, objects, and environments. Concept artists are an essential part of a game's previsualization, and provide the development team with an aesthetic target in development. Environmental artists, by contrast, focus on the geometry, textures, and lighting of the game environment, always with a keen eye to prescribed technical limits (e.g., polygon count, engine capabilities) and design metrics (e.g., in-game surfaces available for player interaction). The job is also extremely collaborative and typically paired with level design. Visual effects artists (aka VFX artists) occupy the most highly technical art position and are responsible for generating a range of particle, camera, and animated effects (e.g., muzzle flashes, billowing smoke, and lens flare).

According to the 2014 Gamasutra Salary Survey, art personnel earn an average annual salary of $74,349 in the aggregate ("Transitions" 2). Artists with fewer than three years of experience earn an average of $50,000 annually, while those same personnel with six or more years of experience earn an average of $82,230 per year (Ibid.). By comparison, lead artists/technical artists and art directors with six or more years of experience earn an average annual salary of $87,576 and $110,000, respectively (Ibid.). Additionally, US-based artists earn approximately 16% more on average than their Canadian counterparts, and 44% more on average than European artists (Ibid.). Finally, male art personnel average $76,054 per annum, while female employees average $55,909 annually (Ibid.).[1]

Victoria Sarkissian
Artist

Victoria Sarkissian is a 2D artist with Turbine, a wholly owned subsidiary of Warner Bros. Interactive Entertainment. Previously, she worked for dSonic, Plaor, Moonshot Games, and Asmadi Games, and held the positions of artist intern, UI artist/illustrator, level skinner, concept artist/illustrator, and temporary UI artist. She has also served as an independent contractor for a variety of external clients, and has produced board game art as well as video game art. She holds a BFA in illustration from the Massachusetts College of Art and Design, and her shipped titles include *Infinite Crisis*, *Mega Fame Casino*, and *Third Eye Crime*. Samples of her work can be found on her personal website (http://victoriasarkissian.com).

* * * * *

How did you come to work in the game industry?

During college, I worked at a GameStop, and after graduating I decided to pursue a career in video games. I happened to get really lucky, and the first internship I applied to hired me for four months to create art assets for a small mobile game experiment. After that, I searched again for a few months and eventually went to a networking event for a local game studio. Thanks to an acquaintance of mine who worked at the studio and who I'd met at a previous event, I was introduced to four art directors at the company and was able to show them my portfolio. Several months went by and then I got an email from one of the directors I'd kept in contact with—they were looking for a temporary UI artist. That was my foot in the door to my first contract work and to the industry.

What sorts of mentoring have you received in your career?

Everywhere I've worked so far I've learned a new skill or technique. Starting out, I came from a traditional illustration background, and a lot of the work I do now was mostly self-taught with a little bit of mentoring here and there. I studied art in a trade program in high school and went on to study illustration in college. I hadn't received any formal training for game art or design before joining the industry. I was definitely interested in pursuing this career path for a long time, though. One of the interesting things about the game industry is that it's very digital. You have to be a computer whiz in order to get by. I ended up teaching myself how to do digital painting as a result. My high school classes focused a lot on drawing fundamentals and graphic design, while my college classes were heavily focused on illustration fundamentals. I learned a lot about traditional media, design theory, figure drawing, oil/acrylic painting, and so on, but digital painting was something I had to figure out on my own. Every day I would practice on the side, and I feel that this is what enabled me to transition into video games—I was able to develop the specific and required skill set. After graduating college, I built a portfolio that was both physically printed and viewable on my website.

My portfolio definitely helped me get my first internship, but I still had to break out of my comfort zone and learn new skills. During the interview for that internship, the interviewer really liked my drawings but said that the company was also looking for someone who could do visual effects. After the interview was over I thought, "Oh my god!" and I practiced like crazy how to make some effects in the program he showed me. About a week later I had some examples to show—I made a bunch of things explode, emailed them to him, and said, "I can do this, I swear!" A few emails later, I got hired on for four months.

When I started the internship, I was mentored by a coworker—he taught me a lot about how to work with software tools and the asset integration process. I started to learn how to integrate my art into code, how to work with an art director, how to use project build software like *Perforce*, and how to work in a game engine. It was a unique experience because I got to see so many different aspects of development.

I've received mentoring on different art pipelines at my current studio as well. One of my main duties on one of the last big projects was to make icons and solve a major visual problem. It was my first experience with UI design and I had no idea how to make icons, or the procedures for connecting them to the rest of the development process. While my art directors coached me in the direction to go, I also had the freedom to figure out a process. What I ended up doing was researching how the industry as a whole deals with UI design, as well as what other games did that I thought made their icons successful and interesting. I also learned things from different coworkers about VFX, concept art, 3D art, animation, and so on. It was all different levels of art. You can learn from anyone at my current studio—when I first started, one of my leads showed me cool tricks in *Adobe Photoshop* that made my life so much easier and my output faster.

During that time, we also had weekly critiques from the UI team, and that was where we would all discuss what we were doing, what was working and what wasn't. It was really wonderful because everyone was working toward the same goal: making the best product possible.

What part of your job is most professionally rewarding? Why?

I'd say working with other people and solving problems. It feels so good to work together as a team to come up with ideas and push them beyond their limit. Getting to see what you've imagined suddenly functional and in-game is also super rewarding. You can show your friends once it's shipped and say "I made that!" I also really love seeing new features added throughout the process, and being a part of the experience of a game taking shape is absolutely amazing.

How does the collaborative component of game development connect with your individual desire for artistic expression?

I feel there's definitely some level of conflict between collaboration and that desire. For example, when I was tasked with redesigning 240 icon artifacts for a large game we were doing, I had a lot of freedom to figure out and solve the design problem, but under extremely tight constraints set by the UI leads involved in the process. At the same time, I ran into potential visual issues with the art director, the designers, and the leads. In terms of artistic expression in games, I feel like you have to compromise, or you have to sacrifice something for someone else, and the same thing goes for them. There's a lot of back and forth work. It's best to not cause problems or have an attitude or ego when working as part of a team. You can't say, "It's my idea and this is my thing," because it's really not. Everything in game development is collaborative. The process as an artist is mostly visualizing on screen someone else's idea and then iterating on that idea to make it all work. Sure, your input is important, and you're usually allowed—even encouraged—to share your ideas and give input on almost everything. But I think there's a fine line that shouldn't be crossed when it comes to certain things . . . unless it's something that's super good and will really improve the project. That's when I think it's good to discuss things. But if your suggestion gets shot down by the person in charge—like the art director or the lead—you have to get over it. You can't hold a grudge, you can't be angry that your vision isn't the one being realized. You have to trust that whoever is in charge will make the best decision possible.

But that doesn't mean you always have to agree. Someone on a lower level of the hierarchy just simply doesn't have the power or control to change the final decision.

Is compromise fundamental to the game development experience, particularly for artists?

Yes, I would definitely say that's a given, but there can still be moments when someone gets upset if their idea isn't used. Based on discussions I've had, it's pretty universal that we all wish our ideas were used more often. Everyone wants to be heard, though I do feel that everyone does get heard in some way or another. The ideas just end up getting merged with everyone else's. It's part of being on a creative team and part of the development process—not everything can get used at the end of the day. While I love the work I get to do professionally, I still do my own personal work during my free time. I definitely feel fulfilled as I get to be my own art director, my own designer, make my own rules and decisions. But that can also make the personal projects harder to complete.

I also think that artists, at times, feel like their artwork gets compromised during the game development process because their art isn't solely theirs. It gets taken to a whole different level while being worked on by someone else, with iteration being an important factor. The work you may have started isn't just yours anymore; it's now five different teammates' collaboration. Someone makes a 3D model, then a concept artist paints over it, and then the 3D modeler goes back and addresses other things. You're letting go of control little by little and leaving it in someone else's hands. One person's art becomes the work of the team, and that could be why artistic visions sometimes feel compromised. Whose art is it? Is it mine because I did the concept work, or is it someone else's because they refined it for the final game? But my art director told me the direction to go, and the designer actually cooked up the idea. So whose art is it?

Where in the development process do the various kinds of art duties (e.g., concept, splash, UI) occur?

Various art duties can occur at almost any point in the production and pre-production pipeline of game development, and you'll see them consistently throughout until the end of a project.

Some studios work on an "at the moment" basis, while others have more of a planned action . . . though this isn't necessarily always the case. Sometimes on a bigger project you'll be divided into separate teams and work in sprints. Sometimes you'll just work on milestones and do whatever work needs to be created. Big projects often have littler projects associated with them, like a mobile game. Just doing concepts in pre-production and then going into full production isn't how most pipelines work, either. It's more like concepts are still happening through production. With a live product—even if it's just a small-scale mobile game—you're doing pre-production and production at the same time because you're constantly pushing out new content.

A lot of iteration occurs at these various stages, and a lot of changes are made throughout each process. Sometimes things will be developed side by side and feed off of each other, while other times one thing might be developed first and then worked on later. Concept art and design that's being done might not be related to what else is being done in production at the same time. UI, animation, 3D—they're all working on stuff that was established beforehand.

On *Third Eye Crime*, the people I worked with had already made the UI and done all the fundamental programming when I joined to freelance. My job as an artist was to skin the levels, which basically meant taking the premade art assets and placing them in the game so that they looked good. It was like attaching everything to a blueprint, an already designed layout. It was the final polish for the game, the last step.

I also worked for a studio that created casino game mobile apps, and the various art duties there were constant all the way through the project. When we were making slot machines for *Mega Fame Casino*, we had a two-week deadline for each individual new slot machine addition, which is very fast. There were about four artists on the project, and the producers would have the tasks set up ahead of time to get the work done. I would go and create the ideas for what we were going to do for icons and a background, while someone else was preparing to skin all the UI menus and buttons. We were constantly collaborating on creating the assets. After we made everything, we would then attach the slot machine to the code, while someone else was finishing the animation. Then the slot machine would be ready to go live. The various art roles functioned all at once in that timeline.

Do artists change companies and geographies with the same frequency as other developers?

I feel like changing companies and moving between various locations is definitely one of those things that happens in our industry. I'm not so sure if I can accurately depict the frequency for artists, as people are always leaving companies for different reasons. Layoffs are definitely one factor, and general personal reasons for leaving tend to vary. However, I've seen people from all departments shift around, not just artists. Massachusetts, for instance, has lost a lot of game companies over the past few years. A lot of people have been laid off, and a lot of people I know have had to move to new places. For some reason, this area just doesn't have that cushion of other local businesses to go to if a job dries up. As a result, a lot of people are unfortunately forced to move to other states to find jobs if they want to keep working in games.

Personally, I feel like I'll end up on the West Coast at some point in my career, or another location. I feel it's unavoidable, especially if I want to keep working in this industry. At the same time, I've focused on Boston opportunities in my career because I like the area, and I'm close to my family and friends—they're very important to me. It's definitely hard to imagine a different life in the future, but I know I'll have to make a change. I also feel like I still have a ways to go in terms of my own art, and I'm excited for the future and thrilled about where my career will take me geographically.

However, I do feel to some extent that artists can be expendable, and can be as easily let go as they are hired.

Why are game artists so fungible?

It depends on the project and its long-term needs. Sometimes a project will stock up on extra hands and when the work is done they let folks go. There's also no shortage of talent out there, and a lot of times one artist can do another's job and more.

I didn't really know until I started working in games that the industry can be unstable. Jobs ending suddenly has mostly been my experience so far. Either there's no more need for art at a certain point, or the projects run short on funding and someone has to get cut. Companies can always pick up artists later if they need them and if funding comes in. Freelance work especially is like that, and I never expect to be freelancing on one job for long.

Being laid off happens to a lot of people. In fact, I'm pretty sure that most developers who work in the gaming industry—artist or otherwise—have experienced a layoff at some point in their career.

In many industries, being laid off is a mark of shame, something difficult to talk about on a résumé or to have to explain in a job interview. Given the depth and frequency of layoffs in the game industry, do they carry the same stigma as in other fields?

No, at least not in my experience. It's definitely not shameful at all. It's just the nature and economics of the industry. This isn't the case everywhere, though. Not every studio has layoffs. However, a common situation is when a game ships, a studio lays off people, because there might not be work to do or there's no need for the extra help.

How does that impact the work environment?

When it comes to the work environment, it depends on how honest the company is. Maybe sometimes you see it coming, other times not. It's definitely crazy and nerve-wracking in the sense that you can be laid off at the end of a project, or at any moment—there's always the possibility. I don't find myself thinking about it too much while I'm actually working, though. At places that I've worked, management has been really good about controlling that tension and keeping negative feelings at bay. The work environments for me have always felt safe and happy. I've been on both sides, though—part of the layoff, and also as someone who has been kept on while other people have been laid off. It's pretty unsettling either way, because you've either just lost your job or watched your friends lose theirs and you feel guilty.

As unsettling as it can be, everyone helps each other out when layoffs happen, and I think that's one of the most amazing and neat things about the industry. Sometimes they'll know some other people looking for skills that you have and try to hook you up with them. Friends pass your name on and reach out to help you land on your feet.

One thing that's interesting to think about is you're going to wind up working with these people again at some point, at some other company. You'll be working with people you didn't expect to work with again. I feel that's a very important aspect to remember: keep in contact. In this industry, it's all about who you know. If you get laid off, or some of your friends get laid off, maybe somebody gets a job somewhere else. Since they know your skills, and they know what you can do, maybe they'll be in a position to hire you at the new place, and you'll end up working there with them.

During one layoff I had, my boss at the time said he knew someone at another local company looking for a UI artist and that I should email them. My boss said he'd recommend me. Because they knew each other, and because I was also an acquaintance of the person he was talking about, things worked out. It really instilled in me a sense that I could land on my feet and get my next job. It was interesting because my last day was on a Friday, and on Monday I started my new full-time job in a completely different environment. It gave me the confidence that there are always other opportunities, and you'll get another job at another place. It's very reassuring, even though it sounds unstable and risky. You might have to relocate, you might have to upend your life, but if you want to stay in this industry, it's expected that you'll move around a lot and never be stationary for too long.

At one point in your career, you specifically chose to do contract work rather than work in a studio. Why is that?

In the past, I picked up contract work because that was what I was able to grab at the time. Part of the reason, too, was because I'm still trying to figure out what I want to do with my career. Even though I've been in the industry for a while now, I'm still really just starting out, and so I've had to take different opportunities in order to transition to where I am now. Even though contract work can be risky and not as secure as being full-time in a studio, I've really enjoyed it because of the variety of things I've been able to do. It's actually super hard to land a full-time job in my experience. You really have to fight for it due to the competition. There are always people with more experience out there than you—there's a lot of talent. Sometimes you just have to wait for the right opportunity and be persistent. It's definitely a case of being in the right place at the right time and who you know.

What are the most significant internal challenges you face in your job?

I'd say a big internal challenge is hoping that I've done good work and pleased my boss. Also, staying up-to-date with the ever-changing industry, especially the techniques used to create game content. It's sink or swim.

What are the external challenges you face in your job?

A big external challenge while working full-time is coming home and gathering up the will to just relax and play a video game. But mostly, the challenge is life in general—keeping on track, figuring out that balance, doing things for myself outside of my job that make me happy.

In addition to submitting a résumé and a portfolio, artists are often asked to take art tests as part of a job application. How do these tests work?

Art tests are pretty standard. Almost all the potential inquiries I've ever had from applying for an artist position have asked for an art test. In my experience, the tests have generally been really simple: someone on the team for the project you'd be hired onto communicates with you through email. They send you the art test documents and give you a time frame for when they want them completed. Depending on the position you applied for, the content of the art test will vary. It could be anything from character design and background concepts to UI artwork that matches an already existing style for an existing product.

I've taken an art test before where I worked with the art director on the assignment really closely, and he helped me push the artwork to its full potential. I really enjoyed it and learned so much in the process. I feel like art tests are conducted as a way to see how you fit into the pipeline of an established studio. It's also really important to take the art tests so the hiring team can feel confident in the artistic ability of the person they want to hire. They want to make sure they're hiring the right person, and that you can actually do the work.

How much time does an art test take?

The length of a test depends on the studio. Most of the time it's pretty reasonable, around two weeks. A few of the ones I've taken have been around a week. It's interesting when I'm given a good amount of time because I try to get the work done as quickly as possible while also putting in my best effort. After finishing the test, the waiting is the hardest part—very nerve-wracking. Sometimes I've gotten responses right away, and sometimes I don't get a response at all. Sometimes it just didn't work out, and I've had to learn how to cope with rejection. It wasn't always easy for me, but you learn to deal with it and then grow from it and apply it to your next experience. It burns less every time.

Before I started working in the game industry, I thought it wouldn't be so hard to break in, that everything was flowers and rainbows. I didn't realize that it was so full of challenges. It's not easy work, and there are so many people dying to do it.

What makes the industry so attractive that people are willing to endure constant vicissitudes?

I think it's attractive because a lot of game devs grew up playing games, are really passionate about them, and get to draw on that inspiration in their work. Games take you to different worlds. You can be anyone you want to be. You can do anything you want. You can kill monsters, fight on a spaceship, and you're controlling the experience. It's not like a movie where you just sit back and watch. I think a big part of the attraction is the idea that "I get to be a part of that." There are so many people who have so many different backgrounds, so many different experiences, and so many different things to teach you—and they're all talented and amazing. I think a lot of developers feel passionate about what they do, so the sacrifices and the hoops they have to jump through in their careers aren't too bad. You put all these people together in a building, creatively collaborating to make a product that people get to experience—that's what I find so rewarding, and I think other developers do too.

You keep an active professional/personal website where you are constantly posting new artwork. Is this kind of up-to-date electronic presence a necessary part of being an artist in the game industry?

Your online presence is very important, especially as an artist, and a portfolio can get outdated really easily. Options like blogs are great for us because it's an extremely convenient and intuitive way to keep your body of work up-to-date. Plus, it's a really great way to see someone progress and get better at what they do. Depending on the non-disclosure agreements an artist has signed, it can be hard sometimes to publicly promote the work you've done professionally. So, most artists post art on their blogs that's personal and made for fun during their spare time. I keep a personal blog to keep myself productive and always improving. It feels good to me because I feel like I'm charting my own progress. Professionally, it's good to keep an up-to-date presence, as it's really important to have your name out there. I feel it makes you more approachable, trustworthy, and likely to be hired. If your art is exciting to a lot of people, it looks better to a potential employer. Art is a business and is used as a means to communicate with an audience, so when your work has that effect it's great.

What sorts of workplace changes would you implement if given the opportunity?

In the workplace, there's honestly not much I'd change. Game development has its process down to a science, even though sometimes it's not always perfectly organized. However, depending on the situation/workplace, I'd implement more organization and meetings to critique work, which would open up the flow of communication.

How is the work you do in the game industry different from the work you have done elsewhere?

I'd say the work I've done is different because it's a job, but it's also really fun. Sometimes it's hard to believe that what you're getting paid to do is actual work. My background was mostly in retail prior to games. Retail sometimes isn't fun, but it does teach you basic social skills and how to do a job. I feel I could never go back to retail or have a standard office job after this experience.

Is there a programming component to producing game art?

I haven't really had much experience with code directly, to be honest. I'm more artistic than technical when it comes to UI and 2D art assets, and have always had a supportive role on the visual side. That said, I've done some integration with the source code. In my first internship, for example, I attached most art assets that I made into the code via Extensible Markup Language (XML).

It's actually common, though, that UI design is very technical. Even though I don't have the most knowledge about integration or programming, it's something that I'm interested in learning. I haven't really had a chance yet to hone those skills, but I know some basic things. So, it's not a definite requirement for an artist to be technically competent, but it does up your chances of working somewhere, especially in mobile or on a AAA project. I feel like when the majority of places look for UI artists, they don't look for someone who can just paint pretty pictures. They want someone who can function in multiple areas: illustration, icons, coding, wireframing, creating art assets, etc. One of the only setbacks, though, and depending on the project, can be that you end up doing more of one thing than another. You can get pigeonholed easily.

On a large game we did, our UI team had about twenty people, and everyone had their own distinct role. There were UI coders, folks who made the wireframes, UI designers, and the artists. Some people just had one job/major task, but everyone was working on the same thing: the UI. On a smaller team, you might find people filling multiple roles and getting to do a whole variety of tasks. You aren't as specialized there.

What does being an illustrator/2D/UI artist mean in the context of game development?

In my experience, an illustrator/2D/UI artist can be anything. The job class includes concept art, UI, graphic design, splash art, promotional art—it's the core of everything visual, and you can expand from there.[2] Most of the work an illustrator/2D artist does is seen in the final product as in-game assets. Your work is a very important component to the identity of a game or game system—think of the final painted icons a player sees/collects/interacts with inside the game.

UI's main focus is making the interface as engaging as possible for players. You're skinning menus that someone else already designed for you . . . which is still fun because you can theme them in really beautiful, illustrative ways. Sometimes UI will involve making wireframes, but I haven't had an opportunity to do that yet.

How would you describe the management structure in your company?

Working in a studio, it's professional but laid back. You know who your boss/bosses are, but at the same time you can have a friendly chat with them, maybe even a drink after work. Sometimes you'll have multiple bosses who manage what you're doing. A producer will assign tasks, an art director will give you direction, art leads will further expand on the vision of the art director, and sometimes the designers will get involved. A lot of the time you need approval from the art director to move forward, and a lot of suggestions and ideas don't move on.

As a contractor working remotely, you're your own management. You're given direct tasks, and maybe have a meeting on *Skype*. You mainly have discussions with the art director, who is usually your client.

How would you describe the workflow in your company?

Workflows in the places I've worked have ranged from consistent and planned to in flux with what's needed at the moment. I feel like it's pretty important to have proper organization, with your schedule and workload planned out for you and everything prioritized in advance. When this happens, a lot of stress is removed because you know what's expected of you, and this also encourages the best possible work because you feel very focused.

I've also experienced times when I'm given tasks but then more tasks are piled on and I need to be able to switch at any given moment. Someone will throw me a new assignment that needs to be finished immediately, or a marketing asset is needed for someone from the graphic art department. This method is kind of interesting as it always keeps the job unpredictable and alive.

Freelance for me has mostly been a single task—or sometimes several assignments at a time—and the work needs to be done by the deadline set by the client.

How does the workflow differ when working on different types of games (e.g., different genres, AAA versus casual games, etc.)?

Working on a larger project/game, you have a defined role. Depending on the project, it might even be just one job. Your job is very focused and you work within your team, making sure you execute your part. Working on a smaller, more casual/indie game, your job potentially will vary and sometimes you need to fill multiple roles and create a lot of assets. You might end up being a jack-of-all-trades.

How is it that you are able to include actual game assets on your website (e.g., the icons you have done)?

I consulted with my boss about when I could post the icons to my online portfolio, and he said, "As soon as we put it in the next update, you get to show it." I was allowed to publicly share my work so soon because the work was made public knowledge.

Concept artists normally have to wait awhile to show their work. I feel that's one of the advantages to making in-game assets. The assets you create, you get to show relatively soon after the game goes live, as long as you have approval and aren't violating any non-disclosure agreements. If the project you're working on gets canceled, though, you don't get to show anything from it at all.

How do artists contribute to a company's ability to be both profitable and innovative?

Artists contribute by helping influence the visuals of a project. For instance, Gearbox Software produces very beautiful, stylized games, and I think that has a lot to do with the art direction and artists they have. *Borderlands* has a really playful and creative, comic booky, cell-shaded style that fits well with its context. The characters and world have a lot of appeal and personality. Because of that, it was visually striking and fresh at the time when it launched. Artists are really important when it comes to visualizing, making ideas a reality, building worlds and characters, creating moods. It's one of the most important parts of a game. And direction from art directors and designers also plays a big part, helping push those ideas further. The work not only needs to look great and connect with players physically, but also emotionally. Art sometimes can be what sells the game.

The beauty of being an artist is that you can often be really innovative. The designer will come to you and say, "This is your brief. Your job is to make it as interesting and unique as possible." So the artist's job is to make characters or icons that push the boundaries of what's possible.

A lot of the time, I feel like projects are crippled by the business side of things. You can only have so much innovation, because at the end of the day the product still has to be created within the time frame. Art is where innovation can happen that doesn't jeopardize the bottom line.

What are some of your notable quality of life issues, both routine and exceptional, that you encounter?

I think the most challenging thing is finding the right balance and remembering that you and your health are important. It's very easy to get lost in your work.

While working in-house at a studio, I feel like I have a more structured life, more of a routine. I wake up, get ready, drive to work, and am away from

my personal life. Every day on my way to work, I think about what I'm planning to accomplish that day, how much harder I can work at my job because
everyone around me is so inspirational and working super hard. I look forward to hanging out after work and socializing with friends. I feel that maintaining a social life is much easier with this routine, as coworkers naturally
become friends. It's nice, too, because even at the end of the day I still have
motivation to pursue personal projects.

Working from home is a little more secluded and I feel like your social life
can take a serious dip if you don't find the right way to balance things. Your
cat automatically is your only interaction with life that day. There were times
when I was freelancing that I found myself waking up and just heading straight
to my computer in my pajamas and working until the work was "done." It's
really easy to never leave your computer when you freelance. I'd often forget
to eat or I'd overeat if I was stressed about a deadline. It's not that you become
lazy; it's more of a struggle to separate work life and your actual life. When I
freelanced, this was more of a quality of life issue for me than anything.

What are some of your notable career progression issues?

I'd say my personal career issues are figuring out what direction to take and
having the patience to get there. Finding enough work when you're freelancing is also a challenge, especially if you're ever out of work. I feel it can definitely hinder progression. Sometimes I'll doubt myself, but you can't give up.

The artist community in general is very competitive. There's a lot of talent
around, but not a lot of opportunities to harness that talent. You can make
a career, but it may be a rocky one. In order to make progress, you have to
make sure you're always on top of what you're doing and be up to industry standards. I feel the pressure of taking a step backward and knowing
that there's always a supply of talent in competition for your job—it really
drives you to be in survival-of-the-fittest mode. I definitely feel hopeful at
the beginning of every new adventure, though. Each one feels like the next
step, taking me a little further ahead.

What is it like to be a woman in the game industry?

I think it's pretty awesome being a woman in games. I mostly feel I'm
just one of the guys, so at the end of the day I feel like I'm treated pretty

equally. I've never felt I've been treated unfairly because of my gender. The game developer community in Massachusetts is also really great. Everyone I've encountered is very respectful of who you are. We have a lovely and amazing Women in Games (WIG) community.[3] It's a nice monthly gathering held around Boston that mainly focuses on a lot of wonderful, interesting topics. They'll choose a topic, and a woman who works in games and who's had all these great accomplishments will come and talk. It's very empowering, and guys go there too. There are two other local monthly game dev events I've attended: Boston Indies and Boston Post Mortem.[4] They have some really nice women speakers who also present at WIG every so often. I couldn't be happier or ask for a more supportive community.

You have worked in both video game and board game development. Are there connections you can draw between the two?

I'd say there are similarities, but differences too. If I could strip everything down, the core is illustration and having the knowledge of design principles. So as long as you understand color, composition, and other design basics, it's very easy to transition between the two. It's all about making a good image that does its job.

Back when I was freelancing for a board game project, my boss gave me a list and said, "We need this character in portrait with this facial feature, as well as one with this different facial feature." It's very similar to UI art for video games and making icons. UI is interesting because it's all about engaging the user, and it's the same thing with board and video games. You're making stuff that will engage the user, will keep them interested, and will point them in a direction: what to do, where to go, etc.

What are the challenges facing the industry over the next decade?

I think one of the biggest challenges is where the industry is headed, how it'll stay profitable while also making innovative games without oversaturating the market. It's common to hear some uncertainty about how most AAA studios might disappear, and indie/casual/mobile games will ultimately be more profitable in the coming years. Consoles are dying and the PC will be everyone's main platform. There's a lot of fear circling the industry, and games are only getting more expensive to create.

Jerry Chan
Animator

Jerry Chan is a visual effects (VFX) artist at Toys for Bob, a wholly owned subsidiary of Activision Blizzard. Previously he worked for BioWare, Turbine, and HitPoint Studios as a VFX artist, associate VFX artist, and animator, respectively. Because his father was an information technologies consultant and software reseller, Chan had early access to software such as Adobe's *Photoshop*, *Director*, and *Flash*. Consequently, Chan became an accomplished animator even before pursuing his BFA in art/animation with a minor in information technologies from the University of Massachusetts Amherst. While at the University of Massachusetts, he worked as an intern with Bit Films and created character animation for the award-winning short films *The Incident at Tower 37* and *Caldera*. His shipped titles include *Star Wars: The Old Republic*, *Infinite Crisis*, *Adera*, *The Secrets of Arcelia Island*, *Guardians of Magic: Amanda's Awakening*, and a variety of advergames. He also worked on the BioWare RPG *Shadow Realms*, which was canceled in 2015.[5] In his spare time, Chan maintains a blog titled "What's it like working in a video game studio?" (http://workinginavideo gamestudio.tumblr.com).

* * * * *

How did you come to work in the game industry?

When I was a sophomore in high school I decided that I was going to pursue my dreams of becoming a character animator at Disney, and I started studying everything I could that was animation related. I had been animating in *Flash* since the seventh grade (back when the company was still Macromedia and not Adobe), so by the time I started college I had a pretty good head start.

The second semester of my freshman year at the University of Massachusetts—I'd just successfully fought my way into the art program to get into the animation program—I found a flyer in the dining hall that said, "Come take a character animation class." So, even though I was already halfway through the semester, I made my way over to the class. It only had two other students in it, and I talked my way in because I'd already studied the textbook, *The Animator's Survival Kit*.

As it turns out, there were two animation programs at the University of Massachusetts: one run through the art program, and the other run out of the computer science department. I'm not entirely sure what the story is behind the two programs, but I think I was the first student from the art department to take a class in the computer science animation program.

When I was finishing up my internship with Bit Films, my animation teacher—who is now a producer at HitPoint Studios—asked if I wanted a paid gig doing hand-drawn background animation for downloadable point-and-click games (also known as "hidden object games"). With school loans looming, I took the job and found that I enjoyed doing VFX way more than character animation.

I never considered myself a VFX artist until Microsoft approached HitPoint to do a game for the launch of Windows 8. Until then, I'd been doing mostly hand-drawn work in *Flash* and some minor *After Effects* stuff. But with this game, I'd essentially be the guy in charge of making all the cinematics and big effects in the game.

I didn't get into real-time effects until early 2013, however, when I joined up with Turbine to work on *Infinite Crisis.*

As to exactly how I got into the industry, that goes all the way back to middle school—that's when I discovered Richard Williams's *Animator's Survival Kit.* If I hadn't found that book and started studying it, I wouldn't have been able to impress my friend who was teaching a character animation class. This is the same friend who would eventually go on to be one of the head producers at HitPoint.

So in my case, it was an instance of knowing the right person, but I also did a lot of the legwork myself to impress the right people.

Prior to joining Toys for Bob, you were a contractor for BioWare. What is the difference between contract work and full-time employment?

Contracting is pretty much a full-time job without full-time benefits. When I interviewed with BioWare, I was interviewing specifically for a contract position in the studio. So, I knew that I wouldn't have full-time employee benefits, such as paid health care, vacation days, or a severance package were I to be laid off. That said, as a contractor, I still had access to health insurance and other benefits, but they weren't as heavily subsidized by the studio and so they cost me a little bit more. On the plus side, I was paid on an hourly basis, meaning that during crunch time I earned overtime pay. Had I been a full-time employee, I would have just earned my regular salary, even if I put in a hundred hours of overtime.

Working as a contractor also meant that, while I was located on the Bio-Ware campus and reported to BioWare employees, I was employed through a temp agency that oversaw my payroll and deductions. While it might sound like a weird setup, I've seen this same thing done at other studios, and it just makes life for the human resources department easier. HR only has to manage one group of employees rather than two, and abide by only one set of rules.

Every studio I've worked for has had contractors. It's ultimately a question of who they can hire full-time or how many full-time positions they have. It's also hard to justify hiring people for more than a contract job if the studio doesn't have enough work to do once the project is finished. So, it's not uncommon for studios to hire contractors on as needed, and then let the contracts expire once the work is done. This isn't some kind of underhanded process—the nature of this kind of employment is usually well defined when you're taking on the job.

Beyond the vacation days, health care, and limits of the contract, I haven't seen much difference between full-time employees and contractors. In fact, contractors may actually have a little bit more freedom when it comes to working on side projects. It's not entirely out of the question to do side work as a contractor so long as the nature of that work doesn't compete with your contract obligations. As an artist in games, I could probably start a webcomic and be in the clear, but producing art for a competing game while working under contract at a studio probably wouldn't be a good idea.

What part of your job is most professionally rewarding?

First is the collaborative process. I often need to go talk to a designer or character animator or environmental artist about how my effects fit in with their work and with the grand scheme of things. The constant back-and-forth process between artists and designers is where a lot of the magic happens—like solving problems—and is one of the more enjoyable parts of the job.

Second, there's that moment when someone sees my work for the first time and they have that "whoa" reaction. I do a lot of things with color theory, shapes, timing, and other psychological shenanigans in order to elicit emotional reactions, and when I've done my job correctly, anyone who plays the game is going have a "wow" moment.

What are the most significant internal challenges you face in your job?

Recently, I've had to integrate into a new team—adjusting to a new process, a new workflow, and trying to insert myself into a well-oiled machine. It's one of those things that will get better with time as I learn to work with a new studio.

What are the external challenges you face in your job?

Not thinking about work is often one of my harder challenges. As a VFX artist, a lot of what I do involves problem solving, and if I can't figure out a solution by the end of the workday it ends up bugging me for the rest of the night.

What sorts of workplace changes would you implement if given the opportunity?

Nap rooms and office cats and dogs would be amazing. There are times where taking something silly like video games very seriously can be stressful, so things to alleviate that stress would probably boost my morale a ton. That said, my morale right now is pretty darn high. Also, it may be illegal to have sleeping facilities inside an office, since having them would imply that you're working enough hours to warrant not going home.

You have worked for both large and small game development companies. How does scheduling and workflow differ according to studio size?

A smaller studio may not have a lot of project management experience, and even though everyone means well, the pipeline may be a little rough. At Hit-Point, for example, sometimes the designer would change the design after all of the artwork was finished. Because the art was mostly hand painted, we'd have to re-render the background, an artist would have to hand paint details and foliage onto it, color correct everything, and then that'd get passed back to me to redo all of my effects. I always felt bad for the sound guy who was at the very end of the pipeline—the last person after me—because he'd have to redo all of his work. All of this, by the way, came when we were trying to finish up other sections of the game and sticking to the same schedule, so we'd have to do all of this rework while also trying to get new work finished.

There wasn't any maliciousness associated with the design changes; it was more a question of how do you learn what you've never been taught? Or, rather, how do you learn how to do things the right way without having seen what can go wrong? Most of us at HitPoint were fresh out of college, so we were still learning the ropes. The big thing to keep in mind with HitPoint was that we were a brand-new studio. Nobody really had any industry experience. A couple of people had worked at Codemasters for a while, but that was it.

There was a big mobile boom while I was at HitPoint. Another studio had become successful and was making waves with their use of microtransactions and social media integration. My bosses understandably also wanted to run a successful studio, so our games started to push toward the same model of social media integration and microtransactions. The problem was that our studio didn't have the years of research and development that this other successful studio had. We were copying models without understanding why they worked, but they worked for us in some ways so we kept at them. As a result, we hired more people so that we could keep on making more of these games and make them faster. At the same time, we were making a big title for a big client that was pretty much along the same lines as these other games, with an emphasis on social media integration. As this project got bigger, we hired more people, a phenomenon I later learned is called the "people hose." With the people hose, you just open up the tap and add people. At HitPoint, we went from thirty employees to seventy in the course of a year.

Unfortunately, the client canceled the big project, and because we hadn't diversified our offerings, there weren't any other projects for us to turn to. Meanwhile, games you'd normally play on social media were declining in popularity, so in order to survive, the company had to lay off more than half of its staff, including me. As it turns out, we'd been following a trend and data that were years old by the time we could act on them, and so we were years late when we finally got our products to market. In Massachusetts especially, there were a bunch of Web-based mobile studios that tried to do the same thing, and we all ended up in the same boat with layoffs, downsizing, and closure.

Were you required to sign an exit contract as part of your layoff?

Yes. Severance packages are usually tied to an exit contract, and the contract basically says, "Don't reveal company secrets, don't badmouth us, and we won't badmouth you."

As far as layoffs go, every company I've worked for has been as nice as possible to their employees who are being laid off. I've never been part of anything like when security guards are positioned around the studio and employees are told to pack up their things and leave. When I was at HitPoint and there was a big layoff, everyone went and got drinks afterwards and no one made a big fuss. There was some crying, for sure, but we were able to pack up our things, our computers weren't locked down, our accounts weren't frozen immediately.

It was similar at Turbine when they announced layoffs. Employees were told to return to their desks and certain employees would be contacted to schedule an exit interview. But they didn't kick us out of the studio. We all stayed and supported each other. Many hugs were given. Again, there was a little bit of crying—I'd be lying if I didn't say that I was one of many teary-eyed game developers on that day—but we were all able to stick around and support our now former coworkers who were leaving.

Is the "people hose" model of staffing up and then laying off common?

I've heard that it was a lot more common back in the early days of the industry, but a lot of studios have realized that you lose valuable talent by constantly hiring and laying off people. At Turbine, for example, as *The Lord of the Rings Online* was ramping down a little bit, they tried to find places for everyone on *Infinite Crisis*.

From what I've noticed, the bigger studios keep a closer eye on their finances and production schedules. That is, the bigger studios I've worked for really try to only hire people that they absolutely need, and hiring is more about the long-term health of the company and the product. They try to keep you on schedule as best they can so that you're not keeping someone down the chain from working, and thus wasting money.

How do organizational structures and workflow processes differ between small and large development studios?

In general, smaller studios have less structure and less solid pipelines compared to big studios. At HitPoint, we pretty much had the attitude of "Do whatever it takes to get it done." Since we were a small team to start with, even though I was an animator—and later an effects artist—I also knew some programming, and so I ended up helping code some small advergames even though that wasn't in my primary job brief. There were also times where, as an effects artist, the art director told me to create chunks of backgrounds, or that I had to supply my own backgrounds for cutscenes because the other artists didn't have the bandwidth to get something done. I also did a lot of the final renders and final composites for outsourced cinematics. So, at smaller studios, you often wear many different hats.

At bigger studios, you tend to stick more to your role. As a VFX artist, my primary concern at Turbine and BioWare was effects. At Turbine, we had a rigid workflow process built around Scrum and we worked in two-week sprints. Part of the Scrum system is that you take a certain amount of time— say X hours—and you make your calculations based on X (i.e., "This is how many hours I think this task will take, and this is how many tasks I think I can get done"). Our producer made sure that we stuck to that schedule, and she also shielded us from any more work and rearranged things if something up the pipeline would delay us from working.

Does studio size have a perceptible effect on the feel of the work environment?

Not really. HitPoint started off feeling like a small studio, partly because we were crammed into a former tobacco barn. I'm not going to say we were shoulder to shoulder, but my desk was almost right next to the art director's desk, who was right next to the producer. At around fifty people is when I stopped knowing everybody there on a first-name basis. I just had a really hard time keeping up with people because we expanded so rapidly, and I didn't interact with most of the people. I worked mostly with the art director and the sound designer, and by the time I'd leave for the day almost everyone else had gone home.

Turbine was much bigger—about 500 people—but I knew everyone on the *Infinite Crisis* team, and it was a big team. It felt like a much smaller studio than HitPoint, even though there was also a *Dungeons & Dragons Online* team, a *The Lord of the Rings Online* team, a marketing team, and administration. I had more opportunity there to interact with more people on a daily basis, and so I got to know way more people by name, some of whom I still keep up with. Even though we were in a really big corporate office— my first week there I kept getting lost—it felt like working in a small studio because everyone was really friendly.

How is the work you do in the game industry different from the work you have done elsewhere?

Compared to film, I find that games are, at a technical level, much more challenging than most film effects artists think. This isn't to take anything away from film, but since game graphics are processed in real time, you're limited not only by time and budget but also by how much the engine and platform can handle. This is especially important for VFX. An explosion in film done in post can be created with billions of particles, pre-rendered, and then composited into the original shot. In video games, anything more than 100 particles per effect often gets you the stink eye from the rest of the team as their systems lag during playtests (because it's that 100 particle effect plus many, many other effects firing off at the same time). If I'm working on something like a waterfall effect, I can't simulate the waterfall by pouring out millions of virtual ping-pongs and creating a mesh based off of that—that's nearly a million polygons. At most, I want something like 500 polygons, because the engine needs to be able to render that as well as the rest of the level at the same time. I could create a new huge texture for each effect to make it beautiful, but I need to be mindful of the file size because that impacts both download size and memory usage size. Again, this isn't to say that film effects artists lack any sort of skill, because I couldn't do what they can do. I just have the additional challenge of weighing visual definition against performance on a daily basis.

That said, similar to film and stage productions, video games are a massively collaborative effort. You work in tandem with so many other people that it's amazing that more toes aren't stepped on regularly. And the level of communication required for this sort of coordinated production is mind blowing. It's definitely something that school doesn't usually prepare you for.

There were times at Turbine when we were looking for more people, and there were folks in film effects applying for the job. We looked at their effects and they were all simulated. The applicants had no real-time experience. When they had an explosion cloud, it looked really good, but they used five million individual particles that were pre-rendered. When everything's pre-rendered, it's drawn frame by frame and played back as a pre-rendered video. Whereas in a video game, you actually have people walk around this thing. You need to run the game at 60 frames per second in order for it to look smooth, and you can't have five million particles because no engine can handle five million particles firing up, plus shaders, plus characters, plus the rest of the level, plus the other effects at the same time. That's the big difference in approach between video games and film, but games are starting to reach that same quality bar as far as how things look. The film standard is definitely coming.

How do you keep up with the increase in visual standards?

I personally don't keep up with it on a regular basis. The VFX leads are the ones who have to keep up with the latest developments. They're the ones who keep on pushing harder to get better-quality work. They're the ones who keep track, because I'm the one who is heads-down in the work. They're the ones who have to say, "Okay, these new engine features are coming out soon. Let's see if we can make something really cool using them." So, I'll get assigned to that, and I'll push as hard as I can, bounce it back to the lead, and he'll say, "Can you tweak this thing a little bit?" And it's back and forth until we get something really polished. For the most part, my knowledge of game effects comes from getting pushed by my leads, or by stealing knowledge and know-how from my peers. For the most part, the only reason I know about new developments is because the quality bar keeps rising and I can only hope that I can keep up with it.

What are the challenges facing the industry over the next decade?

I'm not sure I could sum them up as succinctly or as well as Mark Harris did in his article titled "The Day the Movies Died," or as Steve Jobs did in the video titled "Steve Jobs Foretold the Downfall of Apple!"

Studios, being moneymaking entities, will look to other successful studios for clues about success strategies. Sometimes copycatting works, but from what I've seen, many times the copycatter doesn't fully understand why the original product was successful, so the copy fails. Just look at the rise and fall of free-to-play games with microtransactions. *Dawngate* and *Infinite Crisis* were shut down because they couldn't capture that fire in a bottle that made other free-to-play games in the same genre successful.[6]

What are some of your notable quality of life issues, both routine and exceptional?

I usually joke around about how it's hard driving back home at night after staring at bright glowing, swirling effects all day on my screen, but beyond that I don't think I have any notable quality of life issues that aren't faced by anyone else with a full-time job.

But I can't emphasize work/life balance enough. I could be going full throttle ahead with all things games, but as filmmaker Brad Bird says, in order to create the illusion of life you need to actually have one. That's been one of the bigger life moves I've made since I got out of college. I worked really hard, got the job, started doing good work, and then I was like, "Oh, maybe there's more to life than this."

One of the good things about the game industry is the opportunity to have a really good work/life balance. I'm not at the studio right now. I'm not punching in like I used to. I'm about to cook myself a really nice brunch. I'm sitting in my pajamas. I have plans for later that aren't game related or television related. I can adjust the amount of time I spend around games and computers adequately.

I used to work with a guy who had a kid who meant the world to him, so he'd go home and spend all his free time with her. And my VFX supervisor at BioWare came into work early so that he could leave to be home with his daughter after she got out of day care. I don't know if that's a side effect of everybody in the industry getting older and realizing that we need to be able to live our lives, but there's actually a really good work/life balance in many game studios. The biggest issue is getting the job in the first place. There's fierce competition to get in.

Let me give you another example of good quality of life. At all of the places I've worked, everyone is pretty much gone between Christmas and New Year's. When I was working on *Adera* for Windows 8, most of Microsoft ended up taking off the second half of December. I'm not sure big holiday breaks are common in the game industry, because I've heard a lot of horror stories and I've lived through one myself. But I think with bigger studios, because the age demographic of people working there tends to be a little bit older, employees want family time, which is why I think management tries to design the schedule so that everyone can take time off to be with their families around the holidays.

In my experience, project managers do their best to make sure that everyone can take the time off. When I was working on *Infinite Crisis*, we still had work that needed to be done during the holidays, but because the project managers could establish the pace, they just said, "Okay, we're probably not going get any work done right now, so let's just push the schedule ahead about two weeks." I think that was really good project management that was meant to take care of the workers. And that's one of the things that has really surprised me about the game industry. I had the option of jumping ship over to film or staying in games, and being treated well is why I've stayed in games. It seems like the project managers and the companies tend to care a little bit more about their workers than the horror stories I've heard about film (e.g., constant hiring and laying off of people when a movie or television show is complete, and whether or not they can actually afford to pay their staff, much like what happened to Rhythm & Hues Studios when it filed for bankruptcy and laid off a bunch of people).

I've only been working in the industry for a few years, so I don't know if this is a recent development. I can say from working at Turbine and BioWare, the demographic seems to be that most people are married, most people have kids. I'm one of only a handful of people who are in their early to mid-twenties who doesn't have kids, isn't married, isn't in a long-term relationship, and could work crazy hours. It might just be because everyone's starting to get a little bit older in the industry and they're realizing, "Oh, you know what, it's not healthy to work really long hours." In fact, I think one of the first things I was told when I got to Turbine was that crunch is a failure of project management. Right there is a management philosophy that shapes the environment. It also might be that the industry is new and the management process is getting more refined.

Why do you think the industry demographic skews older?

If you think about it, a lot of these industry vets who have been working in the industry for ten to twenty years at this point started off when video games were brand new. And while back then the games were just as fun, they certainly didn't have the huge production values or scope that a lot of modern games have. People trying to get into the industry then probably didn't have as much competition as people right out of college have right now. The unfortunate thing for people today trying to get into the industry is that they're competing against these veterans who've had years of experience to hone their craft. The current jobs are limited, and if you were in charge of a studio and you had a deadline coming up in a year, would you hire someone fresh out of college with no experience, or would you hire a veteran with years of proven skills under their belt?

As a slightly related example, there's a great 3D animation done by Victor Navone in the late 1990s of an alien singing Gloria Gaynor's "I Will Survive." While it's incredibly well done, by today's standards it's comparable to what a good student would be able to produce in school. Back in 2001, this short helped land him a job at Pixar. If a student were to submit something similar to this to any animated film company today for a full-time animator position, there's a good chance they'd be passed up for someone with a better reel.

It's really hard for schools to keep up with the new technology and methods. I'm not saying anything against schools, but they have the impossible task of trying to hit a moving target with an industry that's constantly changing. As a result, even at the University of Massachusetts where I graduated from, there are really only a handful of us that ended up making it into careers as professional artists—maybe less than a dozen out of a hundred people in my Art Foundations class. As much as I love my professor—and I'm still friends with her—we didn't really learn what we needed to learn from classes alone.

At one point at Turbine, we were looking for more VFX artists and we were getting some stuff from people straight out of school. They either didn't have an understanding of timing or texture, or they didn't have that thing we were looking for. It might just be that the game industry is too picky. Maybe you really do need that two years of experience that most of the job postings ask for.

Getting back to your question, more young people don't work in the games industry because they don't have the higher degree of skill that's needed in a live production environment. That said, I know that when I was working over at HitPoint, they were hiring people straight out of college, and I got hired straight out of college. A lot of the smaller, independent, or mobile studios would hire people right out of college a few years ago because they needed the work to get done and they didn't have a need for—or the ability to pay for—experience.

Are there other things beyond specific technical skills and work experience that young developers seem to be missing?

When I was in college, I had the good fortune of taking a class with Chris Perry, who was a tools developer at Pixar during *Toy Story 2* and *A Bug's Life*. That was a crazy, crazy time in tools development for Pixar. One of the things he talked about was how the formal education system doesn't actually teach people to collaborate. It was in his class that we did a full-fledged short film, *The Incident at Tower 37*. It was an independent film, but most everything was done by students. I had the role of an animation fixer on the project, meaning I would polish and touch up existing animations. It was the first time I was ever exposed to working in a collaborative environment. There were other people doing shading, compositing, and lighting, and I had to learn how to talk to them to get the job done, be it queuing up my new animations for render, hooking up a newly rendered sequence to the final composite, or figuring out why something broke. That was the only class I took in college where there was that kind of collaborative effort being done with expertise and guidance from somebody who'd been in the industry and knew what it was like. Other group projects I worked on never went nearly as well, because in those classes everyone had a similar background (imagine a bunch of artists trying to figure out technical issues).

I went to college thinking I was going to be a character animator, and I came out thinking I was a character animator, but in my first job I found out that I enjoyed animating effects more than doing character animation. It's hard to know what you want to specialize in, because people just don't have that experience, they don't have that exposure. Again, this is partially because the industry is so new—how do you design a curriculum to account for all these things that can be tested and be reliable, and also say that this is the skill set you're going to need? I don't want to say school sucked, and I don't want to say the education system is failing kids, but educators have a really difficult task of hitting this moving target. For example, my position right now—VFX—is in high demand. There aren't many games effects artists out there, because if you look at where games were ten years ago, effects weren't really anything more than a couple of cloud puffs, maybe some sparks. Now

VFX are gameplay feedback, and this is just something newer to games. A decade ago you couldn't have the visual fidelity that we have today, so effects artists had to find other ways. But now that we do have the visual fidelity and more complex systems, I don't even know how you'd possibly get all the skills you need to know to be a VFX artist just by going to school. You need character animation, you need texturing, you need modeling. There are a lot of things that go into making a VFX artist that four years of school unfortunately doesn't seem to be able to cover.

Is it expected that new employees already know how to collaborate, or is learning that skill something studios understand they have to facilitate?

I'll give a double answer. I think technically, all the companies I've worked for assumed that I knew how to talk to people. There weren't specific instructions to "meet now with the designers, talk to them about this, about the character design, about what this spell's supposed to look like." I actually had to go over to those folks on my own initiative, poke my head over the cubicle half wall and say, "Hey, guys, I just wanted to know before I started working to see if you had any specific requests."

At the same time, the development schedule doesn't take that conversation time into account—it's not built in. At a good studio, people just come over on their own and there's a lot of open communication. It's kind of like self-driven communication. It's half assumed that you know how to talk to people, but people also give you the benefit of the doubt, especially if you're new. When I started at BioWare, I sat in my little corner for a bit because my desk wasn't moved over with the other effects artists. So, I had to walk around and ask people questions—how to do certain things, or what the process was for one thing or another. There wasn't any time scheduled for that, but everyone was incredibly nice, straightforward, honest, and kind with their answers, and they didn't berate me by saying, "Why don't you just read the game design doc?" They just explained stuff to me in a very straightforward manner when I went to their desk. There was no resentment, no "Aw, man, you're taking time out of my day." So, people are typically nice at studios, but you do already need to know how to collaborate. It's assumed that you know how to get up and talk to people.

And I think it just kind of happens. My bosses definitely didn't hold my hand and say "You should really go talk to this designer to see what the gameplay feedback is." That came from the experience of having work come back my way with comments saying, "The gameplay feedback doesn't match up with what's expected. Can you please change the effect around?"

Basically, collaboration in the industry comes not only from a place of being nice to people and being productive for the sake of the project, but it also comes from a place of learning how to avoid pain. And that's the pain of constantly having to redo your work later. As an example, at my first job I was pretty much handed static background images and told to animate them. Before I had the common sense to check in with the designers or the art director about what they were expecting and what the ultimate goal of this set piece was, I'd just hammer away at it. In my defense, it was partially because we had a really aggressive schedule and none of us actually had the time to get the work done, let alone meet up with each other and take away from valuable production time. But what would end up happening is that I'd get feedback later that they were really expecting something else, or that the design of the game had changed and they needed to redo things. In many cases, I had to go back and redo all of the work, which drove me nuts because of how much time we were wasting by constantly redoing all of this art.

Communication is a skill, but the good news is that skill can be developed in college. That's where I got most of my communication skills. When I was doing my thesis project, I found that the people who gave me the best raw feedback in terms of story, framing, and composition weren't the students in my animation program but the students who hung out in the science fiction library on campus. Those people are my audience. They're the ones who'll be enjoying whatever I produce, so I was just able to bounce ideas off them. That's where I learned how to ask for feedback. I think that's one of the benefits of going to college if you want to work in the game industry. You have access to all these people, and it's a safe harbor in which to experiment and learn how to talk to people. I can't go up to any random guy in a coffee shop right now and say, "Hey, what do you think of this explosion?" without getting a really weird look.

What are some of your notable career progression issues?

The biggest challenge I think I went through is that to get an entry-level job somewhere, you usually need two years of experience. So, you need experience to get experience. At the same time, it's so hard for students to get a job right now because most school programs don't adequately prepare students for those jobs. Again, this isn't because the schools are bad, but because the industry changes so quickly that it's hard for academia to keep up. I've actually written a couple of blog posts on the subject.

Once you're in the games industry, and once you do the two years at a studio where you do good work—in two years, you launch a title—it's so much easier to find more work. Even though I have a job I really like, I still get emails saying, "Oh, by the way, we still need VFX over here." I either refer my friends or I turn them down. My guess is that because the quality bar has gone up so far and project deadlines are tight, studios prefer experienced people on the team who know how to work in that environment and have a proven level of skill. Not every studio has the luxury of saying, "Okay, we can take a little break now to train up a new person while also taking on the new deadlines." When you have the option of hiring somebody who has real-time particle experience and already knows all this stuff—and is already really good—versus a brand-new employee who doesn't quite have that sense of timing, or they don't know how to properly optimize effects, most studios will opt for experience.

But, at the same time, the benefit of being a new college graduate without any experience is that you don't cost nearly as much to hire on as someone with a ton of experience, especially if you're young and don't have kids. I don't have four kids to take care of like my parents did, and I don't need to buy or rent a huge place to live. Most of the senior folks in the industry do need that money because they have to support families and pay a mortgage.

It's proving that you can actually do the work in the first place that's the hardest thing. The biggest reason I got my first job was because I knew somebody who was a producer over at HitPoint and I was a student in a class she taught.

I have a friend in the industry who is almost entirely self-educated. Before he got in, he was working a day job and teaching himself *Maya* at night. He went to get art feedback from one of the VFX higher-ups at Turbine and that's how he got his job. There's so much extra effort needed beyond school in order to actually get a job in the games industry.

For games, specifically, it's really hard to hit a moving target, especially when the target doesn't go at a constant speed and you can't predict how that target's going to change. If you asked anybody ten to twenty years ago what game graphics would be like today, they probably would've had no idea what kinds of things we'd now be capable of or what kinds of tools we'd have access to. So how do you prepare to teach for that kind of changing environment? That much-admired college animation professor I talked about earlier is a good example. She left Hollywood in the mid-1990s to start teaching. She had a huge filmography, and I'm pretty sure she's on a first-name basis with George Lucas and James Cameron. But when it came to teaching us *Maya* and *After Effects*, she had to hire other people or she had us do online tutorials because that software wasn't what she used when she was in the field. That's nothing against her; I learned a lot from her and I wouldn't be where I am today without her. But at the same time, workflow changes constantly, so it's really hard for anyone who has to teach this to keep up with the rapid changes happening in the field.

d. Koy vanOteghem
Lead Artist

d. Koy vanOteghem is lead artist at Blind Squirrel Games. Previously he was senior environmental artist at Blind Squirrel Games, and before that lead artist, senior artist, junior artist, and prop contractor at inXile Entertainment. He holds a BS in architecture from the Georgia Institute of Technology and has taken postgraduate coursework in game development from Santa Monica College's Academy of Entertainment & Technology. His shipped titles include *Evolve*, *Disney Infinity: Marvel Super Heroes* (aka *Disney Infinity 2.0 Edition*), *Wasteland 2*, *Choplifter HD*, and *Hunted: The Demon's Forge*. He also worked on *HEI$T*, which was canceled during alpha in 2010.[7] He is a husband, father of two young girls, and a military brat, as well as a gameplay-deprived developer and ex-architect. He is determined to stay in Los Angeles, California, for as long as possible.

* * * * *

How did you come to work in the game industry?

After leaving the architecture profession, I returned to school to pursue illustration. I ended up in a game design class because I was interested in the design software the industry was using. I thought it might be interesting to see how game design could assist me in my pursuit of illustration technique.

My instructor liked my work and ethic and invited me to start contracting with his studio as a freelancer. I jumped at the opportunity, and shortly thereafter took a full-time position as a junior artist there.

What are the job duties for the different artist positions?

Prop contractors are, no surprise, artists who build the props for a game: chairs, beer bottles, garbage cans, and so forth—all the things in an environment that make it look lived in. They're usually contract workers, and there are a variety of people who might hold this position. Often, prop contractors are students looking to break into the industry and who want to get their hands on real-world applications. There are prop contractors who are freelancers too, people who've been in the industry for a while but for whatever reason have decided they're not really into the full-time daily grind and want to work independently. So, the title of prop contractor doesn't necessarily imply inexperience, but it often does. Prop contractors tend to work for little money, and the position is really designed to provide the experience necessary for securing a full-time job. Prop contracting is often handled by a prop house, which can be a large organization with hundreds of artists who specifically only build props on a contract basis. Even when they're not part from a prop house, prop contractors aren't full team members, nor full-time employees. They just work on a specific project for a specific contract.

A junior artist position is typically held by someone who's new to the industry. It might be filled by someone who had an internship somewhere, a student coming right out of school, or someone who moves from a three-month temporary job into a full-time position. Junior artists are on the bottom rung of the full-time professional ladder, so they end up doing a lot of tasks that are much more production oriented. They tend to be involved in the grunt work, where they're actually modeling, texturing, and working through discovery. What I mean by "discovery" is that a lot of times there's a research component to art development. We call it discovery because it requires someone to do things like researching something online to understand how it operates, figuring out what an object should look like, fixing a problem with a specific asset, or determining if an asset is appropriate for multiple locations. Discovery is the process of looking for, identifying, and cataloging instances of something in a game. Discovery can also involve figuring out which props should be used in which levels. Typically, discovery tasks are given to junior artists because more senior people don't have the time to comb through a game at such a micro level.

A senior artist, as the title would imply, is someone who's been in the industry for a while. They have a few published titles under their belt, and they're typically tasked with things that have a higher level of responsibility. They're most often still involved in production—building props and assets, developing artistic styles, and things of that sort—but they're more autonomous in nature and their tasks are usually larger. For example, a senior artist might develop new tile sets or engage in world building from a higher level. They aren't necessarily placing clutter or anything like that within a level, but they might be doing more level design–oriented tasks. Senior artists will often have a junior artist or mid-level artist assisting them in their endeavors, and that's usually sort of a trial run on managing people. A senior artist might have one or two people who help out and do some of the grunt work, but for the most part senior artists do whatever tasks have been delegated to them.

A lead artist is where the management really starts to come into play, and there are different kinds of leads. You can be a character lead, an environment artist lead, a UI lead, and so forth. These are the people who manage those smaller sub-teams within the art department. In my current role as lead artist, I actually supervise the leads of those sub-departments. I work directly under the art director, but I'm the only person at my level. Typically, you have an art director and then you have a lead artist who liaises with the rest of the art department. Leads tend to spend about half of their time managing personnel below them and half of their time problem solving and developing pipelines, doing content creation, and conducting research.

What are your day-to-day responsibilities as lead artist?

Well, for one thing, I'm out on the floor a lot. I'm not at my desk much because I get pulled away constantly to problem solve. In fact, I'd say that's the best description of my job. I'm a problem solver in the sense that artists often need guidance, not just in an artistic direction but in terms of technical direction too, as well as in terms of strategies to take when approaching a task. I'm often called in to coordinate multiple artists or artist/engineer teams who are trying to solve a problem. I spend most of my day jumping around the studio, involved in small group meetings with two or three people who have a specific task ahead of them, and they need somebody to sign off on their strategy. So, I'll listen to their ideas on how to tackle something. I also do a lot of coordination through email with outside vendors and with various department heads, and as a result I spend very little time producing anything. As lead artist, I don't do a lot of content creation but I'm involved with the people who do.

A lot of the aesthetic and stylistic choices of a game are established pretty early on in the project, and the art director has the ultimate say in which direction that goes. As lead, I coordinate the artistic approach on a daily basis, and then when things get to a good spot, they can be presented to the art director. My job is to make sure that neither the artists nor the art director get caught up in the minutiae of the day-to-day development. Often, I'll get a little hands-on as people are working through content creation. I'll inject myself in their pipeline and talk about best practices, or give them feedback on a specific asset they're working on to try to achieve what I understand to be the art director's intent. I try to help and guide them in their efforts so that their reviews with the art director are less problematic.

As I mentioned earlier, a big part of my job is coordinating with other departments and outside vendors. We have a design department, an engineering department, and of course executive-level team members. As part of my daily responsibilities I have what's called a "daily stand up" where the leads from the departments assemble and we discuss problems that we're having, things we need to coordinate—basically progress status report–type stuff. I work daily with the engineering lead trying to address technical issues that we face, and often what we're doing is trying to hook up the right team members—the right artist with the right engineer with the right designer— to make sure that those people get into the right room or the right conversation to solve a problem or take on a task.

As lead artist, I'm essentially the management grunt worker. I'm the one who's on the floor, who's scheduling, who's looking at bug lists and *JIRA* [bug tracking software] tasks. The art director is less involved in that component of production and much more involved in the discussions with the executive team, defining what's happening in the various projects, the artistic approach, staffing, budget management, and software acquisition.

How do your job duties change over the course of a game's development?

We might begin a project and be short staffed in the sense that we haven't yet filled all our seats. In that case, early on in production I might be responsible for doing a lot of the front-end work that a lower-tiered artist would ordinarily handle: a lot of that discovery that I referenced earlier, some initial tests on art style, asset development—that sort of thing. I'll take a lot of that on myself to better understand our technical limitations and be able to provide some things to the engineers so that they can get started on their work. Then, as we staff up and expand our team, I start letting go of some of those responsibilities and start taking on more of the day-to-day managerial stuff. As we get toward the end of the project, I move into a role where I'm reviewing the whole body of work on a daily basis. By that I mean I'll play through the game trying to use my artistic eye to figure out where we need to focus for the last stages of polish before release.

The truth is, my job changes pretty dramatically over the course of a project, and every project I've ever worked on has been extremely different from the others. They all have differences in scheduling as far as when you staff up and when a project is greenlit. I've come into some projects that have already been in production and so I've just had to hit the ground running. Other projects I've worked on from initial concept through publication and overseen ramp-up and ramp-down in its entirety.

But this isn't to say that there aren't certain signals that a shift in my job duties is coming. Here's an example: let's say you're taking an original IP that you've developed within your studio internally and you've put together a pitch document. You've got an art style that's maybe not fully established but does have some tooth to it. You've got your gameplay sort of laid out and designed, your pitch document is complete, and you're farming it out to publishers. You really have to have a skeleton crew at that point. You might have only three or four people working on the project at that time because it's not revenue generating. Once a project gets greenlit by a publisher, or maybe even when they start to express real interest in it but haven't necessarily signed on the dotted line, you have to evaluate what's been happening in the employment market. The project I'm on right now is a good example. The project fell into our laps a little too quickly, and because of the way the employment market is right now, it's actually quite difficult to find senior-level and mid-level talent out there. We'd hoped to staff up by fifty or so people—all senior, mid-level, and junior artists and engineers—within a month or two of initiating the project, but three months in we've only had maybe twenty people we were able to hire. It's very competitive out there now in terms of hiring, especially in Southern California, which is definitely a hornet's nest of developers. So we've ended up having to outsource quite a bit of our work as a result. We have a pretty good team internally, but it's a smaller team than we anticipated. The ramp-up for the team was accelerated and thus somewhat problematic. Typically you can't staff up for a project until it's greenlit, when you've got a publisher saying, "We'll pay you X amount of dollars at such and such a time." Otherwise you risk hiring people who then have no work to do.

What are some of the common interdepartmental interactions you facilitate as lead artist?

In the art department, you have artists who are content producers. They make assets, which might be a 3D model, a texture set, matte paintings for a sky dome, etc. But you also have technical artists. These are people who didn't necessarily go to art school and don't necessarily produce content, though they often do. Instead, their focus is more on the technical side of things such as dealing with animation systems, integrating art into a game engine, developing pipelines for production, and developing tools specifically to help artists do their jobs better or faster or more efficiently. There's a lot of interaction between technical artists and artists on a daily basis. They coordinate on things that are pipeline oriented.

But when artists—and I'd include technical artists in this group—have to coordinate with engineers, programmers, and people of that nature, there are a couple of different phases that occur in any project. During the bulk of production, this coordination is usually about interactive objects in a game, whether it's something that's animated or if the player will need to interact with a machine that does something, or an artificial intelligence that's providing feedback to the player. Anytime you have that type of coordination, you really have to get artists and engineers in the same room so that each side understands limitations, what is and what isn't possible, best practices, and strategies on how to approach any type of problem-solving exercise.

There's also another phase at the end of the project, which is an optimization phase. Often it's at the point of the project when you're trying to hit things like frame rate and performance-oriented metrics. And it's here where engineers are telling artists that they have to reduce their footprint. Whether it's memory budgets that are overflowing or particular types of assets that can be very expensive for the processors from a performance perspective, engineers will have to coordinate with an artist to make sure that things are brought into a reasonable budget. It could be the triangle count of a particular asset, the complexity of a shader that's being used within a scene, the complexity of an animation, the file size, etc.

Are artists given resource budget information ad hoc or are there established parameters in a design or technical document?

Both. The truth is that although we're provided with general guidelines and artists know the budgets on processing power and storage, over the course of a production things evolve. Engineering may need to cut back on one area in order to afford something else in another. So, it's an evolving process and often you're told something is perfectly fine and then three months later engineering is telling you that you've got to take it out because the project can't afford it. It's an ongoing back and forth.

And the performance/technical budget depends on the department. UI artists have a very different type of budgeting that they need to deal with than character artists or environment artists. Character artists are typically worried about the one character they're working on, so their budgets are usually pretty clearly defined. Similarly, an environment artist who is world building is worried about how much is on the screen at the same time (e.g., How many things are being culled out in the distance? How thick is the fog?). So, their budgets are looser but more important because they affect game performance much more. UI artist budgets boil down to memory constraints for the most part because they have to fit all of their images and artwork into a specified memory budget. Again, it varies by department and over the course of the development cycle, but the base budgets are pretty well understood.

How would you describe your management style?

My management style actually comes from my architectural background. The public generally perceives architects as artists, as people who sit around and make fancy drawings of buildings. The truth is that architects really are just coordinators. They coordinate among a lot of people and disciplines, whether it's engineers or clients or the government. Architects are the ones who bring the project together. I've carried that sensibility over into my game development career. I'm very much a team builder. I can't possibly know everything, and certainly I don't know the latest trends in technology or art pipelines. It would be impossible for me to keep up with all of that. So I rely very heavily on the people who I build a team with. I rely on their expertise, and I defer to that expertise as often as possible. I'm not the type of manager who puts his foot down and says that something has to be done a certain way. I find that flexibility has benefits from a production standpoint: it allows us to be forward thinking as a team, and team members respond quite well to this way of working. They like the feeling that their opinion is valuable, and they also know that I hold them accountable on that opinion. As a result, they're genuinely sincere when they propose something. It's a relationship that I try to build with all of my team members, where they know how valuable they are to the team and to me. They know I'm going to rely on them constantly, and they feel valuable in that sense.

I've seen other types of management play out in other studios and they breed a lot of dissent and create disgruntled workers. As with any large organization, cliques develop among employees, and I've jumped around in a few of them. It can get pretty ugly when management is heavy-handed. This isn't to say that kind of management can't be effective; there've been a lot of games released that are fantastic and were developed via that conduit. But it's just not something that's in my nature, and I've never seen it successfully executed personally.

I'm not a Scrum master—I don't have that certification. But I do see value in a lot of those strategies, especially with small teams that are well integrated— you might have an artist, a designer, an engineer, and a programmer all working together on a small team on specific tasks. I really like that system. It helps break things up a little bit and helps break up the cliques that you'll see form. I spend a lot of my time working with people and trying to coordinate those efforts to make sure that everybody is getting along.

How do you go about placing the right personnel on the right teams?

Expertise is the first and foremost consideration. You need to have the people with the right skills working together. Personality does come into play—there's no doubt about it—but that's not unique to game development. That's any industry. You have a lot of different types of people working in close quarters, and as a result personalities can clash. You have to be mindful of that when team building, but I wouldn't say that's been a primary concern of mine. We're a midsize developer, and we're quite selective in our hiring practices. We make sure that we're looking at people who fit into our corporate culture, which is family oriented, friendly, and open. So, when it comes to putting together teams, it's not too hard to find people who work well together internally because we're like-minded. We're passionate about what we do and passionate about the projects we work on.

What part of your job is most professionally rewarding and why?

Coordinating across disciplines is pretty cool. I like to see the joining of the three primary creative disciplines—engineering, art, and design—with production. At that level, it's interesting to see the moving parts and how they interlace to produce a shippable product.

Crafting and producing environment art is also very rewarding. Laboring over the design and the construction of set pieces, tile sets, and larger systems is a lot of fun and gratifying in the sense of seeing your efforts realized onscreen.

What are the most significant internal challenges you face in your job?

As an aging professional, staying current with trends in the profession while not getting bogged down in them is a difficult balance to strike, especially with a family, where "free time"—which in my case means the opportunity to watch job-related tutorials—is limited. With students graduating with increasing technical capabilities and software proficiency, it's often easy to feel inadequate. They're improving daily-grind pipelines, and you're sitting in a meeting about scheduling and budgets.

Nevertheless, discovering and learning enough of an emerging technology is important. As a lead, you need to be able understand its full impact and assess its risks. Familiarity with the topic is essential if you're going to effectively discuss the pros and cons of a particular pipeline component or an approach to and recommendation of a particular technique/strategy. That kind of familiarity is only gained through personal dedication to continuing education.

The art discipline is unique in that there are no stages of certification, which is a little odd for me coming from an architectural background where certification is everything. In architecture, you have continuing education credits that have to be fulfilled every year. For artists in game development, no such thing exists. We're left to our own devices to further educate ourselves in order to advance professionally and artistically. Most artists rely quite heavily on the variety of art-oriented websites that are out there (e.g., ArtStation). We spend a lot of time browsing through them to see what other artists are working on.

As far as developing technique goes, that's most often handled via tutorials. Artists will often put together tutorials on YouTube or through various tutorial distributing websites, either for profit or as freeware. Other artists watch these tutorials and work through the exercises to develop their technical and artistic knowledge. Usually you do this during free time, maybe at lunch or at home, because most of your day is spent actually producing content.

It's different for engineers. They have certifications on codebases, meaning they can get Microsoft certified, C++ certified, and so forth. They have a much more rigorous continuing education structure than artists, which definitely affects their hiring practices and ability. Artists are really in a unique position in that sense. We just have to do it ourselves, and it's most often done off the clock.

Do studios ever run training workshops or host guest lecturers?

Sometimes. Blizzard Entertainment has a very robust internal development program where you can go and take structured courses right on campus. You can learn how to be a better artist or programmer, and that's part of your promotion pipeline. Midsize studios like mine have a smaller staff and annual budget, and so we're less inclined to do that type of internal development. What happens in midsize studios is that continuing education is often organized by artists themselves. For example, we have a sketch club that meets once or twice a week at lunch. The members sit around and talk about technique and the like. We also have people who organize external events at local pubs where they bring other studio professionals in to hobnob, talk about industry politics, and stuff like that.

What are the external challenges you face in your job?

The same as every other American: there's never enough time in the day. The game development industry is fairly demanding in terms of time, especially for mid-level through executive professionals. Most often it's late at night where the majority of the real labor is done.

What sorts of workplace changes would you implement if given the opportunity?

Though our industry is plagued with issues regarding hours and compensation, I don't suffer from them currently. I'm lucky enough to work at a studio where employee well-being and retention is a high priority, so I have no complaints there. Short of promoting gender diversity in our industry, there isn't a lot I'd like to see widely pushed as a professional issue.

One thing that our studio stresses is transparency. In any given industry, any given company, there's often a clear distinction between management and boots on the ground, and communication between those two components of an organization can be rough and not flow freely. One of the things that we strive to do at Blind Squirrel is to maintain transparency about what's happening at the executive level, and our executive team is very much involved with staff. They get to know everybody's names, they're out on the floor pretty regularly, and they're always quick to accommodate people's physical needs.

For example, our chief operating officer is currently ordering forty standing desks for employees who think that they might want to stand during the day instead of sit. It's at great cost to the company, but that's the type of perk that they want to provide employees to engender the sense that they care. It's not a false notion; they really do. You see it play out in simple things that affect your daily life, like getting a soda machine installed in the kitchen so that employees can mix their own fun flavors, or making sure that people have the right equipment at their workstations so they aren't constantly frustrated with a slow computer or software that crashes all the time. And this attitude and attention cascades many different levels down to the lowest-level employee. So not only is that effort made, but those intentions are made clear as well. We have pretty regular studio-wide Q & A sessions where the executive team addresses the whole company in an open forum where we talk about challenges that we face, projects we're trying to move forward on, and what's happening in general. The executives are very transparent about the budget the studio has and how much cash is on hand so that people don't need to worry, "Oh, the end of this project is coming up. Are they going to lay me off?" Every employee has an understanding of where the company sits financially, and that's why I'd describe it as a family-oriented studio structure. Everybody is involved in and aware of as much stuff as possible. Obviously, the executives are making deals with publishers that they can't disclose to the employees for legal reasons, and so questions like that are often answered with, "Well, we can't talk about that." But people understand. That open communication between the executive team and the rest of the studio makes us all feel like we're part of things.

If I were to single out something identifiable and common in the actual workplace that I'd like to change, inter-communication/cross-discipline coordination is always the greatest source of delay and complication. It'd be nice if people had better training/skills regarding communication, whether it be writing skills, sketching, diagramming, group think, or documentation development. This should probably be part of the educational curriculum and is my single biggest gripe with incoming junior staff.

How is the work you do in the game industry different from the work you have done elsewhere?

As far as the daily grind goes, it varies from my previous career in architecture very little. Both are industries where distinct disciplines and groups of people come together—art and science, design and engineering, clients and production. Coordination of these things is not particularly unique to game development and has more similarities to, rather than differences from, most other creative production businesses such as film, music, television, industrial design, graphic design, and so forth.

Which companies or ways of working (both within and outside of the game industry) do you look to for inspiration?

The most productive and pleasant way of working for me thus far has been the Scrum-based team structure, so I've done some study there and prescribe it whenever it makes sense.

How would you describe the management structure in your company?

Fairly traditional, with an emphasis on team building and employee retention. I don't think our studio is unique in that. I'm sure you're familiar with the Gamergate controversy and the game industry's history of excessive overtime or crunch periods, which employees are not just asked to do but are required to do in order to retain their jobs. Our studio, like a lot of studios that are growing right now, not only wants to avoid that kind of thing from a legal perspective, but it's also not the type of studio that we want to be. We want to hold on to our employees, and we have a core belief in our studio that if employees are being asked to work overtime excessively for long periods of time, that's a failing on management's part: we didn't adequately schedule a project, we didn't know what we were getting into, and so forth. Asking employees to make up for missteps like these by tapping into their personal time is wrong and should be avoided whenever possible. Often, if you're below a certain salary threshold, your overtime is an issue, that is, whether or not you qualify for overtime compensation. You can see it in the difference between artists and engineers. Engineers are technically and legally classified as nonexempt employees, whereas artists are exempt employees.[8] So for artists, there's no limit to the hours that they might have to work. But in our studio, we don't want people working more than forty to fifty hours a week. It's not necessary if we manage things properly, and it keeps people happy. They have personal time to go do the things that they enjoy doing outside of the workplace. It's a critical component to any studio's hiring and management practices if they want to hold on to people because of what you see happen time and time again in studios that hire for the project. They just demand death marches of excessive overtime—sometimes seventy to eighty hours a week just to hold on to your job. If you're not willing to do it, there's somebody else who will; this really burns people out. They can do it for a couple of years, but then they're just done, and they often leave the industry entirely. They don't just switch companies; they get out of the business altogether. I think that's why, historically, our industry is so transient. I think it's changing, but probably not quickly enough. I like to think we're a studio on the forefront of change. We ask people to go home at the end of the day; we don't want them to stay at work, because we want to keep them happy and productive.

Do the different employee classifications (i.e., exempt and nonexempt) cause any friction internally?

There's certainly a very different mentality between engineers and artists about what they do during the day. Of course, artists are expected to be productive, but they're a more free-spirited bunch, and they tend to socialize a little bit more during the day. They're not under the gun as far as productivity goes. They're expected to get their job done, but their tasks may span several days or weeks and so they sort of budget their own schedules. And art is subjective anyway—whether or not something is done is debatable.

Engineers, on the other hand, are more nose-to-the-grindstone people. They tend to work a little harder as far as productivity goes. They always take advantage of their lunch breaks to research games or do something professionally related. There's a much clearer distinction between their personal lives and hours of production at work, and that's just kind of generally understood. I think everybody knows that's the way it is, and there's no animosity generated by that at all.

How would you describe the workflow in your company?

Top-down, cascading.

How does the workflow differ when working on different types of games (e.g., different genres, AAA versus casual games, etc.)?

It often involves differing ramp-up times, as well as learning new software, techniques, or artistic styles. There's also adjusting the bars of quality or scope to fit the schedule footprint.

What are some of your notable quality of life issues, both routine and exceptional?

Small bouts of crunch time are unavoidable and unpredictable but not necessarily an inevitably painful burden. Often they can be the opposite—they can energize a team to push hard together, if not routine and excessive in their duration or levels of external pressure. But, long and late hours are sometimes necessary to succeed over the long haul.

What does crunch time look like for you as a manager?

I'm in a unique position in the sense that I work from home twice a week, and so on any given day, crunch or not, I'm often home. I'll leave the office maybe a little bit earlier than everyone else because I want to come home and see my kids, but then I jump back on my home workstation and I'll put in a few more hours to try to wrap things up. Because I often spend my day managing people, at night I do the work that still needs to be done. It's a little unique for me in that sense, but even when I haven't had the opportunity to work from home, I'm very much a team player in the sense that we're all in this together. I've never been one to ask everybody to stay just because a few people have to work hard. I give the people who are working for me the opportunity to manage their own schedules. They set their own time budgets, and if we agree that those budgets are accurate, I let them work on their own timelines. As long as they're hitting their marks, then I'm not one to dictate and micromanage their schedules. When crunch time comes around—and it does for every studio (even in a studio like mine, although we try to minimize it)—and the work needs to get done or we need to get something to our publisher by a certain date, then yes, the expectation is that people will put in the extra effort and hours to get it done. If I have the opportunity, I'll stay at work just to help out or at the very least to keep people company. I like working, so it's not a burden for me to stick around. And, having been on the other end of the stick, I never had much taste for managers who were out the door by 5:30 p.m. and saying good luck to everyone who was going to be there until midnight. I make a concerted effort to be present as much as possible. Even when I come home to wrap up things on my end, I'm on *Skype* and checking my email. I'm still coordinating with the team even if I'm not physically present in the studio.

What are some of your notable career progression issues?

Finding a studio that promotes from within, yet does so only as part of a larger meritocracy, can be difficult. Many studios have discernable glass ceilings for various positions and departments, hiring outside the team for upper-level positions. Others can promote too rapidly from within, without merit, which complicates not only the production process—due to lack of experience and gross talent gaps—but also causes faults within one's career, making it difficult to transition between jobs where steps down in title become inevitable.

As far as advancement opportunities and glass ceilings go, the game industry is like any other: the smaller the studio, the more opportunity you have to take on new tasks, to take on new responsibilities. Often, things will come up and there's just no one else to do them, so you end up taking on those responsibilities. Growth opportunities in a small studio are bountiful. During my architectural career, I worked at small and mid-sized studios, and I saw that same phenomenon play out in that industry. So when I decided to make my midlife crisis career shift, I made a very strong decision in my mind to avoid a large game studio because I didn't want to wind up in a situation where I was just a cog in a machine and growth opportunities were less prevalent. I knew that because I was starting in an industry in my thirties where most of the people coming in were in their twenties, I was already a step behind, and so I specifically targeted smaller studios to give myself that opportunity to advance quickly.

This strategy isn't without its pitfalls. Advancing quickly often means that you shorten the amount of time that you have in any of those lower positions, and so sometimes you're less equipped to deal with things. You haven't spent the time in those lower positions to gain a full understanding of them, and as a result you have to push a little harder to make sure that you get the necessary knowledge and experiences within those compressed time frames. It's no mystery in our industry, and there are no misconceptions about working at a larger studio and how long it can take to climb the ladder. Your competition, quite simply put, is more fierce and more abundant.

You might be in a studio with fifty or a hundred other artists doing the same thing you're doing. It's hard to get noticed, and you have to work that much harder to get a promotion. And a lot of times, as I noted earlier, a larger studio will hire externally for higher-level positions as a general hiring practice. With smaller studios, when a position opens up, they're more inclined to look internally to see who can step up and fulfill that role.

As far as career progression goes, I don't worry about it too much. I'm an organic growth kind of guy. I'm a team member in my studio and I strive to provide the team with the services that I'm best able to provide. So in that sense, if my manager, my art director, or my chief operating officer were to feel that I could step up and take on some new responsibilities, then I'd be happy to do that. But I'm not the type of career-oriented person where I have my eye on some specific prize. I've never been preoccupied with being an art director or creative director or running my own studio. In fact, the opposite is probably true. I've seen people run their own studios, and they seem miserable with all of the stresses that come with that. Long term, I probably see myself moving into a director role or something like that, but that's not what drives me.

Is there an upper limit to the career trajectory of an artist?

I'd say typically an artist can and should expect to reach the position of art director if they stay in the industry long enough and work hard enough. To push beyond that, you'd move into a role that is known as a creative director. Creative directors tend not to work on a specific project but are more executive level because they're overseeing multiple projects within the studio. They guide the overall artistic approach for the studio, and that can influence the art style of any given project. Certainly, creative directors have the authority to step in if they don't like the art direction of a project, and they do work pretty closely with the art directors. But again, it's much more of an executive-level position.

What are the challenges facing the industry over the next decade?

Budget, schedule, and project scope control. Production scale, cost, and time requirements have increased unbelievably for AAA productions, and so too has the expectation for quality by the consumer. And although advancements in tools and software have reduced the time necessary for many tasks, there's the extra burden of maintaining the highest quality levels our industry has ever seen. Outsourcing has done a lot to mitigate this overhead, but it presents its own unique challenges and isn't always the best choice for a given production.

▶ DISCUSSION

While the question of whether or not video games are art continues to be debated, there is no doubt that many of the people who produce the visual elements of games are themselves artists. Yet even this is a complicated designation. Far from the (largely imaginary) view of the artist as an isolated creative genius painting away in a boho-chic studio, game artists tend to be one part art nerd, one part game nerd, and one part pragmatist. They work in a variety of digital and analog media, are versed in a range of styles and aesthetics, know how to work within financial and technical budgets and project deadlines, can multitask, and often prize problem solving and collaboration. They are jazzed when their art is integrated into larger and evolving projects, and they recognize that these larger projects combine art, business, and impactful human communication to create engaging, playful experiences.

It could be argued that most of these qualities belong equally to all the other disciplines that comprise the game industry: programming, business, and so on. In the game industry, employees are necessarily creative, collaborative, and industrious. The art discipline, however, is unique. For example, to be hired, prospective artists are often first assessed with an art test as part of the job application process. That is, artists are obliged to demonstrate their abilities beyond the evidence provided by their portfolio and résumé, and this demonstration responds to a specific work brief issued by the hiring company. Such assessment is not uncommon outside of the game industry, or even within the industry in certain disciplines—consider a conventional typing, data entry, or programming test—but game art assessment has a peculiar flavor. While the artist test taker may not be remunerated for the art test (though s/he can be), the test results can wind up as in-game assets in some instances. In other words, the applicant's work (and not necessarily the *successful* applicant's work) may become an actual element of a game currently in production.[9]

Part of the rationale for the art test may be due to the fact that artists are not always able to show the game work they have done—concept art may not have received clearance for public dissemination, or a project may have been canceled prior to release and therefore there are no assets to (legally) show. Likewise, because so much shipped game content is collaborative, it is often hard to tell which employee did which work. Art tests thus offer companies a process for protecting themselves against hiring weaker artists. It is possible, for example, to have a concept artist whose concepts were heavily revised by a subsequent artist and yet the concept artist still claims the concepts as her own. Often, the art test is a way for the development team to get a clear look at what a prospective artist is capable of as an individual contributor.

Ironically, of course, almost no artist at a mid- or large-sized studio works alone, as Sarkissian notes in her discussion of why keeping one's ego in check is a game industry necessity. Indeed, as she so succinctly puts it, one person's ideas "just end up getting merged with everyone else's." This is also part of what makes artists (and perhaps most other positions) so expendable. A paradox of the industry within the art discipline is that in order to break in, one must prove one's individuality, but once a job is secured, it's one's ability to conform that secures work long term.

Regardless, uncontracted (and thus essentially free) work is being done in instances where art test results may wind up in-game, creating a radically unequal scenario in which tangible labor power (i.e., that which is ultimately commodified) is being offered up in the hopes of securing future exchange value. This, in turn, may help explain why art salaries are noticeably lower than programming salaries in the aggregate—why pay for that which you can get for free (or for cheap), if not in assets then at least in unprotected labor power?

Similarly, Sarkissian points to the "passion" involved in game development (as do other interviewees in this book), raising a troubling but important concern. Games have entered an age of industrial sophistication in which new employees have not only grown up with the medium but are able—and in many ways are obligated—to create ever higher-resolution experiences. In fact, we would argue that the modern games workforce often finds itself being subtly pressured to work more and harder, based on employees' "passion" for what they are creating. Have artists internalized their roles as contributors of "passion," rather than of highly specialized and vital skills? They tolerate an unstable industry, long work hours, the extracurricular demands of social networking, and the challenge of separating professional and personal art projects. But why? The emerging narrative seems to echo that of film, television, and music, where work conditions are complicated by the medium's artistic and social pervasiveness. If an employee considers games her passion, at what point is she a volunteer willing to do whatever it takes to create an amazing experience, and at what point is she a paid employee deserving of rights and fair remuneration for her work and time?

Along these lines is the issue of exempt/nonexempt employment, particularly as the issue appears to be subdivided along technical and artistic lines. There are certain legal protections available to nonexempt employees that exempt employees such as artists do not receive (e.g., a cap on the maximum number of hours worked per week), which creates an overtly stratified workforce. In other words, some development disciplines appear to be valued more than others, at least in the eyes of the law and ledger.

Also, while professional networking is important to every discipline, it seems especially so in art. Skill alone is not enough to secure and maintain employment, and reliable and diverse industry contacts are essential, even for established employees. And because professional networks often require substantial care and feeding, artists are effectively required to engage in a secondary and shadow labor market—growing and managing their professional networks in their off hours—on top of the formal one in which they work.

The paradox of collaboration presents another challenge for artists. Collaboration is essential to game development, and yet there is little to no time allotted for it in the production plan. Time to chat, to bridge disciplinary culture gaps, to get everyone on the same page aesthetically—these are not always built into the development timeline, which raises the question: Does this unaccounted-for-yet-essential time contribute to issues of crunch and other generally undesirable workplace phenomena?[10]

Returning to the technical aspects of game artists' work, it is important to highlight that while technological development is well covered across the interviews in this book, particularly noteworthy is that even artists describe an inability to keep up with technological advances in games. This suggests a curious phenomenon: developers (artists included) take aim at a technological target they do not fully understand—nor ever have time to fully ascertain—long before that target is visible. Professional certifications are one way of preparing for this odds-against endeavor—such continuing education is meant to keep one sharp, expansive, up-to-date, and intuitive—but there is a shortage of industrial certifications and continuing education for game artists. There simply are not, in other words, the same kinds of formal opportunities for skill development (and thus career advancement and salary boosting) that exist for other disciplines (e.g., programming).[11] Also, not every studio is able to offer in-house training, resulting in a structurally defined knowledge inequity and competitive disadvantage among employees in the same position class. This is colloquially known as "tribal knowledge," and is a common hindrance.

Significantly, it is the artists who highlight the perennial problem with higher education as vocational training. The challenge for game development faculty of staying current and thus being able to adequately prepare graduates for the job market is intensified in games thanks to rapid technological development and aesthetic expectations, and this problem continues within the industry itself. Because art and engineering work hand-in-glove during production, this differential treatment in terms of continuing education presents a major disconnect: while technical employees are expected to attend workshops and obtain new certifications, artists—whose software tools are as complex and evolving as the development environments of programmers—are required to keep up with the technical developments of their disciplines in their free time. If they do not, a younger, hungrier, more technically savvy artist will be hired (probably for less money) in their stead. Sarkissian describes the workplace zeitgeist this pressure creates as "survival of the fittest." It is easy to see how, under conditions like these, the work/life balance can be thrown far out of kilter.

The evolutionary metaphor of survival fitness is apt. As interviewees in other disciplines note, the only thing maturity brings in the game industry is vulnerability. In the high-stress, highly transient, highly dynamic world of game development, qualities such as being family oriented, life-balanced, and geographically stable are hindrances not advantages. Even at the most socially progressive studios—workplaces where family, work/life balance, and stability are overtly supported—there is a tacit understanding that such qualities are socially but not industrially valuable. In an industry built on a challenging business climate, expensive but short-lived technologies, and a fickle consumer base, it is nearly impossible to be both good to your employees and cutting edge. As a result, every studio determines the extent to which it will compromise on its own corporate values, from issues related to crunch and overtime, to diversity hiring, to fiscal transparency, to career advancement.

Artists deal with an additional issue related to work/life balance that may well extend to other disciplines, but if so, it is far less pronounced: being an artist is generally considered to be a vocation rather than a job. As a result, artists are artists no matter where they are, work or home. This creates a set of labor and legal issues that are thorny to say the least. With non-disclosure agreements and other legal restraints securing the work of artists—who, again, have been hired precisely because of their unique artistic skills—how are they to express themselves artistically when they are off the clock? This question remains one of the enduring problematics of the industry—and indeed of capitalism itself.

The interviews with the artists in this chapter highlight one of the grand challenges facing game industry scholars, as well as game industry employees and employers: game production processes vary widely, even within the same studio and across similar projects, which makes generalizations about the industry's labor practices difficult to document. Timelines, staffing, milestones, and creative processes are highly context dependent, making it hard to paint a refined picture of how game development in general works. While there are established management styles and production practices (e.g., Scrum, Agile, Waterfall), the vagaries of the various agents—developer, publisher, player, technology, economy, law, and so on—make pan-industry specificities hard to ascertain and improvements to quality of life harder still to argue for and implement.

▶ NOTES

1 *Nota bene:* Art salaries can vary considerably in range, in part due to the fact that technical artists can command a higher base rate due to their technical skills.

2 Splash art includes ancillary imagery for purchase, such as character skins, illustrations, and personal items.

3 For more on the Boston area Women in Games community, see https://wigboston. wordpress.com.

4 See http://www.bostonindies.com and http://www.bostonpostmortem.org for more information.

5 For a brief history and description of the *Shadow Realms* project, see https:// en.wikipedia.org/wiki/Shadow_Realms.

6 For details on the development and cancellation of *Dawngate*, see https:// en.wikipedia.org/wiki/Dawngate.

7 A brief history of the development and cancellation of *HEI$T* may be found at https://en.wikipedia.org/wiki/Heist_(video_game).

8 For a concise discussion of the differences between exempt and nonexempt employees, see http://employment.findlaw.com/wages-and-benefits/exempt-employees-vs-nonexempt-employees.html.

9 It is important to note that this is exceptional rather than common practice, both because of the ethics involved (or rather, the lack thereof) and the challenge of reliably generating art assets from an unpredictable number of qualified applicants.

10 While crunch is typically seen within the industry as undesirable and inevitable, vanOteghem notes that some periods of heightened activity can also be energizing to workers.

11 This is not to say, however, that there are no formal avenues for artists to develop their skills. For example, organizations such as the Association for Computing Machinery's SIGGRAPH (http://www.siggraph.org/) and the Game Developers Conference (http://www.gdconf.com/) have conferences, tracks, and workshops dedicated to the advancement of graphics and animation. In this respect, artists are afforded similar opportunities for dialogue and discussion as other game development disciplines.

▶ WORKS CITED

Bibliography

Harris, Mark. "The Day the Movies Died." *GQ.com*. Condé Nast. 10 Feb. 2011. Web. 10 Oct. 2015. <http://www.gq.com/entertainment/movies-and-tv/201102/the-day-the-movies-died-mark-harris>

"Transitions: Gamasutra Salary Survey 2014." *Gamasutra: The Art & Business of Making Games*. UBM Tech. 22 Jul. 2014: 1–8. Web. 10 Oct. 2015. <http://www.gamesetwatch.com/2014/09/05/GAMA14_ACG_SalarySurvey_F.pdf>

Williams, Richard. *The Animator's Survival Kit: A Manual of Methods, Principles, and Formulas for Classical, Computer, Games, Stop Motion, and Internet Animators*. London: Faber and Faber, 2001. Print.

Filmography

A Bug's Life. Dir. John Lasseter. Perf. Dave Foley, Kevin Spacey, and Julia Louis-Dreyfus. Pixar Animation Studios/Walt Disney Pictures, 1998.

Caldera. Dir. Evan Viera. Bit Films, 2012.

The Incident at Tower 37. Dir. Chris Perry. Bit Films, 2009.

Toy Story 2. Dir. John Lasseter. Perf. Tom Hanks and Tim Allen. Pixar Animation Studios/Walt Disney Pictures, 1999.

Gameography

Adera. HitPoint Studios. Microsoft Studios, 2012. Personal computer.

Borderlands. Gearbox Software. 2K Games, 2009. Multiple platforms.

Choplifter HD. inXile Entertainment. inXile Entertainment, 2012. Multiple platforms.

Disney Infinity: Marvel Super Heroes. Avalanche Software. Disney Interactive Studios, 2014. Multiple platforms.

Dungeons & Dragons Online. Turbine. Warner Bros. Interactive Entertainment, 2012. Personal computer.

Evolve. Turtle Rock Studios. 2K Games/Take-Two Interactive, 2015. Multiple platforms.

Guardians of Magic: Amanda's Awakening. HitPoint Studios. HitPoint Studios, 2011. Personal computer.

Hunted: The Demon's Forge. inXile Entertainment. Bethesda Softworks, 2011. Multiple platforms.

Infinite Crisis. Turbine. Warner Bros. Interactive Entertainment, 2015. Personal computer.

The Lord of the Rings Online. Turbine. Turbine/Midway Games, 2007. Personal computer.

Mega Fame Casino. Plaor. Plaor, 2014. Multiple platforms.

The Secrets of Arcelia Island. HitPoint Studios. HitPoint Studios, 2011. Personal computer.

Star Wars: The Old Republic. BioWare. Electronic Arts, 2011. Multiple platforms.

Third Eye Crime. Moonshot Games. Gameblyr, 2014. Multiple platforms.

Wasteland 2. inXile Entertainment. inXile Entertainment, 2014. Multiple platforms.

Softography

Adobe After Effects (http://www.adobe.com/products/aftereffects.html)

Adobe Director (http://www.adobe.com/products/director.html)

Adobe Flash (http://www.adobe.com/products/flash.html)

Adobe Photoshop (http://www.adobe.com/products/photoshop.html)

JIRA Software (https://www.atlassian.com/software/jira)

Maya (http://www.autodesk.com/products/maya)

Microsoft Windows 8 (http://windows.microsoft.com/en-us/windows-8)

Perforce (https://www.perforce.com)

Skype (http://www.skype.com)

ZBrush 4R7 (http://pixologic.com/zbrush/features/ZBrush4R7)

Videography

Schwartzentruber, Jared. "Steve Jobs Foretold the Downfall of Apple!" Online video clip. *YouTube.* YouTube, 2 Nov. 2014. Web. 15 Oct. 2015. <https://www.youtube.com/watch?v=ZBma82g3Uag>

Thomas, Iowan. "Victor Navone—Alien Song (I Will Survive)." Online video clip. *YouTube.* YouTube, 20 Sept. 2006. Web. 15 Oct. 2015. <https://www.youtube.com/watch?v=duOoqDu2H70>

3

Design

▶ **INTRODUCTION**

In many ways, design personnel are the architects of the end user experience. They are involved to varying degrees in almost all of the aesthetic and technological practices of development, from art and story production to sound design and AI engineering. Their principal purpose is to conceptualize and craft a playful and pleasurable end product.

Design personnel typically occupy one of two primary position classes: lead designer and designer. As the title suggests, lead designers can be responsible for the design of a complex game component (e.g., a series of interconnected levels), the game as a whole, or they may work in a supervisory role and manage a group of designers. In some instances, lead designers may report to a creative director or executive producer, who helps keep the vision of a game consistent across multiple disciplines.

Certain game types (e.g., action games, platformers, first-person shooters) make use of specialty design positions, such as level and systems designer. A level designer's job is to block out a game's playable spaces and control pacing and challenge. Level designers may also perform relatively simply coding as part of their duties (e.g., to trigger events and enemy appearances), and often work with 3D modeling software (e.g., *Maya*, *3ds Max*) or proprietary 3D development tools (e.g., *Unreal Engine, REDengine, Unity 3D*). Proprietary tools are often preferred, as they are built specifically for creating and prototyping game content. Tools distributed through free or open source licensing (e.g., *id Tech 4, Torque 3D*), by contrast, generally require special scripts, plug-ins, and other adaptations and modifications to make them functional in various design environments.

Systems designers, by comparison, often take charge of developing and fine-tuning specific in-game systems such as scoring, level advancement, and combat. Systems designers commonly work with proprietary tools that enable real-time adjustments to character animations, the activation/deactivation of hitboxes that simulate melee combat, and the firing characteristics of weaponry. Games with complex systems (e.g., real-time strategy, simulation) require many and deep statistical tracking controls, and in these cases the systems designer is expected to make sure that such elements work harmoniously and synergistically to achieve the player experience goals established by the lead designer.

Often, designers do not begin their careers as "designers" but enter the discipline after first spending time in another game development area (e.g., QA, programming). As it can be difficult to determine what constitutes good design skills ahead of time, hiring preference is typically given to candidates who possess a quantifiable skill set in another discipline. Furthermore, because design is highly subjective, designers typically use a multitude of intuitive evaluations (e.g., "feel" and "fun") to make iterative decisions and improve the quality of their software (Kaufman).

According to the 2014 Gamasutra Salary Survey, design personnel earn an average annual salary of $73,864 in the aggregate ("Transitions" 3). Designers with fewer than three years of experience earn an average of $53,000 annually, while designers with six or more years of experience earn an average $77,768 per year (Ibid.). By comparison, creative directors/lead designers with six or more years of experience earn an average of $101,944 annually (Ibid.). Additionally, US-based design personnel earn approximately 18% more on average than their Canadian counterparts, and 54% more on average than European design personnel (Ibid.). Finally, male design personnel average $74,448 per annum, while female designers average $70,000 annually (Ibid.).

Andrew Rubino
Designer

Andrew Rubino is a senior game designer at BioWare, a wholly owned subsidiary of Electronic Arts. Previously, he was a senior designer at Gazillion Entertainment, a senior AI designer at SuperBot Entertainment, and a lead designer and combat designer at Liquid Entertainment. He holds a BS in game development from Full Sail University, and BAs in English and theater from Lehigh University. His shipped titles include *Marvel Heroes 2015*, *PlayStation All-Stars Battle Royale*, *Karateka*, *Thor: God of Thunder*, and *Rise of the Argonauts*. He is currently working on *Mass Effect: Andromeda*.

* * * * *

How did you come to work in the game industry?

I wanted to work in games my whole life. I knew it even as a young child. In fact, I sent Nintendo a letter when I was eight years old explaining how I thought they could make a game based on Tim Burton's *Batman*.

Upon graduating high school, I wanted to go to DigiPen, but my parents convinced/forced me to go to a regular four-year school. They said that if I still wanted to get a more industry-specific degree after I graduated, they'd support me.

They were surprised when I suggested just that in my last year at Lehigh. They actually fought against it initially, saying that it was just too expensive. But to their credit, they agreed to do some research about Full Sail and the games business in general. They even called some companies, like Blizzard Entertainment and EA, to ask if they hired from Full Sail. Eventually, my parents agreed with me that it was the right call, and I got to go.

Obviously, Lehigh and Full Sail are very different places. Lehigh is a standard, four-year liberal arts school: dorms, people of all sorts with all different kinds of majors and interests, etc. Full Sail is much smaller. There are no dorms, and everyone is working on some permutation of an entertainment degree. And whereas Lehigh requires a specific GPA and SAT score to matriculate, all Full Sail cares about is that you have a high school diploma and the money to pay the tuition. That's actually both a positive and a negative. A lot of the kids who went to Full Sail with me didn't do so well in high school, and a standard college education wouldn't have been the right choice for them. Full Sail provided a way for them to go to school and get the education they needed or wanted and not be held back by their high school grades or lack of interest in other subjects.

What I mostly saw at Full Sail, though, were people right out of high school who were in no way ready to be unleashed the way we were in that program. At Full Sail, every month was a new class. You went to school five days a week, forty hours a week. Usually it was four hours of class, then a break, and then four hours of lab. And classes could run at all hours of the day. Sometimes a class would end at 1 p.m., and other times classes would start at 5 a.m. New enrollment happened every month; I started in September, and in October there was a new group of students. If you failed a class, you were held back, and you had to repeat that class right away. If you failed the same class twice, you had to pay to take it again. And if you failed the same class three times in a row, because of how the credentialing worked, you were basically booted from the school for a year (at minimum) before you would be allowed to take the class over. In other words, you couldn't spend the year taking other courses at Full Sail. Keep in mind that Full Sail is pretty expensive, and the tuition doesn't include room and board. Also, full tuition had to be paid by six months into the program, so if you failed after six months the school still had your money.

Now, you could come back in a year and take your classes over—your check would still be good—but almost nobody did that, because what are they going to do? Live in Florida for a year? Go back home, sit on their hands, and then come back in a year? And the classes and schedule weren't easy. Within the first three months you had to take calculus and programming, which is tough even if you're a good student. I started with sixty-four kids in my class. Twenty-one months later I graduated with thirty or so other students, and only maybe eighteen of us were from that original cohort. Everyone else had either failed at some point and been held back from a later cohort, or was gone from the program altogether.

The attrition rate is so high because Full Sail doesn't really check to see if you're ready for the program. And a lot of kids aren't ready. They may be immature; they may not have the discipline; they may not have the necessary academic foundation. I consider myself a relatively smart guy, and I was absolutely scrambling the first six months at Full Sail to pass my classes. I'd never taken heavy math before, and I'd never taken a programming course in my life. I was basically begging anyone I knew in those classes to help me. While Full Sail says they offer tutors, there are very few. In the end I think I got a 74% on my Programming 2 final exam, and I couldn't have been happier. I doubt it's intended, but the stress level at Full Sail is actually not unlike that in the game industry.

To be fair, I got some really good things out of my time at Full Sail, things that helped prepare me for working in games. First, from very early on, Full Sail is up front about how the industry works: "You know that awesome game idea you have? You're never going to make it. Not because you're terrible, but because the chances of anyone caring about it are very low. That's not what the business is like." They often joked that our first job after graduating was going to be working on a *Barbie Horse Adventures* game. It's brutal, but true, and if you can't deal with that then you might be in the wrong place.

Second, halfway through the program you do your first group project and make a 2D game. Basically, each group has to pitch a game and add enough features from a provided list to earn a certain point total, with each feature having a dedicated point value. The instructors know that you're going to bite off way more than you can chew, and, in fact, they're planning on it. Every two weeks you have a milestone where you have to show how much work you've accomplished. But, there's the "spinning the wheel of destiny" to contend with, which is basically a series of envelopes containing some random occurrence, and you pick one of the envelopes. One we got said, "Good news! They want to publish your game in France. Now you have to complete a French translation of your entire game, meaning that you now need to produce two versions." It was a bunch of work that we never anticipated having to do. But, by the time we finished the course, we had a really good idea of how easy it is to scope-creep yourself to death, how the simplest things can have the biggest knockdown effects, and how hard it is to work in a group.

Those lessons got blown up with the final project for the degree. That project lasted five months, and again the challenge was to build a game with a team. Fortunately, there was no monkey business with that. The instructors really wanted us to keep things focused because the idea was that the final project would become our demo when we went out into the industry. It was a great way to really understand what the game industry is like, because when it's your project on the line, you're going to work eighteen hours a day because you want it to be great. But after two weeks of those kinds of hours, you're going to realize how much crunching hurts.

Full Sail was definitely a pressure cooker and a bit of a grind, but it was helpful. My first job told me flat out that without the Full Sail degree and the experience I got there they probably wouldn't have hired me. I was extremely lucky to be hired by Liquid Entertainment as a designer in my last few months at Full Sail. I'd met their lead designer at the Game Developers Conference job fair that year, and they took a chance on me (one that I think worked out pretty well for them, too). I'll always be grateful.

In light of all of this, I want to quote my first boss, because it's instructive. He said that guys who come out of Full Sail are mechanics. They know how to work on the engines that they've been taught to work on, and that's fine. However, he preferred to hire computer scientists because they're engineers. They may have never worked with a particular engine, but since they know how an engine works, they can figure it out. They'll be able to be really versatile whereas the mechanic from Full Sail is doomed if anything out of the ordinary comes his way. He's never going to figure it out.

What makes a good designer?

For the most part, designers are the people who come up with the content and concepts that the rest of the development team is going to execute. For example, the concept artist is going to tell me what a monster looks like, but usually it's a designer who's the person who comes up with the idea of the monster to begin with. As a designer, you're the start of the train; you're going to determine what other people are doing with their time. The stereotypical designer is the guru on the mountain who types up his sheet and then throws it off the cliff (and never looks at it again) so the people below can build it for him. Obviously, this stereotype exists for a reason, because some people probably do that. That's not a good way to get things done, though. Game development is a collaborative business, and not just because it has to be. Games are better when the development process is collaborative. I could write a document and tell the coder that this is exactly what I want him to do. But it's almost always better to say, "Here's the goal of what I'm trying to do, and here's why I made these decisions—what do you think?" I don't know code the way a programmer does; I don't know art the way an artist does. You get a better product if you get people working together and taking ownership of the work. Real collaboration is important, and this is exactly what I've been taught by the better designers that I've worked with.

One of my old bosses told me that the job of the lead designer/creative director is to define the vision for the game, to make sure that the team stays on track because there are so many people involved and so much chaos. Someone has to be there to say, "These are the pillars. This is what we're trying to do and why we're trying to do it." The designers are the torch-bearers for the lead. As a senior designer, I'm not necessarily the tip of the spear, but I'm there to ensure that we hew to the pillars of the project and to ensure that the people around me understand and buy into our objective. If you explain your goals to your team and your team thinks they sound terrible, you may want to rethink your goals. A good designer will be able to do that; it's really what the job is. In fact, that's why there are some studios that don't have many designers. They have producers instead, because the producer is doing a similar thing in that respect (though usually not doing a moment-to-moment implementation like a designer would). A producer, however, might be relying on other people to determine the quality of the work or to make more of the design decisions. At any rate, there's a lot of overlap between producing and design, though obviously I feel that having dedicated designers is important.

What part of your job is most professionally rewarding?

Easily the most rewarding part is watching other people have fun playing a game that I've worked on. That's the whole point of my job—to ensure that the game is fun. Every game presents new problems to solve, which is actually one of the main reasons I enjoy my job. I spend a tremendous amount of time and energy thinking about the best solutions to these problems and helping implement solutions, so when the game is finally done and people are enjoying it, it's just the best feeling. It's immensely satisfying to know that all the hard work paid off and people really like the results of that work.

I know it sounds strange that every game presents new problems to solve, so let me give you an example. At BioWare, we're currently working on the next installment of the *Mass Effect* series. While there are three previous games in the series, we're now using a totally different engine. So even though we're going to have some of the same mechanics in the new game that we had in the previous ones, we don't have any of that old material anymore. You can't just grab code and cut and paste it into the new engine. Someone has to sit down and rethink the process, even if the end result from the player's perspective is exactly the same. The code has to be different because it's a different engine.

That's just a minor example. In game development, you're constantly faced with new challenges, even if they're old problems. That said, overcoming these challenges comes down to experience (and talent). The more experience you have, the easier it is to make the right guess. For example, my very first game was *Rise of the Argonauts*, and I helped design the combat. That combat was very different from the combat we did in *PlayStation All-Stars Battle Royale*, not just in implementation but in what we were trying to do, how it was going to look, and how it was supposed to work. Despite their differences, however, there was still plenty I could bring over to *Play-Station All-Stars Battle Royale* from *Rise of the Argonauts*. Certain things are always the same: When does the collision turn on? When does the collision turn off? How far out of a character's collision cylinder is the actual impact happening? What kind of reaction does it cause? Even though it wasn't a one-to-one translation between *Rise of the Argonauts* and *Play-Station All-Stars Battle Royale*, there was still a lot that I could draw on from my previous experience.

Now, this doesn't mean that I can look at a problem and instantly have the solution. But it does mean that I have a decent idea about where to start. So, instead of just scrambling in the dark, it's like being able to get to the end goal more quickly. Ultimately, I think that's where a lot of the game development process is, at least from a design perspective—not knowing the answer, necessarily, but knowing how you need to proceed to arrive at the answer.

What are the most significant internal challenges you face in your job?

Personally, I find the biggest challenge to be the unknown in every new game project. Even if you have a good idea of what the game should be (e.g., a fighter, a melee-combat game, etc.), there are still so many unanswered questions, especially in the details of implementation. There are questions of every shape and size, from "How should the player move around?" to "What player skills are we looking to challenge?" to "How do we communicate this mechanic?" or even something as general as "Who is this game for?" In most cases, there's no definitive answer. As a designer, I'm effectively a professional guesser—I'm hired because my bosses believe that I'll come up with good answers in a reasonable amount of time. But getting to those answers takes a lot of iteration, which is a fancy way of saying that we're going to fail a lot. Getting to those answers also requires a great deal of help; in AAA development, there's little someone can do by themselves.

I find these kinds of leaps of faith to be challenging. Internally, I'm constantly questioning my decisions, especially when those decisions are going to cost other people their time. Still, it's those leaps that make the job exciting. I'm often looking for solutions to problems I've never encountered before, and sometimes for solutions to problems that no one has.

What are the external challenges you face in your job?

Our industry is constantly changing due to technological and interactive innovation. Add to that the fact that every game is its own unique entity because of the technology used, the people involved, and a million other factors. The net result is that there's no single proven or definitive way to make a game. We don't have a universal process; no one perfectly understands how to make a game from a production standpoint, because every game is a special snowflake. On top of that, it's difficult to get a group of people working toward the same goal in general, and in AAA game development you're dealing with hundreds of people, often across multiple locations. It's insanely hard. And while we spend a lot of time talking and working on process, we still waste a lot of time because of these complexities (which, it should be noted, is both frustrating and largely unavoidable).

I've often joked that one of the main reasons you don't see many authentic behind-the-scenes documentaries on game development is because players would be shocked and maybe a little terrified to see how game development actually gets done. From the outside, I'm sure it looks disorganized and wasteful, because oftentimes that's exactly what it is. Inefficient processes in development cause frustration within the team, result in features being cut, and definitely cause crunch. Sadly, there's no obvious solution because of the constant change. I don't see this becoming radically different anytime soon, though we can get better at managing the chaos.

How do human and monetary resources factor into your design decisions?

I'm in an interesting position because for me time is money. The major resource, the number one thing that we spend money on, is people. When I'm designing a creature, for example, the budget is always on my mind, because I'll need help from other people to build it, and the design is unique—it's not like we can just go out and buy what we need. Now, we might buy a piece of technology, but that would only make sense if we used it so much that it'd ultimately save us a lot of time. So anyway, for a creature's design, it all comes down to how long in man-hours it's going to take to build. If I cook up a crazy octopus creature that's got all these tentacles, that's going to require an animator to spend a hell of a lot more time on it than something simpler would take, because it has all these different joints that need to be animated. If I'm going to request something complicated like that, then I better be damn sure that 1) it's what I want, and 2) that we plan accordingly for the animator's labor, because that creature is inherently going to be more expensive than, say, a normal biped, which has many fewer joints to animate.

Keep in mind that no one usually comes to me and says, "You have 500,000 dollars. Make it go." Instead, what happens is that a creature has to be completed by a certain date, and we'll come up with an initial design that isn't stupid or extravagant. When we have a rough idea of the design, I'll present it in a kick-off meeting in which I talk to the other departments about what we want to do. That would be the time for someone in another department to talk about the labor cost. Then I'd have a conversation with the producer, and as part of that, the first question I'd ask myself is "Do I really need this? Is it really important to me?" Let me give you a rough example. Imagine I'm designing a zombie enemy in a game. A feature that'd always be costly from a labor (and thus a money) standpoint would be if the zombie's body falls apart as you shoot it. If you were to shoot his hand, it would fall off; if you were to shoot him in the shoulder, his whole arm would come off. Right away my modeler or maybe my animator is going to tell me that the feature is going to be really expensive. So, I'd then have to ask myself: "Do we need that? Is it really important?" For a zombie game, the answer is probably yes—it'll help sell the concept and I might even invoke our competitors when I want to justify the expense. Then the conversation would switch to a question of time. That is, how long would a deconstructing zombie take to make? At that point, the animator/modeler would either have a rough estimate already or be able to calculate one quickly. The producer would then have to decide if it was something that we'd be able to fit into the project. It might turn out to be a question of "Are we willing to sacrifice something else in the game so we can spend more time on this character?" Of course, this is a simple way to put it, because it's not always an apples to apples comparison. We can't cut level design time to make a creature fall apart, because we're not using the same resources.

You've heard the expression "seeing the forest for the trees." In game development, we have to constantly look at a root, then look at the forest, then look at a root, and then look at the forest. You do that over and over again because a game is the sum of its many, many parts. You've got to build a game by thinking about both the small picture and the big picture, but the big picture is ultimately more important. I can give you tons of examples of games that have fun little details that really don't matter, or that people don't notice. It's the big picture—the game as a whole—that's the key, and that's also the most difficult thing to see when you're building a game.

For a lot of the development process, games aren't fun. You're adding all these individual components and the game isn't fun to play. Because of the way an open world works, for example, play consists of a loop between all the systems, and they all need to be there at a certain level before the feel of the game clicks in. You can have driving and combat sorted out for a *Grand Theft Auto*–type game, for instance, but that may not be enough. The world might still feel empty if you don't have all the pedestrians and their behaviors working, so that makes development difficult. With every game you have to have a certain amount of faith that what you're doing is the right decision, because it's going to take a fairly long time before you can look at what you've made and understand it. You hear the same type of thing from people in the film industry, but I'd say it's even more of a challenge in games, because in a movie you can film the scene and then you can look at it immediately to see how it plays. In games, it's more like "Okay, that enemy is cool, but how does he interact with the environment? How does he interact with the player, or with players of different abilities? What about multiplayer situations?" With games, it's hard to look at things in isolation and understand how they fit into the whole. Sometimes you just have to take a guess and have faith.

Does this ability to have faith come with experience or is it innate to one's personality?

I think a common thing you see with new people in the industry is that they're so excited, passionate, and have so much faith that they're willing to put themselves through the grinder to get a game done. It's really an industry stereotype, and it's the reason companies can take advantage of people. The problem, more often than not, is that this faith can be severely tested. Maybe you work 80–120 hours a week for a year. If the game that came from that work isn't a super smash hit (or even if it is), you might not feel it was worth it. I think a lot of people find out within the first five years in the industry that faith isn't enough. It's not worth it to people when they start realizing the cost on their personal lives. What I think you learn from such experiences is what I would call a more measured faith. You gain a more realistic understanding of what life in a project is all about. You have more reasonable expectations of what it's going to take, where you're going to end up, and what it's going to cost you.

How is the work you do in the game industry different from the work you have done elsewhere?

My only jobs as an adult have been in the game industry. Before that I worked in food service while I was in school. There's a kind of fantastic efficiency that you can't help but notice when working at McDonald's: assembly lines in the trenches, objectives are clear and short, and everyone has well-defined work roles and responsibilities. Everything is optimized for speed and production. Game development is (optimally) not like that because the product, as well as the motivations of the producers, are more dynamic and creative. It's a tough and necessary balance in the context of the bottom line, which requires you to consider the tried and true and also push for the innovation necessary to make something novel and to keep staff engaged (or just to keep staff). It's a relatively small industry if you stay in it long enough, and you hear about studios that lean toward hyper-efficient factory models of production, with all the factory culture . . . and the inevitably shitty results.

At its core, the very nature of our business is antithetical to creating a standard set of practices. The arms race of technology and features, as well as the unique components specific to the game you're working on, means that there's no way to determine exactly what needs to be done to complete the project, nor can we accurately plan out how long it's going to take. Each project is a unique entity built of unknown/untested components. How can you adequately plan for that?

I'm not suggesting, however, that we throw our hands up and stop looking for better processes. Far from it. I think it's critical that we find ways to waste less time/money/energy and figure out how large teams can work better together. I have no silver bullet answer, though, and if I did I'd be selling it. What I can suggest, though, is that we accept the chaotic nature of our business. We can't plan everything out, and we shouldn't waste time trying to. Instead, we need to build in iteration time with the understanding that a project could take far more or less time than we anticipate. We need to find ways to keep entire staffs busy on productive work at all phases of a project so we can avoid wasting money, or worse, instituting layoffs.

My guess is that change like this will require publishers to be more flexible with release dates, as it's impossible to perfectly guess how long making a quality game will take. I'm not sure how that would affect the business side of our industry, though, which requires some amount of planning and predictability in order to keep the lights on. You can't tell investors that a game will come out "at some point." Plus, your marketing team needs to have an idea of when to start the hype machine (as well as when to get the money to run that machine).

It's also important to note that whatever solutions we come up with may only be possible at large companies (i.e., those with the resources to handle multiple projects). Alternatively, I can imagine there are production practices that are really only applicable on the small scale with smaller studios.

Having a litany of processes and possible solutions readily available, then, becomes important. If there's no one-size-fits-all solution, then it's paramount that good managers and producers have a variety of tools to draw from and, as studios innovate, we as an industry need to share what's worked and what hasn't. We already do this to an extent at events like the Game Developers Conference, and I'd love to see even more of it.

I want to add that I've seen forward momentum on this within EA and BioWare. At a minimum, there's a growing acknowledgment that some of our old practices (like crunch) aren't working, and there are company-wide initiatives to help implement new processes.

If it is impossible to plan in game development, why is planning such an important part of the process?

Because the reality is that if you don't try to plan, you'll fall into the chaos. You have to plant stakes in the ground and make an attempt to say that you're going to get things done by such and such a date. That's valuable information. What often happens, though, is that new information pops up. It's always useful to have at least a rough idea of how long something is going to take, because then you know where you stand. And people need deadlines to keep them honest. That pressure is helpful to make sure things get done and that people are working efficiently. You want people looking for solutions and not just floating around in exploration mode. If I told you that I need an enemy design from you in six months, you'd probably spend a lot of that six months fucking around and exploring. But if I told you that you had six days, you'd be real focused and try to get the design done as efficiently as possible.

You also have to deal with dependencies, which are a big part of what production needs to figure out. Say I have until the end of the month until someone is expecting a particular creature to be done, and I know it's going to take me two weeks to develop that creature. But I also need a piece of tech from a coder (e.g., certain animations) and I need some VFX [visual effects] . . . and the people who need to do these things are doing a whole bunch of other things as well. Someone has to figure out the order of operations in terms of what's most important. What needs to get done first? Everything is going to have an effect on when everything else is going to get done. Someone has to put all that together, especially when you think about outsourcing (which is really common). With a company like BioWare, which has multiple locations, that organizational piece becomes even harder. It's almost as if we're a boat in the sea. There are storms all around us, and these are the people working the sails to make sure we stay on course. Someone has to do that; someone has to plan. Otherwise we'll just end up in the middle of nowhere.

How does the workflow differ when working on different types of games (e.g., different genres, AAA versus casual games, etc.)?

Every studio I've worked at has had different workflows. That said, work on *Marvel Heroes 2015* was very different because that game was live, multiplayer, free to play, and not on a console. Our concerns and goals were different from those of most other titles. The main difference for me, having previously worked on console titles, was speed. Getting something from the idea phase to in-game took a lot less time, and because we could update the game, we were more relaxed about little issues. We wanted to get it on the test server ASAP so players could get their hands on it and give feedback. This was critical for two reasons. First, we wanted the community to feel like they had a hand in the creative process, and we'd often make adjustments based on their responses. Second, while small issues were acceptable, as a live game we had to be sure we weren't creating new bugs that'd crash the game or otherwise severely impact a player's experience. Frequent updates meant that the players had new content to enjoy (as well as establishing the fact that they could expect frequent updates), which hopefully meant that they'd be more willing to buy something from us. And while it had its problems, I think this workflow ultimately was right for the project. *Marvel Heroes* launched with a 50-something Metacritic rating. A year later, when we rebranded as *Marvel Heroes 2015*, our rating jumped into the 80s.

What are some of your notable quality of life issues, both routine and exceptional?

Probably the most typical issue I encounter is stress. In AAA, there are so many balls in the air it's impossible for one person to keep track of them all, so you're constantly vigilant for new issues. You've got a lot of people depending on you, and you on them. You don't always know the best solution for every problem, so you're risking wasting time, and there's no set process to make this juggling act much easier. It's a pressure cooker. I love the people I work with, I love the energy, but when I come home at the end of the day, I'm fried. For me, it's better at BioWare than any other place I've worked, but it's still an issue.

What are some of your notable career progression issues?

A key issue has to do with "lead" experience. For game designers, it seems like the only way to advance past a certain point is to enter management—to become a lead. I've already experienced a catch-22 around this in multiple places, though: I can't get a lead position because I don't have enough lead experience, but I can't get more lead experience unless I'm already a lead. This also creates something of a career dead end, even if you have a lead position. Once you're a lead, there are fewer and fewer positions above you to go to, so you end up stagnating for long stretches of time. Personally, I enjoy what I do, so I wouldn't have a problem having the same position and responsibilities for years. But position oftentimes determines compensation. Getting stuck in a position may mean no longer getting meaningful raises.

This reinforces another career progression issue: it's easier to get a higher position at another company than it is at your current one. I've seen and experienced this over and over again, and it's a shame, because I've seen good people leave companies simply because there's no higher place there for them to go. I'm not sure why this is exactly, but overall I'd say that most of the companies I've worked for aren't terribly concerned with an individual employee's professional development. If you can already do the job that they need, then great, but otherwise they're more likely to try to hire someone new who can do the job rather than train up someone from within.

Lead experience is the only cut-and-dried experience I've ever personally encountered where it was flat out "You don't have this experience and therefore we won't even consider you for this position." What I've found in design is that the higher up the chain you go, the more specialized they want you to be and that you have to become. For example, if I wanted to be a creative director on an MMO, I'd better have a crap ton of MMO experience on my résumé. Employers won't even consider me otherwise, and they probably shouldn't for that kind of position. At the same time, you can be too specialized for the market. I have some friends from back when I worked on *PlayStation All-Stars Battle Royale* who are extremely talented designers, but all their experience is with fighting games. That's it. There's one studio in the United States that makes fighting games: NetherRealm Studios. As a result, these guys may have a hard time finding work if they need to—there just isn't the demand.

Of course, fighting games mainly involve combat, and that experience could transfer to any game that has a lot of combat. Now, if you took those same guys and put them to work on *FIFA 16*, I think they'd have a problem. I'd have a problem, in fact, and I've worked on all kinds of games. I'd have no idea what to offer a sports game like that. Some skills just don't transfer. It doesn't mean that you can't learn, and it doesn't mean that you're not a good designer. It's just that most companies above a certain level are looking for someone to fill a specific kind of design spot. "We need someone who's really good at player movement. We need someone who's really good at multiplayer. We need someone who does shooters." Because they don't have a person with that kind of experience in-house, or they don't have the time to train somebody up, they look to the market for someone to hire. It's a fast way to bring a ton of experience into the studio.

How common is it for designers to move between companies of various sizes?

It's the rule. Just think of the reasons why anyone would switch jobs: compensation, interest, the possibility of new experiences. What ends up happening at a smaller company is the need to maximize resources. A small company doesn't have a ton of cash to throw around to get top talent, so they're often more willing to take a chance on someone who doesn't have exactly what they need but has a lot of experience and is willing to work for what they'll give them. Oftentimes it's not about money; it's about risk. If someone from an independent studio contacted me and offered me a job as creative director, I'd have some things to think about. Maybe the studio doesn't have a long track record; maybe they don't have the backing of a huge publisher who can help them financially if things go awry. If I took a job like that, I might be risking walking into an insane crunch fest that may not pan out at the end. But I'd get the management experience I need, and that could be useful. The project might be great, and the environment might be fun to work in as well. People will go down and work for a smaller place to get the experience they want, after which they'll return to a large company and be in a position for a promotion.

Now, while I've personally never seen anyone from a very small studio go directly to being a lead at a big studio, what it really boils down to is success. Look at Notch. Notch was an independent guy working on *Minecraft*. As far as I understand it, he had no AAA game experience. You're telling me that a year after *Minecraft* came out and he wanted to be a lead at a big AAA studio, they would've told him no? Hell no. They would've taken that guy in a second because he sold a bajillion copies, and good for him. Obviously that's an exceptional case, but what I'd say is that there's not a defined ladder, per se. It's not like you go from a tiny studio to a mid-sized studio to a big studio. I know people whose first job was at a big studio. There just happened to be a junior position there. So you don't have to climb the ladder in that regard. But what you'll find is that it's often easier to get a leadership position at a different studio, regardless of size.

I should add that the size of the company doesn't have anything to do with the quality of their games or the quality of the work experience. Every studio is different. And some developers prefer to work at larger or smaller studios, and they can be equally successful at either. It comes down to what you want to do and where you think you can best do it.

What sorts of workplace changes would you implement if given the opportunity?

If I had total authority over a workplace, I'd start by eliminating crunch. Data has shown that crunch doesn't actually make a team more efficient. In fact, crunch hurts the team both physically and mentally, and causes attrition. I'd also create time for employees to play the game they're working on.

I'm shocked by how many developers don't play the game they're working on all that frequently, other than to implement and test their personal contributions. They miss the big picture. Playing the game takes time, yes, but I've seen countless examples of it making people better at their jobs since they have a better idea of how what they do interfaces with the other parts of the game. And let's not forget that our success is based on the entire game, not just one piece. You should care how it all comes together . . . and give feedback.

Finally, I'd institute maternity and paternity leave. Obviously this is difficult for smaller studios, but the industry is getting older and a lot of us are starting families. At many places, there's no support for this whatsoever. And without maternity leave, how can you expect to get more women in the industry, not to mention hold on to more senior, experienced staff?

Why is it rare for developers to play their own games when designing them?

They don't have time. Everyone has meetings and all these other things, so time to play is time away from other things. Making games isn't like making a pizza, where you know it's going to take ninety minutes for sure so you can budget something else in. A concept artist, for example, doesn't know exactly how long it'll take to get a particular concept to work with the design restrictions, or if the lead is going to like it, or what they're going to have to iterate on. As a result, it's very hard to budget time to play the game because no one wants to risk not making the deadline. Sometimes you get managers who have the same problems, so they don't push their teams to play the game. The bigger the game, the more pressure there is to get your stuff done because there are all these other people waiting on you. It's a problem.

The thing about regularly playing the game you're working on is it would make the development process more efficient. People would be able to get and give feedback, even on stuff they don't work on.

What are the challenges facing the industry over the next decade?

First off is the growing development cost, especially in AAA. It costs a lot of money to make a game, and the price for the customer hasn't budged. It's made us extremely risk averse, and while we've found some success with other revenue streams (e.g., downloadable content, microtransactions, etc.), they're not a one-size-fits-all solution. It seems like we make fewer and fewer games each year, and I'm not sure what's going to change. Can we raise the price of games and have them still seem like they're a good value? Can we lower costs in a meaningful way? Can we find other ways to make money off a game after it's been purchased—ways that aren't exploitative and still feel like a good value to consumers?

Secondly, developers are getting older. I don't have hard data on this, but anecdotally it seems like the average age of developers is going up. I see a lot more people in their thirties and up than before, and that means teams have different concerns. We want to raise families. We can't regularly work seventy-hour weeks anymore. We're looking for more stability, which isn't something the industry is particularly great at providing. BioWare seems to be adjusting for this, which is great, but I wonder about other companies that haven't been around as long or aren't as large.

Third is the change in platforms. There are some people who wonder if this is the last generation of dedicated game consoles, which seems very possible. At their current rate, smartphones will likely be more powerful than the Xbox One or PS4 before their assumed ten-year life cycle is over, and what happens then? That'd be a major shakeup, especially for AAA, as our business model has been based on dedicated consoles since the late '80s. At a minimum, it'd mean that developers would have to support even more platforms than we currently do, which means spending even more money, something that'd only make financial sense if the audience of gamers continues to grow.

Finally, there's the move to digital. Regardless of platform, gamers will always need good content to play, but at the moment our business model is still very much tied to the idea of people buying discs at a retail store. We can already see that changing in a big way; it's hard to guess where we'll be ten years from now. If most people buy their games online, will retail stores still want to sell consoles? If not, what does that mean?

How do you see the industry responding to the challenge of crunch?

Crunch happens because you overestimate or underestimate how long stuff is going to take, and/or you get screwed by random stuff happening. You're always going to get screwed by random stuff, because that's just the nature of the business. Because of the hard deadline associated with a game's release, you end up being put in a spot where you inevitably have to cram ten pounds of shit into a seven-pound bag. There's just no other way to do it. The only options you have are to gut the game (leaving it a shell of what it's supposed to be), doing a really crappy job, or crunching. The only real way to be successful is to put out a quality product, something people want to buy and play. So you end up in a catch-22; it's impossible to avoid because there's no good way to plan. I always feel terrible for our producers because it's their job to manage the schedule. The moment they hit the save button on the spreadsheet it's wrong. It's outdated because you never know how long stuff is going to take. Some things take longer, some take less, and inevitably something pops up that you didn't think about. Games are so insanely complicated and interwoven that one little change here might mean a huge change there. If you can't plan accordingly—which you can't—you're almost always going to go over budget, because you have no way to know that you're over budget until you are. You combine that with an inflexible release date and the outcome is inevitable: you crunch because that's the only way it's possible to do more work in less time . . . unless you just decide to put out a bad product.

As I said before, though, the data shows that crunch doesn't actually work. For the first two weeks you'll be doing more man-hours than you did previously. Then, at about the two-week mark, it starts to drop and you end up doing less work than you were doing before. You're doing less because your people are tired, and you're doing less because people are making mistakes and now you have to correct those mistakes. You're also doing less work because people expand to fit the space they're given—I think it's only natural for some people to think, "I'm not going to work as hard because I know I have to be here for another eight hours." That's just human nature.

Why are maternity and paternity leave uncommon in the game industry?

The industry historically has had a lot of new people wanting to get into it on a regular basis. And I think the industry has deliberately built itself in a way to make games on the backs of very young people willing to sacrifice a lot more of their time than older, more experienced people would. This creates a situation in which you have studios with a handful of senior staff who figure out what a game is going to be and how the core mechanics will work, and then you have legions of entry-level developers actually doing the physical work of making the game. You don't have to pay these entry-level people much, and you don't have to worry about maternity/paternity leave for them because they're so young they're not thinking about starting families yet. From a paper standpoint, it's a very efficient way to do things. You can just simply throw bodies at the problem, and these folks are so young and passionate that they're willing to do it. When they get older they don't want to put up with that anymore and often leave the industry. When someone like that leaves there are plenty of other people to take that spot.

What I think the most successful studios realize, and that the industry as a whole is starting to realize, is that because fewer and fewer games are being made at the AAA level, your experienced people are more valuable than you think. They're able to solve problems better and faster, and when you lose them, it hurts the entire studio, because the next time you have to solve a problem, you don't have as many people who've done it before. You're working from scratch again. AAA games are getting so big and complicated that these losses can be a huge detriment. I've heard of games in which there was just one programmer who worked on vehicles. He was the only one, and he left the studio. Now there's no one there who understands how the vehicle tech works. Literally no one. That's a massive problem.

Ara Shirinian
Lead Designer

Ara Shirinian is a game designer, consultant, and the former co-host of Chatterbox Video Game Radio. He is currently employed by WePlay Media, and previously he worked for DreamRift, THQ, Acclaim Studios Austin, Konami, and Nicalis in a variety of capacities, including as principal designer, lead designer, senior designer, designer, and consultant. He graduated from the University of Maryland, College Park, with a BS in computer science, and through his studies he discovered that his greatest affinity and love was for the psychology of games rather than their technical implementation. Prior to entering the game industry in 1999 as an associate editor and then senior editor for *Tips & Tricks Magazine*, he worked as a software engineer and as a graphic designer. He has developed games for consoles and mobile devices, and his shipped titles include *Epic Mickey: Power of Illusion, Dood's Big Adventure, MX vs. ATV: Untamed, Cars Mater-National Championship*, and *The Red Star*. He was also a designer and consultant on *NightSky*, a WiiWare game that was a Grand Prize and Excellence in Design finalist at the 2009 Independent Games Festival. His current project with WePlay Media is the official *MotoGP* mobile game.

* * * * *

You describe yourself as a game designer and a consultant. What exactly does a consulting designer do?

As a consultant, I don't have a single employer. I take contract work wherever I can find it. Right now, I very much like and prefer consulting to working a regular job in a studio. There are a couple of reasons. First, I've seen a lot of project failures, and the thing about project failures is that they often take a long time to collapse. For me, consulting seems to be the most sustainable thing, career-wise. So many projects I've been on haven't made any money, so it seems like the best way for me most reliably and consistently to make a living is in the capacity of work-for-hire. That way, my survival need not hinge upon the success or failure of a single to a few significant projects, as is the way for many game development companies.

Importantly, contract work is always different. Sometimes I work at an hourly rate; sometimes I work for a flat fee. I prefer to do hourly for the main reason that the amount of effort required in game development always tends to be much greater than anyone ever estimates, even with the most earnest of intentions. And often I have to scrape around to try to find jobs, 99% of which I get through personal contacts. Within the past few years, I haven't made any effort at all to do any kind of cold calling or sending my résumé out to companies, because my successive tenures at many studios have so frequently ended because of company bankruptcy or layoff due to lack of funds (Acclaim, then THQ, then DreamRift). So in large part, I'm adapting my career behavior to my discovery that there are no guarantees of stability in this business. Also, what really matters to me as a designer is what project I'm doing, and I have the impression—for good reason—that the vast majority of projects that are happening in studios these days, particularly the more corporate studios, are really not that interesting to me any longer because I've already done that kind of work so many times; I hunger for new challenges so I can continue to grow professionally and creatively. If the odds are high that my employer is going to fail—as has been my experience—I may as well take the risk of uncertainty myself and seek individual projects that inspire me, instead of jumping on a large ship where I have marginal influence over whether we all sink or swim.

I've reached a point in my career where I have enough experience that if I really wanted to seek "just another studio job," it wouldn't be hard. One reason I prefer contract work is because I'm no longer as willing to move as I once was, having relocated many times in the past for studio jobs. And if I got a studio job, it would feel too much like what I've done in the past. I don't feel that I'd learn as much, and there are just certain things that appear common among large corporations that extinguish the pleasure of making games. Corporate life seems to do a really great job of killing the rewarding part of game development. I told myself that if I ever got a full-time job again, it would be one where I would have enough authority and power to do things on my own terms, so that I can be most directly responsible for successful outcomes. When you're tied to a studio in a corporate culture, you don't have much freedom to choose your projects, and you're bound to all kinds of idiosyncrasies.

What are the duties of the position(s) you have held in the various companies you have worked for?

My duties have covered a pretty broad range, and in general they fall under implementation, management, planning, and design. The designer's role is interesting because, in my experience, I have at various times (and sometimes all at once) had to be an evangelist for the game's design, a coordinator and communicator between the other disparate roles in development, and a peculiar sort of manager where you have no direct authority over—and yet are responsible for the coordinated output of—artists and programmers. One of my favorite ways to work is to directly implement the game experience itself by way of middleware or proprietary tools that are implemented by programmers. This is in opposition to the situation where the designer simply makes plans and only programmers and artists perform the direct implementation of those plans. I've had a lot of experience in both varieties, and nothing beats being able to directly implement your game. There are so many communication challenges in development in general. The more people an idea must pass through before the result of implementation, the more it inexorably transforms in idiosyncratic ways. It's the famous "telephone game" in action.

Of course perhaps I could have aimed to become both a skilled programmer and a designer, but I think splitting my efforts and concentration between the two wouldn't have allowed me to become as good a designer as I could be. And furthermore, I would've had to endure an aspect of development that I don't have a great affinity or liking for: low-level implementation of structures and patterns, and management of everything under the hood that's not directly related to the psychological and cognitive experience of game playing. I took a gamble early on that specializing myself so narrowly would be the best chance for my success. I'm glad I did.

How is the work you do in the game industry different from the work you have done elsewhere?

Working effectively as a designer requires competence in several disparate skill sets, which can also vary a great deal from studio to studio. In particular, a good designer must have a solid sense of cognitive psychology, social psychology, art, and engineering. What's more, the designer must be adept at communicating and be socially well calibrated. Incidentally, these talents are totally at odds with other aspects that are required for competency, such as a good sense of and understanding of game design by way of actual implementation. The latter is usually developed through years of solitude, while the former can only be developed through equal time practicing social behavior. Game industry work is unique not only because it demands these disparate skill sets, but also because it's quite rare to find people who actually possess such sets, as you might expect. It's also unique in the sense that there's a culture of overwork, which is totally justified and necessary in one sense, and completely debilitating in another.

Another unique dimension of game development is that it involves three completely separate disciplines: programming, design, and art. At the same time, an effective game design can only be achieved when the contributions from these disciplines are systematically coordinated. When it comes to game development, a great designer is also a good artist and programmer, a great artist is also a good designer and programmer, and a great programmer is also a good artist and designer.

An inherent problem with this reality is that most people have extensive training in one discipline and are naive about the others. Plus, by virtue of the fact that most people have such deep knowledge in their respective disciplines, there's an inherent distrust or minimization of value of the other disciplines whenever there's a conflict. And conflicts are unavoidable because making a great game requires systematic coordination of great design, great execution, and great art. It's the worst for the designer, largely due to the fact that the designer's expertise is just less salient to outsiders than programming expertise or art expertise. You can immediately tell if art is great or not—just look at it. You can almost immediately tell if engineering is great or not—just look at how smooth the execution is. But design takes longer to apprehend than any other aspect because you have to experience the game for some time before you can understand its nature and quality. Actually, the designer has it even worse than that, because your expertise as a designer is the least salient to insiders who are on your team. Any design has little worth until it reaches its near-final implementation, and by then, you have to wait months or years before you develop to the point that the true nature of the design can be known.

Discounting all that, as a designer you're also under constant great risk of the design being judged on the quality of the art or the engineering, things which you may have no control over. So we get people who seem like great designers who may be terrible designers because they're overshadowed by a great team of artists and engineers. We also get people who seem like terrible designers who may in fact be great designers, but they're overshadowed by a terrible team of artists and engineers. Why must this overshadowing be so, and why doesn't it work symmetrically in all directions? It's because of the saliency differences previously mentioned.

Game industry work is different from other kinds of work, too, because unless you're making a clone, game development is like inventing a bridge for the first time. Other domains of work are more like building a bridge, where the whys and hows are much better known. With games, there's a tremendous amount of novel invention inherent in the process that's more extreme than other creative processes, even film. Games are more complex than other media. You can think of a game as a container for all other forms of media, plus the interactive component, which just makes the complexity of the thing skyrocket. When you're doing something new in a game, you may not have any previous work to look upon for reference.

At the same time, game development is also unique from other inventive, creative processes in that it requires a tremendous amount of work, which is often split between a large number of individuals. This aspect also causes a kind of stress that's fairly unique to game development because of the complexities of integration and coordination. I try to ameliorate this for myself by working on smaller-scope games and with smaller teams. On the business side this is often ameliorated by working on creatively "safe" projects—if you deliberately limit how much creatively uncharted territory you're venturing into, you get the added benefit of being able to rely upon a large volume of previous works for reference, and your path won't be as risky. Of course, if you take that principle to its furthest extreme, you end up just cloning another game. Maybe you'll make some money, or a lot of money, but cutting out too many risks this way leads to its own risks, some direct and obvious and some indirect and subtle. Your product won't be well differentiated, so if the market is already too saturated you risk making even less money. You also contribute in small ways to a cannibalization of your own medium with respect to the long-term sustainability of the overall industry business and simultaneously its meaningfulness to our culture. This kind of thing isn't a problem or even noticeable until we reach a critical mass of clone-y products. The insidious thing about it is that since it's a result of lots of independent agents acting in their own self-interest, we won't realize just how bad it is until we've been in it for some time, and by then it'll have a massive amount of its own momentum.

One of the things that was starkly surprising to me when I worked at Rainbow Studios is that I found it incredibly difficult to work with some artists. And I spent a lot of time trying to figure out why it was so hard to work with them. Eventually I realized that in large part it was because their values seemed diametrically opposed to mine. This isn't endemic to all game artists, but in my situation a lot of artists considered working in games as second-tier work. They would have rather been making creative work for film; they considered films to be aspirational, and games the second-rate thing they did while biding their time until they could work on their Hollywood blockbuster. The problem is that these media are so different, and several artists I worked with didn't appreciate the differences between them. This is a critical mistake, and the crux that causes a lot of conflict between team members.

So here's what happens: suppose there's this artist, and he's been trained for many years to make art. Maybe he works as an artist in the game industry for ten years. He's got tenure that validates his belief in his ability, values, and opinions. The problem is that so much development happens at the mechanical level, outside of artistry. But suppose this artist has remained focused on his particular branch for all this time without studying or interacting too deeply with the other two branches. As a result, you can have a situation where artists are doing work without due consideration of the interactive nature of the medium because they don't know any better. Their experience in games has remained narrow. Some artists who work in the game industry—though this will become less true over time—still have the baggage of their traditional training, which does not incorporate consideration for the interactive nature of games. They aren't trained to make art for games, art for an interactive space; they're trained to make art for a non-interactive space—every medium except video games—and then they decide that they want to make art for games. Since art is the most salient aspect of a game—that's what people notice first and the most—it gives the artist a distorted sense of their own importance, which is only exacerbated by the length of their tenure. You can't possibly tell someone who's been doing something for ten years that maybe they haven't been taking the right approach.

I know all this may sound biased from a designer's perspective, so let me just say that I have no intention of discounting designers from their own peculiar issues that give artists a hard time. But art for interactive spaces and art for non-interactive spaces are totally different things, totally different domains. They call for different things. So, when interactive art for such an artist is outside of her/his purview as practiced, it's difficult for that artist to appreciate what they're missing. When someone like me comes along, someone who's been studying the psychology and dynamics of the mechanics separately from how they look, the artist isn't used to it. It's threatening, because it goes against every single thing that they've been taught up to that point. It causes a lot of friction. This is why it's so important for every expert in her or his discipline to have some depth of knowledge about the others.

For example, on *Cars Mater-National Championship*, one of the things I was responsible for was designing and implementing the shape of the tracks—where does it go up and down, how does it bank, how wide is it here, how wide is it there, and so on. Once I'd built and tuned a track, it was the artist's job to make art around it to fit it. This is normally a point of friction in game design because oftentimes an artist wants to do things that conflict with what the designer wants to do. The problem arises because the artist doesn't have the perspective to understand where the designer is coming from. The artist may not even have the background to be able to relate to where the designer is coming from. It's a huge problem. Anyway, the way that we built *Cars* was that the edges of each track would function as an impenetrable wall. It would extend all the way around the track, both inside and out. That's how we defined a track. For a player, the most important thing in gameplay for a track is that you have to know where the edge of the track is at all times. You have to be able to see it, to read it. The artist thought it looked really stupid to have a fence going around the entire track. What he preferred instead was to only install visual barriers sporadically in order to not upset the visual pleasantness of the scene he was creating. It became an intractable issue and got escalated to levels well above us because we couldn't agree on a resolution. I tried to explain to him that his preferred way of building the environment would be more appropriate in the context of a painting or a poster, but in this context it's of critical importance for the player to know exactly where the edge of the track is at all times because that's the means by which the player is making decisions. I failed to communicate the importance of these qualities to him. In the end, it came down to somebody above us resolving the issue, and we eventually decided to wrap the fence all along the track. Although it wasn't the most aesthetically pleasing solution, it was the right one because readability is more important than aesthetics in games.

In this case, I think it was the artist's limited experience in the psychology of design, plus all the other things previously mentioned, that led to an inherent distrust of his designer teammate. It wasn't just a disagreement to hash out; it was a clash of disparate values that made it difficult to find a path forward in unison as teammates. There's another essential problem here for designers: because so many aspects of design knowledge aren't salient, it's really hard to convince people that they're real. And that's the central distrust between designers and everyone else on the team. They can't tell that what the designer is saying, recommending, and evaluating is based on a lot of experience. In defense of the artists and programmers, at their worst designers do say, recommend, and evaluate based on caprice and whimsy instead of experience and deep consideration, and narrowly experienced artists and programmers won't be able to tell one from the other.

Games have an essential problem, where the deepest part of them is the least salient part. This is intrinsically bad for the game industry because you often can't sell people on the thing that's the best thing about a game. You can only sell people on the thing that's most noticeable about a game.

What are some specific practices that you pursue as a designer and a manager to negotiate these kinds of cross-disciplinary, collaborative moments?

At Rainbow Studios, I learned that the best way for me to appeal to people who don't understand what I'm saying is to speak purely objectively. For example, I'd make sure to always have an objective reason for any design decision, and present possible solutions for any potential issues. I had to come up with good justifications for things that were really convincing to people who had a very different background from me. I learned how to talk to people without making them feel threatened or without making them defensive on a topic they might be passionate about. I also learned to drop my own passion, to put it aside when talking about an issue.

You have had the misfortune of working on a number of games that have been canceled. What is the cancellation or failure rate in the industry?

If I was pressed to say a number, I'd say around 50%, though of course that depends on how you frame "failure." I'd guess that the failure rate for independent games might be higher, simply because I have the impression that independent developers—at least in the aggregate—are not as good at finishing game products as corporations. That owes to the inherent self-discipline required to actually finish a project when it's under your own auspices. On the other hand, corporations will also kill projects for idiosyncratic reasons that don't even apply to independent developers (e.g., "Oh, we noticed this quarter that other racing games on the Wii aren't making money anymore, so we're going to kill your Wii racing game project.")

What challenges—if any—exist within the organizations for which you have worked that hindered you from performing your duties at an optimal level?

Needless to say, the challenges are numerous. The first has to do with communication and politics, and are the typical issues in any kind of corporate environment. In particular, not enough attention is paid to establishing expectations. There's also an inherent distrust of any designer, which is a side effect of the "everybody's a designer" phenomenon as well as the saliency issue previously explained. This is problematic because designers in general face substantial undue scrutiny compared to the other disciplines, and these things hurt the quality of the game in several ways that go completely unnoticed by the people who are involved. It doesn't help that a lot of designers are in fact woefully unqualified (in large part due to them not having sufficiently deep experience in the other two disciplines), which leads to stereotypes and concomitant problems.

There's also often an inherent distrust of the development team by the publisher or funder, which is almost the same as the above but on a different scale. Most often, the publisher can only see what's right in front of them as far as the state of development goes and doesn't have the experience to understand how development may proceed forward from the present moment. Plus, the publisher often has no idea what's actually involved in the nitty-gritty of development, so their assumptions lead to additional friction. This is exacerbated by the fact that a high-production game often only seems to become "fun" at the very latest stages of development. Until then, the developer must play a high-stakes game of managing and reassuring the publisher's expectations. Then there's the issue of micromanagement, which is a side effect of the previous items, and which is also insidious because it leads creative, productive people to shut down both creatively and productively.

In addition, there are a lot of young people in development who aren't emotionally well developed, and this leads to all kinds of issues. These kinds of things produce an inevitable tug-of-war between publishers and developers that results in both substandard products and overwork.

Finally, there's a significant contingent of employees who are enamored with the idea of game development but possess neither the talent nor the work ethic (more importantly) to operate as a highly functioning member of a team. And unfortunately, we often see two extreme styles of game development: the "director" style, which is better described as a dictator style, and the "team" style, where matters are so overly democratic or undefined or informal that nobody on the team is really sure who is in fact responsible for which decisions; and when decisions are settled upon, it's too often just an idiosyncratic result of politics instead of measured, thoughtful analysis of what's really best for the product.

In corporate, there's both value in and fear of novelty. There's fear because novelty is unproven. Corporate operates in this weird space of equivalence where they treat everything as a statistic and they don't want to bother to understand the system (or can't) in order to qualitatively understand what it could be or do. Nobody wants to take the risk of being first, of being truly novel, but everybody wants to be second, as soon as the novelty has been proven a moneymaker.

As far as new methods of distribution go, it's not the delivery method that determines whether something is popular or not. If it were, it would imply that we won't sell a lot of games via traditional means, which still happens anyway. I don't think newer distribution methods make development costs any cheaper, unless you're also making a much smaller game at the same time. The lesser risk is coming from the smaller game, not the new distribution platform.

Outsourcing comes at great cost most of the time, and it gets worse the more creative and novel your product. It's very easy for a lot of the subtlety of a game to get lost in an outsourcing situation. You can get outsourced work that doesn't fit the project properly, you might have to redo things a lot of times, etc. In my experience, outsourcing results in much more effort than it's actually worth.

That said, I suppose as a consultant I'm kind of like an outsourcer. The difference is that I generally do systematic designs of products, as opposed to creating a single asset or asset set. The people who perform outsource work don't see the whole picture; it's probably omitted in part for efficiency reasons. Unfortunately, omitting the big picture can produce a lot of risk. Even if I work remotely, I'm intimately in communication with the team and intimately familiar with the entire product systematically. I believe that in order for a team to make a good game, ideally every person on that team needs to have a very good systemic understanding of the product. That's primarily lacking in outsource situations, never mind language issues and such.

What challenges—if any—exist external to the organization for which you currently work that hinder you from performing your duties at an optimal level?

Well, there are challenges, but since they're external they have no bearing on my—or I would expect, anyone else's—duties. That said, there's unfair scrutiny and manipulation about the political aspects of games (e.g., war, violence, sexism, subject matter, etc.). A lot of special interest groups seem to be jockeying for influence on games overall. I tend to favor inherently respecting any person's or team's work as a creative production personally meaningful to them, and therefore worthy of existence on its own terms, even if that production just looks like babes in bikinis. The problem with the arguments that complain that there are too many sexist games, violent games, unpleasant subject matter, and so forth is that such an approach disrespects the concept of the game as a work of art. I don't believe it's fair to tell people how they can or can't creatively pursue their time. But, one can decide for one's own self what that variety of creative pursuit or content is worth to them.

Furthermore, efficient economic behavior by corporations is resulting in a kind of scorched earth pattern of game selling that disrupts the sustainability of selling. This is because most marketers in the game industry treat marketing and sales as a black box, and are neither interested in nor considerate of the sustainability of a sales process. They go for what works now, milk that until it's no longer sufficiently profitable, and only afterward consider figuring out what to do next. Plus, the public corporation aspect applies not just pressure to be profitable, but pressure to be increasingly profitable year after year. You can see the inflation of expectations in the press, too: when overall industry profits for a given year were comparable to that of five years ago (which were much bigger than five years before that), the press framed it as a catastrophe, just because the industry had an abnormally good run for some years and then that bubble burst. The overall trend over the longer time frame was still impressively positive.

Another interesting aspect is that corporations don't care about making what we game developers and designers value about games. They just want to make generalized entertainment products called "games," which are very, very different things. It's fair enough, though, because the mass markets don't really want games either. They also want generalized entertainment that we call "games" and that doesn't demand too much from players in terms of labor and attention. This is a very different culture than mine and that of the early video game industry, which was fundamentally based on skill and learning games. Skill and learning games will always inherently be harder to sell because they make demands on players. Demands are considered barriers to accessibility. The game economy has exploded because of its ability to cater to bigger and bigger markets by removing barriers to access. In the process, the industry has also gradually eliminated not only skill in many games, but also the effectiveness of games as learning devices.

The market is completely—and I can't emphasize this enough—oversaturated with product and totally undersaturated with consumers. This is clear from the constant pattern of layoffs, start-ups, and closures, and the reality is that while most successful companies spend much more money on marketing than development (because they have to, in order to have a chance to break through the oversaturation), many games—maybe most—don't make money. There are too many people making games and not enough people interested in games. Consider that there were almost seven hundred entries in the Independent Games Festival in 2013, which was yet another record-breaking year of entries.

Selling games is required for survival, but what sells is often not so good.

How does the use of licensed content affect creativity and risk taking in the industry?

Well, THQ very much preferred licensed content because the executives considered the game industry to be extremely risky. They believed that the best chance for success was to find the biggest franchise around and tie into it. Even though they'd have to pay royalties, it would mitigate the risk of losing tons of money. Sometimes it worked out for them extremely well (e.g., the *Cars* franchise). A few years ago, personally I thought it was riskier to go down the licensed IP road, because there are just so many more variables involved. On the other hand, discoverability is such a big problem now, and is ever growing, that maybe it's becoming more and more risky to make the totally original IP, and maybe the advantages of having an original product these days are already becoming outweighed by the licensed IP approach.

Another factor as to why THQ preferred licensed content was because the executives—the people controlling the direction of the company—didn't seem to have a good grasp of not only what games are (beyond products that were appealing because the IP tied to them was appealing), but also what could be good about a game. In other words, they couldn't recognize a game as being intrinsically good when they saw it. They had a way of looking at games strictly in economic terms, without considering, for example, the specific things about how a game worked or played that could be appealing.

Part of the reason for this was something I perceived from below: a lot of overweight management structure. There were a lot of people in corporate who did very little except act as middlemen. As a result, there was a lot of political momentum around the top. I got the distinct impression that there was a lot of posturing going on to make sure that things appeared good (as opposed to actually being good in terms what was best for the company). There seemed to be a surprising amount of second-guessing about what such-and-such executive did and didn't want, and in a climate where the safest thing to do is to say "no" or "stop" or "it's a bad idea" and the riskiest thing to your job security is to say "yes" or "proceed" or "it's a good idea," you end up with a culture where everybody is working to protect themselves and their station over what could bring the company the greatest potential. In other words, nobody wants to take a risk. Of course, when you don't want to take any risks, you miss opportunities left and right.

I don't believe that a concept makes a game good or bad. It's the actual details of exactly how a game works that make it good or bad. The problem is that these details are among the least salient aspects of a game experience, while the concept is the most salient, especially for people who haven't yet played the game. So, I can understand corporate behavior to a degree: if you want to sell something, you need to select an appealing concept. The problem at

THQ was that this kind of attitude bled into all the other aspects of game development, instead of being relegated to the concept level.

Of course, as developers we would modify our own behavior in an attempt to adapt. For example, we'd present a concept that we thought would be appealing to executives specifically, which is different from what we thought would be appealing to the mass market—the mass market isn't the folks greenlighting the game. In other words, we'd present what we thought the executives would think would be popular. Sometimes, when it would come time to present details to the executives, a not uncommon tactic involved leaving in some obvious error that was easy for an executive to spot. You might consider this kind of error like a "dead dog." The analogy is this: suppose there's a film scene that someone is evaluating, and a dead dog is just sitting right there in the middle of the scene. The evaluator would then say, "Hey, there's a dead dog in your scene," and the creator could respond with "Thanks for pointing that out. That's such a good catch." The evaluator could then feel good about meaningfully impacting the product, and the creators could feel good for not having to compromise their values.

The unfortunate thing is that we experienced so much micromanagement of that kind that we felt that the executives didn't trust us. It was so bizarre—why wouldn't you trust the experts who've dedicated the majority of their lives to the craft? A corporation can only function if all the levels of the corporation trust each other.

Let me give you an example of how development was micromanaged by corporate from afar. One of the *MX vs. ATV* games we made—one of the later ones we published (and we published a lot of them)—was about two weeks away from completion. The creative director got a question from corporate asking, "Why are the riders standing up? That looks wrong." The creative director then had to stop everything he was doing and—I would argue unreasonably—spend time collecting references to prove to the executives that riders as depicted did stand on their bikes correctly according to what actually happens in the sport.

What sorts of workplace changes would you implement if given the opportunity?

I'd go for clarity of roles, expectations, communication, and goals as part of the process of establishing a team or bringing in a new member. This includes mutual agreement on the intensity of work. The biggest problem I see about working in game development is that the specific expectations and culture of a given team are often not communicated well to a prospective team member, and even if they are, most people are so desperate just to get into the industry that they'll take any job they can get. They then find themselves in a position where far more is demanded of them than they want, and then they complain. The problem is that both parties were keeping their heads in the sand because the prospect of a position in the industry is just so scarce.

Generally I see two opposing fundamental attitudes toward game development. First, if you want to make anything good, the competition is so cutthroat that you have to work insane hours and put in Herculean effort just to have a chance at success. The second attitude is reflected in the idea "I have a life/family/kids/hobbies and want to balance these with work." I think both of these attitudes are valid and truthful, but perhaps they aren't compatible on the same team. Some people love game development so much that they want to be total workaholics about it, and those are usually the ones who make the best work. That's not just a coincidence. However, that level of dedication is too much to ask from everyone; it takes a special kind of person to work with that ethic and not be damaged by it. Conversely, the problem with the second attitude is that while it values the comfort and health of the worker above the job itself, many people who I've met who have this attitude actually aren't passionate about their work or career, and that makes it difficult for these people to produce exceptional work. There are a lot of gray areas, but we only hear about the extremes, which discredits its true nature.

Another workplace change I'd like to see has to do with compensation. Overtime isn't generally paid, and this is a huge mistake. I don't believe salaried compensation makes sense for game development; hourly rate does, for all levels of staff. Corporations are taking advantage of salaried rates by exploiting employees for extra time without extra remuneration. In a sense, they're taking advantage of this exploit because game projects are so often financial disasters altogether. In this way, they have funds to complete maybe a few more projects before the money runs out. Or maybe this is the only way that makes a single project tenable with available funds in the first place. The problem isn't easy to solve, because if everyone were paid what they deserved, there would actually be less work as a result. Maybe the solution is to treat the team more as partners who each get a bigger chunk of the pie on the backside when success occurs. That arrangement, however, usually means an inconsistent wage.

Distribution of salaries is also too lopsided, even considering actual value brought to the project. Perceived value overshadows actual value in the game industry.

How would you describe the management structure and workflow in the companies you have worked for?

I've worked in multiple different structures. I've worked in a corporate structure with a creative director, multiple teams, and an upper management exerting all levels of micromanagement upon the product. I've also worked in a relatively flat structure with a small team, as well as in teams where I've had final say versus managing multiple stakeholders in a morass of confusion.

Concomitantly, I've worked in multiple styles of workflow roles. I've been a designer only doing writing or documentation, and coordinating with multiple artists and programmers who do the actual implementation. I've also done both high-level conceptual and low-level specific design. I've worked as a designer performing direct game implementation using proprietary tools, and interfaced with upper management and clients about progress, goals, and so forth.

In your experience or estimation, how does the development process differ when working on different types of games (e.g., different genres, AAA versus smaller games, etc.)?

In general, it's very different from game to game and studio to studio. Production on a well-established game type or series is more like making another bridge instead of inventing the bridge for the first time. Making a novel game, by contrast, is incredibly hard with a large team, because it's impossible to convey a novel vision efficiently to a large team. People don't want to admit this. Communication gets harder as team size expands. At the same time, the volume of work per person seems to go down as team size expands. The frequency of people who don't contribute adequately also increases, and that creates new problems of inequity among team members. Pretty much all social, political, and interpersonal risks are minimized with a smaller team. Truth be told, from what I've experienced, many in the AAA space aren't really that passionate about their jobs, and the industry space seems to facilitate that.

In your experience, there seem to be ample opportunities for mistrust in game development. What impact does mistrust have on the development of a game?

When there's mistrust, things take longer to accomplish. It also directly impacts the quality of the work, as well as the ability of people to get better at their jobs. And that, of course, compounds over time and also if a company is under financial duress. Let me give you an example. I was working with a user interface (UI) artist who was a badass. He was great at his job, he had a lot of experience, and he had obvious expertise. As a result, he was used to relying on his own faculties to differentiate between good work and bad work. I'd been working with him for several years, and we worked well together. It was a good team dynamic, with lots of trust but also the freedom to challenge each other when necessary. Unfortunately, what happened is that management saw the screenshots of the work and began to micromanage the UI design, giving feedback to him directly. Feedback in this way is not a suggestion, it's not offering up critique and allowing the expert to process it and come to an expert decision. It's a covert mandate. As a result of no longer being able to depend on his own innate and critical faculties in the job, the UI artist became prostrate. He just gave up and checked out. In the span of a few months, I saw this guy go from producing fantastic work to producing garbage. He just gave up. Imagine what it does to your attitude to have the skills you've developed over years—everything that you know—absolutely dismissed. Things just degenerated into "Tell me what to do next." I've seen this happen to a number of other people as well . . . me included. And I'm just talking here about the output of work. I'm not even talking about someone's motivation to continue doing what they consider to be their chosen career.

The reason I got into making games—and I think the reason a lot of my peers got into making games—is that we're really emotionally passionate about them. The problem is that we're so passionate that we believe that the way that we think about them is the best way to think about them . . . and everyone else is wrong. If you get a job titled "game designer," it validates the passion and the thinking it spawns. Every game designer feels that they've made it, and by virtue of that it's difficult to have objective conversations because people will fight for things without having good enough reasons.

And so you waste a lot of time in a battle of wills instead of in a measured discussion about pros and cons and a final determination that weighs all of them fairly.

Are there model companies or ways of doing your particular work (both within and outside of the game industry) that you look to for inspiration?

Yes, but since I haven't actually worked at them, it's impossible to know if they're just fantasy tales or not. Toby Gard—the original *Tomb Raider* designer—had the best philosophy about organizing teamwork in game development: everybody needs to have a box that they work inside of, and a subset box of that where it's understood that they have full responsibility and control. Without this, people check out mentally and don't feel in control.

Conversely, the biggest problem I've seen is the opposite, where creative employees are dictated to from above. This is very dangerous, as it leads to highly effective people becoming totally ineffectual at their jobs. They begin to doubt their own expertise and faculties, as idiosyncratic demands are foisted upon them by a source that doesn't appreciate the problem set fully. As I said, I've seen the quality of people's work actually get worse and worse in this process, because after a certain amount of exposure they just go into "tell me what to do" mode. In that mode, they're no longer thinking for themselves and using their own skills and abilities they've honed over the years.

What are the challenges facing the industry in the next decade?

They are, specifically: 1) rising and staying above the status of junk food; 2) the maturation of marketing to better understand player psychology and the consumer as a dynamic, learning agent in the game economy; and 3) designers earning the respect their profession deserves. That is to say, the challenge for us as an industry is to understand more deeply just how critically the precise design of a game impacts its quality and success.

Everybody experientially does video games. The easiest thing in the world is to believe that your emotional reaction to a video game is the same as someone else's. The hardest thing in the world to realize is that your emotional reaction in the experience of playing a video game may be very different from somebody else's. Owing to the fact that people are now playing games for many more reasons than we typically suspect, the most important thing for us as developers to remember is that we need to maximally appreciate these differences in perspectives without losing the internal passion that drew us toward this pursuit in the first place.

▶ DISCUSSION

Among the most significant aspects of the design discipline from a labor perspective are its timeline and salience. As both Rubino and Shirinian note, the quality of a given game's design becomes apparent only after many months of development. A significant amount of faith in design (and in designers) is thus required by everyone in, and connected to, a development project. Concomitantly, it can be hard to measure and communicate design skills in the way one can with programming and art, where tests and certifications are common. This immeasurable quality of design not only makes seeking employment difficult, but can roil the act of game work itself. Design decisions, for example, can sometimes be difficult for other disciplines to grasp because the design is structural and developmental rather than immediately tangible in the way that art, sound, and programming are. These more accessible elements can thus come to overshadow design, an oversight that can prove devastating to a game's ultimate playability—and therefore its attractiveness—in the marketplace.

Importantly, Shirinian notes that design's unavoidably delayed assessment works in the other direction as well. Because it is so difficult to determine the effectiveness of design until late in the development process, a poorly designed game may well not have its problems discovered until considerable resources have already been committed to it. As he puts it: "The thing about project failures is that they often take a long time to collapse." When this happens, the necessities of the market—publish or perish—dictate that studios, their personnel, and ultimately consumers succumb to the skill (or lack thereof) of designers and the circles of trust they are able to sustain among the development team. The uncertainty of design is what (along with easier discoverability in an oversaturated market) makes established IPs so attractive to publishers, of course, but such properties translate into tedium among designers driven by novelty and a passion to innovate.

Shirinian and Rubino also describe the need for design personnel to coordinate and collaborate across disciplines, but in Shirinian's words, "Making a novel game . . . is incredibly hard with a large team, because it's impossible to convey a novel vision efficiently to a large team." Given the risk-averse nature of the game industry, and particularly its AAA components, this impossibility necessarily constrains the type of new experiences players can be offered. Both interviewees address this disciplinary communication problem, observing that it signals a paradox at the heart of game industry work: to create good games, one must be simultaneously devoted to one's own discipline and committed to learning about, appreciating, and relying upon the work of disciplines far outside one's wheelhouse. For this paradox not to destabilize the industry, it seems to be regulated by another paradox, namely, that innovation must be standardized. Given this twin conundrum, it is hardly surprising that intra-studio friction is relatively commonplace and that it plays out in a variety of spaces, from the politics of open floor plans to the differential pay both among and within all of the industry's job categories. It may well also be impacted by employee age, where young people are perhaps somewhat more malleable when it comes to holding these paradoxes in productive tension than more experienced employees who know what kinds of ambiguity they are and are not willing to tolerate.

Certainly an important question to ask after is how this affects the overall potential audience for mainstream games. In addition, if the market cannot support the sheer number of games being created—and it does not seem to be able to in its current configuration, or else there would be far fewer studio closures—in what ways can developers reimagine their design approach to attract new audiences? Or is there a somewhat finite player ceiling ultimately, meaning that the potential innovation space is limited?

The concept and permutations of *cost* are clearly central to game work of all kinds, and especially so in design, which is arguably the source of this work. There are monetary budgets, asset budgets, labor budgets, and more, all of which have their costs and compromises. Chief among them is the human cost, the physical and emotional budget of the developer. This budget is often severely mismanaged and overrun—frequently by the passion of developers themselves—and can lead to unpleasant labor conditions, burnout, and attrition. And yet, the human cost seems impossible to manage under the current market structure, where technological and economic change is constant and quintessential. So where does that leave laborers who (in the most demanding situations) do not have time enough even to play the very games they are building? And where does this leave the products of their work? To put it another way, how has such an unsustainable industry managed to sustain itself for so long, especially, as Rubino notes, given its inherent incongruity with the formation of standard practices?

Along these lines, we were struck by the seemingly inherent arbitrariness and alchemy of game design, especially in the context of the multisite and several-hundred-person teams and hierarchical organizational structures of AAA development. Rubino describes designers in this context as "professional guessers." That is, they are essentially employees who expect to fail (i.e., iterate) many times and on most occasions in their work tasks, tasks that are fundamental to the highly routinized and deadline-dependent game development process. Design, in other words, contravenes producing, despite the fact that the two disciplines often overlap in purview. Producing is very much about routinization and proceduralism, despite the seemingly intrinsic forces that work against them.

It is important to note, too, the failure spectrum in game labor. Failure can be relatively instantaneous, such as when a game build will not compile properly, or be drawn out, such as when a game project or even an entire studio collapses. These more extended failures are well documented across the interviews in this book, but particularly by Shirinian, who cites project/ studio failure as central to his decision to become a contract worker. Oddly enough, in the case of this designer, contract work has proven more stable than studio work, which raises an interesting question: if contingency is essentially reliable and secure, what then is stability?

Finally, the way in which Full Sail University approaches its students' futures is both notable and astonishing. On the one hand, the high-stress curricular environment echoes the high-stakes, deadline-driven experience of AAA game development, and is thus to be lauded for attenuating the transition between workforce training and workforce occupancy. As Rubino notes, the school is also up front about the nature of the industry, and the fact that new employees will likely not get the opportunity to pursue their own design ideas and aesthetics initially. On the other hand, Full Sail's scholastic approach appears machinic and even usurious, producing few and narrowly skilled laborers who have been trained to accept the workplace conditions the game industry both depends upon and reviles. And though the industry is beginning to look for ways to remake itself, such revision seems unlikely when the workforce is being trained into accepting and perpetuating the status quo. Students, in other words, are being trained into exploitation, building first on their infatuation with the medium and then disciplining that desire through education in a set of corporate processes that bind creativity to ever-increasing demands for productive labor.

It appears that it is precisely this phoresic commensalism—the profit motive hitching a ride on innovation (or is it the other way around?)—that confirms Rubino's claim that in the game industry, not everything can be perfectly "optimized for speed and production." Instead, innovation and profit are yoked in an uneasy collaboration, and it is designers who define— but ultimately cannot control the route toward—a studio's revenue-ludic goal.

▶ WORKS CITED

Bibliography

Kaufman, William Ryan. "GSCPP: Recursion, Revision, Response." The 33rd Annual Conference of The Southwest/Texas Popular Culture Association/American Culture Association. Albuquerque, NM, February 8–11, 2012. Conference talk.

"Transitions: Gamasutra Salary Survey 2014." *Gamasutra: The Art & Business of Making Games*. UBM Tech. 22 Jul. 2014: 1–8. Web. 10 Oct. 2015. <http://www.gamesetwatch.com/2014/09/05/GAMA14_ACG_SalarySurvey_F.pdf>

Filmography

Batman. Dir. Tim Burton. Warner Bros., 1989. Film.

Gameography

Barbie Horse Adventures: Wild Horse Rescue. Blitz Games. Vivendi Universal Games, 2003. Multiple platforms.

Battlefield Hardline. Visceral Games/Electronic Arts Digital Illusions Creative Entertainment. Electronic Arts, 2015. Multiple platforms.

Cars Mater-National Championships. Rainbow Studios. THQ, 2007. Multiple platforms.

Dood's Big Adventure. THQ Digital Studios Phoenix. THQ, 2010. Nintendo Wii.

Epic Mickey: Power of Illusion. DreamRift. Disney Interactive Studios, 2012. Nintendo 3DS.

FIFA 16. EA Canada. EA Sports, 2015. Multiple platforms.

Grand Theft Auto. DMA Design. BMG Interactive, 1997. Multiple platforms.

Karateka. Liquid Entertainment. D3 Publisher, 2012. Multiple platforms.

Marvel Heroes 2015. Gazillion Entertainment/Secret Identity Studios. Gazillion Entertainment, 2013. Personal computer.

Mass Effect: Andromeda. BioWare. Electronic Arts, 2017. Multiple platforms.

Minecraft. Mojang. Mojang, 2011. Multiple platforms.

MotoGP Racing: Championship Quest. WePlay Media. WePlay Media, 2016. Mobile.

MX vs. ATV: Untamed. Rainbow Studios. THQ, 2008. Multiple platforms.

NightSky. Nicalis. Nicalis, 2009. Multiple platforms.

PlayStation All-Stars Battle Royale. SuperBot Entertainment/SCE Santa Monica Studio. Sony Computer Entertainment, 2012. Sony PlayStation 3.

The Red Star. Acclaim Studios Austin/Archangel Studios. XS Games, 2007. Sony PlayStation 2.

Rise of the Argonauts. Liquid Entertainment. Codemasters, 2008. Multiple platforms.

Thor: God of Thunder. Liquid Entertainment. Sega, 2011. Multiple platforms.

Tomb Raider. Core Design. Eidos Interactive, 1996. Multiple platforms.

Softography

3ds Max (http://www.autodesk.com/products/3ds-max/overview-dts?s_tnt=69291:1:0)

id Tech 4 (https://github.com/id-Software/DOOM-3-BFG)

Maya (http://www.autodesk.com/products/maya/overview)

REDengine (https://www.cdprojekt.com/pl)

Torque 3D (http://www.garagegames.com/products/torque-3d)

Unity 3D (https://unity3d.com)

Unreal Engine (https://www.unrealengine.com/what-is-unreal-engine-4)

4

Producing

▶ INTRODUCTION

The producing discipline varies widely in scope and degree, not only from studio to studio but also from project to project. In the simplest terms, a producer oversees a project's development budget and schedule. The position is organizational by definition, and therefore heavily dependent on project management tools (e.g., *Microsoft Project*, *JIRA Software*) and practices (e.g., Scrum, Agile) to coordinate disparate sets of data related to personnel, milestones, and timelines into a larger picture that visualizes everything from workflow to profit margin.

Producers typically hold one of three titles—assistant/associate producer, producer, or executive producer. Assistant/associate producers (APs) handle the day-to-day tracking and management of the production schedule and work closely with discipline leads and other team members on task management. As a result, APs tend to be in charge of various communication channels and asset pipelines, as well as of maintaining team morale and well-being, including such mundane but important tasks as ordering in food during long work days.

Producers typically have larger oversight than APs, and their duties include planning and tracking game milestones, coordinating with other management personnel to schedule resources for creating content in a timely manner, navigating third-party submission processes, overseeing the design and development of specific game features, organizing product testing and feedback, updating executive staff on project progress (including discussing contingency plans when necessary), and assisting the creative team in making scoping modifications. In some studios, producers may even take on a creative role, overseeing and organizing content developers and rallying them around a specific feature or core vision of the game.

Executive producers, by extension, have still broader supervisory powers and responsibilities, often including accountability for the profit and loss of a game or series, paying outside vendors, approving budgets for voice talent, outsourcing to expand art and programming department capabilities, and so forth.

According to the 2014 Gamasutra Salary Survey, producers earn an average annual salary of $82,286 in the aggregate ("Transitions" 3). Assistant/associate producers with six or fewer years of experience earn an average of $59,079 annually, while those with more experience earn an average of $61,912 per year (Ibid.). Similarly, producers with six or fewer years of experience earn an average of $73,500 annually, while those with more experience earn an average of $93,160 per year (Ibid.). Executive producers earn at the top of the scale, with an average salary of $126,833 annually (Ibid.). Additionally, US-based producers earn approximately 17% more on average than their Canadian counterparts, and 32% more on average than European producers (Ibid.). Finally, male producers average $84,151 annually, while female employees average $75,726 annually (Ibid.).

Charles Babb
Producer

Charles Babb is the chief executive officer and principal at Fairchild Consortium, president of Harves Interactive Media, and a principal at JetSetter Fresh/Underground Live. Previously he was senior associate producer at Spark Unlimited, producer and associate project manager at Sony Computer Entertainment America, production coordinator at Neversoft Entertainment, associate producer for Gorilla Systems Corporation, assistant project manager for New American Dimensions, and marketing coordinator for

TOKYOPOP. He holds an MS in interactive entertainment from the University of Central Florida's Florida Interactive Entertainment Academy and a BA in international studies from Morehouse College. He has developed games for multiple platforms, and his shipped titles include *Yaiba: Ninja Gaiden Z*; *PlanetSide 2*; *inFAMOUS: Festival of Blood*; *inFAMOUS 2*; *Killzone 3*; and *Guitar Hero: Warriors of Rock*.

* * * * *

What are the duties of the position(s) you have held?

I've managed multiple internal and outsource teams, monitored budgets and resources for internal and outsource teams, created engineering and art development plans based on game designers' needs and desires, solved development bottlenecks, and improved art production pipelines with team members.

Before a project goes to an outsource team, the producer—the overall stakeholder and purse-string holder of the project—will say something like "We need to outsource these certain things. Try to get it done for under X amount of money." The person who monitors the budget—usually the associate producer—then executes based on those costs. At times, though, the costs will change. The outsource team might be taking too long, they might need to add more members, or the project's actual needs change. So if monitoring the budget is your job, you need to keep on top of what's being spent. Monitoring a budget isn't just about the money spent, though. More important is the manpower used. You can always try to find more money, but you can never get back the manpower and time spent on the project.

The process is the same for the internal team. The producer is the person who sets the budget, and the associate producer monitors the use of the money.

In terms of manpower, *Yaiba: Ninja Gaiden Z* had roughly sixty-five to seventy people at its highest capacity. That included some outside contractors, our internal team, and the QA team. We were a pretty small team, but the localization contractor was probably huge because the game had a lot of motion comics and dialogue and thus a lot of story to cover. The localization of the game involved translating all of the dialogue and written text throughout the game, and the game was filled with hints, tutorials, upgrades, and side stories about the other characters and the world that became viewable when unlocked. *Yaiba* also carried an internal dialogue throughout the motion comics. On top of all of this, we had the usual game dialogue, and all of this material had to be translated into Japanese, Mandarin, French, Italian, German, and Spanish. To make things even more complicated, the game's story was still evolving as it was being translated, thus making it difficult for the localization team to power through all the text. There were all kinds of shortened deadlines and changes too, but this is common with games. The nailing down of the story is always the last thing to finish. Like movies, the editing is where the story finds its magic.

How do you go about finding and integrating outsource workers?

The Internet, and you reach out to colleagues you've worked with in the past and ask if they know anyone. Integration—negotiating the team dynamics around outsourcing—happens in a lot of different ways. On *Ninja Gaiden*, for example, we were fortunate that our Japanese publisher and co-creators (Comcept) were able to come over to the US once a month. That was thanks to Craig Allen, the owner of Spark Unlimited. Typically, though, you don't do any traveling to your publisher and co-creators in situations like this. In fact, there really aren't a lot of independent studios of this size doing projects anymore. You have Gearbox Software and a few others, but being independent means being independent. You work with what you have. When Spark did *Lost Planet 3*, the Japanese publishers became open to working with Spark and Craig on other projects. Craig said, "We're going to talk to the Japanese and help them understand what we're doing." The Japanese were trying to figure out how to learn from the West, and Craig was there to say, "Hey, we're willing to teach, but we want to learn from you all as well." It's a two-way street, and the Japanese really opened up based on Craig's overtures. We didn't want to have the attitude that "You really need to come to us. You need to let the Westerners build your games. We know what we're doing. Give us all your money." Craig was able to say that the collaboration could be a two-way street—that everybody was going to learn how to develop and do business in the global economy.

I actually think this technique of collaborating internationally on projects is one of the new ways of doing business in games. On *Ninja Gaiden*, the Japanese weren't outsourcers, per se. They were co-creators. They had opinions and shared them with us. In the US, if our team is too small, we'll budget pieces of the game out to other studios. Maybe we could do some of the motion capture but not all of it, for example, and then we'd just find somebody who could help us. But with Comcept, they said, "We're not built for development. We're built for creative processing and designing, and that's what we can do on this project."

How do producers conceptualize and budget for unexpected moments?

Often there are times when it's easier to find a compromise than just to flat out say no. If you say no, it affects trust. It affects so many other things too, including the process. If you ask seven times and get denied five, you're not even going to ask anymore. You're going to go around the person who's denying you. So, as a producer, it's easier to say, "Well, we can't do this, but let's find a compromise on what we can do." Sometimes when you don't have the internal resources to handle something properly, outsourcing is the solution. It's easier to get to a solution than to deny the problem. We all understand that design and creative directors want to do what's best for the game. We just can't let them destroy the game in the process of trying to find out what's best.

On *Ninja Gaiden*, my boss was a master at *Tetris*-ing the money, so we didn't have to go back and ask for money when we wanted to outsource. You never like asking for more money, because that doesn't solve the problem. What solves the problem is figuring out how to get what you want within your means, to get things to a level that you're willing to live with. You want to ask for money when the project is falling apart, not when there's a wall in your way. You want to ask for more money when you *need* more money, not when you want it. You ask when you can't ship the game any other way: "We can't make Microsoft certification if we don't do these things, and we need more money to do them." If you're the guy on the street who has his hand out, you want it out because you need something to eat. And you hope you never become that guy. Publishers respect that. If they see that you're working well within the constraints that you have, I think they're likely to give you more money. On the other hand, if you treat them like a sugar daddy and ask for more stuff, well . . . .

When setting up the budget for a new project, do you establish cost numbers for external development as well as internal development?

Yes. Hopefully by the end of pre-production, as you enter into production, you know what you're building, and then it's just a multiplier at that point in terms of budget calculations. After that, you set aside the rainy-day money, and that usually ends up being the outsourcing money. It's not just outsourcing, though—you may need to hire more people to the team, and sometimes that's a better solution than outsourcing. I've been on projects in which we've outsourced but in hindsight it would have been cheaper to have hired someone for the internal team and done things in-house.

The thing is, producers are like doctors. Just like doctors practice medicine, producers practice game development. We look at the symptoms and try to resolve the problem in the simplest way. Sometimes the symptom isn't even connected to the problem, and we have to figure that out.

How is the work you do in the game industry different from the work you have done elsewhere?

It's pretty much the same. I've been in entertainment production and marketing the majority of my career, and I've always been in management positions. In fact, I actually don't recall ever not being in some kind of leadership position. In high school, I was the general manager of our television station and I also directed plays. I've always had a supervisory role, even though I've bounced around in a lot of career fields and done a lot of different projects. When I decided to get into games, I didn't want to start at the bottom. I was in a cushy, even posh position in another field and I didn't want to give up those management perks. I decided that the best way for me to get where I wanted to be was through education. I wanted to go back to school anyway at that time; I felt like I was getting stagnant in my job. So, I went to school for production and art at the Florida Interactive Entertainment Academy. The production stuff came quite naturally, while the design stuff was more challenging (though it eventually became more natural to me, and I grew passionate about it).

Is that pathway to leadership common in the game industry?

I've seen people get into leadership from all kinds of backgrounds—engineering, tech, art—and their knowledge base and sensitivity is constrained by that training. For example, an engineer producer can be quite rigid, quite structured about things, and therefore the little details never get glossed over. I've also seen art producers come in whose emphasis is on art, and they push toward that rather than overall project details. They already know a lot of the process since they spent time going to school or learning it on their own, whereas the engineer producer probably came up through the ranks. It's the same for QA. I've watched QA folks go from QA to designer to production. Those are the people who usually—if they're fortunate—become game directors. Maybe doing production management for the first time is something they have a hard time dealing with, but they love building things.

For me, I want the project I produce to be something we can all hang our hats on. I don't long to do art, nor do I long to engineer. Actually, talking about this reminds me of when Michael Jordan was the general manager of the Washington Wizards. He still wanted to play basketball, and he was really hard on his players. I don't have that. Where I'm coming from in my leadership style is more external to the development team: "I don't know exactly what you do, so I'm going to let you walk me through it. And I'm going to be your advocate once you explain how it should be done." Compare this to someone who comes from an engineering background. They might say, "I know what engineers do. I was a lead engineer. I was a great coder. I know how all of this works. This is the natural process." They won't take the time to learn, and they don't really encourage growth and learning in their department from their perspective. The hard skills definitely place them at an advantage as far as knowledge and capturing and eliminating any misinformation, but my ability to look at things with a fresh perspective and give my leads and their teams trust encourages them to arrive at the solution the best way they know how. My biggest concern is that the tasks are done right and done on time.

Of course, the people I manage always look at me and wonder what I bring to the table. I'm not an artist; I'm not an engineer. And hey, if I were them, I'd wonder too. Here I am telling someone with fifteen years of experience how to do their job. Basically, I need to earn their trust. Fortunately, I'm very personable. I have no problem telling people what I think and what I feel. Sometimes I can be political and diplomatic, and other times I can be all-out bullish: "You're absolutely wrong, and I'm going to explain it to you, break it down for you. We can agree to disagree, but I think there's a better way to do this."

It's important to understand that the game industry is unique, and therefore has unique personnel management issues. When you're working on television and film projects (which I've done), everybody has similar goals. Your lighting guys see the project the same way that the people in wardrobe do. In gaming, an artist and an engineer can be very close or they can be very far apart, and they don't even speak the same language. As a game producer, you have become bilingual, trilingual, even denial-lingual, where you deny people things all the time. A game development team is like a bunch of small tribes that are forced to live in the same country. The producer is the diplomat who tries to get all the various tribes to work together. In film and television, people might go to school for a certain thing (e.g., lighting, cinematography, visual effects), but they can change where they fit on a production team if they discover something else that they like. In games, it's almost impossible for an artist to become an engineer, and when that happens we usually make them tech artists. And vice versa.

What are the strategies you deploy to manage your teams effectively?

You have to communicate—*actively* communicate. It's a push/pull system, meaning sometimes you have to push things onto a team and other times you have to pull things from them. As the producer of an Agile team, you learn that a key is to stay out of the way. You can actually be the cog that breaks the gear, and you don't want to be that. You can either be ahead or behind everybody . . . pulling or pushing. You don't want to be in the middle. If you're ahead, you're preparing everybody for what's going to come, and if you're behind you're pushing on the other end.

Let me give you an example. With *Ninja Gaiden*, we initially had a limited number of in-game characters. At some point, we decided to increase that count. We didn't have the character concepts, but we did have a milestone to hit for the additional characters. However, the tech art team had no intention of rigging additional characters; instead, they wanted to do a second pass on the characters they had, and they wanted to fix a few of the characters' animations. Basically, there were new characters about to come online based on design specifications that we really weren't sure we'd hashed out, while our existing characters were still at different stages in the pipeline, with some we weren't quite happy with. My job was to figure out how to get the old work done and prep the new characters. So, I got my concept team ready to go, and I got my animation team on board: "Hey, those three characters you're working on there? Animate a little faster because you might get another one sooner rather than later." I told the tech artists, "You know those characters that you're still having issues with? I know you guys want to do another really good pass on them, but we need to live with it. We'll prepare the publisher for them as they are." To 3D art I said, "I need you to push through the characters you're currently working on, because you're about to be hit again from concept art in a couple of days." And I just scheduled everyone out. After all that up-front planning, I came around on the back end. When it was time to kick it off, I kicked it off. I'd push and say things like "Where's that thing that's due?" And we actually learned to optimize our pipeline based on pulling and pushing stuff through it.

What is the general response to this push/pull technique?

I think a lot of folks just learn to live with it. You have to get the trust sale. I know what the team is doing and we're trying to get the best thing possible made. With most teams, the members have shipped polished products, but just because something's polished doesn't make it good or fun. There are lots of examples of beautiful, beautiful games and the gameplay isn't there. Those games are beautiful because they had a rigid creative process with checks and balances to move forward. Now, there are other projects that are rough—they're not polished at all—but the game is just fun. At most as a developer, you hope to get somewhere in the middle. You want to get something that's highly polished yet very fun. As a producer, you want the development team to understand why they're doing what they're doing. It might not be the most résumé-building thing they're working on at first, but we hope to come around to it again so they can make it that way in a later development cycle.

When you play a game that someone else has designed, are you able to divine from the audiovisual assets and game feel what happened during the production cycle in terms of the development team's management?

No. Every game is like a launch title, and they're all different. We all set sail for the new world; some of us get there, and some of us don't. I've seen projects come out with their first demo, and that initial showing to the public is gorgeous. Then they'll come back around later after the project budget got cut in half or they lost a couple of key players on their team and things have just gone downhill. You can tell a project's production quality based on who is on the team and how fast they were iterating. A game that has a lot of iteration cycles usually comes out pretty good. A game with few iteration cycles, not so much. A lot of games go through different iterations, and iteration doesn't just stop at internal cycles. It could happen through serialization of the game. When you think about *Grand Theft Auto V* and how big and magnificent it is, you have to remember that Rockstar has four iterations of that game—the first four titles in the franchise. And that's not including the mobile versions, or *Red Dead Redemption, Red Dead Revolver, Bully, Bully: Scholarship Edition,* and every other Rockstar game that has similar mechanics. Rockstar has been able to polish the game type for a long time, and then they still drop a hundred million dollars on making the next game a better version of the last. They made the *Midnight Club* series so they could figure out driving mechanics and play.

Is there skill transfer across (not just within) titles?

Yes, and one thing Rockstar has had to do is weather the loss of team members and the intellectual history and know-how they have. Team members can get tremendously burned out; they can also move on to other opportunities. But if a company can maintain that intellectual history and knowledge base, they'll be okay. More and more studios are figuring out how to build and maintain core teams.

On the topic of preserving the intellectual history and knowledge base over time, it's the producer's job to remember what the project team did and how they did it. Anybody could do it, really, but the producer is the one who should have time to record it. Most postmortems, in fact, get "producerized," meaning they go through a producer. The producer might do the first draft, or come in and polish a draft from a creative director or game director.

Where did you acquire the skills to become an effective manager in the game industry?

I think through a combination of schooling, on-the-job training, and my own abilities. Diversifying across projects—being in manga at one point, dealing with music artists and trying to get a musical product out at another point—you learn things, you learn key performance indicators that help you figure out how things should look. You discover that something works, and so you can use it again; something else failed, and so you don't do it again. There's a lot of trial and error; every team is different, and every project is different. You can have the same team on a different project and it feels different. It feels brand new.

Regarding innate abilities, I believe that everyone has some, and it's usually your ability and willingness to learn that's most important. Your personality? That's not learned—you have that. That's definitely DNA, but introverts can be extroverts at times (and vice versa), and knowing that should be a management tool: "Charles is always talking. He's really quiet now, what's going on?"

Are there certain types of projects that suit your particular skill set?

I like Agile projects because they're always a wild ride. You never know what you're going to end up with. I'm not a person who worries too much. I approach things with the attitude that "It's going to get done. It may not be exactly what we want, but it's going to get done." I always smile throughout an Agile project because I have faith in my team that we'll make it happen. Agile methods allow the team to be open, and we glom together a little bit more than we would under other types of management. I like being able to pop from department to department and have high-level conversations. I'll even get into the meat of it when it's needed, or when we decide that the meat needs to be cut. There's also a lot more dispute, a lot more doubt, and a lot more argument in those types of projects, and it's the producer's job to push those things away.

With Agile projects, it's always the producer's fault. When push comes to shove, if something's not working and someone's trying to get something from someone else, I always say that I didn't schedule it properly, that the problem is my fault. You don't want that person to get angry at the person they're trying to get something from. You want them to be angry at you, and then you're going to figure out why the person isn't able to deliver what they need to. You shouldn't be the source of tension; you should be the punching bag. You need to have a thick skin and not let your pride get in the way. You take the blame and resolve the problem, because as a producer your job is solution navigating. It's not to restate the problem over and over again and point fingers.

As a producer, your relationship to the game isn't over after the game ships, either. You're still there in it and have to deal with marketing, public relations, and the publisher. You have to try to get the game serialized (for the sequel), or maybe explain why it didn't get the Metacritic score it was supposed to. Your job as punching bag is never over.

Don't get me wrong—you can throw some punches back. You just have to make sure that they're aimed at the right target. The development team is invested in the project—they have heart in the project. Publishers want to tell you that money is the only skin in the game. Development *is* the skin in the game. So, you don't go out and yell at the development team.

How long do producers usually last before moving on to a new position or industry?

The thing you have to remember is that producers have a long time to heal. I can sit at the computer and say, "You know what? I'm going to chill for a while." And it's not like I'm taking verbal abuse all the time; often it's just self-checking things. When your technical director tells you that you could do something better, he's more than likely right. Sometimes you just don't know why something would be better if it was done a different way. Taking the technical director's criticism as constructive makes you a better person.

The number one criterion for succeeding as a producer is the ability to take abuse, though. You know that as a manager, people are going to come crying to you. The same person could be hugging and loving you one minute, and punching you in the head the next. You have to know that's what's going to happen as a producer. But we have the easy job. At the end of the day, all of the hard skill people put their life into the project. When people ask me what I made in the game, I tell them "the schedule." I'm not the person getting trolled on the Internet about a character that sucks. I'm not the artist who has to live with the character and the comments.

How does the development process differ when working on different types of games (e.g., different genres, AAA versus smaller games, etc.)?

Every studio is different. Some studios have a development methodology, others don't. Established studios have formalized their processes and are well versed in their practices, while younger studios can be very experimental. Experience curves the edge, yet produces quality results. Each genre of game calls for slightly different processes, too. I've worked on Wii-exclusive games, Nintendo DS games, rhythm games, first-person shooters, third-person shooters, and hack-and-slash games. They've all had a different set of demands and requirements, which force teams to utilize different processes to achieve the game design goals.

Are there model companies or ways of doing your particular work (both within and outside of the game industry) that you look to for inspiration?

I find inspiration in Pixar, Apple, Valve, Platinum Games, Naughty Dog, Rocksteady Studios, Klei Entertainment, Tesla Motors, Toyota, Nike, Zappos, and Bad Robot.

What is the advantage of running a studio over working for someone else?

You see the ship sinking before it sinks, and you have more chances to try to deter it. Even as a producer, some things are out of your control, out of your power. The ability to see the ship sinking means a lot to me. To see the change happen, the changing of the guard, I want to be in on that. And there's also the whole thing of job security. As a producer, you're the first one who gets cut . . . all but the head producer. They keep that guy around. There's a reason why he's the head. If it comes down to the animator and the project manager, I'm going to keep the animator. He's hard skilled and I may need more animation. I don't need more scheduling after a certain point.

What are the sorts of things one has to think about when setting up a game development studio?

Initially, you plan on more than one project. The number one thing you want to find is the business within your business. You have twenty engineers, you ship the project, and then you have three months in which marketing is running full throttle based on the publisher's schedule. During those three months you want to use that engineering team; you don't want to outsource the engineering team as an independent studio. You want to go on to another project that's mobile or whatnot and retain your talent. So, the number one thing to consider when setting up a studio is retaining great talent and filtering out bad talent. And you want to filter out bad talent quickly. The more you have poison in your studio, the more it kills the project and the studio. Bad talent turns good talent bad.

I tell everybody that I want hardcore veterans working for me, the ones who've been doing this for twenty years. They remember the first PlayStation and when they first saw a 3D model pushed on a screen. But I also want other seasoned people who are thinking about starting families. As a result, I'm always thinking about ways to retain this kind of talent. For example, why not create a paternity plan, where the father takes off three to four months after the baby is born? If you need longer than that, we'll give you an extra month of online access to the workplace. In this scenario, you have four months where you're away from work, but you have to be available for that last month. Or you have to be available during certain days in your three months at home, and when you're tired of listening to your baby crying, you can come back into the office any time.

If you're going to be in the game business, you have to create packages like that, and then you have to figure out how you're going to afford those packages. If you decide to not have an office and instead have your team work remotely, how do you maintain that? How do you manage that? I think that's the way of the future, actually, where I'm not forcing everybody to come in all the time. As long as things keep moving through the pipeline, that's all we need.

What are the big work/life balance challenges for developers at the moment?

There's too much work that's life. Crunching is a huge problem. I believe that one day we'll get to a place where crunch time is optional, not mandatory. On *Ninja Gaiden*, I was fortunate to have a boss who never truly made crunch mandatory. You could work long hours of your own volition. I think he was at the point where he realized there was a way around crunch time. If you've been on a project that's been on crunch the majority of time, you don't like it. Work/life balance is very important, and as a producer you want to send people home.

When I worked in the Apple Store in Hawaii, you weren't allowed to come into the store on your day off—"You're off twelve days in a row? Don't come in the store. It's Hawaii, go do something else." They just pushed people out of the store. Apple as a company doesn't like people hanging out at work if they're not working. If you're at work, you're at work; if you're at home, you're home.

The game industry is throwing harder and harder restrictions on teams and not really paying teams back the other way around. They're not thanking the teams for the work. You can't give me two years of development time and then cut four months out toward the end of the project. We weren't made for that. So, get your shit together. I've heard of teams having things like that happen, where publishers have a marketing meeting, realize the game isn't going to return the projection, and then cut the budget with the expectation that the development team will still deliver the same quality.

Work/life balance is a matter of managing people's day and night life, their time at work versus the time when they're not at work. Sometimes you work nights; sometimes you work days. Sometimes you take off—your daughter has a ballet recital, tee-ball game, or school play that you have to go to—and the team has to understand that that's the way life works.

Is creating a good work/life balance difficult in an Agile environment?

It is, but it's easier when you have a team of force multipliers. It helps, too, when the team is proactive about when they're going to be out, and getting work done beforehand . . . even if that means staying late or coming in on weekends. Patience is key, and so is the ability to wear many hats. That means you can step in when folks are out or behind.

What are the challenges facing the industry in the next decade?

First, moving from physical distribution to digital distribution. Second, the diminishing return on developing games at a higher and more costly production value. Third, the emergence and boom of the mobile game market. And fourth, the devaluing of games presented by indie game developers (free-to-play or play-to-win models). Indie game developers work three months to a year or two on a project, then they throw it out in the market for free. It makes the consumer think that everything should be free. If you walked into a candy store and Pixy Stix were free, and they were always going to be free, would you buy a jawbreaker for five dollars? Would you buy the chocolate? Just the concept of "I'm going to get some of this ad revenue money" or "Hopefully a publisher will pick me/my team up for my next project" is devaluing games. That game took 16,000 hours to make, and you need to reflect that cost in the price of the game for the consumer. You don't see Louis Vuitton giving away key chains. Imagine if they did. You come into the store and they give you something. We're treating our gaming studios like we're the Gap and whatnot. We need to treat them as high quality because they're high-quality entertainment. I think movies are more like the Gap because they're experiences you can just walk away from. Games, you drop twenty, thirty hours into them. You get way more use out of them. I can rewatch my favorite movie if I want, but my favorite games I'm continually playing.

Now, I think indie gaming has been a great thing. It's really opened the industry up to be more like the Wild West, which I like . . . no one is safe. I love knowing that publishers are quaking in their shoes in fear of a ten-person studio busting its tail for two years because they can't break into the industry and they release something like *League of Legends*. They have a bunch of interns and a couple of visionaries, and they're too young and too hot-headed to stop. Everybody says, "Watch these young kids fail. They're stupid. They don't know anything. They're not being controlled by us, so they're going to fail." I love indie development, but I do have an issue with indie developers who work on a product just for a piece of the ad revenue. But some people just want to be noticed. They want to be famous—they don't need to get paid for it.

In light of the fact that the producer's duties include interfacing with the marketing team, are marketers now pushing the idea of free-to-play games—or games as marketing tools—back to producers?

Yes, everybody's pushing that idea back to you. It's a catchall for games they don't feel like marketing very hard. They see it as a way for everybody to make money (and continue to make money). Think of the advergame; everybody wants that return, that *FarmVille*. I actually have an issue with calling *FarmVille* a game, but that's another discussion. Nobody questioned Chair Entertainment for selling *Infinity Blade* for $6.99; people went out and bought it. *XCOM: Enemy Unknown* on the iPad is another one. People waited until it went on sale from $19.99 to $9.99, but that's still $10 per sale. So it's just a matter of how we handle things, of what we're doing. We need to figure it out. If you do free-to-play, how do you feed the people who worked on the game? They put in a year on the project and you give it away—how do you feed them?

Nate Schaumberg
Senior Producer

Nate Schaumberg is Director of Web at 2K Games, a wholly owned subsidiary of Take-Two Interactive. Prior to joining 2K Games, he worked as a senior producer and program manager at Zynga. He has also worked at Accolade, LucasArts, Planet Moon Studios, and Bigpoint in a variety of capacities, including as lead designer, project manager, senior producer, producer, art producer, associate producer, assistant producer, production coordinator, and technical support representative. Schaumberg has developed games for consoles, personal computers, and mobile devices, and to date has shipped eleven titles including *Tomb Raider: Legend*, *Star Wars: Galactic Battlegrounds*, and *Tangled: The Video Game.*

* * * * *

What are the duties of the position(s) you have held?

The title "producer" has different meanings depending on the company you're working for. In my various roles over the years that have been categorized as "production" or "producer" jobs, I've been a game designer, project manager, team leader, Scrum master, product manager, and program manager. Sometimes all of these things at once. The expectations of a producer basically come from two different camps, which I refer to as the Electronic Arts (EA) model and the LucasArts model. In the EA model, the producer is the owner of the product and the creative leader, the person ultimately responsible for the overall quality of the product. In the LucasArts model, the producer is the owner of the budget and schedule, and ultimately the one responsible for delivering the product on time and on budget. At EA, the LucasArts producer would be called a development director, and at LucasArts the EA producer would be a creative director. So, with that in mind let me now talk about the duties I've had over the years.

I started out as an assistant producer at Accolade on *Test Drive Off-Road 2*. In this role I was very much a hands-on game designer, working in the engine to set up car physics, tournaments, scripting AI, replay cameras, environment maps, and so forth. After Accolade, I joined the producing department at LucasArts, a department that was very much built around project management and being guardians of the process. As a project coordinator and assistant producer, my main responsibilities were to create and maintain asset-tracking databases, put together detailed asset lists, and gather estimates from artists and animators, which were then assigned, tracked, and reported in and against the database. I was also liaison to the quality assurance, sound and voice, localization, public relations, and marketing teams, and I integrated various cross-organizational requirements and deliverables into the game schedule.

As an associate producer, I split time between external and internal production. As an external producer, the role involved a lot of milestone validation, meaning validating and clarifying milestone plans coming from developers, and validating milestone deliverables against the established plans. As an associate producer in an internal role, I started to take on more responsibility for driving project scope, owning milestone deliverables and accountability for establishing reliable schedules (which in turn drove asset-level estimations), as well as some additional responsibilities in tracking technical and engineering tasks and feature pod ownership.

Moving into an art producer role was very similar to the work I had done at LucasArts but with a little less support from the team all around. *Tomb Raider: Legend* was a massive project with a huge team for that time in game development: at its peak it was probably 120 members internally, or 150 including QA and contract resources in both the US and UK. In *Grand Theft Auto* terms, that's small—AAA blockbuster games these days probably scale up to around 500 people, with teams distributed around the world. The challenge with the art producer role was not in establishing a detailed asset list but of keeping the art team working toward meaningful goals while the engineering and design teams were still figuring out the fundamentals of the game. The work in this role was more about establishing a process that would allow artists to contribute valuable assets to the teams working on feature development, while at the same time also keeping artists working toward shippable content.

At Planet Moon Studios, I took on my first role as a producer in charge of a full project. Our team was built on the LucasArts model, and I was responsible for schedule, budget, and timeline. This was the first project in which I was able to put all I'd learned up to that point into play, and I established my own style. I worked with the creative director to make sure creative decisions were being made and communicated to the team regularly, and I worked with the art and engineering leads to translate creative decisions into actionable tasks for the remainder of the team. One of my main focuses there was establishing best practices around game development to ensure both product quality and team health. Through this project I began implementing some of the fundamentals of Agile development, and by the end of the project we were close to using Scrum. The next project and all subsequent projects at Planet Moon Studios were developed using Scrum as the methodology, and I operated as Scrum master for my projects. I also created documentation about the overall creation process for the studio, working team, and studio leadership to establish game development process (GDP) requirements, best practices, and recommendations for all phases of development at the company. In the majority of my time at Planet Moon, I was in charge of scheduling for the entire team (in collaboration with team leads), tracking projects, establishing milestone plans, delivering milestones and supporting documentation to publishers, developing staffing plans, and driving the process and associated meeting cadence (daily Scrum, weekly check-ins, postmortems, scoping sessions, milestone reviews, and so on).

When Planet Moon shut down, many of us landed jobs at Bigpoint, which was just staffing up a US office at the time. We took a lot of the process fundamentals with us to Bigpoint, though my role changed quite a bit. At Bigpoint, my role was in the EA model—I was in charge of creative and quality—so my day-to-day duties were very different. They revolved around writing feature specs, managing the nuts and bolts of a small design team, and doing creative reviews for features and the overall games I was working on. The most challenging element of this role was coming to terms with creating games in a free-to-play (F2P) space, as well as understanding not only the aspects of planning for long-term development and the content/feature cadence that goes with a game development process that continues after a traditional launch, but also the monetization aspects involved with building F2P games.

At Zynga, I was in a very different role than any of the previous ones. That was the first time in my career that I was not on a game development team, though the skills I picked up along the way definitely translated to the work I did there. Initially, I was in charge of managing the game launch process for Zynga's data center teams (Network Operations). This role was, again, really about establishing a process that pulled together many different tasks, dependencies, and competing timelines into an understandable and repeatable process. Through that role I moved into a position where I managed and maintained the process for game launches for Zynga as a whole. I coordinated various partner teams, shared service teams, and game teams, as well as managed dependencies and requirements across the entire company. This involved a lot of follow-up with the partners to verify the validity of information that we were putting in front of game teams, and a lot of follow-up with game teams to make sure they were aware of all company-wide launch requirements and recommendations.

How is the work you do in the game industry different from the work you have done elsewhere?

I'm lucky enough to have been in the games industry for all of my professional career. When I joined Technical Support at Accolade, I left a job driving a forklift in a janitorial supply warehouse. I washed semi-trucks with a power washer on the weekends. So, there's very little manual labor in my games work compared to that, and 100% less forklift driving.

Given your long and diverse work history, is there something that connects all of the positions you have held, something consistent in the game industry?

The craft stays the same, despite all the different types of games and technologies that are produced. Ultimately, it's the craft of delivering high-quality content. It's visual, there's some interactive and entertaining element to it. To put it in simple and bland terms, if there's anything that stays the same in the game industry, it's the product. You've got a group of people who are looking at the way users are interacting with a given product (or set of products). They're looking at the way it's going to be presented visually. And then you've got the business that wraps around that, which is getting the product to market, getting eyes on it, and getting people to play it. For me, the thing that ties the industry together over time is that there are teams of creative people making content. That's the constant.

Is there anything that you know now about the industry and how it works— its aims and objectives—that you wish you had known earlier on in your career?

Yes, there's a lot. I wish I had understood more about the business when I was toiling away on games as a designer and junior producer just trying to get stuff built. I wish I would've known more about the way sales and marketing look at projections, and how/when they were putting games on the market. It would've been great to know more about how games are distributed, and I've had a much better glimpse of all of this in the latter years of my career. Part of it is just due to my position: I grew into a position where I got the opportunity to look at these kinds of things. I think early on I looked at games as products that I consumed—I played a lot of games. I wanted to make games, and it was very much about being in a game environment and building a game. I didn't have much insight into why we were building a given game and what the ultimate outcome was expected to be. I'd hear about it—people would say, "We think we're going to sell X amount of this game"—but really not much on how that gets broken down or how I could impact that goal. Knowing things like "Can I move the unit sales number one way or the other?" would've been useful.

What is the general sense in the industry regarding this knowledge and lower-level positions?

It all depends on the position. As an entry-level producer, you're getting ramped into your ability to know holistically what's going into a game.

Usually you're given some small subset of the game to oversee (e.g., managing QA schedules or managing schedules for artists). You're meant to try to get your head around something small, and then you can get another portion of the game or the development cycle added to your to-do list. These might be things like "How do these art assets that I'm tracking fit into what the level designers are building?" You just sort of chip away at your lack of knowledge like that, and eventually you get to the point where you can even look at engineering, for example, where there aren't really any concrete deliverables—nothing you can see or play—and see how the code is making things work. You can't say anything except "This is fun" or "This is not fun," and it's all subjective. That's the most difficult part, and it usually comes toward the end, as you're getting comfortable with other skills.

As far as knowledge of the budget goes, it's hard to put everything into context when you're slotted into a lower-level position. If you're a production artist and you're painting textures on buildings, the budget doesn't matter. It matters to the producer, who says things like "You need to get one of these done every two days because we have fifty of them due and one hundred days in which to do it."

My personal feeling is that it's important to let junior members of the team know the budgetary situation and why what they're doing and how they're doing it is meaningful. My philosophy is that I want everyone to know why they're doing something, even if they don't like what they're doing. Working at Planet Moon as a third-party producer, where I had a publisher who was paying us for a product and expecting a certain quality on a certain timeline, there were definitely conversations I had with the publisher that I wouldn't share with the team. There's plenty of information on that side of things that would just have been distraction and noise for people who were creating content. For example, a harsh negativity can come from publishers when they're looking at what you're delivering. Maybe they don't feel like it's meeting the quality they expect, maybe they're concerned about your timeline, or maybe they're just concerned about what they're getting from your team for what they're paying. Publishers can deny payment for deliverables if they don't feel like the product is meeting their interpretation of the milestone. And I think softening that blow for the development team is important. You say, "It seems like maybe we're behind a little. Let's figure out a way we can turn this around and deliver a stronger milestone or show some progress over the next couple of weeks."

In describing the positions you have held, you differentiate between internal and external producing. Can you parse the distinction for us?

As an internal producer, you really need to know the nuts and bolts of what goes into making a game and be able to ask the right questions of the team so that they can be successful. Ultimately, you're responsible for getting people in a room and saying "What are we going to build, how are we going to build it, and how long is it going to take?" As an internal producer, you're responsible for the team delivering on the promise.

As an external producer, you're responsible for making another team deliver on that promise. A lot of external producing is about setting expectations. Having knowledge about how games are built is helpful but not critical. You need to have an idea of an acceptable scope for the project, the technologies the team is using, and their relative expertise with those technologies. You need to be able to squint your eyes and get a good idea of what they can deliver to make sure that they're not overpromising or under-promising. As far as the day-to-day goes, an external producer is driving the bigger deliverables rather than working on the minutiae that lead up to those bigger deliverables.

How does the art of determining and enforcing milestones work?

It depends on the project, your project management style, and the different ways to approach managing milestones. It also depends on your organization's structure, or the structure of the organization that's paying for the game. And, of course, it depends on the tolerance of the stakeholders. For instance, when we were working on *Tomb Raider: Legend*, the budget was essentially whatever it took to get a high-quality game done. Milestones were loose at best. We had target dates that we were trying to deliver content for, but if we didn't feel happy with the content halfway through a milestone we'd toss it out, start fresh, and say, "Hey, we need more time." And there was a high tolerance for that.

On the other side of things, when you have a publisher who has a chunk of money that they've committed to pay you for a product that you've committed to deliver within a specific time frame, it's definitely more important to make sure you're determining specific milestones that match the content you're expected to deliver. The way I do that generally is I'll sit down with the leadership group of the team early on and get a general sense of what we're building for all disciplines—for engineering, art, and design. We'll get some ballpark figures, too, for audio and animation. If there's any outsourcing, we'll try to factor that in as well. Generally, we just try to put some broad ideas around the whole of the game so that we start to understand what it'll take to build the product from start to finish. And for me, that's usually with a one- to two-week tolerance. So, we might want a feature in which two characters hold hands and run around, and we'll ask how long that's going to take to engineer. You'd get a ballpark estimate out of that—a best guess that's hopefully within a week or two—and then you do that all the way through the feature set for engineering. We'll move on and talk about how many levels we think we want, how many characters we think we want, and put ballpark figures in terms of time. We might estimate that it takes four days to build, skin, and rig a character, and then three weeks to animate a hero character, a week and a half to animate secondary characters, and one week to animate any supporting characters.

After that, you start plugging in all those numbers—I use *Microsoft Project* for that part. I plug them all in, set up dependencies, and set up the timeline to see if it works for what we said we were going to do. And if doesn't, then you go back and negotiate for features and content and try to get the plan to a point where your gut-check look at the game feels pretty good. Then you reverse engineer from there, and say, "This is the date we said we're going to deliver it. We need about six weeks for QA. We need four to six weeks for a beta period. We need four to six weeks for an alpha period. That means that our production ends here, which means our production needs to start here. And we'll spend two months in pre-production getting everything together." That gives you your basic timeline, and you chop that up into six- to eight-week blocks and say, "Based on the timeline, these are our tentative milestone dates, and based on what we said, these are our tentative milestone deliverables." As you go forward, you add detail to those milestones, and adjust as needed. But really, that gives you your gut check, your basic template for project milestones. As you move along, you can adjust: "We're moving into this milestone in the next milestone period, and we need to figure out exactly what we need to do to deliver on that milestone." At this point, you're just adding in detail.

While I use *Project* at the beginning to get the snapshot and make sure everything works, I don't use the *Project* file to manage the project. I have in the past, and there's some value to managing parts of a project this way—it's good to keep going back if things change and shift to keep your high-level dates and expectations in check—but as far as adding detail into it, I usually don't use *Project* for that. Instead, I'll create milestone documents in a *Microsoft Word* file to the effect of "Here are our goals for this milestone, and in order to achieve those goals here are some details." As far as the tasks themselves go, there are many tools out there. I've used *Microsoft Excel* in the past, and at Planet Moon we built a proprietary database. You can use *JIRA Software* or any project management or task-tracking tool to track the day-to-day stuff.

From what you describe, game development sounds like a holistic process, beginning with the idea and then moving fairly steadily toward the deadline. Are there instances in which it is not?

It happens all the time when there are movie releases or a tie-in product and the deadline comes first before any planning happens. There are also things like the Christmas season, and you'll have those times where you sit down and say, "Two years from now we're putting a game out for Christmas for the Xbox One . . . what can we do?"

This doesn't change the planning process much, though, because what you're doing is starting to brainstorm from there (as opposed to starting from completely blue sky). You put a bunch of really great—and really bad—ideas out, and you wrap those in stone: "For this idea I think it's going to take this much engineering, this much art support, this much animation. We're going to have to deliver this kind of audio content, and there's going to be text and lip-sync." You just dig down to the details that you'll need to do in order to support that, and what tools you need to build versus what tools you can license. You start to put all those pieces together, and put times and costs against them and see what shakes out. Ultimately, you're still plugging everything into a *Project* file to see if it says the target date at the end. If it doesn't, then you need to think about what can be sacrificed, what can be added, or what can be compromised. For example, you might have a situation in which initial estimates for a particular feature come up huge, with the feature projected to take a month and a half to engineer and be supported by three artists for two months. You can take a look at that and ask what's important about the feature and if you scale it back can it still be something good that's also going to be more reasonable resource-wise. You chip away at the great things you don't want to lose, you cut some things that were perhaps on the fringe anyway, and maybe you even decide that the whole idea was bad and replace it with something else. A lot of the job of the producer is just asking the right questions at the right time of the folks who are in the room. Ideally, you've got a group of strong leaders on the team, and you can say, "What if we fake the characters holding hands? They don't have to touch—does that uncomplicate animation and some of the technical aspects of it?" You often just start out asking really stupid questions, but sometimes really good questions. I've told people who are looking for production advice in the past just to ask their question. Chances are no one's going to be pissed that they have to answer it, unless it's a really difficult question to answer. And if that's the case, then it's probably best that you asked it anyway.

Really, the kind of pre-production sitting down I'm talking about is a way to make decisions about what's in a game and what's not. The *Project* file is the guiding document for the eventual development.

What kind of support and resources do producers and other managers have to draw on when they need to make difficult decisions (e.g., employee termination, budget overruns, project shutdowns, and so on)?

As far as support and resources, it really depends on the structure of the studio. When making those big decisions, you're likely to have studio and/or company leadership involved in any and all of those conversations. The producer is going to be the one who comes to the table with the data that supports the proposal, but ultimately it's the executives who are going to make and/or broker those decisions.

At what pay grade, so to speak, do these types of decision-making responsibilities occur for producers?

Once you get to the level of producer and are looking at the entirety of the project. Or if you're a lead, if you're managing a team of developers or artists, you'd assume some of those responsibilities. At the associate/assistant producer level you're impacted by it, but you probably wouldn't be a part of the conversation. The decision would be made above the producer level, at the general manager or executive producer level. As a producer, you'd say, "We're going to need to adjust our budget/headcount/whatever in order to meet our commitments as they've been laid out. So let's pull all the key stakeholders and the team leadership into a room and figure out how we can achieve this."

Sometimes, though, it happens at the purely executive level, where they decide that they just need to reduce staff and they're going to do it by cutting a specific initiative or project. When I was at Accolade, Infogrames purchased Accolade and they needed to cut the cost of that studio, so they started canceling projects and laying people off.

It is not uncommon for large game companies to have multiple domestic and even international offices. How does employee colocation or its absence impact the work of game development?

Personally, I feel it's very important. It's tough to have people who are working on the same feature separated by ten desks, let alone by several time zones. There's definitely an art to outsourcing, so if you're going to outsource content, there's a special skill set associated with understanding what that takes and what to ask. You need to know how to set the right expectations for the outsource group and also the internal group as to what you're going to get and what your investment is in the assets you receive from the outsource group. But outsourcing is really a separate topic.

Getting back to colocating, when I worked at Zynga, the games were almost exclusively developed in the US, China, or India. We didn't actually do much development in India, but rather handed off games that were toward the end of their life. The folks in India would continue to maintain the games, add content, and make sure that the games were supported until they were eventually taken down. But nearly all the development that went on at Zynga was almost exclusively colocated, the exception being outsourced materials or tools, which would eventually be distributed among the whole team.

As long as it's managed well, outsourcing can be beneficial. Of course, you need to know what you're building, what you're asking for, and what to expect. Managing and working with outsourced assets could be the subject of an entire book.

Are there particular game genres that lend themselves well to outsourcing?

I don't know that there are any specific genres that are best for outsourcing, but in my experience the type of content that's most easily outsourced tends to be objects that don't animate. Environments are a good example, but maybe not even full environments. Levels are probably the thing. The objects you put in there—light poles, garbage cans, newspapers—you can outsource stuff like that pretty easily and then just drop it in to populate the level. But you want to craft the gameplay of an environment in-house, with your own hands.

What challenges—if any—existed within the companies you have worked for that hindered you from performing your duties at an optimal level?

When I was at Zynga it was a very large organization—around 2000 employees spread across offices in San Francisco, Seattle, India, China—though it could be nimble. When the company was being nimble, it was tough to get everyone who was going to be impacted by a decision or strategy shift on board, often just because there was little to no awareness about who might be impacted. That kind of thing can lead to fires, where someone will find out about a new initiative late in the process and will have to respond quickly in order to not be a blocker.

Feeding into that was the fact that Zynga was very supportive of employees managing their careers, which was a great thing. That meant there were a lot of personnel shifts in the company, and so there was a lot of institutional knowledge that moved around and ended up getting lost in the shuffle. Add attrition to that and you have the main contributors to the lapses in communication or lack of understanding around dependent organizations.

On the subject of attrition, you have had multiple experiences with studio closures (Planet Moon Studios, Bigpoint) and workforce reductions (Accolade, Zynga). Can you talk briefly about attrition in the game industry?

Games don't need a huge team during the early phases of development, but they do need a lot of people to close out the project. Headcount can be managed if you've got more than one team in place. You can spin up a small concept, prototype, or pre-production team while the majority of your staff is working on closing another game, and then move those people from production to production. If you're just a single game studio, though, it's really tough to keep an entire team meaningfully busy throughout the entire process. If anything goes sideways during development, especially on a very large game, a studio can find itself with a big part of the team sitting idle while the project pivots. That's a tough situation to justify if you're the one who's responsible for maintaining a budget, especially for publicly owned companies.

What challenges—if any—exist external to your work that hinder you from performing your duties at an optimal level?

Do kids count? It's tough to work in such a fast-paced and demanding industry and maintain a strong relationship with family. I'm lucky enough to have the opportunity to work from home in the evenings when required, but family is the main external distraction.

What sorts of workplace changes would you implement if given the opportunity?

Removing any sort of business requirements, I'd like to see more ideas taken through the greenlight process. I'd like to see more chances taken on creative pitches and purely creative games—figure out how to monetize them later.

In your experience, how does the process of game development differ when working on different types of games (e.g., different genres, AAA versus smaller games, etc.)?

Processes can vary wildly depending on how big the game is, the culture of the company, and the style of the leaders who are driving production. Smaller games are generally much easier to manage, as you've usually got a pretty small team. Processes can be simpler, as you're probably all in pretty close proximity and in constant communication about the details of the game, so there's less risk of details being lost in the shuffle, and mistakes or tangents are usually caught pretty early and communicated quickly. On larger teams, there's a lot more overhead and a lot more communication needed. This usually means there are more documents, more meetings, and stricter processes to be followed in order to remove risk.

Are there model companies or ways of doing your particular work (both within and outside of the game industry) that you look to for inspiration?

Creatively, I'm always inspired by the way Pixar approaches their projects. Their visualization methods are outstanding, and it's easy to take inspiration away from the way they approach decision making through preproduction. From a game industry perspective, I have a lot of admiration for the way Double Fine Productions approaches development. They've really been able to weather the "traditional games are dead" storm and come out stronger on the other side. I'm not sure anyone has been as successful at establishing a culture that encourages taking risk and delivering on the promise of that risk, though I'm not sure they've been wildly financially successful for it.

How do you view the proliferation of distribution channels in recent years?

I think it's good for game creators, but also raises a lot of questions around game business. Game creators have lots of different avenues through which they can fund and distribute content. They can take a great idea, get Kickstarter funding, build the game, and launch it on multiple platforms. If the game is done right, then you've got a very successful game that you've been able to build from the ground up and found a company on. That's outstanding.

For EA and Activision, however, it's difficult, even though those publishers have an iron grip on the console market. *Call of Duty*, *FIFA*, and *Battlefield* are always going to do great. *Assassin's Creed* is generally always going to do great. You look at some of the original IP games, though, and they could be tentative. You look at the ability of any studio to move into the console market and become a major player and the likelihood is really low. I think that's probably the root of what I'm trying to say here. Naughty Dog can build whatever they want, people are going to buy it, and it's likely going to be something original. They're one of the few who can do that. You have to have a brand in order to build a big, AAA, unique console title. Or you have to have a franchise that's already established that you can leverage, like *Call of Duty*. There are several franchises out there that attract consumers, and there are some studios as brands that attract consumers as well. They're going to have the lion's share of success in the console market.

But then you have Xbox Live and stuff like that, where there can be occasional breakout hits. I read a statistic that said there are as many new games launched on the App Store each month as the entire N64 catalog. Maybe one of these each week will end up being popular. Chances are that you're going to see the same game week after week at the top of the charts in the App Store.

What constitutes risk in the game industry, and how does the understanding of risk vary from company to company?

It can ultimately be broken down into development costs versus potential revenue. That's the crux. There is a third, much shorter side to the risk triangle, though, which is intellectual property (IP) potential. If you can establish an IP and it costs you a lot and doesn't make much revenue but over the lifetime of that IP the financial benefit has a lot of potential, that'll be taken into account when thinking about risk. In some cases, then, you're looking at development costs over many years and many titles versus potential revenue over many years and many titles. These kinds of projections will green-light or red-light a project.

Questions regarding IP potential can happen early on if the conversation gets started early on. With *Sam & Max*, we could probably add a fourth leg to the aforementioned triangle. When we were looking at that IP at Planet Moon, we were looking at the LucasArts brand and trying to latch onto some of the nostalgia for the brand. Essentially, we started developing a *Sam & Max* game and there was a lot of the projection talk going on within sales and marketing. Their answers to the question of viability were very different. Part of it was our distribution platform; we were trying to develop episodic content that would be distributed online in the same way that Telltale Games (who took over the franchise) does today. The marketing team was excited: "Oh, this is great. People are going to love it. *Sam & Max* is an old school, LucasArts-style adventure game using one of the most beloved franchises ever built. People know it; they love it. It's funny. It's going to be awesome. We're going to sell a half-million units of this." The sales team was confused: "We don't know how to sell this. You can't put a shelf talker in Target that tells people about the game. We have no idea how to do this. We think we're going to sell fifteen thousand copies." We'd sit in those meetings and say things like "Which is it? Should we keep developing this game or not?" It was a really weird conversation, because we were looking at risk versus reward, we were looking at the development costs versus potential revenue, and we had two very different ideas as to what the revenue was going to be. Ultimately, it came down to the fact that the sales team was unable to determine how they'd sell it, so we had to bank on their sales projection, which killed the game.

So I guess there's a "fifth leg" to the risk triangle: the business model. In the case of *Sam & Max*, LucasArts wasn't willing to commit to a different type of business model, so there was no wholesale buy-in to the project.

There was no "We want to distribute content episodically online." There wasn't even "We want to distribute content online." When Planet Moon was signed to a project with Microsoft, we were signed under something called the "broadening initiative," which was basically trying to tap into the mysterious "casual" demographic (families, women, and housewives), getting them to the Xbox 360, and convincing them it was something that could become a staple in the family room. When we got to the end of eighteen months of prototyping, the business model for Microsoft had shifted to the point where what we were building wasn't valuable to them anymore. So, if business requirements change during development, that definitely impacts discussions of risk. What's the risk of shipping a family-focused game on the Xbox 360? Well, it turns out it's high. You can do your best job as a producer and figure out profit/loss and keep the budget contained, but if the relevancy or perceived value of the project to the publisher changes, there's nothing you can do.

As a producer, how do you gauge and manage team health?

It can't always be managed at the team level. It's got to be something that the organization as a whole buys into. I'll go back to my first producing job on *Test Drive Off-Road 2* for an example. We had a terrible quality of life. It was horrible. I worked seven days a week, I worked at least fourteen hours every day, and my producer was ruthless in enforcing the time commitment. That, in many ways, shaped my career going forward, and I've subsequently been a champion for team health and quality of life. I've sought out companies that were also interested in maintaining employee quality of life.

I think you approach the question of team health in part by assuming you have organizational buy-in, and you can stealthily improve the quality of life on your team by ensuring good working hours through solid planning. Really, you've got to put in place some sort of health plan, an agreement with the employees. Planet Moon was one of the first places we were really able to do that. We committed to never crunching for more than two weeks in a row, to never working a Sunday no matter if we were crunching or not, and wherever possible we'd give advance notice of crunches. And we'd make it a goal to try not to crunch. I worked places previously in which producers would say, "We're going to do overtime, we're going to crunch, we're going to work this weekend." When I'd ask them the reason for the crunch, the answer was "To make progress." Progress toward what? Are we just building more content, building more stuff and just hoping it falls into place? Needless to say, I'd get pretty mad.

As a result, I've always been one to advocate for employee health. There were times, especially on the Microsoft project with Planet Moon, that Microsoft was really aggressive with us in saying "You guys need to put some skin in the game." And we had to push the team harder than we wanted to. During those periods we were very transparent with the team and said, "We're being pushed. We really need to step up and deliver, and that's going to mean extra hours and we're breaking our contract with you. But we're going to have beer at 5:00 p.m. every Friday, and I'll be in the kitchen making breakfast burritos every Tuesday and Thursday." I'd just try to do things for the team to let them know that while I couldn't make any 3D models, do any scripting, or code features, I was there to support them and say, "We understand that it's not easy, but we're trying to take care of you as best we can."

The thing is, there are angry people on every team. They're mad about crunch or they don't like what they're working on. As a manager you can be as transparent, friendly, and supportive to those people as possible and they just may not come through it. In that specific instance with Microsoft that I mentioned—the six-week, real hard push—I spent a lot of time focusing on culture and quality of life. There are people who were on that team that today still comment on how nice it was even though it sucked in the moment. We can now look back on it and it seems like it was a good time. It's a story to tell, we pulled together, and we're all still great friends.

What are the challenges facing the industry in the next decade?

The industry is still struggling to come to terms with the shift to mobile, which leapfrogged the shift to social. Mobile games are becoming the bread and butter for game companies, and this presents different challenges for different areas of the industry. From the perspective of console developers, game development is becoming a riskier business with huge teams, long timelines, and massive budgets. There's a huge amount of risk taken on a handful of high-profile titles. The AAA console title business hasn't been as dependable as it's been in the past, and I believe that there'll be even less tolerance for risk going forward. Development costs increase with each console cycle, so there's a real risk that this business could implode, with companies unwilling to take risks on high-profile titles that drive console sales. With fewer consoles out there (and thus fewer delivery platforms like Xbox Live and PlayStation Network), independent developers will have less exposure, which then puts their business at risk also. I believe that we'll weather the storm, but it's certainly going to be a challenge.

On the social games front, there's obviously been a real shift to mobile for these consumers, and that business has taken a huge hit. Many developers of social games are also in the mobile market, so I think the challenge for them is to find the right games for a broader social platform.

▶ DISCUSSION

Producing is paradoxical work. In its exacting and persistent calculations of time and money, and its prognosticating about—even planning for—potential surprises, obstacles, and miscalculations, producing is both concrete and speculative. Producers are also essential and expendable; without them, projects can meander wildly until withering away, but outside the walls of the studio, producers' work is largely invisible, while inside it is often considered superfluous compared to the work of artists and programmers. Finally, producers are expected to parlay the wisdom of past experiences to advance present projects, even though it appears to be common industry knowledge that—due to the transience of personnel, changes in technology, variations in design, and the idiosyncrasies of development teams—game development is never the same thing twice. If we were to broadly characterize the work of producers, then, we would say that it is grounded in the expectation of insufficient planning and it aims to optimize this spectral system through good communication, trust building, and calculated risk taking.

Like other game development disciplines, the skills of and demands on producers vary widely depending on company size, culture, and the nature of the assigned work. A by-product of this variability is that, as Schaumberg describes it, a change in employer—but not in title—may well necessitate a substantial shift in job scope and duties. Significantly, the interviewees here directly or indirectly point out that despite this variety, the craft of game development itself remains largely constant. That is, in spite of all of the technological, economic, and industrial signs to the contrary, game planning and production—the producer's purview—are ultimately and relatively static. In brief, this means that game development projects need to be guided from start to finish, constantly accounting for and adapting to changes related to time, money, vision, and project goals. The idea that this is a "craft"—Schaumberg's term—seems right to us. Situated somewhere between art and science, the craft of game production appears to require a bit of each, equal measures of inspiration and engineering.

For producers, the creative nature of game development essentially necessitates a pre-production phase that in some ways is more important than the organization of the production phase itself. This is because it is in pre-production that the major project elements of scale, scope, budget, schedule, and human resources are largely determined. Producers translate the fantasy of a game into a blueprint for its methodical creation, knowing full well that many details in the blueprint are always already wrong. As with all good craftspeople, however, their expertise is signaled not by perfect technique but by their ability to create excellence out of the imperfections and mistakes that arise throughout a process. This is precisely what producers try to do. They are problem solvers, often working simultaneously on local project issues ("By Wednesday, we need asset X completed in order to stay on schedule"), corporate issues ("If my teams are going to stay productive, they need to have weekends off"), and external industrial issues ("How is anyone going to make money when the free-to-play model is changing consumer behavior in fundamental ways?"). Babb goes even further, noting that producers are increasingly required to facilitate international collaborations involved in their projects—the result of localization requirements and outsourcing—suggesting that the craft of game development is soon to routinely entail the shaping of play around multicultural and multilingual contexts.

Thinking about the work of producers as a craft also helps illuminate the fact that—despite reportage that condemns poorly designed multimillion-dollar AAA titles and heroizes addictive titles made on shoestring budgets—from a producing standpoint, the bottom line in development is not money but labor. As Babb notes, additional development financing can often be found if needed, but expended labor cannot be recuperated. This may explain the prevalence of the proverbial "money pit" in game development, that is, the point in a project's life cycle when developers are loath to give up on it despite numerous signs indicating that this is precisely what is called for (e.g., *Duke Nukem Forever*). It also likely explains the prevalence of draconian milestones and overtly buggy releases (e.g., *E.T. the Extra-Terrestrial*). Simply put, a game must get to market to have a chance of recovering the production expenses it has incurred, which in some instances leads to the problematic assessment that shipping an inferior product is better than shipping no product at all.

Thinking about game producing as a craft also highlights the soft factors of producing—keeping productivity and morale simultaneously high, for example—and reveals how producers must find ways to be both humane and machinic as they cope with fluctuating personnel, differential job proficiencies within the same rank and classification, project changes born of iterative design methods, and work/life balance. Again, as the interviewees here reveal, while money is more or less fungible in the game industry, personnel are not. Removing or adding core personnel is difficult and disruptive—especially when the producer has invested much work into developing strong corporate communication skills, built transparency and trust within the development team, and created a personnel-specific project schedule that accommodates hundreds (even thousands) of tasks, timelines, and production dependencies. No doubt it is precisely the complexity of such potential disruptions that has led, in part, to the industry's growing reliance on outsourcing and the cultivation of strong team dynamics. The former helps to engineer the vicissitudes of asset production out of the development pipeline. The latter fosters product quality even as it prioritizes workplace health.

Given how production methodologies can vary from game to game and studio to studio, it can be hard to delimit the extent to which producers' skills can be tangibly felt in the game as final product. Both Babb and Schaumberg remark that as producers they do not consider themselves critical to the creative or technical teams. They also point out, however, that they perform crucial functions, from finding additional personnel, money, and time to messaging disappointment or concern from executives or publishers. In part, this paradox is attributable to what has elsewhere been termed "apportioned commodity fetishism," the tendency to believe that one has a comprehensive understanding of an artifact's labor relations due to passing familiarity with a few high-profile examples of labor connected to that artifact. In the case of video games, for example, it is common knowledge that they are built by talented programmers and artists, which enables a kind of metonymic perception that labor in the industry is fully understood. Apportioned commodity fetishism suggests, however, that this partial and common view of game production has emerged largely to prevent a more comprehensive—and in many ways, more reprehensible—understanding of the industry from reaching the general public.[1] Clearly, producers are among the many people in the game industry whose work is disappeared, which raises the question: at what cost? Producers ensure that more visible personnel—artists, programmers, musicians, designers, and voice talent, for example—produce their work, stay on task, and get paid. Arguably, then, producers are the lifeblood of the game industry, which means that they are among the most well positioned to change many of the objectionable characteristics of the industry that almost everyone we interviewed for this project wishes would change: overreliance on crunch time, lack of employee diversity, and work/life imbalances.

Producers, of course, are well aware that they hold some of this power, that they have the means—to some degree—to wrangle many of the variables and processes that collectively comprise and intervene in game development. Indeed, many producers are experienced (and sometimes specifically trained) in the deployment of formal production methodologies designed to control everything from budget overruns and feature creep to personnel problems and technology failures. The interviews here underscore, however, that it may not always be obvious how a producer's chosen production methodology can affect a project's end result. A schedule-driven methodology such as Waterfall, for example, might help the development team understand where to scope down and scale back in order to stay close to the projected cadence and finish on time and within budget. However, such a methodology might be too rigid to respond to vital processes of discovery and iteration once the game is in production. Similarly, Agile development allows a development team to verify and estimate its own schedule and permits innovation and course correction. However, some publishers may be uncomfortable with the lack of concrete end dates and final feature lists that can accompany an Agile workflow. Ultimately, the results of the production methodology involve not only the producer's choices, but also how the development team and the publisher react to these choices and work with or against them. Clearly, then, producers hold some power over the development process, but they are also working in the middle of a complex production schema that involves the money givers (publishers) and the money takers (developers), all of whom are interacting in direct and indirect ways to advance a range of professional and personal agendas.

All that said, if the producer's job was as simple as driving a project forward in the midst of organizational incongruity, game development might still be challenging but would also be relatively straightforward. What really seems to complicate the producer's job are the external factors that impinge on all the internal dynamics. At present, the primary such factor is the rise of mobile computing. It is hard to overestimate the impact of the mobile market—especially the free-to-play segment—on the game industry as a whole and particularly on the job of producing. The emergence of the mobile sphere has not only significantly lowered the barrier to entry for development and created a variety of alternative success metrics (e.g., payment as a percentage of advertising revenue on the back end), but it has forced even the largest game companies to reevaluate their business strategies. Unsurprisingly, this upheaval is reflected in the day-to-day job of the game developer, with producers, for example, having to come to grips with a development environment in which there may be no money for salaries. Instead, they face a funding model that can orbit around microtransactions and advertising revenue rather than the conventions of unit sales and production costs, in some ways redefining what it means to "produce" a game.

It is precisely this changing nature of the "producer" that makes summarizing their import and impact on the industry so difficult. In fact, of all the interviews we conducted for this volume, the ones with producers were the most curious. Their work is clearly foundational to the industry, yet not only is their work largely invisible and paradoxical in the ways we have discussed above, it is also at turns elevated and abused. Our interviewees spoke repeatedly about their feelings of satisfaction at having navigated the chaotic waters of a full development cycle, pushing and pulling their colleagues to produce their best work in a timely and budgetarily conscientious manner. They talked candidly about how their work relies on gut checks and expert guesses that are informed by computed metrics and enforced milestones to produce a final product that is both planned and surprising. At the same time, however, the obvious pleasure producers find in choreographing game development projects is blunted by the fact that, due to the very nature of their organizational positions, they are at the center of their projects and thus most exposed to its many points of disappointment and failure. In fact, our interviewees accepted their almost official duty to serve as project "punching bag" and scapegoat, and to go down with the ship while ensuring everyone else's safety. Similarly, they spoke of being multilingual diplomats among cultures at odds with each other, the implication being that, should war break out, the producer will always be to blame.

Babb notes that, to some degree, one's chance of success as a leader in such an environment is determined by one's own disciplinary orientations—artistic leaders will lead one way, engineers another. We do not disagree, yet it seems to us that there is more to successful producing than coming to terms with personal management proclivities. It also necessitates patience with, and perhaps even enthusiasm for, the innumerable unexpected interventions in one's plans, not to mention fortitude in the face of unavoidable—not just accidental—failure born from these unexpected interventions, including those that emerge from the very hierarchies, funding models, and social systems within which video game development occurs. A significant question that remains for us and the producers we have interviewed here concerns the extent to which producers should allow their patience and fortitude to abate their responsiveness to the serious quality of life issues that plague the game industry. This is, of course, an old conundrum in middle management, the group of people both best- and worst-positioned to initiate industrial change. To their credit, our interviewees seem to be headed in a good direction with such matters given their emphases on smooth communication, managerial transparency, and a willingness to resist inhospitable treatment by those who control a project's purse strings. *Tempus monstrabit.*

▶ NOTE

1   For more on apportioned commodity fetishism, see McAllister, et al.

▶ WORKS CITED

Bibliography

McAllister, Ken S., Judd Ethan Ruggill, Tobias Conradi, Steven Conway, Jennifer deWinter, Chris Hanson, Carly A. Kocurek, Kevin A. Moberly, Randy Nichols, Rolf F. Nohr, and Marc A. Ouellette. "Apportioned Commodity Fetishism and the Transformative Power of Game Studies." *Examining the Evolution of Gaming and Its Impact on Social, Cultural, and Political Perspectives.* Ed. Keri Duncan Valentine and Lucas John Jensen. Hershey: IGI Global, 2016. 96–122. Print.

"Transitions: Gamasutra Salary Survey 2014." *Gamasutra: The Art & Business of Making Games.* UBM Tech. 22 Jul. 2014: 1–8. Web. 10 Oct. 2015. <http://www.gamesetwatch.com/2014/09/05/GAMA14_ACG_SalarySurvey_F.pdf>

Gameography

Assassin's Creed (franchise). Ubisoft. Ubisoft, 2007-present. Multiple platforms.

Battlefield (franchise). EA Digital Illusions/Visceral Games. Electronic Arts, 2002–2015. Multiple platforms.

Bully. Rockstar Vancouver. Rockstar Games, 2006. Multiple platforms.

Bully: Scholarship Editions. Rockstar San Diego. Rockstar Games, 2008. Multiple platforms.

Call of Duty (franchise). Infinity Ward/Treyarch/Sledgehammer Games. Activision/Square Enix, 2003-present. Multiple platforms.

Duke Nukem Forever. 3D Realms/Triptych Games/Gearbox Software/Piranha Games. 2K Games/Aspyr Media, 2011. Multiple platforms.

E.T. the Extra-Terrestrial. Atari. Atari, 1982. Atari 2600.

Farmville. Zynga. Zynga, 2009. Personal computer.

FIFA (franchise). EA Sports. Electronic Arts, 1993-present. Multiple platforms.

Grand Theft Auto V. Rockstar Games. Rockstar Games, 2013. Multiple platforms.

Guitar Hero: Warriors of Rock. Neversoft/Vicarious Visions. Activision, 2010. Multiple platforms.

inFAMOUS 2. Sucker Punch Productions. Sony Computer Entertainment, 2011. Sony PlayStation 3.

inFAMOUS: Festival of Blood. Sucker Punch Productions. Sony Computer Entertainment, 2011. Sony PlayStation 3.

Infinity Blade. Chair Entertainment. Epic Games, 2010. iOS.

Killzone 3. Guerrilla Games. Sony Computer Entertainment, 2011. Sony PlayStation 3.

League of Legends. Riot Games. Riot Games, 2009. Personal computer.

Lost Planet 3. Spark Unlimited. Capcom, 2013. Multiple platforms.

Midnight Club (franchise). Angel Studios/Rockstar San Diego/Rockstar London/Rebellion Developments. Rockstar Games/Destination Software, 2000–2009. Multiple platforms.

PlanetSide 2. Daybreak Game Company. Daybreak Game Company, 2012. Multiple platforms.

Red Dead Redemption. Rockstar San Diego. Rockstar Games, 2010. Multiple platforms.

Red Dead Revolver. Rockstar San Diego. Rockstar Games, 2004. Multiple platforms.

Sam & Max. LucasArts. LucasArts, 1993–2010. Multiple platforms.

Star Wars: Galactic Battlegrounds. LucasArts/Ensemble Studios. LucasArts, 2001. Personal computer.

Tangled: The Video Game. Disney Interactive Studios. Disney Interactive Studios, 2010. Multiple platforms.

Test Drive Off-Road 2. Accolade. Accolade, 1998. Personal computer.

Tetris. Alexey Pajitnov. Spectrum HoloByte, 1987. Multiple platforms.

Tomb Raider: Legend. Crystal Dynamics. Eidos Interactive, 2006. Multiple platforms.

XCOM: Enemy Unknown. Feral Interactive. Feral Interactive, 2013. iOS.

Yaiba: Ninja Gaiden Z. Team Ninja/Spark Unlimited/Comcept. Tecmo Koei, 2014. Multiple platforms.

Softography

JIRA Software (https://www.atlassian.com/software/jira)

Microsoft Excel (http://office.microsoft.com/en-us/excel)

Microsoft Project (https://products.office.com/en-us/Project/project-and-portfolio-management-software)

Microsoft Word (http://office.microsoft.com/en-us/word)

5

Quality Assurance

▶ INTRODUCTION

Quality assurance (QA) is the testing and tuning process that usually happens prior to a game's release in order to ensure that the game looks, sounds, plays, and feels the way the developers intend. QA personnel—often called playtesters, quality analysts, and the like—are tasked with assaying the aesthetic, technical, and/or interactive elements of a game for possible improvement during various stages of development, sometimes even after a game has been released. QA locates bugs in the software, finds flaws in a game's design or controls, documents anomalies in the graphics and audio elements, and annotates any other potentially problematic phenomena using a set of predefined standards. These standards may be defined by the developer, publisher, host platform or environment (e.g., Microsoft Xbox Live, Steam), rating organizations and systems (e.g., the Entertainment Software Rating Board), and public policy and laws. The standards may be aesthetic (e.g., a studio or publisher's audiovisual benchmarks), technological (e.g., operational stability and connectivity over a given network or service), or moral (e.g., the importance of age and culturally appropriate content).

QA personnel may be an internal and dedicated part of the development team, but they may also work externally, either as contract employees or unpaid contributors (e.g., players who are invited to participate in a closed beta). Finally, QA has been one of the traditional entry points into the game industry, with employees often spending time testing before moving on to other development positions (e.g., design, producing).

Importantly, QA personnel can offer the design and development teams a new perspective on a game, through the eyes of those unfamiliar with the game's mechanics or story. They act as a pre-release defense against the frustrations and confusions that might otherwise be encountered by post-release consumers. In more complex games, the QA team checks that all mechanics work as designed when combined during gameplay. A common task might be the rigorous testing of all object-interaction combinations in an adventure game, or assuring that every weapon or power feature is fairly balanced against every other feature in a title built on player versus player combat. These tasks are in addition to general bug finding, where QA verifies that the software does not crash or trap the user in insurmountable situations.

Typically, QA personnel hold one of two position classes: tester or lead. Testers conduct the hands-on work of game assessment, generally (though not always) through directed and repeated play sessions. Leads act as supervisors, coordinating testing, aggregating and reporting results, and representing QA personnel to the rest of the development team. Leads may also act as envoys to the public, recruiting players through a variety of channels to help test a game.

According to the 2014 Gamasutra Salary Survey, QA personnel are among the lowest paid in the industry, with an average annual salary of $54,833 ("Transitions" 4). QA leads with up to six years of experience average $60,417 annually, and testers with similar experience earn an average of $38,833 per year (Ibid.). Leads with more than six years of experience earn an average of $65,500 per year (Ibid.). Additionally, US-based QA personnel earn approximately 33% more on average than their Canadian counterparts, and 43% more on average than European QA personnel (Ibid.). Finally, male QA personnel average $54,576 annually, while female employees average $56,786 per year (Ibid.).

Carolyn VanEseltine
Tester

Carolyn VanEseltine is the founder of Sibyl Moon Games. Previously she was a QA specialist for Outact Entertainment; game designer for Giant Spacekat; playtest coordinator, Web QA specialist, production assistant, and associate producer at Harmonix Music Systems; and gamemaster at Simutronics Games. She holds a BA in creative writing from Beloit College, and her shipped titles include *Does Canned Rice Dream of a Napkin Heap?*, *Ollie Ollie Oxen Free*, *Revolution 60*, *Dance Central 3*, *Rock Band Blitz*, *Beet the Devil*, *Dance Central 2*, *One Eye Open*, *Dance Central*, *Rock Band 3*, *Green Day: Rock Band*, *LEGO Rock Band*, *The Beatles: Rock Band*, and *GemStone IV*. She is also co-author with Frank Wu of *Revolution 60: The Chessboard Lethologica*. She has received multiple awards for her interactive fiction writing, including a XYZZY Award for Best NPCs (*Ollie Ollie Oxen Free*). She blogs about game design and development on the Sibyl Moon website (www.sibylmoon.com).

＊ ＊ ＊ ＊ ＊

How did you come to work in the game industry?

As a high school student, I was a huge fan of the online game *GemStone IV*, which was a text-based MUD available through AOL. In college, I became part of the game's volunteer staff—working six hours of customer service a week and being compensated with a free account—and then I progressed to a paid, part-time staffing position after graduating from college.

I think I would've found my way into games even without this experience at Simutronics because digital games were always my passion. My dad and I used to play text adventures when I was little, and I remember using graph paper and notebook paper to plan out my own game in fifth grade. My kid self would be terribly impressed by me today.

Prior to getting into developing games, I had a seven-year customer service career. When I was working for Simutronics, I was very excited about getting into the code and exploring the various ways to build a game. But I also had this customer service role. When I found out that Harmonix was looking for somebody to run their playtesting, it was in some ways very similar to the customer service side of working for Simutronics—focusing on listening to the player and documenting the player's needs. There was a very solid skill overlap there.

What are some of the skills that customer service and playtest coordination have in common?

For playtest coordination and customer service specifically, I'd say that it's very much about listening to what the other person is saying, trying to communicate with them very clearly, having empathy for what they're thinking and feeling, and having the ability to really pay attention to the person you're talking with instead of thinking about whatever else is going on. I found all this to be extremely useful when we were running playtesting, because when you bring in players, you want to know what the user experience is. It's very much like software user experience testing. You can't afford to give the player any preconceptions—you have to listen completely to what they're saying, even if what they're saying is "I'm so frustrated I want to flip this table!"

Having had that experience—someone yelling at me across a counter—makes it very easy to stay zen if somebody's having a frustrating experience, or to help lighten their mood. A lot of playtesting is "Here, have this very frustrating experience and tell us about it." That's where I see the main overlap.

What is the difference between playtesting and quality assurance?

It's the difference between "Does the player have a good experience?" (playtesting) and "Is this game functioning correctly?" (QA). Playtesting focuses specifically on the user experience. It's about figuring out how players are going to interact with your game—what they're going to find fun, not fun, frustrating, etc. QA is a paid discipline, and it always should be. It should never be volunteer. QA is specifically about determining whether the product that's been delivered matches the design documents. It's looking for bugs and comparing the game to the spec.

The job of playtest coordinator is a paid position that brings volunteer playtesters from outside a company into the company to see a game. It's a supervisory position in the sense that you're supervising and observing what playtesters do. Being a QA tester is not a supervisory position. It's "I've got the build. Now I have to find the bugs in it." It's generally a paid hourly position.

At Harmonix, I started out in playtest for *The Beatles: Rock Band*, and when that playtest cycle ended, I transferred over to QA. It was specifically for the Web—the company had a console-to-web feature that they needed someone to hammer on. So that was my transition point when I stopped working with externals primarily and started working with internals. By working with internals, I mean that I was working with employees inside Harmonix instead of volunteers from outside Harmonix. Instead of documenting the experience of external users (our players), I was documenting the experience of internal users (our employees). And I was trying to track those issues down before someone else reported them, rather than limiting myself to observing what users observed. So my day turned into chasing bugs, and I became QA.

How do you find playtesters?

It varies. One thing about playtesting is that it's much easier to find people who are good at video games than people who are bad at them. It's easy to find experienced people who are excited to do playtesting for you, especially when you're at a well-known studio. At Harmonix, all we had to do was say "new game" and we'd be flooded with experts who wanted to playtest. What we needed were beginners. So, a lot of the process of acquiring testers there and at Giant Spacekat involved people going around to their trusted, non-game-playing friends—where we knew the information wasn't going to leak, both because we trusted them and because we were going to have them sign a non-disclosure agreement—and say "We know you don't play video games. We have this thing—it's a video game—and we really need someone who doesn't play video games to tell us what the play experience is like and how we can make it better for you." In some ways it was very much a matter of personal networking for that critical beginner group.

Were those beginning testers compensated beyond getting an early look at an unreleased game?

We didn't compensate them. Some studios do compensate their testers, but my feeling is that's a bad plan. If you're paying somebody to play your game, they feel more of an obligation to like your game. But you really want people to be comfortable telling you that your game sucks. It sounds ridiculous, but in some ways that's the hardest thing to deal with in playtesting. You have to explain to people, "We need to know what's wrong. Please don't smooth this over. If we don't hear it from you, we'll hear it from the press, from our players, from people who hate our game. So if there's something wrong, we need to know now."

Obviously, we'd make the testing environment a pleasant one, with free soda, coffee drinks, and pizza. And we'd personally try to be friendly. But having a monetary exchange in testing actually adjusts the way players think about the process. It takes an intrinsic reward and turns it into an extrinsic reward, and you really want the playtesting experience to involve an intrinsic reward, no matter who's playing. So, to get the best data, the ideal playtesting process is along the lines of "Would you please do us a favor."

How did you transition from QA to production?

There was a studio redesign. We unfortunately had some layoffs, and the concept of having a dedicated Web QA department was something that went away. In order to keep me on, and because I'd been steadily expanding my responsibilities, I was shifted over to the production department.

Generally speaking, where in the development process does QA begin and end?

The farther you get into a game, the more QA attention there is. That's because the earlier you are, the less there is to check. The key is unit testing, which involves building a test suite to make sure that various elements of a piece of software work correctly. That's the kind of thing in non-gaming software that tends to be where QA engineers focus. In the games industry, when we talk about QA people, we're usually talking about the people who are end testing instead. They're working on the most compiled form of the game to date.

Early on, the QA contribution is to interface with design, so that QA has a very strong idea of what the game is supposed to look like. This enables QA to put together protocols for the various tests they'll be running down the line. But until you have an actual build, there's nothing for QA to do except for building those test protocols. They're not really going to be getting into the guts of it the way engineering is. So, the closer you get to the shipping date, the more complete a game you have.

Depending on the studio, two months to one week from the shipping date is where QA is in the mix constantly, tracking bugs. You have these very tight cycles at the end of the game development process where you have a bunch of QA people just hammering on the build and trying to break it. You have a producer standing over them trying to figure out whether the errors they're finding are showstoppers—where everything has to go back to production and be fixed—or ones that can be shipped and patched later.

Where in the development process does playtesting begin and end?

Playtest is more like a bell curve in development than a solid increase like it is with QA. There's this concept of finding the fun in design—you don't want to ship a game that isn't fun. If you have an idea that isn't fun, you have to fig-ure that out as fast as possible and make something else. At the beginning of the development process, when things are still being mapped out, playtesting centers around rapid prototyping. You work as fast as you can to make something that'll represent some concept in your game, and then see if it's fun or not. The way you test fun is to drag people into the studio and have them do playtesting. These prototypes might not even be in the final build. A lot of studios do things like make quick *Flash* mock-ups of what user interfaces are going to be like to make sure that they make sense to people. That's not content that'll ever go into the final build, but it's something that enables you to understand what the user experience is like early on. The further you get into the game development process, the more information you can get—but there comes a point where it's not useful to have playtesters anymore. At that point, you understand what the game is; you've solidified its features and ironed out the difficulties. From there, playtesting tapers off because you've made the game and you just need to make it right.

Given the relatively slow ramp-up of QA work in the development process, is there a lot of downtime in QA?

First off, there isn't the same steady need for QA as there is for engineering, or art, or any of the other disciplines. Unfortunately, this lack of steady need isn't handled all that well in the industry. There's an unpleasant tendency for companies to ramp up and ramp down. It's like being in Hollywood or other sectors of the entertainment industry—ramp up for the big project then go to layoffs once the project's over. It's kind of ugly.

However, there are small contract organizations that you can hire to do QA. There are also independent contractors who do QA—this past fall I did a gig as an independent QA contractor. The other thing you see is that there are studios that can balance multiple projects at once to make sure that all the staff are continuously busy, that they have something to do to be paid. Harmonix was very good at that because they produced a steady stream of downloadable content while they were making the *Rock Band* and *Dance Central* franchises. Because there were those constant small pieces of content coming out, it meant that the company could keep their QA people on. At the end of the day, though, it's not financially sensible for most companies to keep a full QA staff on hand. But you do have to have a lot of QA people at the end of each project.

Independent studios typically don't have dedicated QA people. If you look at Giant Spacekat, for example, there were four of us who were full-time. As a result, QA was done internally. We sat down and talked about what we needed to look at and what might be broken. And then we all just played the build like crazy and tried to break it. It was a distraction from the other parts of our job, but it was something that had to be done. It was critically important—the people who don't do QA at all are the ones who produce really buggy games. But ideally you want someone doing QA who didn't build the game.

Are there any other areas in game development as volatile as QA when it comes to staffing?

QA is definitely the most volatile discipline. Studios are always ramping up and ramping down, regardless of size. There are also lots of studio closures—it's something that happens constantly. But if a studio is ramping up and ramping down a lot, then a lot of the people being let go are probably QA. It's not that they don't have the skills to move to another area of game development. It's just that there's only so much work available at any given time, and the kind of work that QA people do is less likely to be available. If things are going well then you'll have people who are cross-training, so that they're not as expendable. At Harmonix, a lot of the people in QA were also musicians and provided some amount of sound support. But in general, QA is considered an entry-level position—an entry-level position which people who are detail-oriented, organized, and focused can do without having specific schooling or specialized skills. Because of this, you can't necessarily move them to art, music, or coding.

What enabled you to transition from QA to design?

I was terribly determined. I know how immodest that sounds, but I knew what I wanted to be doing in the long run, and QA wasn't it. I was very reliably studying, researching, and developing small games of my own outside of my QA work at Harmonix. The company wasn't in a position where they could afford to bring me on as a junior designer. They were in a position where, when they hired designers, they hired senior people. As a result, design was never going to be accessible for me while I was there. But they were willing to do things like let me shadow design department meetings so that I could get some indirect training in design. That was extremely valuable to me.

Design opportunities were the reason I went to Giant Spacekat. Harmonix was very enthusiastic about me being in production but wasn't going to have any design opportunities for me. Giant Spacekat did, and my heart is really in design.

Do the seasonal rhythms of game development (i.e., companies heavily targeting the holiday shopping season for release of showcase titles) impact the market for QA jobs?

Yes. Everyone wants to release across Christmas, and no one wants to release at the same time as a *Call of Duty* game. But I don't think seasonal stuff is quite as impactful as it could be, given the amount of time that goes into making a big game. You have some projects that take a year to make, and others that take three years to make.

You see a glut in the job market when studios shut down. I actually applied for a design position at Bethesda Softworks at the time when 38 Studios closed. I'd sent in my application and then heard that news. I thought, "Oh no, I'm never hearing from them." I saw a bunch of good people get hired as a result, but that's the way it goes. It's a small industry.

Does playtesting have any more longevity than QA, or is it equally volatile when it comes to hiring and firing?

It does have more longevity. Playtesting isn't its own department at most companies—usually it's rolled in with design or production. The expectation is that whoever is organizing playtesting will be working closely with design and production to make sure that the information is flowing through the process, and that this is someone who can be repurposed when there isn't heavy playtesting to be done.

I don't mean to sound cynical, but the dream of just sitting around all day on your butt playing video games is just a terrible one. Playtesting and QA aren't stable positions, they don't pay super well, and aren't highly respected— which is a bad thing. Being good at QA actually requires a very specialized skill set, and it's a real problem that QA experts can't stay in QA and just be good at QA. Our industry would be very different if QA specialists were treated more respectfully, and I think our games would be better for it.

What are QA and playtesting like for independent studios?

Giant Spacekat brought me on specifically for combat design and combat tuning. Combat tuning meant getting people in, having them play the game, seeing what their reactions were, and then tweaking the game accordingly to improve the combat experience. I think every single human being I know must have come to my living room. Giant Spacekat is decentralized—there's not a studio—so when we held playtesting it was actually at the house of one of the people from the company. I hosted, Brianna Wu (co-founder of Giant Spacekat) hosted—I think the only person who didn't host was the lead animator. I begged my friends who don't play video games to make an exception; I sent surveys out through Facebook and to folks I used to work with; I got signal boosts from various people. It was a very similar process to one you would use in a large studio, but note that's because I was trained in the process at a large studio. And that's also the culture of the Boston game development community—the Boston independent community is very tight-knit. There are mailing lists for the Boston indie community that include things like "Hey, I need a bunch of people to come playtest my game. Are you available this evening?"

Does the Boston independent community help with other facets of game development besides playtesting?

Absolutely. Just this morning there was a question that went out from someone who didn't fully understand how to integrate Structured Query Language (SQL) into their codebase. There were four people who answered the question by the time I found it. There's very much a feeling in the independent community in Boston that we can do better as a group than we can on our own, and we make a point of helping each other. So, if I were in a situation where I had a question about legal issues in game development, for example, I'd send it out to the mailing list to see if anyone had good advice for me.

How has the Web work you have done fit into the game development process more generally?

When I was at Harmonix, there was this idea that rather than *Rock Band 3* being something that you just engaged in with your Xbox, then turned off and walked away when you were done, we wanted it to be much more holistic, more community oriented. There were a number of ways in which we integrated our website into the console play. Things like being able to look up the leaderboards at home to see who'd beaten your latest scores, or being able to build a list of songs you wanted to buy after the latest downloadable content came out, were part of that.

My pet project was the *Rock Band* Network, which was a user-generated content project. It was far and away my favorite project at Harmonix because the point of the network was for any musician to be able to put their music into *Rock Band*. The technological and legal systems involved were spectacularly complicated because they had to integrate with Microsoft. Coordinating the interface with Harmonix and Microsoft, making sure the money flowed correctly to the various parties—it was an amazing project to work on, but it was also something that had to be spit shined to perfection so that things didn't get screwed up. When I came on as Web QA there, I was making sure that if I uploaded a song to the website I could process it correctly and have it come out on the console. As beta testers came in, I started working with them, and after the project left beta, I essentially became the Harmonix liaison to the *Rock Band* Network community. For the first year of *Rock Band* Network operation, I answered to Harmonix senior producer Matthew Nordhaus, who was the project lead. Then I became a producer, and he handed it off to me.

The *Rock Band* Network was in some ways a huge success and in other ways not so much. It was a huge success in that it released an astonishing amount of music to the *Rock Band* platform. The *Rock Band* Network released over 2100 songs in its lifetime, most of which were by indie musicians and not big names. It was a triumph for Harmonix co-founder Alex Rigopolous, who had long had the idea that *Rock Band* could be a way of experiencing music.

However, we discovered that people who play *Rock Band* would rather play the songs they already know than ones they don't. When there was a small, steady stream of downloadable content, people were more willing to take a chance on music that they didn't know yet. When that stream became a raging river—at the height we had maybe ten songs coming out each day— we found that users weren't as interested in trying music they didn't know, even with previews and demos. Ultimately, it was an artistic triumph and a triumph for what Harmonix was about, but maybe not an ideal financial venture. To be clear, I never saw the full numbers on the project, but from the leaderboards it was possible for me to see that while some of the songs that came out through the *Rock Band* Network sold 3000 copies, others only sold 48.

Are you able to speak generally about the legal agreements involved in the Rock Band *Network?*

In very general terms, yes. I'm not a lawyer, though, so understand that this comes from my reading of the lay version of the agreements rather than comprehending the contracts in full. I never saw the agreements between Harmonix and Microsoft, Harmonix and Sony, or Harmonix and Nintendo—it was a big project.

The biggest concern was that people were going to upload music that they didn't have the right to upload. That had a lot to do with why we had a Harmonix person constantly in contact with the *Rock Band* Network community. The idea was that if there were ever a problem like that it could be shut off immediately before the content shipped live. It was also to make sure that people didn't upload swear words and the like—the game was rated T, after all.[1] To a great extent, the legal agreements that were finally drawn up put a lot of responsibility on the person uploading the song. If somebody were to upload a song that she or he didn't have the rights to, theoretically the legal chain would have come back to them rather than hitting Harmonix directly.

Despite the fact that the *Rock Band* Network was all about community, we didn't really get a lot of data about users. The information about our player base that we had access to was limited to people who were willing to respond to Harmonix surveys—people who wanted to receive our email, people who wanted to get tweets from us. To those folks we could pose demographic questions. But not the most casual players. All we ever got were sales stats, or at least that's all I ever had access to.

One thing to keep in mind is that the people authoring songs for the *Rock Band* Network were essentially independent contractors. They were getting paid for their work in royalties, rather than by the hour. I wouldn't consider them as being part of the general public, though. They were a very professional group. I really enjoyed working with them because they took it all very seriously. They had fun with it, for sure, but they absolutely knew what they were talking about every time—just this enormous level of expertise. The *Rock Band* Network authors weren't going to give you a hard time just to give you a hard time, which is unfortunately something that you do see with some of the game-playing public. I've spent some time wandering around the Blizzard Entertainment forums and being glad that I've never been in charge of running them.

How much of the work in QA has to consider the game's target rating?

For the most part, that's a production issue rather than a QA issue, but anything related to ratings will still involve QA because the people in QA know the game better than anyone else. If you want to understand what's actually in the game, rather than what's been planned, then QA will know.

There's a heightened consciousness about ratings during the design phase, generally framed as "What rating are we going for?" For *Dance Central*, we knew that we didn't want a rating above T. We also didn't want a rating below T because that might be a problem when we shipped downloadable content that had swearing or sexual innuendo in it.

The person who handled ratings stuff on the production side was one of our producers in Digital Submissions. Digital Submissions goes by a lot of different names—in fact, I'm not even sure that it's always lumped under production. It's basically whoever it is who talks to first parties, works through their paperwork, sends them the build, turns around certification, and handles the other important things that need to be done in the process. Making sure the build would fit Microsoft's requirements was part of our job, and Microsoft's requirements included having an ESRB rating. If I hadn't been busy handling the *Rock Band* Network, ratings issues might have fallen to me, because I was also in Digital Submissions at the time. But there were three of us, so we distributed the workload by who had time and energy available.

What was it like interacting with the public as a company representative?

There's a term for the person whose job it is to interact with the public: community manager. That's something that can be your central title or just something that's part of your job responsibilities. I have community management experience from my time at Simutronics and Harmonix, but community manager has never been my official title. Community management is basically looping back—it's customer service. When you represent your company, you're in charge of personifying the company's attitude, regardless of whether that attitude is quirky and fun, super professional, or whatever it happens to be.

Depending on the size of the company, there may be some kind of vetting or training process before anybody wants you to speak to the public in a professional capacity. When you deal with people who are part of the public and are acting unprofessionally, it's just like being in customer service and having someone walk up to your desk and be unprofessional—you handle it as professionally as you can, with as much grace as you can. Eventually, if it's a serious problem, you tell them you're not going to interact with them anymore or, in some cases, redirect them to legal.

What part of your job is most professionally rewarding? Why?

For me, the most professionally rewarding moments are the ones when it's clear that I've successfully transformed a creative vision into a desirable player experience. It usually happens when I'm watching playtesting, when I get a player email, or when I read a review of my work—but it's the culmination of everything else, when players react and I can see that their reactions are exactly what I was trying to achieve.

What are the most significant internal challenges you face in your job?

Right now, I'm a solo developer. As a solo developer, no one has my back. There's no producer to organize me and keep me on track with my deadlines. There's no more skillful designer to ask for a second opinion. There's no more experienced coder to look at my bugs. There's no legal team to review the contract. There's no office manager to deal with the leaking ceiling. There's no PR person to represent me to the outside world. They're all me. This means that solo development is a constant process of risk assessment and redirection. If I drop the ball, I'd better figure out how to pick it up again—or I'd better be ready to find help. No one else is going to unblock me, so I have to be able to unblock myself, every single time.

What are the external challenges you face in your job?

The bar for achievement is high and the competition is tough. It's not enough to make a good indie game—you have to make a spectacular indie game, and then support it with a strong PR and marketing campaign.

Also, I'm a short, soft-spoken woman in an industry that's overwhelmingly male. There are significant disadvantages to this.

What sorts of workplace changes would you implement if given the opportunity?

Routine day care for the dog. Seriously. I work from a home office, and while it's nice to have my dog here, it does mean that he routinely interrupts my train of thought.

How is the work you do in the game industry different from the work you have done elsewhere?

I had a seven-year career as a customer service professional, first as a parking coordinator at the University of North Carolina at Chapel Hill, and then as an international concierge. Customer service and game development aren't without parallels—for example, the customer service/community management skills overlap strongly, and communication skills are critical to both. But the goal length is extremely different, and so is the way success is measured. In customer service, you typically benefit people on an individual basis, resolving tens or hundreds of individual problems a day. In game development, everything hinges around the long-term plan—everyone spends months or years working toward a single product's launch. It's like being in Hollywood.

Which companies or ways of working (both within and outside of the game industry) do you look to for inspiration?

Failbetter Games, Fire Hose Games, Dejobaan Games, Harmonix Music Systems, Valve Corporation, Pixar, and Google come immediately to mind. I'm also strongly inspired by individual game developers like Emily Short, Andrew Plotkin, and Lynnea Glasser. All of these companies and people strike me as being very, very good at what they do. I have incredible respect for competence.

I look at a studio like Failbetter, for example, which made the browser-based game *Fallen London* and launched *Sunless Sea* in 2015 (which they created from a successful Kickstarter campaign). *Fallen London* is extremely narrative—it's like a giant choose-your-own-adventure, except that you wind up repeating paths all the time. Alexis Kennedy, the CEO and creative director of Failbetter, had this image for a weird steampunk world where London wound up on the shores of Hell and strange Lovecraftian things happen there. I look at his vision, I look at what he executed, and I look at the fact that he did it with a team of maybe 20 people max—I'm just very inspired by his clear, cohesive vision which allowed him to communicate successfully with a group of people. The game has an extremely devoted player base of something like 40,000 people. I have a lot of respect for that drive, that determination, that willingness to innovate, and the competence to get it right.

Touching on my own personal philosophy of game design, I believe in game design as a way to take one person's vision of an experience and give it to another person. That's incredibly powerful. It's a way to teach empathy; it's a way to give perspective; it's a way to make miracles. To a certain extent that's the individual experience, and to a certain extent that's a way to change the world. In some ways, that's why I'm so drawn to the indie space—it's where I see people who see that same potential and who are getting excited about the same kinds of things I'm excited about. But it's not something that's missing from the AAA space, either—that's part of why Harmonix was such a joyous place to be. We were focused on this idea of "How do we give normal people the experience of being a rock star? How do we make normal people feel like an amazing dance champion?" It doesn't have to be something like that, though. It could be sharing an experience of what it's like to be a transgender person, or the only black kid in an all-white school. How do we communicate emotion? How do we communicate experience? Games are the best tool we've ever had for that. They matter. It's not just an industry; it's an art form.

Don't get me wrong: I believe deeply in books and movies. Heck, I believe deeply in music—it's a lovely way to communicate experience. But games are non-passive. You interact with them and they interact with you, as opposed to watching a movie. The movie interacts with you, but you don't reach out back.

How does the workflow differ when working on different types of games (e.g., different genres, AAA versus casual games, etc.)?

I handle all the roles as a solo indie, but that obviously isn't an option in AAA development. There has to be a clear workflow and clear lines of communication in AAA, or everything breaks down in confusion.

During my time at Harmonix Music Systems, the company operated under Agile with Scrum. Projects had a solid development process that started with an initial vision, went through feature lists and user stories, and ended with developed products. Scrum masters (typically producers) and product owners collaborated to turn feature ideas into user stories. The team committed to user stories and completed them over the course of two- to four-week sprints.

When I was part of the Digital Submissions production team, we didn't have sprints because we had an established pipeline. Downloadable content (say, for *Rock Band*) followed a very specific path that took between six and nine months, beginning with the initial song licensing and ending with a packaged piece of downloadable content ready for first-party review (Nintendo, Sony, and Microsoft). My part of that pipeline—preparing the first-party paperwork, sending the downloadable content to first parties, and finally executing the release—took approximately one week to complete. We had new downloadable content coming out weekly, so my responsibilities were identical every week, with only the underlying songs changing.

What is your experience with inter-company collegiality/collaboration?

The two companies that immediately come to mind are Harmonix and Fire Hose Games. Harmonix is obviously quite a bit bigger, and Fire Hose may not even be on your radar. I originally encountered Fire Hose when I came on at Harmonix, and they were only six people big. Harmonix had hired them to do some contract work on the prototype for *Dance Central*. The head of community relations was Shawn Baptiste, an absolutely wonderful human being. He took a leave from Harmonix for a couple of years, and when he came back, he worked briefly at Harmonix, then he shifted over to be a major figure at Fire Hose. I wouldn't go so far as to say that Harmonix and Fire Hose are sister studios, but in my time, Fire Hose was a place that Harmonix absolutely looked to do well by. They had good connections and a good working relationship.

I believe it was in 2011 that the PlayStation Network got hacked and a lot of users' security information was released. The entire network was shut down, and that happened exactly when Fire Hose was supposed to release its first solo title, *Slam Bolt Scrappers*. As a company, not only were we upset because our users were on PlayStation Network too, but we were really worried because we wondered if this was going to mean the collapse of Fire Hose. They were trying to distribute a title that they literally couldn't distribute. I'm pretty sure that the official Harmonix accounts did a social media push for them, and certainly individual people who had HMX official Twitter tags would do reposts of Fire Hose announcements. I've seen back and forth between the studios since then.

There's an argument to be made that, to a certain extent, a similar relationship exists between Microsoft and Harmonix, or at least it did during the period of the *Dance Central* titles. Microsoft was not only the first party for *Dance Central*, but it was also the publisher. We had Microsoft people who were in our office constantly in order to be helpful and to pick up builds to bring to Microsoft for internal playtesting. It was a constant back and forth.

What are some of your notable quality of life issues, both routine and exceptional?

First, money. My last two studio positions considered me to be a self-employed contractor, which meant high taxes and no benefits. And as a solo developer, there'll be no income whatsoever until I ship my first commercial project.

Several years ago I was at a local game development conference where there was a discussion on how to start an independent game company. One of the questions people asked the assembled solo developers was "How on earth are you funding your work?" As they went around the room responding to the question, it turned out that almost everyone had one of two answers. The first was "savings": you make sure that you have enough of a nest egg and an exit plan for when you run out of nest egg. The other answer was "you have someone who is willing to fund you, typically your spouse." The third possibility, which is more rare, is that people do the venture capital circuit. But that tends to be for people who want to found a major studio as opposed to "I want to get three people together and ship a thing."

The second notable quality of life issue is time. As a solo developer, there's no one setting work hours, which is more problematic than might be immediately obvious. It's easy for an eight-hour day to turn into a ten-hour day, to turn into a fourteen-hour day, simply because I work from home and there's no one blocking me. In some very real ways, I never leave work, and that's not good for work/life balance.

Finally, training is a big issue. I'm extraordinarily versatile—I demonstrated that on *Revolution 60*, where my official game credits include everything from combat design to playtest coordination to cinematic scripting to sound design. But there are a lot of things I don't know, and either I have to learn them or find a way around any obstacles created by not knowing them.

What are some of your notable career progression issues?

The needs of the company outweigh the needs of the individual, and training can be very hard to come by. This means that, once you're on a career path, it can be very difficult to redirect. This strongly impacted my career because Harmonix Music Systems really needed me in production, and I really wanted to move to game design. After three years of trying to shift my career path, I finally accepted that I had to pick between the career path I wanted and the company I wanted. That led to me leaving Harmonix Music Systems voluntarily and joining the indie development space.

What motivated you to become an independent developer?

My heart lies in design, and getting full-time design positions is incredibly competitive and difficult. In some ways, the challenges around design are similar to QA. A lot of people think that anyone can do game design, but it's not true. There's a lot of competition for game design positions because design is seen as an entry-level position even though in many ways it isn't. Game design involves not only what you know, but also what your experience is. There's also the need for companies to winnow out the people who *think* they can do game design from the people who actually have experience doing game design. In terms of a large studio, my résumé isn't as convincing as I wish it were. I have a decent chunk of game design experience, but I'm much better situated to land a job in production because I was a producer for years.

The indie space is really hard, but it provides an opportunity for me to prove that I can do design. Someday down the road I'll be able to turn around and say, "Hey, I can do this, I've proven myself," and land a job back with a studio doing what I want to do. For me, indie development started as a means to an end, but I've really come to love the independent community. Sure, it's demanding because you have to be so versatile and self-reliant, but it's not so different in the AAA space. There, you have to ship a product and it has to succeed. There's no room for failure because the budgets are so high and you can't afford a flop. The indie space is much safer for experimental design and for innovators, which is also pretty exciting. I came to independent development to polish my résumé, but I've stayed because it's a good fit for me.

Is the title of game designer understood differently depending on the studio and genre?

Game design is actually an umbrella term. There are a variety of skills that fall under game design. For example, Giant Spacekat hired me to do combat design, which is all about figuring out how to give players a balanced experience that still feels exciting and produces charges of adrenaline. There's also systems design, which is about creating and balancing the various systems in a game. There's narrative design—my official specialty—which involves figuring out how to integrate the story and the game together, how to make them reinforce each other without one being too subservient to the other, and how to make that story grip people and affect their emotions. There's gameplay design, which sounds vague but is about creating and refining the experience of the game within the software product generally. UI design links very closely to art, and makes sure that the interface is accessible and understandable to the user (which makes or breaks games every day). It doesn't matter how good your game is if nobody can figure out how to play it. Finally, there's level design, which is linked to some of the other design domains. Quest design is connected to level design, for example.

So, there are a lot of creative and industrial practices that fall under the umbrella term of "game design." Remember, these are only general categories, and they vary from studio to studio and from game genre to game genre. Typically, companies will advertise for what they need: a combat designer, a gameplay scripter, a narrative designer. When a company advertises for a game designer, they're probably either talking about a person who can design the gameplay experience, or they specifically need someone who's well rounded.

Given the many different kinds of jobs that might fall under design and production, how do applicants go about finding the right positions to apply for?

I was at Harmonix as the *Dance Central* project was getting started, and *Dance Central* was a huge secret. Harmonix was trying to find people who could be QA for *Dance Central*, and one of the requirements of the job was that you had to be able to dance. You had to be competent; you had to know something about it. So how do you get people like that when you can't advertise for a dancer? None of the ads could say anything about dance because that had to be a super secret. The way it worked was by networking. It was very much a "Do you know people who know people?" kind of situation. As it turned out, my friend Caelyn Sandel was a huge *Dance Dance Revolution* fan and loved video games. I talked her into coming in and applying for a job without ever telling her what the job was for. I knew she was absolutely the right person for it, and I literally couldn't tell her why. That took a lot of hard work—she was convinced that there was no point in her applying.

Usually and unfortunately, it goes the other way around. You apply for a job, you don't hear anything, and you find out later it's because you weren't qualified for whatever reason. The advantage of networking is that you can talk to people who know your qualifications and can help you figure out if you'd be a good fit for a specific position.

Based on your description, it sounds as if the game industry has a small-town feel, that everyone knows everyone else. What is it about the industry that produces this feel, especially given its size and growth?

I'd say that a large part of this feel comes from the fact that it's a difficult industry to break into, and it's a difficult industry to get training in. The people at AAA studios are rarely new to the industry. One person I knew used to teach art on the side, and when he ran across promising students he'd see if they were interested in joining the company. It was extremely valuable for him to stay connected to a community outside of game development.

If you've somehow made it into game development, it's probably because you know somebody, frankly. You either knew them before or you made a point of putting yourself out there, meeting people, and networking. It's actually a very tricky industry to be in as an introvert.

One thing that affects all of this is that game developers generally move for the industry. There's game development in Boston, in New York, in Washington—all over. But if you lose a job, you can't count on being able to get a similar job in the same town. I know two people in Australia who moved there because that's where they could get jobs. When people move for a job, the people they know first and foremost are the people in the studio. They're making friends within their studio first, friends who then move on to other places. It becomes a constant, spreading network. Every year at the Game Developers Conference, thousands of people get back together. In many ways it's a critically important conference, but it's also an alumni reunion.

I realize that because people develop good and widespread professional networks, it might seem like once you're in the industry you're in for good, especially if you're willing to move. Unfortunately, that's not always the case. I know a number of people who've been out of work for a long time. It's a very high-demand industry. For any given position there are many people applying, so even the best network is no guarantee of employment. But that's also what makes the networking so important—having someone who will vouch for you at the time you're applying. That's the reality of the industry right now—it's so reliant on interpersonal relationships.

At the end of my time at Harmonix, I was producing the Web team. The reason I was in that position was because I had already worked individually with everyone I'd need to work with. If I needed to talk to someone in systems operations, if I needed to speak with the community team, if I needed to be able to talk with the game team, I was already familiar with them and they with me because I had come up through the ranks. I knew something about their job and experience already. I was in my position because I could clear the lines of communication efficiently. If there was a situation in which two people hadn't figured out that they needed to talk to each other, I could drag one into the other's office and say, "You're blocking my person. Unblock my person. Here's what's wrong. Talk." While there are occasionally some exceptions, game development is a collaborative process. You have to be able to speak to each other. You have to listen to each other. You have to know each other. You have to trust each other.

Does gender play into networking in the game industry?

Yes. The vast majority of people in game development are white, male, and not prepared automatically to think of a woman as their next colleague. It's something that can be very subtle. At one point I was in a meeting where we were planning to hire someone and everybody kept talking about the potential hire as "he." One of the other women in the room actually raised her hand and said, "Look, can we stop saying 'he'—we could be hiring a woman, right?" The response was "We just use 'he' for anybody," and the discussion went right back to using "he." There were fourteen people in the room, but only three of us were women, and while at least two of us considered this a problem, we couldn't halt the meeting over it. We had to let it go. But it makes a difference; it makes an impression in people's heads. It affects the mind-set.

Along these lines, I also had an interesting experience with a group of students not too long ago. I'd been brought in to play their game and give them feedback on their work. They'd created a game that had two characters, one of whom was male and one of whom was female. The students had taken the male character, added "-ella" to the name, and removed a bow tie—that was the female character. It was very visibly a situation where they needed two characters and the female one was an afterthought. I was looking at these four students who were about twenty years old and all male and I said, "Did you consider that this might be a problem?" They looked at me like I was speaking nonsense. I said, "It's very obvious that you didn't make this game thinking about someone like me as a primary player." I was really glad there was a woman professor in the room who came by and backed me up, because the students were visibly dismissing my feedback. The professor came by and said, "You asked for her feedback—you should listen." It was frustrating but not uncommon.

Is the game industry actively talking about issues of diversity as a means for innovating in games?

It's absolutely a conversation going on among indies nationally and internationally. It's really hard to tell what's going on at AAA studios on this issue, except when they release formal statements. That said, I do think there's movement happening in the right direction, though there's still a long way to go, certainly.

What are the challenges facing the industry over the next decade?

Games are the entertainment medium of the modern age, but what we've done with them to date only scratches the surface of possibility. There's an ongoing conflict between experimenting with new ideas and trusting old, successful ideas, which relates directly to the tension between the indie space, where experimentation is much safer, and the AAA space, where experimentation may lose millions of dollars, but where stagnation may do the same.

As an industry, we're also at a major turning point related to diversity and activism. There's a clear stereotype of what a game developer looks like and what a game player looks like, but those stereotypes are horribly out of date—and many of the people who match those stereotypes are resisting the change. As a result, game development and games in general haven't been historically welcoming to minorities of any kind (gender, race, disability, etc.), but people are becoming increasingly aware of the need for change. The misogynistic movement known as Gamergate is the most visible manifestation of this conflict, but there are others, and the minorities working in the games industry have no choice about being caught in the conflict.

Kylie Findlay
Quality Assurance Lead

Nominated as one of the game industry's most important women by the Market for Computer & Video Games (Pacific Region) trade organization in 2015, Kylie Findlay is a quality analyst II at Firemonkeys Studios, a wholly owned subsidiary of Electronic Arts. Previously, she worked in QA at

Torus Games, The Voxel Agents, and Priceless Games. She holds a bachelor of games design from Griffith University (South Bank Campus), and her shipped titles include *Real Racing 3*, *How to Train Your Dragon 2: The Video Game*, *Falling Skies: Planetary Warfare*, *Barbie: Dreamhouse Party*, *Turbo: Super Stunt Squad*, *The Croods: Prehistoric Party!*, *Rise of the Guardians: The Video Game*, and *Train Conductor 2: USA*.

* * * * *

How did you come to work in the game industry?

I was looking through tech-related university degrees at Griffith, trying to decide what I wanted to study. The bachelor of games design popped out at me, as I'm sure it does to most people who love games. It was brand new and didn't have any entry requirements. Once I started, it was apparent that we were going to be the guinea pigs who helped shape the program for the future. At first, it seemed like it might be bad timing because this was during the Australian industry collapse—around 2008. It actually meant, though, that there were quite a few industry professionals looking for work, so some of them ended up being my teachers, and they obviously had actual game development knowledge to share. I wound up with some good industry contacts because a number of the faculty went back into games, as did some of my fellow students. Those contacts eventually helped me get my first job in QA.

I'm not sure, though, if my degree helped all that much in preparing me for and landing a job. We only really started making games in our last year, and even then most of the people in the program were artists and writers. There were a few programmers, but they didn't really know much about programming. We wound up pulling together some games, but I think I just went for QA after I graduated because it was entry level, the job was available, and it's where I got hired. The game industry wasn't particularly big in Brisbane, which is why I moved to Melbourne. Once I moved into QA, I learned a lot of testing practices and how a studio works, which eventually helped me get the job at Firemonkeys.

How many students were in that first cohort at Griffith University, and how many now work in the game industry?

I think we had twenty-five students in that cohort. By the end, there were maybe eleven of us who graduated, and maybe half of those graduates got jobs in games. A few people started their own game studio, and it's still going, so that's cool. I think I'm the only one who went into QA.

How does QA operate generally?

At Firemonkeys, we have Development QA embedded within the game teams. We focus on issue prevention and containment, coordination of the overall end-to-end test verification strategy of a project, and operational planning and execution against milestone approvals and build submissions. We're currently looking to hire some quality engineers in order to help with the technical aspects of QA (e.g., creating tools).

At the company level, we have three central testing studios—referred to as Core QA and located in Bucharest, Romania; Hyderabad, India; and Baton Rouge, United States of America—who are tasked with executing against a project's test plan. They focus on issue detection along with providing various automation testing and metrics gathering.

EA also has central teams that focus on compliance (who facilitate testing efforts against first-party technical requirements and internal EA standards), certification (who provide the final checks before a game is submitted to first-party publishing), localization testing (who verify all linguistic components), and live monitoring and live QA (who assist game teams directly to monitor and identify issues with our live service titles).

QA also collaborates with feature owners to define the test cases for specific functionalities, provide developers with "pre-integration" testing to identify potential issues or reproduce existing issues before they're committed to source control, coordinate build deliveries to external development partners, and measure, track, and create reports for the game team about milestone deliveries.

Back when I was at Torus, QA was hands-on testing, finding issues, and helping send builds out for test. We had external testers there as well. But at Firemonkeys, QA mostly involves sending email, spreadsheets, and status reports, though I still help send builds. My current position is much more administrative than hands-on, and that's a shift I was ready for when I came to this studio. I was really ready to have more responsibility and the chance to learn new things.

As far as the Romanian QA operation goes (which is the one I deal with), it's a lot like you would imagine—a huge building full of people testing away. Now,

EA Romania isn't just QA. It has the console and mobile development units, central project management groups, a strong local quality engineering team, first-party publishing, training coordination, handset procurement service (i.e., buying new devices), and so on. In terms of QA, they have QA project leads and QA project managers assigned to specific projects there, and of course lots of testers who come in and work on certain projects. They go through a test plan over and over all day, looking for whatever request we've directed them to address in the new builds. Examples of things we ask them to check out include any new feature or content we've added that day, or maybe someone on the development team has found an issue and we'd like QA to investigate it further. The *Real Racing 3* test team consists of ten to twelve people, but they cycle through people quite a bit as they're always bringing in new trainees.

As far as when QA typically enters the development process, that depends on the QA capacity of the studio. We're testing constantly for *Real Racing 3* because the game has six-week updates. For a lot of these updates, the planning is already done by the time we're in test. Still, it'd be great for QA to be brought in earlier in the development process—perhaps even at the planning stage—to pre-assess potential problems. We might be able to point out possible problems down the line and prevent an issue from ever being there in the first place (and thus needing correcting). Traditionally, QA comes in to test the build once it's ready to go, but it'd be really good to get QA eyes on a project early to understand how the features are supposed to work in the end product. To be fair, EA is making steps toward getting this to happen. I have some involvement with the early stages of *Real Racing 3* updates, and I know my input is valued. It'd help a lot, too, if I actively tried to be more involved.

Being able to spot a potential problem is something that comes with experience. For example, because I've been working on *Real Racing 3* for so long, I've gotten a good feel for what's going to work with the existing structure. In the game, we have a lot of events/quests that happen on set dates. As you can imagine, we have a big problem with people time changing in our game, because they can change the date on their device. Sometimes, though, this is accidental, with people changing time zones due to travel. But this is the kind of thing QA can see ahead of time, because we know the game so well.

How is QA structured generally?

The entry-level QA position involves pure testing. The person just comes in and tests the game all day, working through the test plan and test cases.

Sometimes the test plan could involve just running at walls in the game, or doing random stuff. This is called "ad hoc testing."

The level up from the entry-level position is a lead, and leads manage groups of testers and tell them what test cases to focus on. In the case of Firemonkeys, our leads are in Romania.

The test cases that the leads manage come from the next level up—the quality analyst—and that's what I do. Quality analysts are the ones who come up with the test plans. We ask the development team exactly how the game is supposed to work, and then we create test plans and cases from that information and our own experience playing the game.

The level up from the quality analyst is the QA manager, who manages everyone in the studio and handles the communication from higher up in the company.

A technically accurate representation of how QA is structured at EA would look like this: we have three QA job trees, and all branch off into different types of QA. First is quality testing (e.g., Core QA lead), which focuses on issue detection and containment. Second is quality management (e.g., Core QA), which focuses on coordinating and executing the test plan. Quality testing and quality management represent a lot of the roles in Romania QA. Finally, there's quality design (e.g., Dev QA), which is focused on issue prevention and containment. My current role lies within the quality design tree.

In terms of my daily job duties, I look at my email when I first get in to see if anything crazy is happening that I need to attend to right away. By "crazy" I mean a serious issue on the live build (i.e., the one in the online store) that's popped up overnight. Having a live service game keeps things very interesting in that way. With a crazy problem, we have the opportunity to push fixes with data or make server changes. If we can't do either of those things to fix the issue and it's serious enough, we might have to fix it in the client and release a hotfix build. Usually, though, things are pretty quiet.

After that, I check to see how many new bugs were reported overnight—we send builds out for test every workday. I'll assign the new bugs to the tech lead, and he'll then assign them to the rest of the development team. We might then have a daily status report so that the team knows how many bugs are open for the update we're working on. It's a standardized report among all three projects in the studio, and it's mostly designed to inform the senior people about project status—if everything is on track or is at risk. I'll also go over the status of every feature we're developing, and I do that by looking at the new build that's been created that morning. There are also the various meetings in between all this and the stand-up meetings with the leads where we just talk about what we're doing that day. I'll also test the current build when I have a chance.

What qualities make for an effective QA lead?

I think you need to be able to learn quickly. You also need to be able to take the initiative, to make sure stuff gets done, because it can be really, really easy to let things fall through the cracks. It actually helps to be something of a microman-ager. Good communication skills help a lot too—especially at Firemonkeys—because we're always communicating with the Romanian team. Even though the Romanians speak English, it's their second or even third language, and so there'll be times when I have to be really careful about how I explain some-thing. Even though a given conversation may happen just through text on a screen, I can actually tell when they're not getting the point even if they say they are. It's really important to make sure something gets tested properly, and good communication skills are key to guaranteeing that happens.

To give you a sense of how much we depend on effective communication, here's an example. Throughout a given day, people will ask me to ask the Romanian team to test certain things that have just been added to the game or to squash a bug. So I'll send the request to the test team. When they get into the office to start their day, they'll have flagged emails of things they need to do. We also have a group chat going with the leads over there, and we'll discuss what's going on throughout the day and what they need to test. We also exchange notes about what they did with the builds that we sent.

How would you describe the management structure in your company?

On my team, it's fantastic. I came onto the project when it was a well-established live title, so I didn't see how things were at the start (from what I've heard, it was a little hectic). We release feature updates every six weeks, which is an incredibly tight schedule if you consider how much stuff we manage to pack into each update. The leads on my team are very aware of our capabilities and really listen to input when deciding on the scope of a feature. When something is looking a bit sketchy, instead of shipping a subpar product, we push it to the next update. It's not a luxury that a lot of game teams have, but we take full advantage of it.

I don't have much contact with management above my leads. We have weekly stand-up meetings at the end of each Friday—beer o'clock—but no real one-on-one situations. That being said, the leads on my team seem quite transparent with stuff happening behind the scenes, and we have a pretty good idea about the future of our project.

I also have a QA manager who I report to directly, and he manages the QA operation for the entire studio (seventeen QA employees, some of whom are regular full-time and some of whom are temporary full-time). He has quite a bit on his plate.

How would you describe the workflow in your company?

Because my team works on a tight schedule, everyone has well-established workflows and responsibilities. We repeat them over and over, and it's become incredibly efficient. From what I understand, the high-level aspect of an update is planned months before the development work begins. A few weeks before we start planning sprints, the leads will break the process down further, although if it's a new feature design it'll have to be fleshed out quite a bit during this period. Then it becomes a juggling act: there are certain members of the team who focus on feature development for a future update, while other members might be bug fixing for the previous one. There are usually spaces in between where we can throw everyone at one thing or another, but those spaces are brief. And while all of this is happening, we might have an issue on the live version in the store that needs fixing. There are bits of the process where it's super chaotic, but I think overall we manage it pretty well.

How does the workflow differ when working on different types of games (e.g., different genres, AAA versus casual games, etc.)?

In my experience, workflow is usually tied to a team rather than the type of game. For example, I worked on seven different titles when I was at Torus Games, and although they were a combination of handheld, console, PC, and mobile games, the development structure was always similar and followed the Waterfall model. I think this was because Torus focused on licensed titles and essentially they were "developers for hire." As a result, they had to outline the entire game in a design document to please publishers. But it's also the way they had always functioned, so it'd be very difficult to break out of that routine.

The *Real Racing 3* team that I'm on now takes more of an Agile approach, and we work in two-week sprints. It's actually very different from the Torus way of doing things.

The QA at Priceless Games was different in another way. Priceless is a tiny studio—maybe four or five people—and I was the only QA person who was available to them on a regular basis. This would be once or twice a week, depending on when they needed me. It was really casual. In fact, I don't even know if I ever had a contract. The job was purely online. I worked from home and logged my hours. But those were also friends of mine, and the job helped me get in at Torus because I had previous experience.

At Torus I was really a hands-on tester. There were three of us—two QAs and a lead—and we simply split up the workload because a lot of the time we'd be developing a game that was going to be released on four different platforms (Wii, Xbox 360, PS3, and DS). It was a lot of stuff to cover.

At Firemonkeys, I'm on the management side of things, which involves much less testing and a lot more sending of emails. The big advantage here is that EA offers a lot of support. If something goes wrong, they'll bring someone in to help. QA and development at a smaller studio doesn't have that, which is why smaller studios have crunch more often.

What are the most significant internal challenges you face in your job?

From my experience prior to joining Firemonkeys, QA isn't seen as a hugely important part of the game development process. For a lot of people, it's an afterthought. As a result, it's always a bit of a struggle to get myself included in discussions—and my opinion heard—during the development process. Getting QA feedback early on is important; QA is coming from the perspective of the player after all.

Another challenge is that it can be hard to approach members of the development team with issues, especially if they've worked really hard on something. They don't want to be told there's a problem with the work they did, so it can be quite intimidating if they respond badly. It really wears you down when you're constantly dealing with the negative aspects of a project, that is, giving people bad news. The key to doing this well is trying to be as nice as possible. Usually, I'll keep an eye on the build as it's compiling, and if I see it fail a few times then I'll say something. Most of the time, people are incredibly apologetic about the fail. Still, everyone's always nervous to see me because they think that something horrible has happened even if I'm coming up to tell them good news. So I just try to be as relaxed as possible, which is something you learn on the job.

Fortunately, my current team is excellent, so I don't have to give them bad news very often. And when I do, they take it gracefully. I also think I've just gotten used to the dynamic of having to be the bearer of bad news.

Does QA ever get credit or blame for a game's success or failure?

Well, with *Real Racing 3* we tend to be pretty anxious on launch day (i.e., when our update goes live on the mobile store), which happens every six weeks because that's our update schedule. We usually try to time things such that the update comes out when we're just getting into work. That way, if there's a serious issue, we're going to know about it pretty quickly and we have the capacity to push a patch or do a hotfix build. But I don't think there's ever been a moment at Firemonkeys when people have pointed the finger at QA for a mistake. We have all kinds of procedures for critical and non-critical things. For example, if we need to release a hotfix build, we have to fill out a form explaining why. Hotfixes almost always happen because an issue didn't appear in a test account (i.e., an account with cheat access). With something like that, there's no possible way to catch the error unless you develop a whole new testing procedure, so there's really no one to blame. Situations like that are still stressful, though, but definitely not the end of the world, and not QA's fault.

What are the external challenges you face in your job?

Obviously it's not great to frequently get the blame for problems making it into the live version. I see plenty of players saying that if there's an issue present in the game, it's because QA didn't catch it. This is a huge misconception. There are deadlines that need to be met, and issues are prioritized based on risk. The issues that make it to the top of the list get fixed, and, of course, some issues never do. The development process is a lot more complicated than most people think, and that's especially true for QA.

Another challenge is that most people outside of the industry—and sometimes even people in the industry—think that I have a dream job, that I get paid to just play games all day. It's kind of frustrating to always have to explain that QA isn't that simple, and that we actually have a lot of responsibility in the development process.

What sorts of workplace changes would you implement if given the opportunity?

One workplace change I'd like to see is more time between game updates. Even two extra weeks per update would give us more time to test and find issues, or help us tackle our bug backlog. Every team handles overscoping/feature creep a little differently, and the process completely depends on the capabilities and dynamics of the team. Even the other project teams at my studio handle the phenomenon differently from my team. We have a tendency to try to fit more and more stuff into every game update. I'd say this is pretty common in development, and it's called a few things, depending on where you are in the development cycle. In the beginning, it's termed "overscoping," and toward the end it's called "feature creep." My team does it pretty regularly, but we've gotten very good at readjusting the amount of work along the way to fit the schedule. We don't move our dates unless we absolutely have to, or if a submission is late. That can happen if Apple, for example, is particularly busy reviewing games.

Overscoping exists in part because the leads from the various development disciplines each want something to be in the next project, and they're not necessarily thinking about what the other leads want. Sometimes that something makes it in, sometimes it doesn't, and sometimes it's brought back later for a future update. There's a lot of give and take, and so even when the feature list is the final one coming out of a planning meeting, it can often end up being quite wrong in terms of what actually makes it into the final build. Ultimately, everything gets broken up into tasks in a planning meeting, the tasks get assigned to people, and those individual people have to determine how long it's going to take to finish their assignments. If the projected time ends up being way too long, then things get pushed back or cut from the scope. The thing is, there's *always* too much. Everyone's so ambitious that overscoping is inevitable. So, even though we try to be wary about where we're going to be time-wise when we're feature complete, we also always expect to be overscoped.

In QA, we plan out testing capacity around this very issue. We follow up with other people on the team when we think stuff is done, that is, when what we see in the build appears complete. We go and make sure with the point person that this is indeed the case, and then we make sure QA jumps on it immediately and tests the crap out of it. Inevitably, stuff ends up getting cut, but it could end up in the next update, so it's not a complete waste of time.

While overscoping happens toward the front of development, crunch happens at the end because people think they have time to do something and it turns out they don't. When that happens, most of the time stuff gets pushed back or out. People don't stay past closing time unless they badly want the feature, because they have to think of how it's going to affect the other people on the team (like us in QA). If things do get tight or a submission is late, Romanian QA will work weekends. They're usually pretty responsive, actually, because they get paid overtime there. When it looks like they're going to have to work on the weekend, we'll tell the Romanians to gather a list of people and we'll let them know by Thursday if they'll need to.

The thing about crunch is that it's really nobody's fault. Overtime for QA is usually just because the build is compiling, and it really needs to be sent out for test. So, we'll stay back, wait for it to finish compiling, and then send it off. The worst possible scenario in that case is if we wait a few hours and the build still fails. Of course, this is only during the week—never on the weekends. At Firemonkeys, we don't work weekends.

Another facet of crunch is that sometimes a given department just doesn't have the capacity to do the work. For instance, until recently, we didn't have enough designers on our project for the amount of work we needed done, and so the ones we did have would always have to work overtime in order to make things happen. With *Real Racing 3*, we've established a quality bar with our fans, and they expect updates to be more than just mere bug fixes. And a bug fix wouldn't make any money anyway, so updates have to come with content. The more stuff you put in, the more expectation you create for yourself, raising the bar even higher. I think people just like to reach for the sky instead of playing it safe.

Of course, in addition to people intentionally coming up with new features to add, there are also things that pop up in development unexpectedly, which can lead to overtime (e.g., a new iPhone hardware/firmware release, where essentially we get the device/update at the same time as consumers and are thus unable to verify things during development; third-party dependencies, such as a new Facebook SDK release; etc.). You could always create a basic update and then plan to put stuff in it if you have more time. The result would be the same, however: overreaching, in this case due to the unexpected.

Which companies or ways of working (both within and outside of the game industry) do you look to for inspiration?

I'm a big fan of Naughty Dog. I love their games, and their work culture seems pretty unique. Apparently, they don't have much middle management because they were acquired by Sony ages ago and have been able to keep a lot of that business side out of development. That sounds pretty cool and is something I'd like to experience. It's the idea of maybe not feeling the business side of things quite so much. It'd be really interesting to be a part of a team that didn't have that pressure, because that kind of business push leads to having to rush into things and pack a lot of stuff into games that maybe wouldn't normally make it to market. There's always pressure to make money, especially coming from executive-level management. So, it'd be cool to not have that and be able to be less rushed and more creative in development and testing.

What are some of your notable quality of life issues, both routine and exceptional?

A routine issue would have to be crunch time, of course. This is a staple of the industry, and a really shitty one. While it obviously depends entirely on the nature of your workplace and project deadlines, I'd wager that everyone who has worked in games has crunched at one time or another or was expected to do so (unpaid, of course). I haven't experienced it much at my current workplace, happily. There've only been a few times when I've stayed back to wait for and send builds. At Torus, it was much more common, and lots of people on the team regularly stayed back to get stuff done. The reason for that, I think, was the team size and the tight deadlines. We were thirty to forty people depending on the day, and we were creating games from scratch and finishing them in three to four months. As a result, we were always under a lot of pressure to make enough money to keep going.

Keep in mind, too, that Torus is a family business. When I was there, the founder would go overseas to different conferences, and he knew lots of people in the industry. So he'd go and get jobs for the studio. His three sons, who worked at the studio, would handle a lot of the development decision making. Each time the founder would get us a job, we'd have work for the next six months. And then he'd have to go out and look for jobs again. So there was always tremendous pressure to get the games done in order to keep the company alive. I don't know how, but some of the guys would work crazy amounts of overtime. I don't know if they got compensated, but I assume they did because they worked there for a long time. Torus had a lot of people who had been there for ten, even fifteen years.

Here at Firemonkeys, we don't crunch like that. Firemonkeys is really supportive about having a good work/life balance. Also, because we're owned by EA, there are always other projects. We're covered by the fact that the company doesn't live or die on a single game.

What are some of your notable career progression issues?

I'm really enjoying my job in QA at the moment, but I think I'd like to get involved with project management in the future. EA is a really big company and so there are plenty of opportunities for transition/progression. Nailing down what you want and which team you'd like to work on is a bit more difficult. I feel like I want to be more a part of the creative side of games, looking forward and making something instead of criticizing it. When you're in QA, you're always on the negative side of things, pointing out problems. A role just came up to be a QA project manager here. That'd still be in QA, but it would be a management role. But there are always positions opening up. We have positions called development directors or development managers, and they're essentially project managers. EA is really good about communicating the possibilities for training and moving into different areas. QA is really good for that, too, because you're always talking with most of your team members as part of your job. There might be an issue with code, or there might be a sound issue, and so you end up pretty much getting friendly with every single person on the team. It's really good for getting a base of experience and a network, and if people have something open in their area, you'll know about it and the people there will be happy to help you. So QA is definitely good in that way.

On another note, I actually love the idea of working on my own games with my partner and friends. Of course, I've seen how difficult that can be, so it might be something I think about further down the line.

What are the challenges facing the industry over the next decade?

Diversity, definitely. We need lots of different types of people making games in order for games to reach lots of different types of people. It's a pretty basic concept, and one that's been talked about plenty. From my perspective, the shift is happening. Even in my studio, I look around and see quite a few women and people with diverse cultural backgrounds. I've also seen more support networks appear every year, and that's really fantastic. For example, I'm part of a "women in games and tech support" group, so I get to see a lot of stuff happening behind the scenes. I'm exposed to a lot more than most people in the industry, and I think that's really awesome. If I didn't have that group, I'd feel a lot more isolated and unwanted as a woman in the game industry. The support group makes me feel like I have people who understand me and what I do. I can even turn to them for advice if I need to. Mainly, having the group is comforting. Seeing other women's experiences in the industry and seeing how those experiences shape them, what they've done about problems, and so forth, is helpful. The women in the group band together to support each other. It makes me feel really good knowing that the group is there if I need them.

▶ DISCUSSION

QA forms a curious and important nexus in the labor of game development. For one thing, the discipline is often an entry point for a number of careers in the industry, largely because no special technical or aesthetic skills are required. Moreover, other disciplines (e.g., design and producing) are readily accessible to people with QA experience thanks to how closely QA works with other production units in the development process. At the same time, QA is also one of the most volatile areas in the industry, with employees often hired quickly during project ramp-up, then terminated just as quickly once the product ships. Ironically, the very quality that so readily enables industrial entrée—minimal specialized skills—is precisely what makes entry-level QA so fungible: easy in, easy out, easily replaced. "Out" does not always mean "out of a job," however. On rare occasions, it can mean "out of QA and into another area of production." In fact, this is what many entry-level QA employees hope for, namely, that QA will be a stepping-stone to more interesting, lucrative, and satisfying work elsewhere in the company or industry.

These interrelated phenomena raise a host of conceptual and practical problematics, not the least of which involve career advancement, employee loyalty, and institutional memory. How, for example, does career advancement occur—and how is employee loyalty cultivated—when employees are let go almost as soon as they are hired? Similarly, where does the institutional and practical memory associated with the QA discipline reside when the outflow of labor and experience is so dramatic?

Along these lines, it is also interesting to note that the employees with the deepest and arguably most important knowledge of a game—that of the user experience (i.e., what the consumer pays for)—happen to be among the least valued economically in terms of salary and retention. We can only speculate about how this impacts game development, both in terms of industrial growth and practice (immediately and over time) and with regard to game content and the play experience. In other words, in what ways does this kind of extreme labor volatility affect aesthetic, thematic, and experiential innovation within game development studios? One place these issues clearly play out is in the hiring and advancement practices in QA, as well as in the rationales that inform those practices.

Consider, for example, that a particularly unusual feature of QA is that it often engages a nonprofessional and unpaid public as part of its workforce. There are playtesters who participate in the QA process simply for the opportunity of a sneak peek at an upcoming game, the pleasure of participating in the development process, and even as a favor to a friend or colleague. And the question of compensation is a challenging one. Certainly, the industrial logic of withholding compensation is understandable: apart from the cost savings, test results may be skewed due to the tester's desire to keep getting paid. Forgoing compensation for the sake of design, however, ensures that game development is always exploitative, no matter how considerate a company is toward its paid employees. The labor power of the volunteer is being monetized, with the volunteer ultimately paying doubly for the privilege of participating in the development process—once in the form of the labor itself, and once for the game should the volunteer choose to purchase it once it has been packaged and shipped.

As VanEseltine intimates, developers often value inexperienced playtesters—or testers new to a specific project—over experts, because inexperienced testers are most akin to the eventual customer of the game. Consequently, employee retention is a low priority in QA compared to other disciplines (e.g., programming), where experience and institutional knowledge have intrinsic value. As QA personnel become increasingly involved in the development of a game, the assumption is that their bias in favor of the existing experience becomes harder and harder to overcome. In other words, the feedback becomes increasingly less likely to resemble that of the "brand-new player." This creates a difficult dynamic, with a project's best and most experienced QA personnel potentially providing the most problematic feedback.

The reality, of course, is more nuanced. Clearly, accomplished testers have the ability to roleplay as a "brand-new player" on demand and in multiple (and very particular) ways: the newbie, the cheater, the completionist, the berserker, and so on. The actual new player, on the other hand, is genuinely green when it comes to assessing a game (and thus has only one way to approach the evaluative tasks), but is also green when, for example, it comes to recognizing undocumented development problems. The value of minimally paid or unpaid QA workers, then, seems to reside at least partially in their ability to do word-of-mouth promotion, a marketing tactic with a potentially tremendous return on investment. By involving articulate, passionate, and largely uncompensated testers in QA, studios can foment good buzz about a forthcoming title by some of fandom's most influential members—all for the price of a few pizzas (if that).

QA employees also often face work—depending on studio size and structure—that is at once expansive and interdisciplinary (e.g., documenting collision detection bugs in the morning, then testing a co-op play mode in the afternoon) and isolating and monotonous (e.g., avoiding discussions with other employees so as not to contaminate their assessments of the game's latest revisions). At times QA needs to exist essentially independently of the rest of the development sphere so that QA personnel can approach a game's systems with a critical eye. This critical distance, however—which not infrequently is accompanied by resentment from coworkers who feel as if their work is under constant QA scrutiny—can sometimes lead to tedium and stress, as well as to professional carelessness due to a lack of connection with the company's other employees. These workplace conditions, too, likely contribute to the volatility of QA, as structural interconnection and dependence generally contribute to both overall and local stability in organizations of all kinds.[2]

Of course, given the general economic and technological transience of the game industry, it is hardly surprising that a number of its basic job classifications—not just those in QA—are equally impermanent. Indeed, one of the themes of nearly all the interviews in this volume is that virtually every job in the game industry has a fugaciousness about it. The game industry is nothing if not unstable, from its raw materials (and especially the commodity prices of those materials) and labor practices, to its shipped products and fan communities.

We also see in these two interviews that QA has become a global discipline, which is to say, both more and less multilingual and multicultural. EA's aggregation of its QA into just a handful of sites around the world, for example, suggests that cultural and linguistic difference may not be particularly important in terms of the business of QA, where English is still the lingua franca of commerce. At the same time, however, even games built under modest budgets are increasingly expected to have gone through a localization process, whether through in-house talent, professional outsourcing, or crowdsourcing. The fact that a game plays equally well (despite language differences) in Singapore, Sweden, or Saudi Arabia is only possible due to the homogenizing effects of globalization . . . and skilled QA teams.

Notably, both of the interviews here separately confirm and together emphasize the importance of excellent transdisciplinary communication skills in the game industry, and especially in QA. Solving problems across international boundaries often pales in comparison to solving problems among corporate divisions (e.g., art, legal, coding, management), so it makes sense that QA—tasked as it is with identifying all manner of problems, locating their sources no matter the discipline, and requiring fixes—has become increasingly responsible for facilitating problem-resolution strategies at all stages of the game development process and across all units. Such increased attention to the importance of excellent transdisciplinary communication skills suggests that the game industry may be realizing that great games emerge out of equal parts inspired design, organized work, and effective corporate communication.

Even when AAA game studios move aggressively in the direction of the Hollywood blockbuster, that is, away from dialogue-heavy drama and plot development and toward less culturally specific experiences (i.e., action and explosions), they are still aiming to streamline their development processes to the greatest extent possible. To do so not only decreases the number of resources needed for localization and finalization, but also expands a game's potential global appeal, opening it up to new and potentially more afford-able QA resources (e.g., digital sound effects rather than voice actors).

The paradox of the economic competitiveness of the game industry and the closeness of its workers and their development communities (e.g., the independent development community in Boston) is also worth not-ing. Despite the widespread use of legal mechanisms for maintaining secrecy and gaining competitive advantage in the marketplace, the game industry is replete with career networking and community resources such as discussion forums, listservs, industry meet-and-greets, and the like, producing what amounts to an underground job economy parallel-ing the formal one.

Finally, we would be remiss if we did not call attention to the fact that both VanEseltine and Findlay mention diversity as a prominent and continuing issue in game development. As other interviews in this book indicate, the issue is hardly specific to QA, and it is certainly worthy of deeper and more sustained study. At the very least, VanEseltine provides some rather telling examples of how male bias tends to manifest itself on a day-to-day basis in the industry and its tributaries. Given the strategic accessibility of QA in most game companies—that is, the ease with which non-professional and entry-level professional consultants can have a measurable impact on how games are shaped—one avenue for diversifying the game industry work-place (and games themselves) is by bringing in more testers and related per-sonnel from underrepresented backgrounds. In so doing, we suspect, the industry-wide understanding of "quality" might expand to ensure the devel-opment not only of functional and fun games, but also of more equitable, diverse, and creative workplaces.

▶ NOTES

1   The Entertainment Software Rating Board (ESRB) rating T—for "teen"—has an age floor of thirteen years old. For more information on the ESRB and its ratings, see http://www.esrb.org.

2   That said, interconnection can also contribute to instability, as ostensibly local problems can become global in an integrated and interdependent system.

▶ WORKS CITED

Bibliography

"Transitions: Gamasutra Salary Survey 2014." *Gamasutra: The Art & Business of Making Games*. UBM Tech. 22 Jul. 2014. 1–8. Web. 10 Oct. 2015. <http://www.gamesetwatch.com/2014/09/05/GAMA14_ACG_SalarySurvey_F.pdf>

VanEseltine, Carolyn, and Frank Wu. *Revolution 60: The Chessboard Lethologica*. Boston: Giant Spacekat, 2014. Web.

Gameography

Barbie: Dreamhouse Party. Torus Games. Little Orbit, 2013. Multiple platforms.

The Beatles: Rock Band. Harmonix Music Systems/Pi Studios. MTV Games, 2009. Multiple platforms.

Beet the Devil. Carolyn VanEseltine. Carolyn VanEseltine, 2011. Personal computer.

Call of Duty (franchise). Infinity Ward/Treyarch/Sledgehammer Games. Activision/Square Enix, 2003-present. Multiple platforms.

The Croods: Prehistoric Party! Torus Games. D3 Publisher, 2013. Multiple platforms.

Dance Central. Harmonix Music Systems. MTV Games/Microsoft Game Studios, 2010. Microsoft Xbox 360.

Dance Central 2. Harmonix Music Systems. Harmonix Music Systems, 2011. Microsoft Xbox 360.

Dance Central 3. Harmonix Music Systems/Backbone Entertainment. Harmonix Music Systems, 2012. Microsoft Xbox 360.

Dance Dance Revolution (franchise). Konami. Konami, 1998–2016. Multiple platforms.

Does Canned Rice Dream of a Napkin Heap? Carolyn VanEseltine. Antholojam 1: A Golden Age Sci-Fi Game Anthology, 2014. Personal computer.

Fallen London. Failbetter Games. Failbetter Games, 2009. Multiple platforms.

Falling Skies: Planetary Warfare. Torus Games. Little Orbit, 2014. Multiple platforms.

GemStone IV. Simutronics. GEnie/AOL/Simutronics, 1988. Personal computer.

Green Day: Rock Band. Harmonix Music Systems/Demiurge Studios. MTV Games, 2010. Multiple platforms.

How to Train Your Dragon 2: The Video Game. Torus Games. Little Orbit, 2014. Multiple platforms.

Lego Rock Band. Harmonix Music Systems/Traveller's Tales/Backbone Entertainment. Warner Bros. Interactive Entertainment/MTV Games, 2009. Multiple platforms.

Ollie Ollie Oxen Free. Carolyn VanEseltine. Carolyn VanEseltine, 2014. Personal computer.

One Eye Open. Carolyn VanEseltine and Caelyn Sandel. Carolyn VanEseltine and Caelyn Sandel, 2010. Personal computer.

Real Racing 3. Firemonkeys Studios. EA Games, 2013. Multiple platforms.

Revolution 60. Giant Spacekat. Giant Spacekat, 2014. iOS.

Rise of the Guardians: The Video Game. Torus Games. D3 Publisher, 2012. Multiple platforms.

Rock Band (franchise). Harmonix Music Systems. Harmonix Music Systems, 2007–2015. Multiple platforms.

Rock Band Blitz. Harmonix Music Systems. Harmonix Music Systems, 2012. Multiple platforms.

Rock Band 3. Harmonix Music Systems/Backbone Entertainment. MTV Games/Electronic Arts/Mad Catz, 2010. Multiple platforms.

Slam Bolt Scrappers. Fire Hose Games. Fire Hose Games, 2011. Personal computer.

Sunless Sea. Failbetter Games. Failbetter Games, 2015. Multiple platforms.

Train Conductor 2: USA. The Voxel Agents. The Voxel Agents, 2012. Multiple platforms.

Turbo: Super Stunt Squad. Torus Games. D3 Publisher, 2013. Multiple platforms.

Softography

Adobe Flash (http://www.adobe.com/products/flash.html)

6

Audio

INTRODUCTION

The audio discipline is responsible for creating or procuring a game's audio assets, which may include sound effects, music, and dialogue. Depending on the size of the game studio, audio personnel may specialize in one or more of these asset areas, and regardless of specialization often work closely with designers and other creative stakeholders on both individual game moments (e.g., a particular sound effect) and across the game as a whole (e.g., the musical score). Because high-quality sound files require large amounts of memory at runtime and on storage media, audio personnel in particular rely on compression tools and techniques to achieve the best-quality work in the smallest possible computational and storage footprint.

Audio work is often done freelance, though some companies are able to support in-house audio departments with multiple full-time employees. Because audio assets can be designed modularly—that is, they are discrete units that can be plugged in where and when they are needed—they can be developed off-site and integrated into a game with little advance notice. To some degree, this is by design: not only are a player's actions difficult to predict (making the apt insertion of long audio elements nearly impossible), but game development itself is a highly iterative process, which limits an audio

255

designer's ability to make final decisions until quite late in the development cycle. Consequently, sound effects, music, and dialogue will sometimes be among the last pieces of content added to a game.

Typically, audio personnel hold one of two position classes—designer or director—with the designer position often subdivided into specialties such as sound design/engineering, music composition, and voice direction. Like the leads or directors in other disciplines, the audio director's role is largely supervisory and administrative.

In terms of audio specializations, sound designers/engineers are responsible for creating any sound other than music or dialogue (e.g., the footfalls of the main character, the firing sounds of alien weaponry, menu navigation clicks and tones), and they source their own sounds (e.g., recording a live gunshot sound at a firing range), rely on preexisting libraries (e.g., taking existing Lucasfilm audio library sounds to recreate authentic *Star Wars* noises), or work with a combination of the two to create a game's soundtrack.

Composers are responsible for creating a game's musical score, either by composing entirely new material or by arranging or adapting existing musical material. Composers working on big-budget and large-scope games may have a live orchestra perform an original score, whereas composers on smaller games will use a MIDI interface to trigger samples of a variety of musical instruments. Music may also come in the form of a licensed soundtrack, especially if a game ties into a well-known film, television series, or entertainment genre with a commonly associated musical style (e.g., a Western-themed game with an Ennio Morricone soundtrack). These tracks, too, need to be edited and fit into the game. An audio designer specializing in music will be responsible for creating and sourcing musical beats, as well as working with designers and programmers to trigger that music at the correct moments. Composers also work with sound designers and the voice personnel to develop an overall audio mix, where the three elements blend together.

Voice directors are responsible for recording any spoken dialogue for cinematics (aka "cutscenes") and AI "barks" (the random unscripted utterances spoken procedurally by non-player characters). Voice directors may also help cast voice actors and direct them in the recording studio, often in conjunction with a game's other creative stakeholders.

According to the 2014 Gamasutra Salary Survey, audio personnel earn an average annual salary of $95,682 in the aggregate ("Transitions" 4). Those with three to six years of experience earn an average of $60,227 annually, while those with more experience earn an average of $118,750 per year (Ibid.). Audio directors with more than six years of experience earn an average annual salary of $109,500 (Ibid.). Finally, male audio personnel average $98,500 per annum, while female employees average $67,500 annually (Ibid.).

Jared Emerson-Johnson
Music Supervisor

Jared Emerson-Johnson is a computer game industry veteran specializing in sound and music. He entered the industry through Bay Area Sound, where he has now worked for more than a dozen years. He has operated in various capacities there, including as a composer, sound designer, and voice director. His current position, music supervisor, involves overseeing the completion of many of the tasks that were once his to complete, and he still occasionally performs some of those tasks himself. Bay Area Sound provides work on contract, and as a result, Emerson-Johnson has contributed assets to games created by Atari, Activision, Double Fine Productions, Electronic Arts, Jantze Studios, Kabam, Leapfrog, LucasArts Entertainment, Microsoft, Sega, Sony, Telltale Games, Ubisoft, Zynga, and others. Among the many titles to which he has contributed are the *Sam & Max* franchise, *Wallace & Gromit's Grand Adventures, God of War, Star Wars: The Old Republic, The Walking Dead, The Wolf Among Us,* and most recently, *Tales from the Borderlands, Game of Thrones,* and *Firewatch.* He holds a BA (summa cum laude) in music from Cornell University.

* * * * *

How did you come to work in the game industry?

When I was finishing up college, I reached out to a handful of game composers and expressed an interest in game music. I was able to do an internship with one of them, Clint Bajakian, and it all sort of cascaded from there. At that time, I was more interested in working with music than specifically working in video games—games happened to be the most immediate opportunity available to me as I was entering the workforce. My background is in audio and music, and growing up I was a performance musician. While I was in college and taking more courses in composition, I developed a love of writing music, and that took over much of my musical life. When it came time to think about my future and jobs, I saw two main paths. If I wanted to pursue music after completing school, one path was in academia, being a music professor. Or I could try to do something in entertainment. My main hope coming out of school was to be able to make a living doing the thing I loved. It's interesting: when I first got into games, I wasn't thinking of it as a long-term career. It was sort of like, "Hey, games are cool. They're getting cooler as far as audio is concerned. There's more live music in games and more and more interesting artists writing music for games, so maybe that's a good option." At the time I saw games as a stepping-stone to film or some other kind of entertainment scoring. Then once I got into it, I fell in love with game audio, and the more I did it, the more I realized that I really liked the unique qualities of game music. So I never ended up actively pursuing a switch from games to film.

Going into the game industry, I was imagining staying for two years—five at the most. It's been thirteen now. That's how I got started. I wanted to work in music, and games seemed like a feasible way to make a living writing music. I liked the idea of writing music to go with stories and characters, so that was a draw as well. Unlike a lot of people who get into the industry because they love games and want to help make them, for me it was more a matter of where I could apply my music education and make a living from it. The love of the games themselves and the love of the unique qualities of game scoring came later for me.

A lot of people—especially people like my parents and older generations— still often ask me if I'll someday do film. I think it's because they relate to film more; they like to go to the movies. They don't really love or know video games well. At this point, my answer to their question is "nope." I've done a little bit of work on some short films and animated shorts, and I enjoyed it, but the interactivity of games is just so unique. What that means for music is that every new project's score is a distinct puzzle to crack, and there's a lot more to think about than just "what's the story, where are the beats, when does this and that happen, okay, now I'm going to score it."

With games, there are more options to consider for how to tackle different challenges, how you want to support the story, how you want to interface with the player. I really like thinking about those questions. I've been doing it for a while, but it never gets boring because every project is different. Each one is a new nut to crack, and I really like that. With film, on the other hand, obviously every movie is different, but you still just get the picture and you score the picture. I prefer working with interactive media that can branch in various ways and reconnect or twist depending on the actions of the player.

What else about the industry makes it a unique place to be a music director or a musician?

Interactivity is number one for sure; all games, by definition, are interacting with the player, and the player is affecting the flow of the game. Sometimes it's fairly linear; oftentimes it's not. Usually a game can go in any number of really wild directions, and the music has to follow and still make sense, still be part of the whole. It has to match pace with the action and mood, while not just cutting abruptly from one piece to another. A composer has to think about what "interactivity" means for each individual game. It's more than just "the player does this, then the game does that, then the player does something else." The medium itself is always changing. What a game "is" varies from one studio to the next. Moving from one project to another can be a wildly different product—it can feel like a completely different medium each time. Film, on the other hand, is always film. Sure, you can have an experimental film and different genres, but the basic scoring process is always more or less the same when scoring a linear medium. With games, the difference between a mobile puzzle game and a storytelling game like those that Telltale Games makes, or a shooter game where you're rampaging around—they're all quite different from each other, and the way the music interacts with the game is just as variable. That's what I mean about it feeling like a different medium depending on the project. I like that from one project to the next it feels like I'm starting a brand-new thing from the ground up. Every job is brand new.

You probably know that music production for a game is usually completely separate from sound effects and other kinds of audio production. I've done—and continue to do—both, and this is another thing I like about my work: even though sound effects and music are separate disciplines, they often need to coordinate with each other. That's why I took the time to learn how to do sound design earlier in my career in addition to music. I figured that it might come in handy if the people who initially hired me to do music for a game could also tap me for sound design when needed.

It didn't hurt that I had Clint Bajakian, who's an outstanding composer and sound designer, as a mentor in those early days. I built sound up into a second skill. It's useful for career purposes to be able to offer more than just one service; but, more importantly, being able to understand (and produce) both sides of the soundscape means I can design them to be complementary. It's not two people working in isolation and throwing their work together at the end of the project; it's integrated. That said, music and sound/audio production are different disciplines, as is voice production. In games, things often hinge on the voice work, which my company does as well. The voice, music, and sound effects are all separate, but there has to be a homogenous logic to the way they work together in the final product. It's incredibly valuable to be able to understand and create content in all three audio branches.

Another important difference between film score production and the audio work we do in games is that with film, composers generally come in at the end of production, that is, after there's at least a cut of the film. The composer may have done some early planning about basic schemes and ideas with the director, but the real work doesn't start until later in postproduction. With games, because of how they're often produced, there isn't usually time to let the audio wait until the end. Instead, you often get rolling earlier in development—well before the game is fully built out—and you can see the whole project (including the audio) taking shape as you're working on it. I like this because I feel like I can respond to the game more that way and be more involved in its mechanics. I also like allowing the composing process to be iterative rather than just getting the finished product and slapping something over it. This isn't always true—sometimes I do get called to plop stuff in at the end—but usually I'm working gradually with a team of people (not just the director and a couple of producers), including programmers, artists, and others, all interacting with the game as it emerges.

At the beginning of the game development process there's very little of the game to see—it's all typically sketches and lists and descriptions. Then you start building the world and sometimes even building the engine the game is going to run on. So early on, the development process in general is quite technical, and then the art starts rolling in. And once the art is coming in, then it's usually safe to start getting some of the first musical ideas in. There's a lot of creative give and take across the departments—at least in the best projects.

Given that you compose, do sound design, and provide voice direction, why is your title "music supervisor" instead of "audio director" or the like?

Bay Area Sound is a small contracting firm. My partner Julian Kwasneski and I split the work we get depending on its nature and our availability; Julian specializes in sound design and voiceover, while I mostly do music and occasionally some sound design and voice stuff. I generally set my own priorities and delegate tasks as necessary. The title of "music supervisor" has worked well for career purposes because it's something that clients can latch onto cleanly, rather than requiring me to explain the various things I do in a given day. There's also the psychology of hiring and attracting clients to consider. Music is often seen as more of an auteur thing with a persona that goes along with it. So my title is really useful for first introductions. It lets me say, "Hi. I'm Jared. I'm a music composer." People hear "music composer" and they instantly get the gist of what I do. Saying, "I'm a music composer, sound designer, voice director, implementer, and general audio manager" would be more accurate, but muddies the waters. It's easier to say, "I'm a music supervisor, and our company handles all aspects of audio production and implementation."

On a more personal level, music is my number one passion. In recent years we've been quite busy, and I've been working on two, three, sometimes even four large projects simultaneously. When you're producing that much music, there's just no time to do anything else. Especially lately, "music supervisor" is the most accurate description of what I do on a given day.

To what extent do game music composers use relatively conventional methods to do their creative work?

Some composers are quite traditional in their approach; others are a little more hybrid. It really comes down to personal preference. There are certainly some composers who never had any kind of classical training. The main thing I've found is that in order to be successful doing this work you have to absorb as many different styles as you can—every new method is another tool that might be useful for a future score. Even if your personal way of thinking about music might not change much over time, professionally you still need to be willing try new things. Personally, even if I'm creating procedural music, it's useful for me to first start thinking about the score in terms of melody, key, pitches, texture—a more traditional approach. I know there are plenty of people who thrive by working differently, who never sit down at the piano to work on something and instead have another method for arriving at their end product. Most of the composers I know still play and perform music, that is, they have physical instruments that they like to play—piano, guitar, violin. Even the specialist electronic composers I know generally play acoustic instruments too. I think most people still come to music from childhood with some kind of acoustic instrument. There are definitely young people who have gotten into the industry just by knowing how to compose on the computer, but again, it's crucial to be able to understand different musical traditions and methodologies when you need to.

To what extent does music theory come into play in your job?

Actually, I rely on music theory a fair amount. It was through my theory studies that I first started composing seriously in school. My theory education gave me a better context in which to understand and contextualize the underlying structures of all these pieces I'd been listening to my whole life. Suddenly I could see music from a builder's perspective. I could see elements coming together and making a whole—I could see the mind of the composer in each piece, and the decisions they made along the way. Once I was able to see all the little decisions that make a piece of music work in one way or another—to cause listeners to react in certain ways—I began to understand how composers actually and intentionally evoked those emotions.

This isn't to say that I sit around all the time thinking about music analysis and counterpoint the way you do in an academic setting, but having that knowledge as a foundation is always informing the way I compose. This is especially true for orchestral pieces because some of the rules of tonal theory really affect musical quality when you're dealing with live performance, orchestration, arrangement, etc. The more theory you know, the more it comes in handy.

The first advice I usually give people who ask me about breaking into the game audio industry is to study and listen to as many different artists as you can—and especially listen to types of music you may not like personally or haven't yet been exposed to. The more educated you can be about all the different choices other composers are making, the more equipped you'll be to give clients what they want (which is, after all, what you're being hired to do). Sure, there's an element of the process where it's you in your little crucible making personal artistic choices, but at the end of the day, you're serving the client. What you make may be cool—and it could even be something that's surprising to them, that they didn't even know they wanted—but in the end, they have to love what you've made for their project. So if they specifically want a bunch of Moog synthesizer parts in the scoring, you have to be able to make that happen. If they want a live orchestra or a jazz ensemble, it's up to you to make that happen for them as well.

Ask any working game composer and they'll probably have at least a passing knowledge of what their colleagues are into. In our field, you have to. It doesn't serve you professionally to close yourself off from the wide variety of musical styles or to specialize in just one. Personally, I like that I can have one project where I'm doing a jazz combo, then go on to another one where I'm doing a big synthy space western score, then another one that's in a traditional orchestral style, then another that's a retro 1980s NES chip tune. In the entertainment industries, it's advantageous to develop that kind of breadth because at some point down the line someone is going to ask you to do something that you've never done before. If you're already prepared with a wide base of knowledge, and if you know how to educate yourself quickly, you'll be able to dive right in and give them what they want.

Even though each project is different, is there a standard operating procedure for audio?

Almost always, the first thing I'll do with a new client is meet with them in person and talk in detail about what they specifically need for the project. I also try to figure out how much they've really thought about the music, if at all. Sometimes they've got it all worked out and they hand you a list and say, "Here's what we need." Other times, they haven't thought about the music at all and it becomes your job as composer to draw out of them what'll work best for the project they're designing. After that, I start looking at as much of the game as they have ready to show. Sometimes it's concept art; sometimes it's just a writer or designer in a room verbally describing their vision of the game. Things may change down the line a bit, but I get as much information as I can, then start making lists of what they need. Sometimes I make a full list of everything needed from the beginning to end of the game, and sometimes I just look at one little section of the game—maybe a small but important moment—and decide if we just need one piece of music or if there are ten different ways it could play out (which means writing a bunch of variations). We also have to figure out how dense to be with the interactivity of the music because that's often a guiding factor for how everything else gets made, sound/music-wise.

Once I've done that pre-production work with the client, I'll come back to my studio and choose a single piece of music that's representative of the game. I'll try to select something that's thematic or that's got something exciting or iconic, partly just to get the development team psyched up about the music. Once the project is underway, I'll be throwing new music at them daily, but the first delivery of music carries a lot of weight because it's going to be scrutinized by everybody. So I like to sit down and take the time to find something that I know will be evocative of the score as a whole. Usually it's a big moment in the game, maybe a climactic scene in a story game, or if it's a puzzle or narratively driven game, maybe the menu theme—anything that cuts to the heart of what the game is really about. Then I'll start sketching out ideas either on piano or whatever instrument seems appropriate and figure out what the theme might be. Next, I'll work on a MIDI sequencer—usually *Digital Performer*—to start building a template of instruments; that is, I figure out what instruments are going to be the sound of the game. Sometimes it's prescribed outright by the genre or the franchise; if it's an orchestral score, I'll just bring up a standard orchestra template. Usually, though, it's orchestral plus something else, or a jazz ensemble plus something else, so I have to figure out how to make it an iconic sound even though the music isn't a consistent genre. That's why putting together the instrumentation always takes longer than you might think it will—you want to make sure the instrumentation is iconic and essential, tailored to the project in question.

After working out a plan for instrumentation, I'll start actually putting the notes down. I'll put the piece together, dub stems of the audio out, then create a mix in *Pro Tools*. Oftentimes I'll do two or three different mixes— light, medium, and heavy versions—to accentuate different things, just to show how a single theme idea can work at different levels of intensity. Once that's done, I'll deliver it to the client; they'll listen to it and usually give me feedback. You hope it's, "Oh man, this game is going to be so cool!" That's the best feedback, but sometimes they'll have specific suggestions which I'll incorporate and it becomes an iterative process after that. I fill in the rest of the missing holes in the music spec, then go in and play a build of the game to see how all of it's working in the game.

For some projects, I'll do the implementation as well. I'll write and produce the music, then actually put it into the game myself and audition it there.

It's this process over and over throughout the course of production. It's going back into the office and meeting with people and getting their feedback on everything, seeing what's working and what's not. Sometimes stuff that was sounding great suddenly doesn't work anymore, because of a change in the design or because of a change in the order of game events. This takes time to fix and test, and there's the period when new stuff needs to be added because the client has come up with new objectives, storylines, and what have you. Sometimes large sections of a game will be cut, and then there'll be a question of what to do with any music that was written for the removed section (ideally, it gets repurposed elsewhere). You keep iterating and eventually you have a score and can play through the entire game, fine-tuning everything. As I previously mentioned, I'll usually end up making alternate versions of a lot of cues, because a piece may work great most of the time, but in special circumstances—say, an environment that should be really quiet—a softer or more ambient version is needed.

I think it was Clint Bajakian who often compared a game score to a series of pipes. Each cue is a different-shaped pipe—straight, U-bends, T-intersections, and so on—and they can all fit together in any number of combinations. The composer's job is to make sure that they all interface with each other in a way that seems like a coherent piece of music when they're assembled in real time during gameplay. When playing through a game, it shouldn't ever feel like a bunch of different pieces are starting and stopping. Instead, you want the player to be going along, experiencing different things, but hearing a through-line in the music, even though the game is actually stringing together different files in response to the choices the player is making. For most games, each piece needs to be able to dovetail into something else, then come back, twist, turn, stop, start. So rather than building a linear score that has a bunch of highs and lows like you would for a film or for a television show, you build a bunch of segments: some are high or low, some are short and shocking, and some are ambient and background-y. Then you just have to make sure that they can all move sensically from one into another. It's not that every piece has to fit with every other piece, but rather that all the known possible combinations will be covered and that their transitions will be as seamless as possible. It's a methodical process. It requires a lot of care and organization to do it right.

The process for doing sound design (as opposed to music composition) is similar, though sound lists are generally much longer. You know you need an entire suite of footstep sounds, for example, and multiple suites of ambient background sounds. It often takes less time to produce the individual assets than it does for musical cues, but there are so many more of them that it ends up being a comparable amount of work. As with pre-production on a musical score, you go in, meet with the designers, assess the client's needs, combine that with your own professional experience, and start creating the files they need. With most games, you can intuit a lot of what'll be needed on the sound front even before talking to anyone. You know you're going to need to make the ambient sounds for each space and setting, and probably footstep sounds too, for instance. The biggest difference between music and sound is that sound is almost always directly connected to something visually occurring onscreen. As a result, it requires extensive playtesting to identify and insert missing sounds in every scene. Since game assets change a fair amount during production, a good sound designer has to constantly reassess scenes to make sure no new content has appeared that requires audio treatment.

How have game music and sound changed during your time in the industry, and how have those changes altered the nature of your job?

Bay Area Sound has been around since 2001 and I've been employed there for my whole career. We've contracted for a lot of different companies over those years, but my paychecks are all from Bay Area Sound, which was founded by Clint Bajakian and my current partner Julian Kwasneski. Clint hired me for an internship while I was in college, and I ended up joining the company full-time in 2003. About a year later, Clint sold his share in the company and took a music supervision job at Sony, which left me as the one music guy. So I inherited most of the musical responsibilities at that point.

There were technical limitations up until the early 1990s that made real recorded audio impossible in most games. Eventually the disk space and streaming issues were solved and higher-quality audio started appearing in games more and more through the '90s, especially in PC games. I started working in game audio during the heyday of the Xbox and the PlayStation 2, and by that time it was finally possible for most consoles and PCs to ship quality audio (though there were still a few gaming SKUs that couldn't). Some of my earliest projects still used MIDI in lieu of actual audio files, just like they did on the Nintendo Entertainment System. I'd create the sample sets and write pieces of MIDI music.

It's also worth pointing out that in my early days there weren't nearly as many solid audio middleware applications as we have now. These programs let us do really cool things with audio, but back then it was really difficult. If you wanted to have a piece that could transition in seven different ways—go in one musical direction over here, another direction over there, or maybe add or subtract instruments to change the mood—all that usually had to be hand scripted by a programmer. And since programmers usually didn't have time to be writing code like this, rarely did composers have the opportunity to develop their work in this way. Now, of course, there are entire companies—for example, Wwise and FMOD—devoted to making software that can take your music and stylistic parameters and do a ton of cool interactive things, more or less out of the box. It's a lot easier to create an interactive soundscape now than it was when I started doing this work.

Interestingly, because it's now easier to produce high-quality sound, I think there's more scrutiny of the audio fidelity. Listeners expect a game to sound like a movie or an album, whereas before there was a lot of leeway and people were willing to forgive low-resolution audio quality because it was the norm. No one complained that *Super Mario Bros.* sounded so chippy. The first game composers were the programmers. At that time, all game audio was functional feedback. So the little "Doonk. Doonk. Doonk," in *Pong* was there to help players know what was going on, not to convey an emotional reaction. That started to change in the 1980s with Nintendo and the other third-generation consoles because they actually had real composers writing themes to accompany their games, but even then the function beneath the music was extremely different. Over the following fifteen years, technologies improved and the role of game audio followed suit. By the time I was starting my career, we were still limited by technology but the quality of game audio fidelity was improving exponentially. Developers and composers were thinking about game music more like they thought about film music. This was part of the reason I wanted to get into the business when I did; I was seeing this change happening. Especially with adventure games like the ones that LucasArts made in the 1990s, music was starting to help tell the game's story. It was thematic and connected to characters and emotional content. Whereas before it had been for background or creating a general mood, it was now starting to become cinematic, for lack of a better word.

What kinds of issues impact the production value of game sound?

The limitations on sound quality differ pretty widely from project to project. In 2007, for example, I was working on a game called *Tales of Monkey Island*, a pirate game that was a new sequel to the old adventure game franchise from LucasArts. In addition to a PC release, we were developing a version for WiiWare on the Nintendo Wii. At that time, most games on WiiWare were simple arcade, puzzle, and casual games. *Tales of Monkey Island*, however, actually had an interactive story and dialogue—thousands of lines and interactions. Because of the system limitations of WiiWare, a game couldn't be more than 40 megabytes, which is miniscule when you're talking about recorded audio. As a result, everything had to be drastically reduced. We ended up producing the whole score for the Wii with MIDI as if it was fifteen years earlier. When the PC release came out, we updated the game so that it had real audio. This wasn't that long ago and we were still being bound by hardware limitations, which is hard to imagine. That's just one anecdote, but my point is that every project has new limitations, some of which may be technical and some of which may be the result of prioritizations or budget. Some studios may not care as much about the audio as they do about something else, or maybe they care way more about the audio than something else. As a composer, what I'm able to do is directly impacted by these decisions. Budget is often a huge factor in how the score gets designed and put together.

What are the processes involved in hiring other musicians to play and record the music you write for a game?

The first thing to know is that long before they're in the studio to record there's a lot of early communication with the musicians about what they're being asked to do. This usually starts with a sampled mock-up of the music, regardless of whether it's going to be recorded with a live orchestra or a jazz combo. I don't think anybody in games is only doing pen and ink on manuscript paper, that is, writing sheet music and then bringing it to a session and hearing it for the first time there—no client I know of would ever approve that level of composer autonomy, nor should they, really. Most clients want to hear the music and evaluate how it's working in the game, even in a rough sampled mock-up. By the time we're booking sessions, everything has usually been vetted to some degree long before bringing the musicians in, and the players usually have had a chance to listen to a version of what they'll be playing. Those musical touchstones I mentioned before, plus a basic understanding of different genres, all come into play in the studio because you can use shorthand in communication with the performers: "It's sort of like an *E.T.* thing with a little *Jurassic Park* mixed in" or "This is like a Charlie Parker sort of thing." And they'll go, "Oh yeah, okay," and nail it. Good studio musicians have a broad repertoire and deep knowledge resources, and they can usually tell what a composer is looking for after hearing a sampled mock-up.

After the preliminary communications, it's the normal process of rehearsal where you're in a session and something isn't quite right, so you correct it in the moment.

Is it the sound/audio designer's job to deal with musicians' unions?

It varies, depending on the client. Sometimes we'll handle the talent contracts because they're coming through our department, and we have a blanket budget for all audio production. In those cases we portion off a section of the budget to go to musician or voice talent costs. More often, though, we keep talent costs separate from our production costs and the client handles the talent contracting and payment.

With voice work, we're often involved directly with the union just in terms of paperwork and such because there are a lot of forms that have to be signed. Since we're the ones physically at the session, it makes sense for us to handle the signing of the actor agreements.

I probably spend about 75%–80% of my time writing and producing music then getting it into the game. A good chunk of this time, though, is administrative. For me, the dullest part of my job is all the extracurricular stuff I need to do like asset tracking, invoicing, scheduling, managing client expectations, technical IT-related stuff, and all the other non-creative parts of the job. This usually amounts to about 20%–25% of the work.

Sometimes, for large projects, I'll manage a small team of people. In those situations, the time spent on actual music creation goes down to about 10%–20%, with the rest of my time going toward management: receiving deliverables from composers and sound designers, and providing feedback. This can be fun—it's always great to work with other audio people—and it can also be a nice break from making music under a deadline. Being a composer is often a solitary life, so it can be really valuable to lift your head up and remember what's happening out in the world. Most of my fondest production memories are of collaborative scores. But there's no getting around the fact that a fair amount of time has to be spent dealing with the more mundane aspects of making a game, especially because we're a small business. As I said, this means that in addition to contracting musicians and writing scores, I'm sometimes doing invoicing, following up with prospects, even doing debt collection. This is typical of client work. I don't especially love it, but I also don't mind it much—it's expected, part of the job. After a while, you don't even think about it; it's all just rolled into the day-to-day schedule.

These administrative duties are typically interwoven into a day of composition and music production. For example, I might be in the middle of working on a new piece when an email arrives, demanding that I stop everything to deal with a pressing client need. Generally speaking, the larger the client, the more predictable their project scheduling is. Smaller clients tend to have more sudden changes and unexpected needs, which can disrupt my own internal scheduling and require on-the-fly calendar adjustments. Being equipped to deal with these interruptions to the creative process without letting them derail my creative flow too much was something that I had a harder time with early in my career, but I'm now pretty good at it. It's a compartmentalizing skill that takes time to learn but is vitally important. Similarly, it's important to develop a sense of when something can be ignored for a while if you're in the middle of something else and you don't want to break from it. Knowing your priorities and not always feeling like you have to respond to things immediately can keep you sane and get the work done most efficiently. Of course, ignoring something that needs immediate attention can cause major problems, so it's critically important to develop a reliable "Can this wait?" barometer.

I'd say that this was the number one struggle for me in the beginning of my career, that is, letting go of the work sometimes, and not letting the franticness of crunch time, clients, and producers drive me into working nonstop and making myself sick. In my first five years in the industry, when someone said "Emergency!" I'd accept that it was a genuine emergency, work all weekend, stay up several nights in a row, whatever it took to get the work done and delivered. But I began to discover that half of the time, the clients who were declaring an emergency would say—after everyone had pushed themselves to the limit—"Oh, actually we're going to push the schedule out, so now there's plenty of time." Everyone had worked themselves half to death unnecessarily.

Going through this same dance again and again really focused my ability to read between the lines to determine which deadlines are *really* important, and which are the invention of someone covering their own ass, trying to look good, or passing down the pressure being put on them by their bosses with no real regard for the overall production pipeline. Being able to look at the whole picture beyond my own individual role, to determine what's really serious, which emergencies actually matter, is a tremendously important skill. This isn't to say that you ever brush off clients or miss deadlines; rather, you actually know when something truly warrants staying up all night to get it done, or when it's worth working a whole weekend or every weekend for a month to hit a deadline. You learn to know when you can go to bed at night knowing that there'll be plenty of time to finish the next morning. You learn that sometimes when a client says they need something in the next hour, if you get it to them by noon the following day everything will be more than fine. Being able to independently assess urgency and to effectively prioritize my work, my health, and my overall well-being was something that took quite a long time to figure out when I was new in the industry. I've definitely gotten better at it over time, but it's still something I need to remind myself of from time to time. I've never missed a deadline, not when I was caught up in client panics, and not now that I'm less so. This is something I tell people coming into the industry for the first time: don't get too wrapped up in the hysteria that can happen during crunch time. Pay attention to where the urgency is coming from and whether or not the panic makes sense in context. Look for the big picture, then decide if an all-nighter is called for. Sometimes it is, sometimes it's not.

Once a composer possesses this skill, it can really help in the workplace, because he or she can say, "Okay, I hear you saying that you need this by X time, but this other thing won't be coming in until that same time, and I need that other thing to produce the thing you want me to do now. Wouldn't it make more sense for me to work on something else until everything I need is in place for your task?" Usually the answer is, "Oh, yes, that makes way more sense actually."

Does working for your own small company insulate you to some degree from the crunch time problems that seem endemic to the industry?

It doesn't remove it all, but it does insulate us a little bit. I think "insulate" is a good word, because we're still crunching just as hard as everyone else on the team. The work is the same; it still hits us, and we still have the hundred-hour workweeks, the all-nighters, the weekends, and so on. The nature of game production demands periods of extreme crunch. The crunch periods often come in bursts, and you have to hold your breath until you can come up for air again. But being able to crunch in the comfort and solitude of my own studio feels better than doing it at a corporate office. The job is about having things ready for the people who want them, when they want them.

As long as I do that, I'm good. In an office environment, there are managers breathing down your neck, micromanaging your time. You want to tell them, "You're going to get what you need when you need it—don't worry." But that's their job, so they do it anyway.

There's so much burnout in the industry because of the way crunch time works, especially as workers move from their twenties into their thirties and forties. They may start a family, and will either need to leave the industry or move exclusively into managerial roles where they're not really able to do the thing that first drew them into the industry. Later in life, there's much less available time for workaholism for someone who isn't fresh out of college and ready to kill themselves for a while until they collapse. All of this is to say that working in a small studio doesn't shield you from the crunches, but it does insulate you because you're able to get things done autonomously in a way that works for your life, not someone else's. The crunch is the same, but it's psychologically much more comfortable.

How do career advancement, merit increases, and the like get negotiated for people working in audio, especially in an independent studio like yours?

It's tricky, and depends a lot on whether you're working in-house at a developer or if you're a contractor. I'll mostly speak to the latter, since Bay Area Sound operates under project-to-project contracts. Like a lot of client-based work, our rates depend somewhat on the ability of clients to pay. There are baseline rates that are pretty standard across the industry, and of course there are some firms that charge five times more, or five times less than that. The baseline rate is roughly what a normal big, successful company ought to expect to pay for music. We use that as our starting point in any financial negotiations; when a client is small or working within a tight budget, we may make adjustments from there. These fee calculations vary depending on the client and the studio. Most commonly, the price will be calculated based on a per-minute-of-music rate. It'll be X amount of dollars per minute of finished music in the game. With some clients, though, it makes more sense to use an hourly rate. This is rare, but I mention it because there are many different ways of pricing out music and audio, and it really ends up depending on what works best for a particular client.

In any case, we have a sliding scale depending on the ability of the client to pay. If we get repeat work from a client for whom we're reducing our rates, and if they've had success with the products that we've been a part of, we try to nudge our number up to get it closer to the industry standard. Having flexibility to work with the client's budgetary limitations is really important. If we didn't have it, we'd have to turn down a lot of work from smaller start-ups and independent developers. There are plenty of composers who do turn down work because the money isn't right, but for us—especially when a client or a project is really interesting—we'd rather work on it with an adjusted rate than not work on it at all. So we try to figure out a solution where if they can't afford even a reduced rate, we can still do something. Maybe they're thinking they need forty-five minutes of music when they may only need thirty minutes. Often we can shift the numbers like this to ensure that the amount of work is fair for an amount of money that they're able to afford. Equally important to being flexible with our rates is guarding ourselves against working for too little and eating our own operating costs.

In terms of raises, that's hard, because once you have a client, they hope they'll pay the same amount forever. Eventually, it's almost always a discussion and negotiation that needs to be had. We keep it amicable, and the less we have to play business hardball, the better. For clients who are able to pay the baseline amount, we keep it there—adjusted for inflation over the years. For the clients who are getting a deal, we make it clear to them that they're getting a deal outright. We want them to know this explicitly, because often clients don't realize how much audio costs and why. They may not realize that our expenses are high because of all the equipment and training we need and all the people we need to hire to make it work—it's a considerable investment. Many young companies especially don't realize these kinds of details, and don't always know how much it costs us internally to produce original music for a game. So we try to educate them about our expenses while still giving them as much of a deal as we can afford, especially if they continue hiring us for subsequent projects. We try to find a way to make the arrangement mutually beneficial. As with almost all client work, everyone has to be flexible . . . unless you're doing so well that you can say "no" to prospective paying work. But as I said, we like new clients and projects because they're often the most fun—as long as the compensation is fair.

The budgeting reality for contract composers and musicians is a different scene from working in-house at a developer. For in-house audio staff, it's a lot easier to get a standard raise because there are all of the usual corporate HR structures in place to facilitate this. You go into the boss's office and say, "I've been here for X years and have done good work. I'd like a raise."

Ultimately, your career path on the music side of the game industry is flexible, varying quite a bit from client to client. You're constantly asking yourself: How much do I care about the work? How much do I care about the project the client is trying to do? What are the people like who you'd be working with? Can they afford something reasonable? There have been clients who weren't equipped to pay anything for the music. For them, we can't do it for free, but we've helped them find a way to get something else that works, or maybe write one piece that they can use for the main theme, and leave them to find the rest through a licensing service or what have you.

Do you ever think about leaving the small studio scene for the more stable work schedules and assigned duties of a larger company?

I've had moments when I've thought about it. They don't usually last long, because even though being in a small shop means doing a lot of hustling, it also means building up great relationships with clients and nurturing those relationships. It pretty much goes like this: you get a job with a new client and you try to work it out so that when the next gig comes around, they want you to work on it. And being independent is worth it due to the fact that I get to set my own schedule for the most part, and I mostly get to do what I love. Even with all of the deadline crunches and scheduling night-mares, there's a freedom in contracting that I wouldn't give up for the world. It's hard to explain how nice that is.

I'm now so used to this way of working that the idea of going into an office every day and working with other people all around would be hard for me, I think. When I'm composing, I'm most productive when left alone, without distractions. If I had to run off to meetings every other hour, having people knocking on the door asking me questions, I'd get nothing done. I'm able to work most efficiently with the small setup we have now. I find that even when I go in for a day to various client offices, it really cuts into my production time. At the end of the day I like feel-ing that I got a lot done, that I was able to check a bunch of stuff off "The List." The creative and collaborative aspects of my job are great, of course. I often say that the best part of my job is the work. The actual work that I get paid for is incredibly rewarding personally, and I love it. I think if I were at a bigger company, I'd get to do less of this satisfying work and I'd go a little crazy.

Jacek Tuschewski
Audio Director

Jacek Tuschewski is audio director, sound designer, and producer for Torus Games and Media Saints. He is also co-founder and audio director at League of Geeks. He holds a BS in computer programming from Santa Ana College, and an advanced diploma of professional game development and an advanced diploma of screen and media from the Academy of Interactive Entertainment. Titles he has contributed to include *Armello, Land Sliders, Crystal Crusade, Penguins of Madagascar, Falling Skies: The Game, How To Train Your Dragon 2: The Video Game, Falling Skies: Planetary Warfare, Barbie: Dreamhouse Party, Monster High: 13 Wishes, Turbo, The Croods: Prehistoric Party!, Rise of the Guardians, Madagascar 3*, and *Monster Jam: Maximum Destruction*. He has also worked on a number of feature films including *A Thousand Roads, Layer Cake, The Passion of the Christ, Whale Rider, Ali, Gladiator, The Insider*, and *Thread of Voice*. In addition, his work has appeared in theatrical productions, print, and other media, much of which can be seen on his website (http://lamaic.com).

* * * * *

How did you come to work in the game industry?

I was interested in design from a very young age and hoped to go into it as an adult but was drawn in other directions. I taught myself BASIC programming on my Commodore VIC-20 and published a few games in magazines. I then began to spend time on music programming and even wrote a few hacking tools. But while I enjoyed programming in college, I realized it wasn't the career for me.

My interest in sound started when I was a teenager, with the music of The Beatles and George Martin's production on their work. Learning to use programs like *MusiCalc* and *Steinberg Pro 16* on my Commodore 64 was a turning point because I discovered that I could make more than music. I could make *sound* and make it the way I imagined.

I've tried to keep exploring these areas—design, sound, multimedia—ever since, and working in games, like working in film, came out of that. The rewarding and exciting part is that every job can be different. I enjoy sound design and sound programming, creating soundscapes, and maybe most of all producing, that is, making someone's music that isn't mine sound amazing so that it blows them away or moves them to tears. I enjoy holding, forming, and growing a vision of the sonic landscapes of an entire project.

Management at game companies I don't enjoy so much. In all the game companies I've worked for, management isn't seen as something that companies need to invest in. The ones that do invest in management change into some kind of corporation, and in my opinion, that's not something that works well for game development. With the exception of Media Saints, management in game development is a huge challenge to get right. I think Media Saints only got it right because the level of camaraderie was exceptionally high.

Part of the problem is the large number of introverts in game development. Programmers, for example, are really hard to get talking . . . period. You might as well forget about trying to get a report out of them because they'll choose coding—the thing they get paid to do and love to do—over something they feel is much less important. They'll even band together, so if they manage to write a report at all, it'll be about not writing reports. That's happened in so many companies it's not even funny, and it's allowed because programmers are usually the stars of the show. Lots of managers find it hard to force programmers to write reports, and programmers will tend to leave jobs pretty quickly where that kind of thing is required. They usually get sick and tired of having their work rejected or prodded or analyzed by a committee that often has no idea what they're talking about.

For big game companies with lots of management, this can be a problem. Many of the bigger companies also hire from outside the industry, so you can end up working with a manager from the fashion industry or someone who's never even heard of *Halo: Combat Evolved*. That's a real example, by the way. Someone like this can still be a good manager, but I think it's problematic to not know the first thing about an industry you work in.

I'm under no illusion that there's a magical company making games in a better way, though. It's the team that makes a game successful, and teams change. People move, people change, but large companies are probably the least attractive to me as models or places to be because they're almost incapable of change. For me, inspiration comes from the people involved in a project and the conversations and meetings of the minds that occur while working on it.

One of the big challenges in the industry is that a lot of people who work in games never analyze themselves. I have no idea if I'm just peculiar or lucky or something else, but I've always analyzed myself and my surroundings. Constantly. Doing so makes communicating easier, and when I have self-aware employees it makes managing them easier. The challenge isn't to manage, really, but to be a friend.

Part of the communication problem in games generally may have to do with age—there are just so many young people and they don't know the right way to do things. For example, here in Australia, internships are a required part of school, and thus I have lots of friends who want me to help their children get internships. The thing is, we get burned because the interns talk, even though we have them sign a non-disclosure agreement. They can't help themselves—they're excited and don't know any better. As a result, we have to fire them—the project is all over Facebook and jeopardizing our contract with the IP holder/publisher. So I can't take on any interns—they just can't keep a secret—which means I can't train future employees in that way. It's terrible, but that's the nature of the industry: youthful excitement isn't always a good thing.

Another part of the communication problem in games is that there are people who get into the game industry just for work, not because they like and believe in games. I know a number of managers, for example, who came to games to manage people, not because of the uniqueness of the product. But it isn't just managers. I'm a musician, and I have lots of musician friends who want to work in the industry. When I ask them about their favorite game, it turns out they don't play games. Gameplay experience is important to different degrees in various areas in the game industry, but it's very important in the composition and sound effects design areas.

It's important for management too, and managing a game is hard. You need to have an intrinsic understanding of games to manage the process. Games can be nonlinear, which is a huge difference from film, music, art, and writing. Games normally don't have demigod directors or executive producers with gigantic egos, and game design can't have personnel with minimal or no idea what their or your job encompasses. Most people in games love and understand games. So if you're a manager who doesn't play games, you've already almost alienated yourself from the start. When you're not playing games and you can't talk about them, who wants to listen to you?

What does the non-management side of your work look like?

Most companies work in an open manner, with no cubicles. They have a huge, open room with tons of desks that move around as projects dictate. Not all companies do it like that, but most of them do. We do it at Torus, and at League of Geeks. So depending upon the project, we just move people around as needed. If you're working with the artists, you just move with them; you don't keep your office or your desk. You move with the project.

That said, I'm the only one at Torus who has a soundproof room. When I started, I used to sit out among everyone, and they grew to hate me very quickly because we were working on shooter games and car games. I'd be listening to the same game sound over and over again—on my headphones—and people several desks away would complain about the noise. So, they got me my own sound booth. I'm actually in a double-walled, double-glazed, special soundproof room inside another a soundproof room. I'm doubly insulated, and that means that coworkers will often step in to talk privately about personal or work-related issues . . . and I'm not getting paid enough to be a therapist.

Everyone working on sound needs speakers or at least headphones in order to do their job. The only time my coworkers hear anything now is when I really crank up the bass. Sometimes the bass leaks out, and when I come out later and say, "I really like the bass," they all respond, "Yeah, we know!" It actually took me three years to teach people to knock on my door before just waltzing in. Usually, they'd just open the door and there'd be a wall of sound, which would startle them. That happened enough that they actually knock now. There's a window in my door—a huge, double-glazed window. Now, they knock on my door and we have to make eye contact before they enter. I usually turn the sound down and then invite them in. It took a while to get to that point, but now everyone knocks. And everyone closes the door when they leave, but that didn't used to be the case.

Most of the time when I'm working with someone on a particular feature, we'll set up the game in my office, where we can play it through the speakers at a good volume. We'll even play a rough version of the game so we can hear it properly. Sometimes I'll play the game with the programmers out on the floor, but we can only do that for a few minutes before the complaints start. It's bizarre, because everyone on the floor has headphones on and is listening to music. They don't want to hear this game they're working on.

It's like a chef never tasting the food he makes. The sound of the game is an interruption to programmers' individual listening sessions.

As a result, I often can't work with people the way I want to. But, we can have a conversation on the floor and they can show me the game and what they're thinking: "This is how she jumps"; "This is what we're thinking about the bicycle." As a result, I go out to the floor for some things, but hold actual audio meetings in my studio. For design meetings, we have a boardroom where the game is put up on the big screen. So, while the audio work happens in my studio, we do design work, preparation work, and audio planning in the boardroom. This work might include talking about what songs we're going to be using, where the music comes from, what kind of feeling we need for the music, etc. Once we've got a plan, I'll go back to my studio to crystalize what we talked about and either send an email or ask people in so that I can play them some music and see what they think. I really enjoy that part of the process.

Usually, audio and sound design planning comes in at the point in time where there's a concept for the game. That's when I have to write a small description of the sound/music before we get the contract. I'll explain what the stuff might look like in its most basic form. If we'll be employing an intuitive music system, for example, then the music will be chosen according to player action (e.g., if you make the avatar run fast, the music is faster, more engaging; if you're exploring an area and stopping to examine things, then the music would reflect that). Anyway, I put these types of things in the document and everyone gets excited about them . . . until they find out how much they cost. Then we negotiate.

What is the typical budget for game audio?

I used to think that most people were educated enough to know that they have to pay for the music in games, but it turns out they're not. I don't think anyone is prepared to pay for music anymore. In fact, I haven't worked on any games lately in which people were prepared to pay for a score. Very few games these days get a budget that allows for recording with an orchestra or even live musicians. It's super rare.

I tend to try to have some live instruments in the music I make, but usually it's just one violinist or guitarist, or maybe a singer or a few singers if I can swing it. And I get them cheap because I know lots of musicians. Most of the time, though, I buy pre-composed pieces of music and I remix them to suit the game because the budget for all of the music in a game is often about $3000. That's the standard, from the biggest companies to the smallest. For a game I did recently that was based on a globally recognizable IP, the music budget got cut from $15,000 to $10,000. So, I literally had to go to the composer—who's my friend—and tell him he was only going to earn two-thirds his regular rate. He's a friend . . . that shouldn't be happening.

Music—like everything else in games—is becoming standardized. With standardization comes shrinking budgets, which means that everyone has to work for less money. It's really sad; it's all middleware now because you can't afford custom work. And there's going to be very little custom work in the future either, except for maybe character design. The animations that are underneath game characters now are the same animations studios have been using for the past ten games. This kind of standardization is increasingly pervasive.

Anyway, let's say my company wins the bid to build a game. In my role as audio director, I don't have a lot to say for the first month or two of development. I go to meetings and talk about music: where it could go, etc. And I give the team a lot of temporary music and sound effects that they can use as placeholders. When we have a prototype level of the game where you can actually walk around and play something, that's when I really get going, thinking about how we can make specific sounds for this and that. All through this part of the process we have weekly meetings, and sometimes more than weekly is the norm.

As the game progresses, I also refine where the whole thing is going, and then about halfway through I engage the musicians. We get a budget together, submit it either to the company we work for or to the publisher we're working with, and they decide what they want to spend. Sometimes the game comes with examples or a preexisting palette that we have to stick with, meaning the composer will have to compose within a particular style of music. That isn't unusual when you're working with a film-based title. The same can happen with sound effects; there's a preexisting palette that I might have to work from.

With *How to Train Your Dragon 2: The Video Game*, I actually used the music from the first film in the franchise—*How to Train Your Dragon*—as a base. We used the music from the first film for the game based on the second movie because—and this happens a lot—games get made so much sooner than the movies they're based on. The film score isn't even written yet. For the film, they're still making decisions based off the rough-cut audio temp tracks, while in games we've actually had to submit and ship the game because the manufacturing time is horrendous. It takes months and months to manufacture cartridges and disks cheaply, and so it's not uncommon for the game to have been complete for almost six months before the film it's based on is finished. We're done with the game just as a composer usually starts composing for a film. So often there's actually no music from the film for us to work with.

This was the case with the *How to Train Your Dragon 2* film, so I asked if there was any sync licensing associated with the first film. DreamWorks owned the score outright, so we were able to use the music from the first film for the game tied to the second movie. Of course, I had to still compose music to match it, but having the original score was fantastic. The game just feels phenomenal with such an amazing score. It's the London Symphony Orchestra playing, which you'd never be able to get if DreamWorks hadn't contracted them for the film. I really enjoyed working with those tracks. Sometimes game development is just beautiful, and the process works really well. That game was one of those times.

At any rate, once everyone is agreed on budget and sound, we create a track listing and the music if it's not from a preexisting source (like a library or licensing service), we put the tracks in the game, and then I do a final balance of all the audio elements. Sometimes we run out of space on different media. The Nintendo 3DS, for example, has a limited card size, so we may only get five pieces of music instead of seven on a game for that platform. We might have to cut some pieces out entirely, or trim their size so we still have seven but they're only half-length. And sometimes the publishers are too cheap to pay for the larger-size cards. Audio is usually one of the biggest culprits in file size problems, even though we're using compression, MP3s, and algorithms like that. It still might not be enough, but the game gets shipped anyway.

How is game labor likely to change going forward in terms of audio?

Game design will still need someone with an understanding of music to do the soundtrack, even though the budgets will be even lower in the future. The question becomes whether or not the industry is going to be able to retain these people for the amount of money they'll be paying. When people like me are thinking of leaving the industry, it isn't because we don't love it.

It's because there's not enough money in it for us to continue. There's talk about automating game sound, but I don't think it will ever become fully automated. In fact, I think the struggle to make game audio cheaper is actually because it's not likely to ever be automated entirely. As a result, there are efforts to save money on the human side where possible.

Speaking of automation, I think animation is one area that's definitely becoming more automated, or at the very least, animation is experiencing something similar to music in the way it can be transferred. With the right software, I can transfer a walk cycle from a frog to a human so that the human hops just like a frog. I don't have to sit there and recreate the animation. It's recalculated and instantly transferred. Of course, even then, with the animation literally just transferred from a frog to a human, it needs some adjustment. It still requires an animator, but now the animator has to spend much less time doing the actual job. She doesn't have to sit there for hours trying to animate a human from scratch to do a frog-like motion. She can just tweak what's already been done, so you can actually hire less qualified people to do the job. You don't need an amazing animator anymore.

I think texturing is going the same way. There's lots of texturing happening in games, and I think that much of it is pre-generated. You can just buy libraries of textures. That happens quite a bit. But again, you'll still need a texture artist on a game project, just not an excellent one.

In contrast, I think coding is getting more complicated, and that's another area where automation will be limited. Pretty much every game now has to talk to a server; there's a negotiation with a server because of the rise of downloadable content and online play. You actually have to be pretty switched on with coding to make a game these days, because the software can involve so much more than just the gameplay. Nowadays a game has to connect with Facebook, it has to connect with Twitter, it has to stream to YouTube. Someone has to write all this stuff, keep it updated, and put it into the game. So, I think coding is one area that's going to be very safe to be in moving forward, even if the coding isn't in games exactly. There's going to be a need to build the third-party tools to make all the social networking and user tracking possible.

How does the audio budget break down between music and sound effects?

On a contract job, the IP holder or the publisher typically pays for the music on top of the budget for the game. It'll be an external contract that the developer will make with a composer, but the services are paid for by the publisher or IP holder. Generally, I find someone, or the IP holder and I agree on someone. Sound effects aren't usually part of the music budget; instead they're part of the game development budget.

It actually took me a long time to get Torus to negotiate for the music budget to be separated out as a standard part of our contracts. It was a problem because if it worked the other way—where music was a part of the game budget—then DreamWorks or whoever could just say, "We want the London Symphony Orchestra!" and Torus would be obligated to pay for that out of the development budget. What a problem that'd be: the LSO is probably booked out for the next three years, and even if they weren't, it'd cost half a million dollars to record twenty minutes with them. That might be most of the game development budget right there. But if the contract says the studio pays, they have you over a barrel. They're paying you a million dollars, and they can ask for the impossible. As soon as the payer switches, though, it becomes "We want the LSO! Oh, it's going to cost us half a million dollars and we have to wait three years? We don't want the LSO anymore. Do you know any cheap orchestras?"

It took me a long time to get that switched, and I think it's become a standard now in most cases. I like to think I pioneered that standard, because it's a nightmare any other way. I think it just has to be like that. Once the money comes out of the IP holder's wallet, it becomes much more real to them. It isn't that they don't want original music or sound effects. It just costs too much and takes too long.

When I can't make original music, I sometimes use a company like Smart-Sound. They give you multi-tracks of everything—the bass, the violin, the drums—and then I can mix and remix everything so it works for the project. Even better is that in this case, I license the world copyrights for the tracks, so I can use them on any project I want. I can remix to my heart's content; I can change the drums, or if I don't like the bass player they used, I can get my own bass player to play on it.

Sometimes the budget doesn't allow for any of that, but just having the flexibility of me mixing is nice. I'm a good producer and mixer, and I've been doing it for a long time. I can make a really shitty track sound really good. But what SmartSound is doing with music is where everything else in games is headed too, and it's not just games. It's happening for movies too. If you go to SmartSound's website, in fact, and look at their examples, they don't use games; they use movies and television shows. They even have a music player on their website where you can actually mix the track yourself right there. It's really a nice service, and I highly recommend it for people who don't have a big audio budget. For three hundred dollars you get maybe four hours of music, all multi-tracked. You probably can't beat that.

If I take time to think about it, it can be a little frustrating to do audio in games, because the music budget for a big film is about a million dollars. That's the norm. If you get someone like Hans Zimmer, the budget goes up substantially. It's a gigantic difference from what we get in games, but publishers want the same sort of sound, which is crazy. Warner Bros., for example, is both a game company and a movie company. They understand how powerful music can be, and so for most of the Warner Bros. games I've worked on they were willing to pay $40,000–$45,000 no questions asked . . . and they think that's a bargain. But most other companies are a lot cheaper. Some will pay fair value, but it's a rare thing.

Remember, though, that film and game production are very different animals. A lot of composers try to get into the game industry but wind up leaving because it's so limited. They can't express themselves in games the way they can in film where the scores are linear (as opposed to games' mostly nonlinear format). It can be hard to find good composers willing to score a game, which results in a catch-22. You just can't get really amazing quality work for a game under those conditions. If you were to approach Hans Zimmer with a huge budget, he might still say no. He might not want the headache of not being able to sync to picture and to work the way he usually works. Finding composers for games can feel like getting a good painter and telling them they've got no canvas to paint on.

Is it typical for audio directors to work with different companies on different projects the way you do?

It's probably not typical for an audio director, but it would be for sound designers or composers because of what the pay is like. I make such little money in games, it's insane. We got paid over $300,000 for the work we did on *Gladiator*, and I haven't made $300,000 in all of my time in the game industry. I still have moments when I'm driving to a gig someplace to make five hundred bucks and think, "I should go back into the film industry."

Don't get me wrong; I love what I do. It's beautiful. But the pay is just terrible in the game industry, and is actually getting worse. I work on so many different projects because you need to in order to make any decent money. For example, one of the projects I'm doing now is going to take me a year and I'll only get paid $5,000 . . . total . . . for a yearlong project.

Keep in mind, too, the rights issues. On every project, I'm fighting a battle for the musician and the composer . . . and I'm losing. There isn't the same kind of artist representation in games that there is in other media. I think what's needed are organizations like the American Society for Composers, Artists, and Publishers (ASCAP), but focused on the game industry exclusively. I think there's something like that in France, but that's the only country I know of that has some kind of game-specific organization. There's also the Game Audio Network Guild (GANG), and GANG is trying to change the process. GANG has a few lawyers involved, but they still can't manage to get the copyright and fees issues to come out fairly, as far as I'm aware, anyway.

It's tough to make even small changes happen. As I said, the composer contracts are tricky because composers are external partners to developers. Because the IP holder or publisher is typically the one who pays for the composer, I'll usually tell the composer to do something specific in the contract negotiation. For example, composers need to ask for a synchronization license. That allows the publisher to use the music across the range of ways they promote that particular game. But if the publisher or IP holder wants to make a different game or animated movie and use the music, or they want to use the music in an advertisement, then they have to pay the composer for those rights. So, in this case, the license has a time-related feature: as soon as there's another game, another IP, or whatever, they can't use your music anymore without paying you for it. I'm trying to make this a standard in composers' contracts.

As I mentioned, Warner Bros. typically pays well—which is great—but they try to get all the rights for the music they can and use the music from a game on everything else: other games and IP. I had a falling out with one of the composers who used to work at Torus over this, and he actually quit. He quit because Warner used his music on products that weren't related at all to the game. He said, "What's going on?" and I had to tell him it was because of the contract that was signed.

People have to be aware that it works this way, and that games don't function at the same level as film when it comes to rights. Music literally isn't seen as something special like it is in movies. We don't really have stars in game composing, or the budgets that go with them. I think Hans Zimmer did a track for *Crysis*, but basically he just composed a piece of music for them to use and that's it. He only did one track. The rest was done by another, less well-known composer who basically mimicked Hans's style.

▶ DISCUSSION

In nearly all of its attendant disciplines, game development is characterized by collaboration, iteration, and by the fact that every project is sui generis. These qualities are perhaps nowhere more pronounced than in game audio. The personnel who make sound effects, for example, are tasked with designing (or at least implementing in new ways) audio effects that will distinguish a game from its competitors, beginning with the interface and extending through every bird chirp, car backfire, and Wilhelm scream.[1] This work entails an iterative process that often only ends because the game must ship or because the resource budget has been reached. For games requiring voice talent, the words of the script may be linear, but the dialogue trees to cover all the permutations of a player's actions may be massive, and so too the cast of characters. Such complexity often requires numerous variant readings that ultimately need to be aligned in an equal number of distinct game moments—many of which will only be experienced by a fraction of the most devoted players. Music is arguably the most distinctive component of a game's soundscape, not only for the extent to which it defines a given title, but also for the way in which it is produced—usually over many iteration cycles—and for the way it can be repurposed (at least in some instances) across the soundtrack. In all of these cases, audio personnel are bound by—if not dependent on— the fact that their industry requires cross-disciplinary collaboration, the production of multiple components simultaneously, and the implication of uniqueness in every project.

Each of these requirements has far-reaching implications for the game industry, but it is perhaps iterative concurrency that is most responsible for one of the more emphatic points of the interviews in this chapter: the importance of experiential breadth—musical and otherwise—for audio designers. Given the need for composers to be able to create scores for a wide variety of scenarios in a game while keeping an overall acoustic theme well supported, the more styles and forms of music the composer is familiar with, the easier it will be for her or him to adapt in innovative and environmentally appropriate ways. Such adaptability also speaks to why game sound design tends to be a more holistic process than in other media. Unlike sound design in cinema, for example, where much of the audio work is done in post-production (i.e., after the visual elements have been assembled), game sound production tends to be part of the main development pipeline, and as a result is often just as iterative and collaborative as level design, plot development, code optimization, and so on.

As Emerson-Johnson and Tuschewski make clear, however, the concurrence of game sound development does not necessarily mean that this work is done within a development studio, nor is it always the case that it is in fact iteratively concurrent. In the former instance, game audio is often contracted to a service provider, an arrangement that can create a long-term (i.e., for the length of a project) work-for-hire relationship and attendant internal/external labor dynamics whereby audio personnel are both a part of and distinct from a game's core development team. In the latter case, though rarer, the integration of music into a game can come quite late in the development cycle, especially for simple or low-budget titles. It can also happen that composers will work with the development team for some time to assemble the necessary tracks, but these beds of music will not be tweaked and inserted into the game until close to the end of the production cycle. This is primarily about avoiding wasted work that can result from embedding sound into an early iteration of a game only to have that part of the game changed or deleted later. This is especially tricky where cutscenes are concerned because such extended blocks of nearly inviolable linear content cannot be easily edited; dropping them into the game thus must be planned very carefully.

Audio development also inherently presents certain physical demands that other development disciplines do not, chief among them being the need for separate and soundproof production spaces. This is at odds with the typical open floor plan environment of most game studios, an environment designed to facilitate the everyday collaboration essential to game development. In Tuschewski's experience, the audio discipline's spatial needs do not necessarily impede collaboration, however, as audio spaces can serve as loci for collaborative opportunities and meeting points where professional and personal business may be discussed in private.

An exception to such bespoke engineering (and ersatz conversation) booths occurs when sound designers work remotely. In addition to the advantages that telecommuting generally affords—minimal commuting time, lower office space overhead, greater independence—working remotely offers audio personnel the benefit of being insulated from the panoramic anxiety of crunch times. By the same token, telecommuting can make it difficult to *stop* working because the dividing line between work life and personal life becomes imperceptible, and can also make interaction with remote colleagues more difficult. This latter issue tends to exacerbate communication problems within and across development teams.

All of these effects are sometimes amplified by the impact of unionized labor, which is felt more strongly in audio disciplines than in other game development specialties, despite the fact that game development in general has little to no union penetration. The inveterate union practices of the film and broadcasting industries are the impetus for this union effect. The American Society of Composers, Authors, and Publishers (ASCAP) and the Screen Actors Guild—American Federation of Television and Radio Artists (SAG-AFTRA), for example, shape musician and voice actor expectations and budgets, and therefore the budgeting and approach of game audio production and game development more broadly. As Tuschewski explains, the union expectation among artists is both important and difficult. Artists need to be paid, but the work and budgets of game audio production are sufficiently different from those of other media that a false expectation can be created among the talent. According to Emerson-Johnson and Tuschewski both, such misapprehensions are also driven by the dilemma posed by consumer and publisher assumptions that 1) the production values of games will be the same as feature-length films, and 2) because sound is digital (i.e., immaterial), it is essentially free to produce. In the end, even though game audio personnel are typically keen to pay established artist rates, they are often unable to because studios and clients tend to de-prioritize audio budgets, which then forces audio personnel into wage compromises, workarounds, and in the worst cases, migration from the games sphere.

Unsurprisingly, as a result of the human resources cost for music, the budget allotments for audio generally, and the prevalence and sophistication of middleware, audio—like many other development disciplines—is moving toward a factory model in which custom work is cost prohibitive. Audio personnel are increasingly able to order sound assets (and the publishing rights to them) directly from third parties, and these assets can then be mixed locally by the audio engineer or audio director to produce a game's soundscape. At the same time—and perhaps as a result—compensation for audio personnel is decreasing, particularly when compared to compensation in other media. There is the associated—and predictable—de-skilling of the discipline to consider too, which when arrayed with the aforementioned negative trajectories depicts a discipline very much in transition. Part of this transition involves the routine departure of many of the industry's most experienced employees, as well as the threat of an organized labor response in the form of a work stoppage or general strike (Futter). In other words, audio personnel do not leave the industry because of the stress or the politics; they leave because they literally cannot afford to stay.

▶ NOTE

1   The Wilhelm scream is an iconic sound effect first used in 1951 that has now "appeared" in nearly 300 films and more than 150 games. For more information, see: https://en.wikipedia.org/wiki/Wilhelm_scream.

▶ WORKS CITED

Bibliography

Futter, Mike. "The Potential Voice Actor Strike Explained." *Game Informer*. 8 Oct. 2015. Web. 10 Oct. 2015. <http://www.gameinformer.com/b/features/archive/2015/09/25/the-potential-sag-aftra--voice-actor-strike-explained.aspx>

"Transitions: Gamasutra Salary Survey 2014." *Gamasutra: The Art & Business of Making Games*. UBM Tech. 22 Jul. 2014. 1–8. Web. 10 Oct. 2015. <http://www.gamesetwatch.com/2014/09/05/GAMA14_ACG_SalarySurvey_F.pdf>

Filmography

Ali. Dir. Michael Mann. Columbia Pictures, 2001. Film.

E.T. the Extra-Terrestrial. Dir. Steven Spielberg. Universal Pictures, 1982. Film.

Gladiator. Dir. Ridley Scott. DreamWorks, 2000. Film.

How to Train Your Dragon. Dir. Chris Sanders and Dean DeBlois. DreamWorks, 2010. Film.

How to Train Your Dragon 2. Dir. Dean DeBlois. DreamWorks, 2014. Film.

The Insider. Dir. Michael Mann. Buena Vista Pictures, 1999. Film.

Jurassic Park. Dir. Steven Spielberg. Universal Pictures, 1993. Film.

Layer Cake. Dir. Matthew Vaughn. Columbia Pictures, 2004. Film.

The Passion of the Christ. Dir. Mel Gibson. Icon Entertainment International, 2004. Film.

Star Wars. Dir. George Lucas. Twentieth Century Fox, 1977. Film.

A Thousand Roads. Dir. Chris Eyre. Mandalay Entertainment/The Smithsonian National Museum, 2005. Film.

Thread of Voice. Dir. Marcus Bergner, Michael Buckley, Frank Lovece, and Marisa Stirpe. Arf Arf, 1993. Film.

Whale Rider. Dir. Niki Caro. South Pacific Pictures, 2002. Film.

Gameography

Armello. League of Geeks. League of Geeks, 2015. Multiple platforms

Barbie: Dreamhouse Party. Little Orbit. Little Orbit, 2013. Multiple platforms.

The Croods: Prehistoric Party!. Torus Games. DreamWorks, 2013. Multiple platforms.

Crysis. Crytek. Electronic Arts, 2015. Multiple platforms.

Crystal Crusade. Torus Games. Torus Games, 2015. Multiple platforms.

Falling Skies: The Game. Little Orbit. Little Orbit, 2014. Multiple platforms.

Falling Skies: Planetary Warfare. Little Orbit. Little Orbit, 2014. Multiple platforms.

Firewatch. Campo Santo. Panic, 2016. Multiple platforms.

Game of Thrones. Telltale Games. Telltale Games, 2014. Multiple platforms.

God of War. SCE Santa Monica Studio. Sony Computer Entertainment, 2005. Sony PlayStation.

Halo: Combat Evolved. Bungie. Microsoft, 2001. Microsoft Xbox.

How to Train Your Dragon 2: The Video Game. Torus Games. Little Orbit, 2014. Multiple platforms.

Land Sliders. Prettygreat. Prettygreat, 2015. Multiple platforms.

Madagascar 3. Torus Games. DreamWorks, 2012. Multiple platforms.

Monster High: 13 Wishes. Little Orbit. Little Orbit, 2013. Multiple platforms.

Monster Jam: Maximum Destruction. Inland Productions. Activision, 2002. Multiple platforms.

Penguins of Madagascar. Torus Games. DreamWorks, 2014. Multiple platforms.

Pong. Atari. Atari, 1972. Coin-operated.

Rise of the Guardians: The Video Game. Torus Games. DreamWorks, 2012. Multiple platforms.

Sam & Max (franchise). Telltale Games. Telltale Games, 2006–2009. Multiple platforms.

Star Wars: The Old Republic. BioWare. Electronic Arts, 2011. Microsoft Windows.

Super Mario Bros. Nintendo. Nintendo, 1985. Nintendo Entertainment System.

Tales from the Borderlands. Telltale Games. Telltale Games, 2014. Multiple platforms.

Tales of Monkey Island. Telltale Games. LucasArts, 2009. Multiple platforms.

Turbo. Torus Games. DreamWorks, 2013. Multiple platforms.

The Walking Dead. Telltale Games. Telltale Games, 2012. Multiple platforms.

Wallace & Gromit's Grand Adventures. Telltale Games. Telltale Games, 2009. Multiple platforms.

The Wolf Among Us. Telltale Games. Telltale Games, 2013. Multiple platforms.

Softography

Digital Performer. MOTU. MOTU, 2016. Multiple platforms.

MusiCalc. Waveform Corporation. Waveform Corporation, 1983. Commodore 64.

Pro Tools. Digidesign. Avid, 2016. Multiple platforms.

Steinberg Pro 16. Steinberg. Steinberg, 1984. Commodore 64.

7

Business

▶ INTRODUCTION

This chapter explores an array of industry positions that are not typically involved in day-to-day game design and development processes. They are grouped together under "Business" because they are usually administrative and/or support positions that enable the hands-on work of game making. Such support work includes organizational leadership, asset cultivation and management (including intellectual property and human resources), sales and promotion, legal consultation and compliance, and so on—in essence, the organizational scaffolding of the industry rather than its explicitly creative or technical side.

Even though the "Business" designation is quite broad—encompassing a much larger diversity of specializations than other employment categories (e.g., programming, design, art)—it can be subdivided reasonably into six principal subcategories: upper management (e.g., chief executives and presidents), legal (e.g., attorneys and their support staff), human resources, finance (e.g., sales, accounting), marketing and public relations (including community management), and information technology operations and support. Regardless of subcategory, however, business personnel work closely with each other and various development personnel to ensure both a smoothly functioning work environment and timely delivery of products and services to the market.

According to the 2014 Gamasutra Salary Survey, business personnel are, in aggregate, typically the highest paid in the industry, with an average annual salary of $101,572 ("Transitions" 5). Marketing, public relations, and sales personnel with fewer than six years of experience earn an average of $73,500 annually, while personnel holding CEO/president or vice president/executive manager positions and with more than six years of experience average $135,735 per year (Ibid.). Business personnel on the whole with more than six years of experience earn an average $156,731 per year (Ibid.). Additionally, US-based business personnel earn approximately 21% more on average than their Canadian counterparts, and 43% more on average than European business personnel (Ibid.). Finally, male business personnel average $104,513 annually, while female employees average $90,250 per year (Ibid.).

Lauren Clinnick
Marketing/Public Relations

Lauren Clinnick is co-founder and director of Lumi Consulting. She is also a digital media assessment panel member for Film Victoria, a committee member on Women in Development, Games and Everything Tech (WiDGET), and a committee member on the Australian STEM Video Game Challenge. Previously she worked for House Communications, Senetas, and Preshafood as an account executive, marketing assistant, and office manager, respectively. She holds a bachelor of business and a bachelor of arts in Japanese language from Swinburne University of Technology, and her shipped titles include *Rogue Singularity*, *Mori*, *Bonza National Geographic*, *Read Only Memories*, and *Crossy Road*. She is a popular speaker at industry events on the topics of public relations and marketing.

* * * * *

How did you come to work in the game industry?

Through grief. I'd had a tough year with a lot of death in it, both among friends and family. It was a reminder that life is extremely, mysteriously short. I was faced with the realization that while I was excellent at my (then) job, I'd been anxious and unhappy about its content and structure, and it was badly affecting my physical and mental health. I owed it to myself to try for something I suspected would make me a lot happier.

I'd been consulting in marketing with Katie Gall (co-founder and director of Marketing and Communications at Lumi Consulting) as a source of revenue outside of my regular public relations job in the tech industry. She and I talked and I revealed that I wanted to try focusing on servicing the games industry, and that I wanted to move to consulting full-time. She, too, was at a crossroads in life. We were both afraid of what the Gamergate controversy was doing to others, but we knew we wanted this.

The games industry in Australia wasn't hiring full-time (or even part-time) marketing, communications, or public relations roles at that time. We decided that we should create a place for ourselves in the gap that we saw. We made arrangements and relaunched Lumi Consulting with a focus on games.

What services does Lumi Consulting offer?

As part of the recent global financial collapse, Australia lost lots of AAA and AA services. What emerged from the ashes were smaller, independent studios. Few of these studios were in a position to be able to afford in-house marketing and public relations services, and many of them didn't come from a background in which marketing staff are prioritized. Everybody was looking for ways to address the gap, and so we stepped in and designed a lot of services that act as marketing support. We're kind of like a tag-in marketing staff department for these companies, and we do everything a normal in-house marketing team would do.

When we start a relationship with a new client, we do an intensive messaging workshop. It's basically a two- or two-and-a-half-hour meeting in which we sit down with the client and do a needs assessment. Either we focus on the studio as a whole, or we focus on a single game, and we concentrate on what we need to know, what the unique selling points are, whether we need to do a competitor analysis, whether we need to do a SWOT (strengths, weaknesses, opportunities, threats) analysis, and so forth. If it's a service that's being marketed or something where the sales pipeline is really important, we look at what the actual process is for getting the service or product sold.

We do a lot of different activities during this workshop, and many of them are tailored to the service or nature of the company. From there, we make a digital report that's equivalent to an internal marketing bible. This bible is necessary because a lot of studios are essentially reinventing the marketing wheel every time they do something—applying for a grant, submitting a game for participation in a competition, going to a PAX showcase, and so on. In the marketing bible we give them, there's a one-line pitch as well as an extended boilerplate for the game. At this initial stage, we're really just trying to get clients to start thinking about core marketing materials.

As far as services go, we also give trailer briefings, so that clients know what makes a really good trailer for different purposes. We do media training, so once a client is preparing to talk to the media or take something to the media, we train them on how to give a good interview (e.g., how to politely decline or redirect a question). In addition, we do public speaking training if a client is interested in starting to get into the process of pitching for speaking engagements. We also help sharpen negotiation skills. For example, say a developer has been approached by Sony but is unsure of how to represent themselves or argue for the best revenue split. We'll conduct intensive negotiation skills training with lots of practice with people and pitching skills. We even give feedback on Patreon and Kickstarter copy. Basically, we do everything that an in-house marketing staff would do back in the days when companies had dedicated marketing departments and staff members. We fill that gap for our clients, and our services are based on what a particular company needs.

A lot of what we find, especially when we're working with indie developers, is that they often prioritize programming and art over everything else. They may even try to make things work with just these two areas covered, and bring on contractors for sound, music, and the rest. It's very tough for people who are trying to make a business work *and* build an amazing product when they don't have a marketing background. These same people are also exhausting themselves and pushing themselves to extremes just to make something that fits their vision. When someone is super exhausted at the end of the day and they're doing what they're passionate about—which might be programming or systems design—they haven't left themselves the energy or mental space to then swap hats and focus on marketing.

In addition, a lot of people are under a misapprehension about when marketing should come into the development picture. With AAA development, it can appear that marketing only becomes a big thing when the game is ready to ship. That's what it can look like from the outside. For us, marketing should really come in as soon as the developer has an idea of what the spirit of the game—or of the studio—is going to be. The ideal time for us to initiate a marketing and public relations relationship with clients is when they have something that's potentially pre-alpha, where there's still a lot of runway left to optimize gameplay, to target a certain market/demographic, and to really think the whole project through: "Who am I making this for? How am I going to reach them? What are the emotional rewards my game is going to offer them? What's going to keep them coming back? What's going to make them loyal to my company?" These aren't things to think about post-release, or even just prior to release.

Thinking about marketing can also be challenging for some people because marketing really is "the machine" of the industry—and there are a lot of parts to it. For example, playtesting is part of what we see as marketing componentry, as are advertising, messaging, and media outreach. A lot of people have the misunderstanding that marketing equals advertising; however, it's one of those things where all advertising is marketing, but not all marketing is advertising. It's a very interesting, fast-moving area, and many developers don't want to put in the effort to keep up with it. They think to themselves, "I just want to hone my craft of being excellent in music or level design." I can definitely understand that. If somebody said to me, "You have to be excellent at marketing, but you must also be excellent at programming," I'd be exhausted and I'd just want to cry. It's hard enough to focus on the one thing that you're really good at already without having to do something completely new on top of it. There's still the general sense among developers that if you make something really good, people will come and play. There are a lot of people who are coming around now and realizing that mind-set actually doesn't work.

Even when developers are comfortable with the idea of marketing, they may not understand it fully. It's not uncommon for developers to say, "I went to Gamasutra. I read lots of postmortems. I know how to market my game." But marketing for games moves so fast that you might read a postmortem for a game that came out a month ago and that recipe actually won't work anymore because the environment has changed. There could be an in-store based change, a new operating system that comes out—that kind of thing. So, effective game marketing can be really difficult, even for professionals.

Where does marketing/public relations as a service fit into the structure of the game industry?

If developers aren't working with somebody like us, there's usually someone on their team who's wearing the marketing hat. We've definitely noticed pressure, especially among independent developers, for everyone to have at least a secondary if not a third skill on top of their primary skill. For example, a producer might also serve as his game's community manager, or an artist who dabbles as a musician might help cover sound. There's tremendous economic pressure to be able to occupy a plurality of roles.

In AAA development, you can still find people who can really drill down into a small corner of development and be a specialist. They can focus in such a granular, tiny way and get fantastic at their bit of the process. But elsewhere in the market, we're seeing that a jack-of-all-trades skill base is what's important.

At Lumi, we term ourselves "service providers," and this includes everything about marketing, public relations, and even user experience. We're spoiled by the fact that we can focus on what we do, but when it comes to the developers we work with, a lot of the time we're seeing the multiple skill pressure phenomenon play out. For example, when we worked on *Rogue Singularity*, the developers wrote all the copy for their own greenlight campaigns. They also wrote all of their own grants. In a larger studio or in the days of old, there'd probably be someone else on the team focused on that, allowing the programmers to concentrate on programming.

Are there service providers in other areas beyond marketing and public relations?

Yes, there are legal service providers, design consultants, and others. For example, we work with Christina Chen a lot, who is a free-to-play design specialist. If a potential client approaches us with a free-to-play mobile game idea, we'll say to them, "What advice have you had for the design of this? How have you gone about the monetization and the free-to-play design?" If they're not super experienced developers, we usually refer them to Christina. Just as we at Lumi offer marketing workshops, Christina offers free-to-play design workshops where she says, "Give me your game. I'm going to look right into it, then we'll get together and talk about what this game needs in order to have better retention and conversion." If someone comes to us with a free-to-play mobile game and they want it to be marketed really well, we could get them the largest audience in the world. But if this audience isn't going to be converted and retained, then the client will be disappointed with the revenue. So we often say, "Okay, here's the assembly line. Go to Christina first." We'll refer them to Christina and take a fee. They'll have a workshop with Christina, and then at that point, they'll either go back and make some significant changes or they'll come to us, and we'll load them up and get them going on an internal marketing document. Getting them to start thinking about who the game is for and how to talk about it puts them in a much better position to have a game that appeals to a specific audience. Doing that also means that the gameplay has been optimized, not only in terms of its monetization strategy but in a way that's most ergonomic, that keeps players engaged and coming back.

Because there was a collapse in the industry here in Australia and a lot of the development teams that now exist are small, experts in certain services are starting to pop up and serve many development studios. There's an agency out of Perth, for example, that works as a matchmaking service between developers and composers/musicians. Again, music is one of those areas where a AAA developer would have an in-house department or might bring in a specialist on a long-term contract. But often, smaller developers only need a little music, or can't take on another team member, and so this Perth agency helps make the connection they need for one-off music work. Another example is Tavern of Voices, which is a matchmaking service between developers and voice actors/voice talent. The emergence of this kind of one-for-many service provider is changing how game business is done here.

Does Lumi work on a traditional fee-for-service model?

It depends on the project. Games are a high-risk industry and many of our clients are taking on a lot of risk to do the work they're doing. Most of the time we take a deposit up front and then get paid the rest within seven days of completion. We keep our payment windows really short because we're a small business in a high-risk environment, and a lot of our clients have cash flow pressures. Our prices are extremely reasonable for what they are, and definitely a lot less than what I'd be charging if I were still back in tech investment and focused on tech start-ups. But that's just the nature of the game industry and environment. So, we're generally project-based in our fees, and can also work on retainer for a period of time. We haven't found that revenue share is very common for us. If we've worked with someone several times and there's a proven track record, or if they have an excellent reputation and thus there's already pre-validation, we might consider a revenue sharing agreement. But it's really just whatever we can do to risk-manage our cash flow.

Some services are slightly different, though. For example, in music sometimes you'll find that the artist will say, "I'll work using a fee-based system, but if you let me keep exclusive rights to sell the music on Bandcamp or as part of my own personal brand, and let me keep the album sales, then my fee is X." That way, the service provider is making money off the project but in a different way. Royalties are very complicated financially and involve heaps of spreadsheets, but in certain service areas they work.

The problem with revenue sharing for us is that game development can be such a glory situation, with people taking on risk and taking pride in it: "I've just murdered myself with crunch and it's so glorious and wonderful." But that's only rewarding for some people. When you have a risk-filled environment based on crunch, the workforce tends to consist of affluent, educated, single men or those people who have someone else supporting them. I work more than full-time, and my partner works full-time as a psychologist. Our house always looks like a bomb went off inside it. If we had an extra house-wife who could support us that would be amazing, and I'd be able to take on more risk, work longer hours, and do crazy crunch. But I just can't. The end result of this climate of crunch is a more homogenous culture, which is what I saw in tech investment too. All of those CEOs are super young guys who can be totally crazy and blow everything up, but you don't find young mums, you don't find people with big families who don't have full-time or part-time stay-at-home partners. It's a really homogenous situation, and I don't think it's healthy.

How does this environment impact service providers?

We've found—and it's been confirmed by other service providers that we've talked to—that service inquiries tend to come to us in quite an immature form. For example, a developer might come to us and ask for what's basically paid user acquisition or pure advertising. As a result, we lose time bringing them up to speed on what we do and helping them develop an understanding of what they need. We've found that this knowledge gap formed after the Australian industry collapsed, with people since then primarily developing their skills in a silo. Because these people have spent so much time in one area, they have no understanding of how game business works. And because so many of them now have to wear multiple hats, they're ill prepared to grasp the subtleties of how to optimize their work and loop in marketing as part of the development process. As a result, a lot of what we do—and something we think is really important—is speaking at industry events to help bring our colleagues (generally speaking) up to speed. We make ourselves highly visible and accessible, and say to developers, "Talking to us is free. If you want to buy me a coffee, I'll fit it in. If you have a two-second question, ask it." I can't always promise that I'll be able to respond to these kinds of requests in a super timely manner, but I prefer that people get a lot of the silly questions out of the way before they're already in trouble or need help urgently. By talking publicly more, we've matured the leads we have coming in. We tell people, "This is how we recommend you design your approach to marketing. These are the things to think about, these are some tips and tricks you can use to get the most out of an industry show." Every time we go to an industry show and a developer isn't capturing emails—they're just letting people walk off after playing their game—I just want to cry. That's their golden opportunity to get another pair of eyeballs on their release, which is so very important to a game's success. So we spend a lot of time on outreach, trying to help people understand how important marketing and public relations are to development.

We also spend time each month doing pro bono work to support women in the industry. We're trying to do what we see as important groundwork and reinvestment into the domestic industry to give people a better idea of what we do, and to make the climate better for everyone. If someone doesn't become my client, that's fine, but I'd like them to do better rather than worse at marketing in any case.

As far as gender equity issues are concerned, there are two main elements that we—collectively as an industry—should be looking at. First, there are more women entering the workforce in technical roles: programmers, software engineers, visual effects specialists, and other STEM (science, technology, engineering, and mathematics) defined jobs. Women are making decisions to work and train in STEM fields at an extremely young age, and we need to be talking to these young women now to show them that the opportunities in games are huge. We can't continue to target adult women and then wonder why they don't want to work in games. In many ways, it's too late to get them to change careers. Instead, we need to pull it right back and talk to super young girls and to schools and say, "This is me. I work in a STEM industry. I don't work in a STEM job but I work in a STEM industry and you can too." You can talk to people about how passionate and happy and challenged women can be in these roles. So that's the STEM/games side of the equation.

There are also women in games who don't have STEM specializations—I'm one of them. They might have soft skills instead, like a business or marketing background. We need to more clearly articulate with these women so that the game industry can use them. You don't have to be a programmer or technical artist. You can be a fine artist, you can be a composer, you can be business minded, you can have a legal background—the game industry is so large, creative, sprawling, and expressive that you can find a place in it with the skills you have. The game industry will actually embrace you and respond to you if you have an unusual background. I thought not having done game design post high school meant that nobody was going to be interested in anything I had to say, but I was wrong. We need to be telling women that the game industry needs them and their interesting backgrounds. That's what's going to lead to more creative approaches and innovative results. We need to say to women that if they choose to learn STEM skills, they can have really rewarding, creative, engaging, fast-growth jobs. But we also need to say to women who don't come from a technical background and don't know how to code, "You can still make a really meaningful contribution to the industry, and there are other women already here. We want you, and we want to help you. Just talk to us." And there are plenty of those jobs. For example, there's a psychiatrist based in Sydney, Jennifer Hazel, who has always loved games. She's a fully qualified psychiatrist, but now she's looking into games for therapy. She's started an initiative called Prescription Pixel, and the website has all these amazing research links and resources for games combating anxiety and posttraumatic stress disorder.

We need to keep taking away the barriers that say a games person looks like this, that the games industry only needs one kind of person and you're not it. That was something that even five years ago was so reinforced. Katie and I are really trying to take down the walls and say, "Take a peek inside. Come and visit us, see it, play with it. Have a look. We're here and we're already doing it; you could be a part of it—just talk to us." It really makes such a difference down the line.

What is crunch time like from a service provider's perspective?

From our perspective, crunch is extremely difficult. It's really hard to work with a client when they're crunching or when they have a culture of crunch. Very often, they have skewed ideas on what's reasonable for other people, and the hours that other people work. Also, the work they do during crunch is often of very poor quality. In response, a lot of what we do on our end is designed to alleviate some of the crunch associated with marketing. There's a bit of a pitfall when developers say, "I'm going to completely make the game and then I'm going to spend a month marketing the game before release. Then I'll market it on release, and then I'm done." If someone has worked so hard to build a game completely, it's crazy for them to try to teach themselves something new or do something they're not comfortable with in the last month before release. We often liken working with a service provider early to going to a gym and engaging the services of a skilled personal trainer. The trainer will spend time understanding you, and all you have to do is half an hour a week of light exercise and you'll be in reasonably good shape. But, if you've never worked out before and you try and pick up a hundred kilogram barbell, you'll hurt yourself, pass out, or die. It's the same with marketing, public relations, and other services. A little at a time over a long period means that you'll be able to do more and more impressive things during the lead-up to the release of your game. When a developer tries to do the equivalent of lifting an enormously heavy weight at the end of the development cycle when they're already fatigued, the results are never good.

So, we try to be that personal trainer for our clients, drip feeding some training and introducing new ideas slowly. We try to get them thinking about things a little bit every week because the results will be so much better down the line. You can't smash out community engagement like you can code. People think, "I can code all night and get it done just fine. I can totally do that with marketing." But it doesn't work that way. You have to have press relationships that you can't brute force, just like you can't brute force building a community. You can't rush building relationships with critics, and you can't rush your ability to seem natural, confident, calm, and happy when you're talking about your game. A lot of these skills are things that absolutely have to be practiced for a long time, and the results are quite bad if things are crammed into the last minute. In fact, if the marketing and public relations on a project are going to be last minute, the developer is better off putting their money into paid user acquisition and pure advertising. You just can't rush the marketing skills.

A lot of what we do for clients in this regard is to say, "If you're going to have to wear multiple hats, you're going to have to do a little bit of training now and again, and you're going to have to do it really carefully." Also, time management and scheduling things are super, super important, which is why a good production pipeline really helps marketing a lot. It's also a good anti-crunch device. If you're having contact with your public when you're totally fatigued and dead from crunch, or if you're talking to the media when you're exhausted, it's just not a good experience for anyone. I'd much rather have someone who's fresh and happy and isn't full of doom, dread, and self-doubt by the time they talk to the media.

In terms of Lumi's services and the flexibility with which they are provided, how do you arrive at a fair pricing model?

The gold standard is to put aside up to 30% of the production budget for marketing, which makes things nicely scalable. It's 30% if you're huge, and 30% if you're small, because marketing covers everything from working with experts like us to engaging in advertising, production development, traveling to shows, and so on. When we recommend to new developers that they put aside 30% of their budget for marketing, they look at us like they want to cry. That's just so much money for them, and they've scraped every dollar and penny just to be able to develop their game. They haven't thought about marketing a lot of the time.

In terms of fair pricing, we're consultants, and consultancy fees are higher than what you would spend on an in-house staff member. But you're paying for the temporary nature of the consultancy relationship, and so having a base rate for a consultant is as long as a piece of string. One hundred dollars Australian an hour would be the lowest limit for a client consult depending on what the role is. The fee can be as high as three hundred to five hundred dollars an hour, or more if the work is extremely specialized.

My partner Katie and I are relatively young, we work in a co-working space, we keep our overhead costs low, and offer an a la carte menu of services. We've worked out a per-hour base rate for these services and arrived at 150 dollars per hour per staff member. That base rate is flexible if the relationship with the client offers a lot of work or if there are non-monetary benefits such as a speaking engagement we're interested in (i.e., being able to present ourselves as a company at industry events, holding a workshop without paying sponsorship fees, etc.), access to data (i.e., access related to alpha/beta testing of graphics, the efficacy of different sales methods and timing/price points, etc.), or something else we think is interesting and will help us with future service or product developments. In terms of that base rate, we price ourselves at the upper point so that about 30% of inquirers say no. When people say no after we've given them a quote because we're too expensive for them, that isn't a bad thing. I'm a lot more concerned when someone quotes me for a service and they're undercharging. To me, that says either their business isn't sustainable or there's some kind of an issue. So, if we can't work with everyone, that's fine—being able to work with everyone isn't our goal.

That said, we do put aside pro bono hours each month for intriguing opportunities. But, in general, we price ourselves until we get 30% knock back because for us that's a good guide. At that price point, people respect how much we're worth and we haven't turned them off by asking too much.

Our pricing formula—if not the rates themselves—is comparable to marketing consulting work in other industries. The actual rates might be higher elsewhere, but we're working in an environment that's money constrained and where people often help each other in different ways (e.g., there's a lot of sharing of data and experience). We're happy to engage in some mutual experience sharing as well and to charge slightly less, but it's definitely in line with our overall philosophy. Nobody would look at our prices and say that they're ridiculously cheap. In companies with a lot of overhead—heaps of staff, a large office in the city, etc.—you can have consultants who won't get out of bed for less than 5000 dollars. We're in a position where we don't need a minimum buy-in of that much work for that much money. We can still pick and choose and be quite flexible. We're also able to do that because the demand is there. We have so many inquiries all the time; we're not in the position where we have just three clients in a year and have to cover all our costs with those three clients. We can earn however much extra revenue we want by taking on more jobs. In many ways, it's best to avoid depending on just one or two clients too much.

What are the goals of Lumi's industrial outreach?

We're working to try to convince the industry that marketing and public relations are not the dark side of games development, the evil thing you don't want to do. There are developers who believe that something can't be art if you have to think about marketing—they just want to make good games that'll be played by a billion people. But for us, we ask, "Don't you want to get paid?" It's completely fine if someone just wants to be a hobbyist, and I don't look down on that at all. If someone is able to make games just for the art of it and be supported in other ways, that's really excellent. Me, though, I want people to be able to hire more people. I want the industry to be able to grow. I'd like to see Australia have a stratified environment where there are indie developers, AA, AAA, service providers, and agencies—and all of them robust. In essence, I want to see greater health in the industry in general, and a lot of that health gets delivered by revenue, and a lot of that revenue gets delivered by sales. You need marketing for sales, and sales mean everyone gets paid. Having a healthy respect for that, knowing that marketing can be fun, creative, and rewarding, that it's the connection point between the studio and the public, and that marketing brings fans and helps games resonate with people—that'd be great. Helping developers realize that marketing and public relations are a healthy, good part of game development and not an evil, crappy, toxic, mean part is one of our goals. We still see a lot of people, especially in the art game space, rolling their eyes about marketing and capitalism. I spend so many hours a week doing pro bono stuff and helping people that when I see developers roll their eyes it hurts a lot. How dare you accuse me of being a soulless sort. We care about the industry so much, and we want our outreach to convince people to leave behind their misguided ideas of marketing as evil.

Another part of our outreach comes from the fact that I want good games to find good audiences. So many games come out that are really good, and they just don't stick because nobody did the back-of-the-napkin math to know the sales they needed to make. It doesn't take a genius to do some rough guessing on how big an audience is needed to have a sustainable product. You have to get your game in front of people in order for it to be successful. The formula to figure this out is to look at your audience on all of your social channels, plus all your audiences through mailing lists, plus all the people who see it at trade shows, plus all the readerships of the outlets in which you receive press coverage, and then sum the numbers. If you know that something like only 1% of people who see a game via any one of these channels will buy it; and that if a game is free to play, only 1% of less than 1% of all the people who play the game will be monetized; and that you can figure out the lifetime value of an average customer in terms of X amount of cents—if you know all this, you can determine if you'll make the money you need to make. It's a pretty simple calculation, but people don't do it. They just put their game out there and think, "Oh, it's going to make enough. It's fine.

It's a good game. It'll take off. It'll go well. It'll make my money back and I can pay everyone." When I encounter that person and say, "How many sales do you need to make? What looks good? What's great and what's amazing sales-wise?" and they go, "I don't really know," it's insane to me. Oh, please, think about things. Make deliberate choices with your games and know that everything you're doing in and with your game has a consequence, and it doesn't need to freak you out. If we could get developers to think in these ways, they'd be much happier and the industry would be much healthier.

Does Lumi offer revenue calculation as part of its service suite?

It depends on the game. If it's mobile and free-to-play, we refer the client to Christina Chen. She can help them work out the game's lifetime value, virality rating, and other analytics so that they can make informed decisions. That kind of thing is better serviced by talking to someone like Christina.

For other types of games, we start by advising our clients to think about the numbers they need. We're not their accountant; we don't know what their profit and loss statements look like. But we start by getting them to think about these kinds of things because if they know what success looks like for them, it makes our job a lot easier. Their numbers help us to know the kind of audience size we need to bring in, and we can give them an idea about what sorts of activities they need to do to grab an audience that size, and we can ballpark the costs to do so. The better informed the client is coming to us, the better off the relationship can be and the better the multiplier of the outcome at the end for them.

What part of your job is most professionally rewarding? Why?

The best part of my job is knowing that the work we do really, truly helps developers and their projects. We make a difference. Our clients come away feeling better informed, supported, and armed with better marketing skills and resources.

What are the most significant internal challenges you face in your job?

The pressure. Being a co-founder of a small business in the service industry means that work is extremely busy and complex. You need to figure out what success looks like, plan for it, and execute. Then you test, evaluate, tweak, and continue. Because I feel a lot of responsibility for the success of the business, and a deep desire to support my clients to the highest degree of quality, I hold myself to very high standards and the buck doesn't get passed.

Given how committed you are to your work, as well as your expectation that your clients are similarly passionate, how do you talk with them about work/life balance and its impact on the bottom line?

It's a funny thing—work/life balance is super important to us as a company, but then I look at the hours I work sometimes and there's a disconnect. I regularly spill over into fifty hours a week—which is a lot for me—but there are developers who work close to double that. I'm still getting a handle on all of the inquiries that come in, or I'm always pushing myself at work to continue to do a lot of learning as I'm working. And I still really try to keep up-to-date with what's happening in the industry. That ends up tipping me over to fifty hours a week, but the goal is to work smarter and pare that down. At Lumi we're also working to mix our offerings between services and products, because products give us incremental revenue and are digitally scalable so that we don't have to make contact with every sale. Being able to get up to the point of building products takes additional time, and we have to carve out the time so that we can scale back our work week in the future.

If we have a suspicion that crunch is a factor for a client because we're seeing extremely sporadic amounts of output, or they're not super responsive, or they were only really steadily able to release certain assets and then they give us twenty at once, we might bring it up in our next call. We could say as little as "How are things going?" or as much as "We're really interested in having a chat about how the team is feeling about the project." We also try to identify bottleneck issues, and when we're talking about what we'd like to see from a client, we might say, "It's not an issue of aiming for the stars so you land on the moon. We're not asking you to flog yourself so you can maybe do okay, but we want to make this as ergonomic as possible. Instead of you spending ten hours in a week getting really frustrated that you're trying to understand how Twitter advertisements work, for example, we're just going to guide you and prioritize a few things." Much of dealing with crunch on both the development and service side is about prioritizing and discarding things that just aren't going to bring the return on investment, and also keeping the return on investment foremost in your mind. Essentially, we try to deal with/prevent crunch by talking regularly with clients about their production schedules. If we feel they'll have trouble hitting milestones, we bring them up. We encourage them to let us know as early as possible if they're having trouble completing required assets on time. If they're crunching, we make sure that we're only asking for the absolute minimum viable amount of work from them. The main thing we do is to make sure regular, even short calls/meetings are a part of our working relationship.

When it comes to marketing, some people might be tempted to focus on what they really like. They might like giving interviews, for example, and getting coverage in the media. In response, we might suggest less of those kinds of vanity metrics, i.e., things that look good on paper and might give the developer a bit of validation but that they probably shouldn't be focusing so heavily on. Media outreach to get press coverage is very expensive and takes a lot of hours. If we do it for a client, we say we need to do a website audit to make sure that when someone clicks through, the client is likely to catch them in a mailing list. Likewise, the purchasing process for the game needs to be completely clear, and we try to help clients reduce as much as possible the number of steps between someone noticing their game and actually buying it. We can get a client a huge audience through media coverage, but if their website is crap, those potential customers will all disappear.

A lot of what we do with clients is ask them to be deliberate about what they choose to do, prioritize certain things, and really concentrate on scheduling. We also try to be realistic about what we as marketing consultants can do. If someone comes to us and says, "I need an enormous advertising campaign," and they don't have the budget or the time, we're quite good at pushing back and saying, "We're really excited you're in this position with the game, congrats on having the beta done. We only have a certain number of hours available this month. What we suggest is prioritizing these activities and then seeing how things look." Our process is really about ergonomically giving clients tasks to do and also being very clear and assertive about what we're willing to do.

Does Lumi have a stable of contractors that clients can call on after they have had a consultation with you?

We're very strategic about how we connect clients with contractors. A common request we get is for a recommendation for someone to handle a developer/game's social media. We can do that, but we prefer to teach the client a minimum viable strategy for marketing so that they can take an employee on and then have us train that person. We don't want to slow down our momentum to do the nuts and bolts work of social media for a client if they can't pay us at our standard rate, which would get really expensive for them over time. Also, it's not super rewarding work for us to make content for someone else—we generally don't engage in that.

We'd love to have more contractors who are willing to be social content creators for clients, as well as perform other services. As I said, we work with Christina Chen on free-to-play, and Tara Brannigan at Boop.Social. Tara is based out of New Zealand and is building up a social strategy and community management services operation. We'll be interested in working more with her because she's focusing on the execution and "Can you do this for us?" side of things.

Again, though, we're careful about how we deploy contractors. You can get into muddy waters when you recommend certain people, or if someone takes on a contractor to execute some work and things don't go smoothly.

What are the external challenges you face in your job?

Generally, the industry has a limited understanding of marketing. The understanding of the value of marketing skills sometimes isn't there, leading to missed communication and the benefits of support in this area. Other challenges include continuing globalization, ongoing discoverability difficulties, and the perceptions of value and fair pricing expectations from a continually empowered consumer group. The ongoing discoverability issues are not so much for our business—our inquiries are really healthy and we get approached a lot—but it is for our clients. There have been massive increases in the number of games released recently—ten games a day getting published on Steam, and more than that getting published on other online app stores. Depending on where a developer is publishing, game discoverability can be a huge problem. Because there's been this democratization of tools and the access to digital distribution is so easy, getting a game noticed can be extremely hard for clients.

There's also the question of how to make a splash in mobile. Honestly, in terms of mobile, what we at Lumi can do is often limited. Clients want to work with a marketer to get a huge audience, and we can work with them to make sure their store copy is excellent. We can help them make sure that their social channels are strong, but virality and size are so defined now by getting a feature from Apple. That's the channel where mobile games are reaching this virality, where the multipliers are. I can't guarantee every client a feature from Apple. The relationships we have with Apple are something that I can't cash in often. I could get someone to have a look at a game, but there's no guarantee of anything beyond that.

And discoverability is a problem for all developers, regardless of their size. The potency of a game's impression has to be so strong now because there's so much out there. Consumers typically have a bunch of unplayed games in their Steam libraries, and to try to sell them on the need to make another purchase is tough.

What sorts of workplace changes would you implement if given the opportunity?

Crunch from developers gets passed on to their service providers. If a client is crunching, very often that stress and pressure becomes an expectation that's put on us as well. Anti-crunch policies and a focus on sustainable work practices would be very welcome. At some point there must be something definitive done about the overtime problem in the games industry.

How is the work you do in the game industry different from the work you have done elsewhere?

The game industry is fueled by passion—gargantuan amounts of it. This is a blessing and a curse, as the work is fulfilling and wonderful to be a part of. Conversely, it's always close to the heart of those performing the work, leading to a very close tie to identity and overall measures of self-worth at times. The passion and love can lead to people pushing themselves harder than is healthy, or to make judgements based far more on emotion than objective logic.

Which companies or ways of working (both within and outside of the game industry) do you look to for inspiration?

I always look for and admire the working lives of those who are happy in what they do, those who have found what work/life balance means to them. It's individual for everyone, and I don't directly emulate any person or groups. The ways of working I admire include making your career work for you, flexible/non-traditional working hours and locations, and working fewer than five days a week.

How would you describe the management structure in your company?

We have a very flat management structure, with no isolated departments. All communication is transparent and frequent. We'd love to be able to partner with more diverse consultants to refer specific work to them, and we'd love to have full-time administrative and finance staff to assist us and our account executive. If expansion makes future sense and we can maintain our vision and mission as a company, we'd certainly consider it, but would err on the side of conservative expansion over accelerated growth.

How would you describe the workflow in your company?

We use *Trello* for a macro view of our client projects, with *Google Calendar* for all due dates and a *Google Doc* for Katie and I to see (and make changes to) our daily to-do list. All items are organized using Stephen Covey's method, which means they're sorted by importance and urgency in a grid. Workflow is done in sprint-like blocks, with breaks over the day to touch base with team members and monitor that all tasks are on track, organized, and signed off on by both directors before being submitted to the client.

How does the workflow differ when working on different types of games (e.g., different genres, AAA versus casual games, etc.)?

It largely doesn't differ, as we're service providers and not title developers. However, our workflow differs slightly if we're providing a one-off service such as a workshop or lecture—which consists of preparation, execution, and reflection—as opposed to functioning on retainer for ongoing relationships, which uses the flow described above.

What are some of your notable quality of life issues, both routine and exceptional?

Routinely, both Katie and I work around fifty hours a week. This is more than we really want, even though we love our work. In exceptional cases, we're forced to crunch due to clients going through production issues, sudden changes, etc. Overall, we work too long and too arduously. It's everywhere in the industry—we all push ourselves too much and without enough hesitation. It's a badge of pride for some, and as a small business owner it can be hard to compete with those who do nothing else but work.

What are some of your notable career progression issues?

When Katie and I wanted to enter the game industry as experienced marketers, there were zero opportunities for us, so we made our own opportunity. If we hadn't been in a position to be able to take that risk, we likely wouldn't be in the game industry today.

What is Lumi's business development trajectory?

Katie and I have a lot of interest in developing the product side of our business because we often find ourselves saying the same things to different people and there are certain templates that are just really useful for people. We're very interested in developing products not only so that we don't have to have contact with every sale, but also because we just want to see a better acceptance and understanding of marketing in general. What we'd really like is to be able to be even more selective with certain clients, and see a maturation of the inquiries we get and the challenges that people have.

We'd also like to work more selectively with certain people and work with companies of different sizes but still be able to tangentially support a lot of people. We really enjoy workshops, public speaking engagements, and being able to have more contact with more people overseas and in more places. So, our business development trajectory is focused on anything that frees up our time so that we can experiment with more interesting things. This year we've traveled to all of the states in Australia (except for one in the Northern Territory) because we love going to the domestic shows and knowing what's happening in the local communities. The interpersonal relationships are some of the things that we find the most rewarding and most special about games. Being able to reach more people with what we can do and be less limited in the number of people we can help is super important to us. That's what we're going for with Lumi in the future.

How is the service side of game development going to change going forward?

That's tough, because the service side of games is still so much in its infancy. Compared to service providers, studios have a more established development history and set of organizational patterns. But I can see certain service providers growing and changing a little bit in the coming years. I think they won't get massive, and we're a long way away from an Australian studio being so large that they make a purchase offer to us or to somebody similar.

I think it's quite likely that service providers will stay independent, but that the service companies themselves might grow in team size. Service providers are a lot less likely to have a huge tectonic shift within the next five years in comparison to indie developers, for example, because indie developers are the ones in the riskier position.

Of course, we could definitely see a larger, outside agency such as Ogilvy & Mather being interested in what we do. I think it could be a tough fit, though, because we've taken this training approach, and a lot of what agencies make money off of is people not knowing what they don't know. A lot of marketing and PR agencies are comfortable with clients being completely ignorant about marketing. So, I think we'd probably have some teething problems if we got approached by an external company. We're not looking for it at the moment, but if there were an organization large enough to give us real funding—to chuck a lot of money into product development and things like that—it'd definitely be something I'd look at, and it might be something that suits us. Depending on the attitude, mood, and culture of the industry at the time, however, being acquired could actually damage our reputation in terms of authenticity and the whole thing of marketing not being evil. That'd be a pity. It just depends on if we thought it could work for the company and if it could help create better products and services.

What are the challenges facing the industry over the next decade?

We're challenged by the ongoing, persistent hangover of the industry treating women differently (both in the workplace and in the subject matter). While the situation is improving, there are still so many expectations and evaluations that women face unnecessarily and unfairly. I just want to be able to do my job and be respected for that.

Tobias Frisch
Sales/Finance

Tobias Frisch is a producer and financial controller at Studio Fizbin. Previously, he worked as an intern in Producing for Ravensburger Digital, the mobile game division of Ravensburger Spieleverlag GmbH. He holds an MA in service marketing from Hochschule Pforzheim, and a BA in business administration from Hochschule für Wirtschaft und Umwelt Nürtingen-Geislingen.

As part of his graduate work, he participated in a study abroad program at San Diego State University. His shipped titles include *Opera Maker, Game of Peace*, and *The Inner World*. He is an avid member of the *Star Wars* costuming group 501st Legion: The World's Definitive Imperial Costuming Organization.

* * * * *

How did you come to work in the game industry?

As a passionate gamer since the days of the Nintendo Game Boy and Super Nintendo Entertainment System, I simply wanted to work in the industry. So I looked up what opportunities there were in Germany, especially in the southern areas, and found Studio Fizbin. I didn't know anyone there and just applied as anyone would. I was aware of the fact that working for a small independent developer would often mean long, hard work, not earning a lot of money (enough to live on and not much more), and doing a lot of work that was to the right and left of my main skill set. In the end, it paid off.

What are your specific job duties?

My job is to keep the business side of the company running, meaning that I have to do everything business related. I'm responsible for financial control of the company overall, which includes planning for each project (no matter how many there are, usually two to five at once), public relations/external communications with clients and the press, all internal financial mechanisms (including talking to the lawyer and the tax counselor), accounting, and human resources (e.g., managing applicants and freelancers we work with). Basically, I work on everything except creating the game, though indirectly I have an effect on that too. The creative director calls me his worst enemy. He always wants (and of course needs) to make the best, most beautiful and content-rich game we can. But my job is to deliver the game on time and on budget. So, that's why I'm his worst enemy—I'm the reason we often have to sacrifice content.

Unfortunately, all of these responsibilities mean that I can't dig too deeply into any one thing. For example, while I have an MA in marketing, marketing is only about 15% of my total job duties. The reason that it's so little is that we have to deal with tons of new challenges every day. This week, for instance, a project was canceled, which is really bad. Now we have to figure out what to do instead of the project we'd weeks ago planned to get started on. No amount of university work can teach you what to do in a situation like this. My job is to respond and adapt quickly to new problems each day, and there's nobody in the company with a lot of experience with these kinds of problems to consult with. Really, my duties include the pure existence of the company. If I fail, so does the company.

As a company, there are two basic areas we work in. The first is our own projects, where we develop the project idea, do the design, and make the game. These projects have to be financed, which is pretty difficult. The second thing we do is contract work. This means that someone else has an idea and we do the design and build the game. The project isn't for us but a client. We usually work three to four months on a big contract project, and if we're lucky in winning pitches and then projects, we do one or two of them per year. At the same time, we're generally also working on several smaller projects, such as finishing up the development of an existing project or doing some prototyping. There might be four to six of these types of projects per year. Unfortunately, our own projects are rare, with usually one per year (or fewer). These projects usually have a larger scope, coming in at six months or more. We're a small team, which is why we usually can only do one large project at a time. We've been trying to get to the point where we can do more large projects in parallel, which means that we also have to grow our team. Just this year we just hired two more programmers for a bigger client's project, and we're trying to start another before the first has ended.

Usually when there's a new project, I sit together with our leads from the technology and design departments and we break down the project and try to plan the game as best we can in terms of development time and financial parameters. I'm the keeper of the plan, so to speak. If there's any change in time or budget that the other areas of the company need to initiate, they come to me.

How do your work responsibilities as financial controller of the company impact your relationship with the other members of the team?

First off, let me say that we've all become good friends at Fizbin. While it's true that each of us has different skill sets, all in all we're the same. We want to make awesome, beautiful, high-quality games. That's a good, thick connection we have. Somehow, we manage to differentiate between the business side of things and the personal relationships we all have together.

Sometimes it's really hard and we have some strong discussions, but afterward we can go out, drink a beer, and talk about something else.

That said, it was really hard for me when I first joined the company. After about six months, I wasn't sure I was doing the right things. I was always having to say, "We don't have time. Cut this out, cut that out." I asked the other directors if we could talk after work about my performance and they told me I was doing a great job. They said, "If we sometimes look angry, don't worry. We're so happy that we have you, but you have to get used to this. So please don't take it personally." We're all really honest with each other, which means that if I have to be the bad guy, they know the reason. They've learned that the decisions I make are strictly financial, and they've also learned to accept when I impose milestones or provide notifications about upcoming dates and release, or talk about how to get things done on time and on budget.

It's important to point out that this kind of professional conflict happens with all of the areas in the company, not just with financial. There's often conflict between concept and technical because there are potential features that just aren't doable. The conflict has been good because it's taught everyone that we have to work very closely together during the conceptualization phase to make sure that ideas and features are really possible given the various financial, technical, and time constraints. We've done some projects in the past where we didn't have this close collaboration during the beginning, and once we got into production we had some serious problems.

That said, things are more complicated with financial because the technical director and the creative director are two of the company's founders, which technically makes them my bosses. At the same time, I have to tell them what they have to do.

What are the other significant personnel components at your studio?

We have a creative director, who is responsible for all things conceptual. We have a technical director, who is responsible for everything programming related. We have an art director, who is in charge of developing the style and graphical assets of our projects. We have a game designer, who helps the creative director in building a structure—a design—for the concept. He's also in charge of building a tutorial for the programmer, which describes what the game is supposed to be. We also have another programmer whose job is to assist the technical director, as well as two new programmers.

What is the average development time frame for your studio's projects?

Three to four months per project, with up to five projects—one to two large ones (with a three- to four-month development time) and several smaller projects—going at once. Freelancers are a must with a timetable like that. We can't keep all of them employed all the time, because each project has different demands. Sometimes we need more animators, sometimes we need more graphic artists, sometimes we need more programmers. We have a huge network of freelancers, which means we can relatively easily get people in and out of projects as needed. All of these people want to work as freelancers. We've really wanted to hire some of them permanently—we always need a user interface designer, for example—but the people we know and work with don't want to come on full-time. One guy told me that he wants to stay free and wants to decide on his own what projects he works on. I'm actually the opposite: I want the security of a steady job.

How did you generate this large network of freelancers?

The base of the network was formed by the founders of Fizbin. They studied together at the Filmakademie Baden-Württemberg, which is quite well known in Germany. During their studies they met and did projects with many different graphic designers and animators, who are now the foundation of our freelance network.

The other important source of freelance talent is fairs and events. That's where we meet new people. I guess at this point, about 50% of our freelancers come from events like Gamescom.

What part of your job is most professionally rewarding? Why?

I was hired mainly to manage the timing, budget, and quality of game projects. The three founders of Studio Fizbin have other key competencies in technology (programming), art (design, concept), and creative work (game design, world design, story). They needed someone to run the business side of the company and help Fizbin survive in the daily, harsh environment of game development. This hasn't changed, and we also have to do lots of contract work to make enough money.

In light of this, there are three parts of my job that I find extremely reward-ing. First, when we win a pitch or when a project is finished on time, with quality, and (of course) under budget. Second, when our company is finan-cially safe for a couple of months—you can never, ever think in longer terms than that unless you're lucky and one of your games is a million-dollar hit (1 out of 10,000 games will be that lucky). And third, when we get nice emails from happy players or great game ratings and awareness. I don't get to do as much marketing as I'd like, so good game awareness means that a small amount of marketing work has paid off.

Can you talk more about the funding process and how it relates to the devel-opment process?

Securing funding for our own games is really the hardest thing I've ever experienced. In Germany, there's some state funding, but it's nothing com-pared to the kind of governmental funding you'd find in northern Europe, Scandinavia, or Canada. It's damn hard to get money, and we've had to delay a game project because we didn't get funding. Thanks to new contract work, however, we're now able to apply for two state funding sources and have the opportunity to get some publisher funding if the state funding is suc-cessful. In general, the money from the German government is game spe-cific, but funded projects have to have an education orientation. It doesn't need to be an educational game made for schools only, but it has to have an educational influence. Our game *The Inner World* is a good example. It's a point-and-click adventure in the style of *The Secret of Monkey Island.* It's not really an educational game in the sense that there's a specific topic that the game teaches. Still, kids learn to think logically, combine objects, and solve puzzles. There's also no violence in the game, which is always good when applying for government funding.

Recently there's been a change to the state funding policy such that games don't need to be educational at all costs. This is a good change. Before, it was sometimes hard to produce a strictly educational game. Sometimes games are just fun and not necessarily educational.

On average, our bigger project budgets—like *The Inner World*—come in at around 150,000 to 200,000 euros, with external funding amounting to 100,000 euros of that total. In terms of government funding, there are basi-cally two kinds. There's small funding, which has a cap of 20,000 euros, and big funding, which has a ceiling of 120,000 euros. Usually you don't get the maximum amount from either source, and the catch is that neither can fund more than 50% of your overall project budget. The constraints can really break your neck, and the application process is pretty tough. It involves completing something like twelve different forms as well as a pitch document. The pitch document needs to be submitted in both paper and electronic copies, and in it you need to describe the game idea from top to bottom. You don't need to have a prototype—you can get funding for prototyping, which is pretty good. But, you have to have a really, really strong pitch document, usually consisting of thirty to fifty pages. Also, you need to submit a basic marketing concept, target group description, and staff list. You also need to address regional factors; we're based in Ludwigsburg in the state of Baden-Wüerttemberg, and we have to spend 120% of the money we receive in the state of Baden-Wüerttemberg, which makes it impossible to work with people in France, for example. Governmental funding is a good idea, but there are so many constraints that come with it that it makes it hard for a German company to become international. All of this impacts the distribution and sales of a state-funded game.

There's also funding from publishers, but quite often the deals are really crappy. If the developer gets a 20% share, that's a good deal. Also, it's really rare that publishers finance your game, and if so, often it's just at about 30% of the total. We're in a lucky position that we've met a really good publisher who focuses on indie studios and they try to help and finance us as much as they can. In the end, both the developer and the publisher need to earn money and want to do business together. So it's all about negotiating.

There are some investors and banks that also provide funding, but they see game development as a very high-risk investment. As a developer, you can't really plan to sell a certain number of units, because video games can be extremely successful or huge failures . . . unless, of course, you have a trademark like *Assassin's Creed*, which is a self-seller. If you're small and you're doing your own IP, it's really hard to plan ahead and with enough detail to satisfy a bank.

There's also Kickstarter, which recently launched in Germany. We have some friends at other companies who've tried it, but they've found that they work all day doing stuff for Kickstarter and still don't get the money they need for their projects. It looks like if you don't have a game celebrity in your campaign or a well-known IP, you'll fail.

Usually, we try to combine some of the state funding we're able to get together with a little bit of a publisher deal and our own money. We don't have a good solution to the funding problem, because we're still struggling with it.

In addition to the procedural constraints associated with receiving governmental monies, what are the international distribution challenges you face?

On *The Inner World*, we worked with a German publisher who has a partner in Great Britain who handles international publishing. We worked with the German publisher to develop a marketing plan for Germany as well as for the international markets. In the German-speaking market, the plan was awesome; I have no complaints. On the international side, we managed to get press coverage from all of the big sites (e.g., *Rock, Paper, Shotgun*), and our publisher was at PAX Prime. Still, public awareness of our game was really low, and we don't know why. Obviously, press coverage isn't the only thing you need to worry about anymore. Maybe we should have done a better job of getting the game played by international Let's Play-ers. The most famous German Let's Play-er played our game, and we saw a heavy increase in awareness and engagement (e.g., with our Facebook fan page) but not really in sales. It looks like a lot of Let's Play viewers didn't buy the game because they already knew the story (which is quite logical). But in the end, awareness is better than nothing at all.

In addition, I think point-and-click adventures just aren't trendy anymore outside of Germany, unless you're doing *The Walking Dead*. The classic style seems to be dead.

At any rate, we're grateful that our publisher helped fund the project. Without them, we couldn't have developed and launched the game. They're a small company, too, but they're awesome. They really worked hard to get the game out. They provided about 50,000 euros of funding and marketing spends, and they also didn't calculate their own working hours. They worked for the game, but it wasn't calculated in their share, which is pretty awesome.

Why is the million unit sales figure so important?

In the traditional games market (i.e., not iOS or Android), one million units is typically what you need to reach in order to make back your investment.

For *The Inner World*, it's the number we got from our publisher, who showed us other games in their portfolio that all circled around one million units when they were at the break-even point. We know that traditional sales for Mac and PC won't come anywhere near that number—especially from a relatively unknown company—which is why we decided to include iOS and Android distribution in our plan. Our traditional sales came in around 20,000 units, which is nothing. Our iOS and Android sales are around 200,000 units, which is pretty good for a paid app. What we still want to do but need to check to see if it's technically possible is to port the game to console. The PC market is dying, but the console market is pretty stable. Maybe porting the game to consoles will help our sales numbers.

As far as digital distribution to PC is concerned, Steam is pretty much the only thing that matters. If you do a PC game, you have to be on Steam. If you look at Steam's price decreases—you can often get a AAA title for 50% off four weeks after the initial release—you realize that's just the PC market. Almost nobody wants to pay fifty dollars or more anymore for a PC game. I don't know why; basically, it's the same game as the one that's on the PlayStation 4, but people just don't buy it. I can only assume that Steam is the reason for all of the sales that people are used to. There's a summer sale, an autumn sale, a Halloween sale, a Christmas sale—you don't need to buy any PC game for the original price because there'll be a sale in which the game is 30%–80% off and people know that. That's why the market is dying.

On consoles, it's much more stable. Fifty to eighty dollars is normal for any game on any console. For any new game that you do, you have to develop it for the consoles. You should do PC too, to get as much revenue from it as possible, but not as a single platform release anymore.

Are you able to calculate for all of these sales in your financial outlook modeling?

That's pretty hard to do. We can do it with our publisher because they have over eighty games in their portfolio and can give us some pretty good numbers to work with. But without past numbers it's almost impossible. When we can't do it, we guess, and maybe we're right 70% of the time. Last Christmas, *The Inner World* sold a lot more than even our publisher thought, and we still don't know why. In that case, the surprise was a good thing, but it can be the other way too.

We can't point to a specific press interaction as the cause of sales. There's always so much coming in—from Let's Plays to streams to reviews to marketing events—and everything impacts sales to some degree. You just can't figure out to what degree.

Together with our publisher, we keep track of sales data with tools like *App Annie*. *App Annie* is a pretty good tracking tool, and it's helpful to look at it after a discount has been offered to see how effective it was. With *The Inner World*, we tested some discounts in the beginning to see what kind of data we could gather.

What are the tools you rely on to do your job, and what are the tools you wish you could add to the company?

I'd like to have an in-app tracking tool that would tell me which users are playing our games, when they play them, and how they play them (i.e., when and where they quit). In Germany, we're very concerned as a nation with the protection of personal information, but I'd really love a tool that provided that data. We had thought about using a third-party data collection application in our last game but decided against it because of the security standards and laws in Germany.

Given your specific technical and financial challenges, what does the business of selling games look like at Studio Fizbin?

We have a really good mixture of the contract work we do and our own games. If you do contract work, you can do the planning pretty well. There's a project budget, and usually your client asks you to set it. Basically, you say, "We can do this and that for this amount of money."

At the same time, we can't exist without doing contract work. Because making and selling your own games is so damn unpredictable, you have to have a stable income side. The contract work is what makes our company plannable. Another way to look at it is that I have two jobs: one that pays the bills and the other that's more personal.

The problem with this arrangement is that your own projects always suffer, which is why it takes a long time to develop your own games. We'll keep taking on contract work until one of our games is a million-selling hit. That'll be the time when we'll have enough funds on our own to do the next game, which will also sell a million units (to do the next game, which will also sell a million units, and so on). Until then, we have to do the contract work to finance our own projects. One out of 10,000 small developers will succeed, and all the rest will do contract work until the end.

I know a lot of other companies in Germany our size—we're pretty well connected. They usually tell me that they have exactly the same problems we have, and according to what we hear, it looks like we're one of the most stable small companies in Germany . . . and we suffer. This makes me not want to know how the other companies suffer. We've been around for five years and it looks like not many other companies our size last that long.

As far as long-term planning goes, that's something we're starting to be able to do more of. Initially, my job focused a lot on putting out fires, because nobody at the company prior to my arrival thought about financing after the release of a game. They were completely focused on finishing the project that was in front of them. What we had to learn is that once you release a game into the marketplace, there's no money coming in for six months or so. Having no money creates a lot of fires, which then need to be put out.

These days, I look at our financial spreadsheet each morning, and I can see that we're able to plan ahead for six months, which is amazing given where we came from. Usually, we have our internal meetings once a week, and I tell everyone the situation: that we have security for six months and then there's no money left. We have to constantly look for other jobs to do.

Is there a solution to the seemingly intractable problem of contract work taking precedence over creative work?

After *The Inner World*, we tried to make another game in three months, which for us was impossible. Our own demands on game scope and quality make it impossible for us to make a full-scale game in such a short time. Unfortunately, we didn't know that at the time. But we did know that we needed more games in our portfolio, which would generate a share of revenue over the months after a game launch. So, one solution is that you need to have enough games in your portfolio at any given time to make for a steady revenue flow.

Another solution would be for classic finance institutions like banks to start investing in small companies like ours. They need to see small companies as revenue generating. More traditional industries can go to investors and banks and easily get money. In Germany, it seems like game developers are still thought of as kids who want to do something awesome. There needs to be a change in that perspective so that the game business is seen as serious business. Until that happens, you'll need good luck so that your game is a hit and you make enough money to develop the next game. If your luck isn't so good, then you're in that circle of contract work.

What are the most significant internal challenges you face in your job?

We're small; we haven't had the million unit hit so far. So, the biggest challenge is to survive financially and to be able to make our own games. The other significant challenge is that no one in the company had ever made games before, so each day is new to us. The flip side is that we gain so much experience each day. As a result, project management is a big new challenge with each project, and we can use new experiences gained in previous projects when we plan for the next one. It's exhausting but awesome.

What are the external challenges you face in your job?

No bank or investor will invest in you or your project if you're small and unknown. It creates a bit of a vicious circle, because if you're known you've had at least one big hit. But to make games (and hopefully get a hit), you need a lot of money, which you don't get without a big hit. So, each and every time you have to prove yourself as externally worthy, both financially and qualitatively.

For contract work, you have to engage in competition with anywhere from several to hundreds of other companies to win a pitch in order to get some funding. Luckily, we're pretty good at that and have had some awesome contract jobs over the last several years. Still, it's hard to get funding for your own games.

We're really lucky because we have one of the best publishers you could imagine—Headup Games—and they try to invest in our development and give us support in sales, marketing, PR, etc. Without them, we wouldn't have been able to make *The Inner World*.

Another big external challenge is clients. Sometimes they just try to squeeze everything they can out of you, demanding more and more content for a project that's already been planned. Some clients just don't understand what costs stand behind a small feature, and some just try to push what they want through without paying the additional cost. This can be a never-ending battle. On the other side, some clients are just great and trust you and your work.

What sorts of workplace changes would you implement if given the opportunity?

We only have one office here, though we also have space in Berlin. Since I make some critical phone calls or hold important meetings (when it comes to financing, for example), I'd love to have a separate room to be able to talk more privately about serious topics. This isn't because there are any secrets, but rather so we wouldn't worry our other colleagues. Sometimes you need to discuss things and the discussion sounds harsh, even though the decision that comes out of that discussion isn't nearly so. So, it can be important that not everyone hears every discussion all the time. Still, I generally love the atmosphere of us being together in one room—perhaps a separate office with a glass door?

Also, I'd love to invest more in new hardware, monitors, and software licensing. Software licensing is really expensive, and we can only cover the basics.

Which companies or ways of working (both within and outside of the game industry) do you look to for inspiration?

Well, I try not to look so much at other companies since we need to have our own way of doing things. I like our sometimes chaotic-looking but pretty fast and efficient way of doing our work. But of course, there's always room for inspiration. I like the atmosphere at Headup Games. They're able to provide a bit more in the way of good office spaces and good development hardware. Even though they're bigger than we are, they're able to keep a sense of fun in the workplace, which is important, as we're all more of a "working family" than just coworkers.

I'd love to create two or more game development teams at Fizbin, and these would consist of small units of various departments that would be able to make more than one project quickly and with good quality. My inspiration for this is Ravensburger Digital, where I did an internship for my MA. They have a flat hierarchy but are able to keep several teams running at once.

How would you describe the management structure in your company?

Extremely flat. We're a small team and, depending on the projects, we tem-
porarily grow. Our management—if you could even call it that—consists of
the leads of the various departments: business, art, concept/game design,
and technology. Together, we do decision making in terms of new projects
and overall company decisions. As the "general manager," I usually provide
all important information and make an action plan. We then discuss it
together, and I execute the decision. This is really important (for bigger decisions) since I act in the name of the three founders, who are also my friends.

How would you describe the workflow in your company?

Depending on the project, we plan each workflow individually. Of course,
some rules always apply. For instance, we usually do prototyping while
developing the game design based on the general concept. In parallel, art
is designed and conceptualized. Only after that pre-production phase is
complete and the game design document is ready do we start production, which usually begins with sketching out the basic technical frame-
work (e.g., game logic). All other departments involved produce assets,
from graphics to animations to sound files. Each of these steps is planned
carefully, with me as head of planning alongside the leads of each main
department. The plan is monitored regularly and updated as needed.
Since we have an overview of each department, we can be very fast if
changes occur.

*How does the workflow differ when working on different types of games (e.g.,
different genres, AAA versus casual games, etc.)?*

The biggest difference is in the number of departments involved. Also, the workload of each department and, therefore, the number of people working there
varies. The basic flow is always the same; it just gets more complex when there's
a bigger, yearlong or so production compared to a three-month minigame.

How do you handle contract negotiations with publishers?

We have a media lawyer who counsels us if need be. What we usually do is
define what we want for ourselves from a given contract and then go from
there. For example, we typically say that we want to keep the IP, and that we

want X amount of money for development—we can't execute the contract for anything less. We really try to stick to the decision we make internally. Sometimes it works, and sometimes the publisher says "bye-bye." You have to be like that; you can't be a publisher's plaything. If a publisher sees that you know what you want, they usually agree to your terms or you find good compromises together.

It's also important that you don't minimize your importance, that you don't think, "I'm the small developer, and they're the giant publisher." You have the idea and the skills to turn it into a game. You're on an equal level with the publisher, and you need to show that. It's really important.

Publishers like it if you've done some thinking about sales and revenue numbers, even if the numbers may not be accurate. They really love it if you're well prepared to discuss every aspect of a game, not just the design side. We didn't do that in some of our early pitches, and only focused on design. When publishers asked us about target groups, performance, and stuff like that, we weren't able to respond.

What are some of your notable quality of life issues, both routine and exceptional?

Since this is my first real job, I can't compare it with other experiences. But working in the game industry in general has been a dream come true, and so my personal happy bar is very high. On the other hand, working for an independent developer is often really hard, with crunch times and sleepless nights about the company's existence, even though I'm "just" an employee. Every time we accomplish another milestone or something like that, it reaffirms my happiness and commitment.

We manage the work/life balance pretty well here, all things considered. I have my fair share of free time and, therefore, can work hard during the normal work days/hours. We've improved things a lot in this area, including for our founders.

During the last months of development on *The Inner World* and for a few months after release—when we had PAX, support emails, and all the PR stuff going on—we could only live for work. There's no other way to say it. It overwhelmed all of us. We had a good time, and we loved it, but there was no room for anything else. It was a total failure in terms of work/life balance.

As a result, we started tracking our working time more closely. In games and other creative industries there are always crunch times. Sometimes you just have to get things done to meet a deadline. We usually have three to four crunch periods per year, and each period typically lasts three to six weeks depending on the project and planning. But we want to reward our people, so we've implemented a policy in which overtime is tracked and then rewarded with free time afterward.

Tracking time has also helped the founders of the company realize just how many hours a day they were working, and they've tried to reduce their own time commitment. They've gone from fourteen hours per day, six days per week to nine hours per day, five days per week. The amazing thing is that they're still able to get things done. We've gotten more efficient as a company because we don't work as much anymore.

Time tracking in general has also helped us improve our estimation of development time for game features, which has helped us reduce crunch times.

Are there university programs that do a good job of preparing students to work in the game industry?

Unfortunately, no. I don't think that any studies can really reflect the reality of a small company like ours. University programs usually concentrate on the basics and on the bigger theories. In some sense, this is okay. When I think back, my studies taught me to think logically, to structure processes, and to make sure to have the right information at the right time.

The real learning in game development comes on the job and during internships. The best thing you can do to prepare yourself for work in the industry is to go through an internship or two just to get a feel for how fast and chaotic the game industry can be.

Sometimes I wish I had a very experienced boss who could draw on that experience to tell me the right way to do something. I could use the counsel. Universities should look to incorporate teachers from smaller companies, not just large ones. The brand manager for Mercedes is great, but Mercedes has very different problems than a small company.

What is your relationship like with other game companies?

We have a good relationship with other companies. There's competition some-times, if you pitch for the same work. But overall, we're more like an under-ground network that's trying to make awesome games. We know a lot of other small game companies and are good friends with them. Unfortunately, none of us can help each other because none of us have any money. What we've been trying to do is make a physical game developer hub with a bunch of developers in the same building, like the Dutch did with the Dutch Game Garden (which is state supported). The guys in the Munich area have succeeded a little bit, so now if there's a big project and they need some additional developers, they can just ask their neighbors. We tried to do the same thing here in the Stuttgart area, but so far it's failed. Without support from the government, we can't do it. Getting a building or some space is really, really expensive. The monthly costs of space, hardware, and services are what really hurt, financially speaking.

What are the challenges facing the industry over the next decade?

We're already seeing rapidly decreasing revenues for classic paid games, especially in the PC arena. Also, the retail market is shrinking, while digi-tal distribution—like the Steam platform or the PlayStation Store—can't be ignored anymore.

In addition, free-to-play, pay-to-play, and so forth present new business models and challenges for both casual and AAA game development. Mobile gaming, too, has become a significant business sector in the last five to ten years. As a developer, you can't ignore those facts anymore. You can't just make a game for the specific platform you want; you have to be able to deliver on as many platforms as possible.

Another challenge is that people tend to spend less and less money for games since there are now a huge number of free-to-play or episode-style games, which cost way less at the time of initial purchase than a full game.

Finally, over the next decade, mobile devices will become as powerful as today's PCs or consoles. We'll also see the mainstreaming of virtual real-ity devices (e.g., Oculus Rift). For developers and publishers, it'll be more and more important to hook players right from the beginning with exciting gameplay and good graphics. It'll be challenging to provide a low barrier to entry and to keep players playing your game over a long time. Multiplayer, downloadable content, and paid add-on features will become much more important than they are currently. Basically, developers will need to be able to deliver a game that has a low entry barrier (i.e., it's inexpensive), but will be able to earn money via additional content and keep players playing a long time. Not all developers and publishers will survive the change.

What is your long-term goal for Studio Fizbin?

We definitely don't want to be just another contractor, because we want to do our own stuff. A good deal with a big publisher would keep us safe for two years and allow us to do our own game. Also, they'd finance the whole production, which smaller publishers wouldn't do. Nothing's decided yet, but it's definitely something we're considering. We have to find the balance.

Kim Soares
Executive

Kim Soares is the founder, CEO, and lead designer of Kukouri Mobile Entertainment. Prior to founding Kukouri Mobile Entertainment, he helped found Nitro Games, where he served as lead designer and producer. He began his career in the game industry in 1996 as a journalist after receiving his diploma from Langinkoski Koulu in Kotka, Finland. He has written game reviews for many Finnish newspapers and game magazines, and in 2000 founded the Finnish gaming website *Peliversumi*, which is no longer active. His shipped titles include *Monsterrific, Tiny Troopers: Alliance, Tiny Troopers: Joint Ops, Tiny Troopers 2: Special Ops, Tiny Troopers, Commander: Conquest of the Americas, Woody Two-Legs: Attack of the Zombie Pirates*, and *East India Company*.

* * * * *

What is the history and structure of your company?

When I started the company, I was the only employee for a few months. Within six months I hired everybody else, and there have been eight full-time people since. Everybody lives in or near Kotka, Finland, with half the team commuting from Kouvola (a small town 60 km away). But we're really flexible and the guys from Kouvola work from home at least once a week.

We also outsource some things, mainly entire projects. As a small team, we can only do so much ourselves, so outsourcing the porting of projects and such enables our team to focus on new games. For example, we outsourced the Windows port of *Tiny Troopers* to a developer in Spain. We've found that outsourcing is doable for us if we outsource the whole process. Trying to outsource bits and pieces of things (e.g., graphics, parts of programming, etc.) creates a lot of work, and you have to dedicate people full-time to supervise it. For us, that's not a good use of our manpower.

Keep in mind that we only work on our own projects and don't do any contract work. That's the strategy we decided on early in our efforts. As a small indie, we're in a lucky position in that we've had an investor who has been with us from the start, and so we haven't had to do any outsourced work for other companies. Many small developers in mobile try to do that—take on contract work as a way to fund their own projects—but it's really easy to get lost in that way of doing things. Suddenly, three years have gone by and you realize you've only been doing project work for others. You haven't made any of your own games.

When I left my former employer, I thought I'd focus on developing PC games. But when I did the calculations, I realized that I'd need a team of twenty people and maybe five or six million euros of investment money for at least three years. Then I did the calculations for a mobile game company that would release one game per year, and the numbers were much more favorable. A mobile team only needed six to ten people and 250,000–300,000 euros worth of investment money. Needless to say, it was much easier to choose mobile.

While the mobile side of the game industry is easy to get into, it's hard to survive once you're there. I was lucky to find an investor: Suomen Viestintärahoitus, which is a small investment company partly owned by other companies. I'm on the board of a company that owns part of Suomen Viestintärahoitus, so I knew the CEO really well. I knew he was looking for new businesses and fields to invest in, and I was looking for investors. Since we sat on the same boards, it was really easy to forge a partnership.

In starting your own company, what were your staffing priorities?

Basically, I was looking for people I knew, people I could trust who were professional and would be up to the task. This was made more challenging because I wanted to build the company in Kotka, and the gravitational pull in Finland is Helsinki. Most people go to Helsinki to look for work in the game industry, and if they go there, it's much harder to get them to move back to a small city or town like Kotka. I hired my first two employees from a trainee program, and the rest I had worked with at another gaming company.

What are the job classes at Kukouri?

We have a 3D animator, a 2D graphic artist, and an art director, who also has a 2D background. We have four programmers, but one is also a producer half-time. And then there's me, the CEO and lead designer. That makes eight.

At one point, we had a marketing guy as well. He was with us for maybe a year and a half but had to resign for personal reasons. That's actually one of the reasons we teamed up with Chillingo, which is a subsidiary of Electronic Arts (EA). They not only publish our games, but also handle most of the marketing for us as well. They have good relationships with Apple and Google, which is really important in mobile games. They also have a good network with the gaming media. As a small developer, it makes sense to team up with a good publisher who can offer added value.

Does having a foreign-based publisher create any particular challenges for you?

That's a tricky question. As a publisher, they want to take part in the design process and an outside viewpoint can be very valuable. So, we welcome any and all feedback and suggestions. The problem is that we have a very agile team, and when we send the build to the publisher for feedback we're already doing the next phase of design and development. In some specific cases—when a key feature is concerned, for example—we just go through the whole thing with them in *Skype* so that we're sure to get their feedback.

Another challenge is that we have to follow the legal advice and requirements that come from the publisher. We want to be safe from lawsuits, of course, but as a Finnish person it doesn't always make sense as to why things have to be so strict. US legal people want to play things really, really safe, and I can understand that: the threat that someone will slip and fall in a McDonald's, then sue the company for a gazillion dollars is ever-present. So, I can see why the legal folks might be paranoid about some things, but as a European I'd be much more lenient generally.

How did you connect with Chillingo?

In 2011, we were looking for a publisher, and I met with the Chillingo people in Paris at an event called Game Connection. It's like a speed dating event for publishers and developers, and you book meetings that last for thirty minutes. The event takes place over three days, so you can have as many as forty meetings with forty different publishers. We had our first game in beta stage, and I booked meetings with different publishers. One of them was Chillingo, and they liked the game so much that they called me back the same evening. We ended up finalizing the contract two weeks later. They turned out to be the best possible publisher for us: they're part of EA and one of the best indie publishers in the business.

Mobile development is different from console and PC development, of course. With PC and console, the publisher traditionally funds a major part (if not all) of the development costs. The publisher is taking a huge financial risk, and even though the developer owns the IP, the developer only ends up getting 5%–15% of the revenue that comes in. Because the production costs are so much less in mobile, developers don't usually need publisher funding. Even if they did, there aren't any publishers who will fund mobile game development, at least not in any meaningful fashion. I know there are publishers who might chip in 20,000 euros, but that's insignificant in terms of the scope of game budgets. In mobile, the only reason you want a publisher is for the marketing side of things. With Apple and Google being the dominant and basically the only marketplaces you have, you have to have a good relationship with them. If you don't, then it's really unlikely that you're going to get promoted in the App Store or on Google Play. And if you do get promoted there, you're going to get millions and millions of downloads, which are vital for your survival as a company. Chillingo and other big publishers have really good relationships with Apple and Google. Big publishers have people visiting Apple and Google offices on a weekly basis and pitching the latest games in their portfolio. That's something we could never do as a small Finnish developer.

Who handles the analytics on your projects?

Analytics is one reason we teamed up with Chillingo. They can tap into EA—especially EA Mobile—and use their analysts to go through the data. One of the key metrics in mobile games is LTV—the lifetime value of your average player. The LTV number tells you if it's feasible to spend money on a user or not, and there are some significant mathematics involved in calculating the LTV. The LTV isn't an exact number; it's more of an abstract estimate. So, if you get a player to download your game, then on average his or her lifetime value is going to be X dollars. Some estimates for Supercell's games come in at about eight to ten dollars LTV, and that's the top in the industry. If you have a smaller game or maybe one that's not so successful, the LTV can be anywhere from a few cents to a few dollars. And when you're considering how to pitch and develop your game, you compare the LTV against whatever the user cost for a single player would be. Let's say, for example, that you can break things down by country, and you know that the LTV in France for your game is five dollars. So, on average, every French player you have will bring five dollars to you. You then take that number as your metric and target French players on Twitter, Facebook, ads in other games, etc., theorizing that it'll take less than five dollars to get one new user for your game. If it costs more than the LTV, of course, you don't do it.

LTV is especially important for free-to-play games, which are about 95% of the games in mobile these days. With free-to-play games, you're counting the players who have downloaded the game and what they're spending on average per day. You then extrapolate from that number to get an estimate of how long each player will play the game and spend money over a long period of time.

LTV calculations are automated to a high degree because they involve millions of data points and hundreds of thousands of lines of numbers. Calibrating LTV is some serious math. There are variables involved because you can't know the LTV of any one person, but you can estimate the variables that you think might hold true for a given scenario. For our first game, we needed three months post-release before we had enough data for meaningful LTV estimates.

How would you describe the management structure in your company?

Extremely flat. Everyone has a say on game design, for example. As CEO, I tell our team very openly about what our board has decided, how investor negotiations are going, and so forth. I do this because that way every team member knows why we're doing what we're doing.

Team members are responsible for estimating their own product schedules and then sticking to those schedules as much possible. In short, we give the responsibility to the employees themselves.

One thing that has enabled us to have a flat organization and to be quick to react is the fact that we only have eight full-time employees. It's very much like what Supercell does. They've organized their teams into ten people or fewer. We're in the process of looking for investment to hire a second team and double our headcount, but that would mean that we would have two separate teams, not one big team doing one game. If you get more than ten people on a team, you can't as easily have a flat organizational structure. You can have a bigger company, but then you have to organize those people into smaller teams.

Your history in the game industry is long and diverse, beginning in journalism, moving into design, and now as a CEO. Is this a common career arc?

I think my background is common, or at least it used to be. Ten to fifteen years ago, many developers I met—especially the designers—had a background in the gaming press. I think that if you critique games, you have a good background to be a designer because you spend your time not just playing games but analyzing them. You try to define what's good about them, and you compare them to dozens or hundreds of other games you've already played.

While I have a lot of experience as a game journalist, I don't have an advanced degree. I tried to get into university twice, once to study English literature, once to study journalism. I failed to get in both times, and at the same time I got my first job at a Finnish games magazine. I stopped trying to get into school and started working. Over the next several years, I went from writing game reviews to making games.

As far as being a CEO goes, I draw on my own experience. I've been an employee myself, and I want to create a work environment that I'd want to work in. That's a fairly new idea in Finland. Supercell CEO Ilkka Paananen is right on the money when he says he strives to be the "least powerful CEO in the world." Basically, that's what I'm going for: I want all of my employees to take charge of their own work and destiny in the company.

Does this create unique management challenges for you?

Yes, in part because I wear many hats. As a designer, I have to have the last word on design issues, just like our lead programmer has to have the final word on programming issues, and our producer has the final say on any timetable or project management issues. In a way, being the lead designer conflicts with my mission as the CEO to empower the employees. But I think the team understands the situation. For example, if we have two opposing views on a design issue or some bigger thing, they cede decision making to me as the final arbiter.

How would you characterize the Finnish game industry?

We help each other out within the Finnish game industry. Maybe it's because Finland is such a small country and historically there have been so few game companies, so everybody knows each other in the industry. Companies are really open with each other about how they do things, sharing their sales figures and information about their distribution channels. I recently talked to two other CEOs from two other Finnish mobile game companies about how much we're making on the Windows phone platform and how we're doing it.

Maybe the best example of how close-knit the Finnish game industry is comes from our last game. At launch, the game had some unforeseen server stability issues. It was a really bad situation during the first week. I sent an email to Supercell's Ilkka Paananen explaining the problem. He immediately got their lead server architect to contact us and our programmers via email. I also contacted the CEO of another Finnish game company, Grand Cru. I knew that they had a server architect who could really help us, and I asked if they could send him from Helsinki to Kotka to help us out. The CEO of Grand Cru, Markus Pasula, was kind enough to put him up in a hotel in Kotka for a week to help us out, even though Grand Cru had projects that needed his attention. Normally, companies within the same industry view each other as competitors. Here in Finland, though, they even share their employees when needed.

How has game development in Finland changed over the course of your career?

I think it's gotten easier to work in places other than Helsinki. Finland is a small country, and 25% of the population lives in the greater Helsinki area. So, historically, everything has tended to gravitate to Helsinki—advertising, newspapers, game developers, and so on. Twenty years ago there were just a couple of game development companies in the whole country. Now there are more than a hundred companies with 2500 employees. The big companies (e.g., Rovio, Supercell) are still in Helsinki, but the mobile game boom has allowed things to spread out a bit. We're in Kotka, for example, and there are a number of small, indie game developers all around Finland.

Given the collaborative nature of the Finnish game industry, what is the general policy regarding non-disclosure/non-defamation agreements, non-compete clauses, and other legal mechanisms designed to protect intellectual property (among other things)?

It's not a usual thing to do or have in Finland. In the US, you can make it really hard for an employee to take a job with another company. You can't really do that legally in Finland. I know of one Finnish company that has really strict non-disclosure agreements (NDAs) for their employees, but I think that company is trying to manage its employees through fear. That doesn't go with the flat organization and empowering environment many companies here try to create. We don't have NDAs for our employees, and we don't have separate sanction fees for the sharing of company business or trade secrets. It goes to the basic legislation in the country that if an employee does something harmful to your company, you have certain legal rights. Of course, people can pretty much do whatever they want, but I'm not the one to force strict contracts on them; that would breed mistrust in my employees. So generally, Finnish companies don't tend to use NDAs. That said, the game industry is an international business, and when we partner with companies from other countries, we do have NDAs to contend with.

What does the larger European game development community look like from your vantage point?

One thing to note is the difference between salaries. In the old Eastern Bloc countries like Poland, Hungary, and Serbia, for example, you have much lower salaries than what you have in Nordic countries or in the UK. If you want to outsource something, it's usually a lot cheaper to get it done from one of these countries than from the UK or Germany. I think that some of the Eastern European countries are even cheaper than India, which used to be the place to go for cheap game development labor. Things have really changed in India, though. For the price of outsourcing there now you can almost hire a person in Finland. Anyway, I think the cost differential in Europe can be polarizing in the sense that you have cheap labor countries and more expensive labor countries. And this isn't exclusive to the game industry. There's a huge disparity in average net salaries in European Union countries. For example, in Poland the average net salary is less than one-third of what it is in Finland.

Do these kinds of issues create challenges as you try to grow your company?

To some degree, yes. I'd really like to expand the company here in Kotka, my hometown. That could be hard because finding eight to ten new people willing to relocate to a town with a population of only 55,000 isn't going to be easy. Given that I'd want to have two separate teams and not one big team, it could be a viable option to have the second team located in Helsinki or even in the UK or Germany. If the teams are separate and they're doing their own games, then they don't have to be in the same physical location necessarily. Then again, I'm not sure that we'd be able to effectively implement our company's work environment, ethics, and way of doing things if we had remote teams.

What part of your job is most professionally rewarding? Why?

At heart, I'm a game designer. Even though I'm a CEO, game design is mainly my responsibility in the company. Designing games—be it specific mechanics, characters, stories, missions, or something else—is a creative process that I enjoy immensely. Often it's the problematic areas of design that give me the most satisfaction: thinking through a difficult challenge and then finding the perfect solution is inherently satisfying. I've also noticed that, at least for me, problem solving through teamwork is more rewarding than working alone. It also brings the team together when people feel they're making a difference and having a say about things.

What are the most significant internal challenges you face in your job?

Time constraints. As a creative process, design needs time; you can't force an idea or solution on a challenge. This is especially troublesome as my other role as CEO has to come first on many occasions. At the same time, I have to get parts of the design ready or else some team members can't proceed with their own tasks. For example, if programmers don't have a design for the workings and rules of a specific mechanic, or a user interface artist needs to know what actions are present in which screens in order to construct the UI, this can create a lot of stress and that's not good for the creative process. It can result in a nasty spiral.

What are the external challenges you face in your job?

Perhaps the most significant ones are macro-level challenges, such as changing legislation. For example, the European Union recently changed the laws regarding refunds on mobile games. The Children's Online Privacy Protection Act also affects the industry as a whole. Naturally, these are issues I can't affect in the least, so it's more about monitoring them and trying to prepare for possible compulsory changes beforehand.

What sorts of workplace changes would you implement if given the opportunity?

Putting some money and time into our office furniture and interior design. As a small company, those are areas we haven't really paid that much attention to. Then again, work culture and social aspects are what really matter, and those are issues I've paid a lot of attention to. When I founded Kukouri, I wanted to do things differently. I wanted to create a workplace that I'd like to work in. I believe that work culture has an immense impact on people's well-being, not to mention on the business side of things.

As I've mentioned, we have a very flat corporate structure. As CEO, I keep the whole team informed on management-level matters. Every employee always knows why we're doing what we're doing and what their role is in the bigger picture. At Kukouri, people are given a lot of freedom and responsibility. There's no micromanagement. Everyone has a say on things like game design, if they want to. Work hours are flexible, and people can work from home at least one day a week.

We're a small company, so perhaps that makes this type of flexible work culture easier for us to implement than a much larger company, where individual teams might have twenty, forty, or even more people.

How is the work you do in the game industry different from the work you have done elsewhere?

In many ways, the game industry is very informal. I think this has to do with the relatively young age of the industry, and also the fact that games are creative products. Even at industry conventions such as Game Connection or the Game Developers Conference, you see many more people wearing T-shirts and hoodies than business suits.

For creative positions and some management positions (e.g., graphic artist, gameplay programmer, game designer, producer, etc.), the game industry is often the place where these people have been eager to get into, and it's their dream job. This shows in their passion for their work. In other areas, like business development, marketing, and strategic operations, you often have people who aren't necessarily enthusiastic about games. The vice president of sales in some big company may have come from some other industry altogether, and to him games are just numbers. A game, a cigarette, a bar of soap—they're all just products to him.

Which companies or ways of working (both within and outside of the game industry) do you look to for inspiration?

Supercell has a very similar work culture to ours. Indeed, many other Finnish game companies seem to share the same orientation toward an informal and flat organization, especially mobile game developers.

On the other side of the coin, there are ways of doing business that are to be avoided. The "EA spouse" incident is quite famous and instructive on what not to do. More recently and maybe the worst example of them all was from *L.A. Noire* developer Team Bondi. Also Konami's practices are instructive on what not to do. Some people, usually in management positions, are eager to tell their employees that crunch and overtime are just part of making games, and that if you want to work in the industry, then you have to put up with both. That's just bullshit. Crunch and overtime are most often the result of bad management and project planning, likely caused by the same people who tell you that crunch and overtime are just part of making games.

Making people work overtime constantly isn't just immoral, it's also stupid and counterproductive. Overtime rapidly starts decreasing people's problem-solving skills, alertness, and creativity, all of which you need in many game development disciplines: programming, design, testing, art, and so forth. In addition, working people too hard is a sure way to damage office morale, and that can have very negative effects over the long term.

What are the challenges facing the industry over the next decade?

In mobile games, the race to zero in the pricing of products has given birth to free-to-play. Free-to-play is now the dominant business model, and there's no going back. This severely limits what kind of gameplay choices developers have. We've been trying to come up with a new game concept for our next big project for some time now. We had several concepts that we were confident we could make into good games, but forcing them into free-to-play proved impossible, so we abandoned them. It's frustrating. Increasingly, it's not about making a good game but about making a good platform for microtransactions (i.e., in-app purchases).

There's also the extreme polarization in revenues, which means that the majority of developers never recoup their development costs. In other words, the current mobile games industry is not a sustainable model for most. To make matters worse for small developers, user acquisition costs have gotten out of hand. Advertising your game in Facebook or other social media or inside other games is getting increasingly expensive. The average cost per download is several dollars, and if your game's LTV is less than that then there are no grounds for spending money to get more users, and your game is basically dead on arrival. If you can't afford to advertise your game, it'll be invisible, no matter how good it is. The App Store and Google Play get thousands of new games every week, and most of those games get negligible numbers of downloads because they're all but unknown to consumers.

This has already led to the consolidation of markets because only big companies have millions to spend on user acquisition. On PC and console platforms, it's both the huge development and huge marketing costs that are the source of market consolidation. With mobile, it's the huge user acquisition costs. So the causes differ a bit, but the result is the same.

From a broader perspective, free-to-play is going to seep into PC and consoles too. This will create challenges for Microsoft and Sony and also big traditional publishers. Nintendo has to really reinvent itself soon if it wants to stay in the race. The Wii and Wii U have been poor decisions, and Nintendo's handhelds have taken a big blow from the rise of mobile games.

What is the relationship of free-to-play games and the mobile space?

As I mentioned, a lot of people are talking about a race to zero in mobile games. In the beginning, I think Apple imagined that games in the App Store would sell in the price range of ten dollars or so. But then they introduced lower pricing tiers. As the competition got fiercer and fiercer in the App Store and in the mobile space generally, companies started making lower-priced games to get people to buy them. It was just a matter of time before developers began to abandon even the lowest-price tier of ninety-nine cents to offer their games for free. In 2011, when we were doing our first game, the race to zero wasn't that apparent. Two years later, though, it was clear that the free-to-play strategy was going to dominate the industry. Supercell, King Digital Entertainment, and others are as big as they are today because they were skilled and lucky, but also because they saw free-to-play before anyone realized what was happening.

What are your goals at Kukouri?

One thing that's setting boundaries for us as a company is that mobile games are getting bigger and bigger all the time. Just the other day, I was looking at some of the games that were around when I started the company in 2011 and they were really small compared to what we have now in mobile games. The teams are getting bigger and the production values are getting better, and there's a lot of consolidation in the market. If you want to be around as an indie, you have to find a way to compete with the big guys. You have to grow, and that's something that I'd like to do. I want to continue to use a small team model, though. This means having multiple teams. A bigger headcount, even with the people divided on multiple teams, means needing support roles such as project managers.

Another emerging role in mobile, especially in a larger-sized company, is the data analyst. Everything is pretty much getting to be data driven in mobile. It's all about user repetition, which drives the marketing we do in mobile. This is a really specialized area. The person doing this work is not going to come from the team members on the development side. Data analysts are specialized support people, and an essential part of our growth plan.

Given your many responsibilities at Kukouri, what does your day-to-day workflow look like?

It's really hands-on. We have an open office floor plan, but I have an office with a door so I can have some privacy when I'm on the phone. Mostly, though, I move around the team. I probably sat next to our art director four times today and maybe spent the same amount of time with our 3D animator. We're in pre-production for our next game, and I wanted their opinions on some design decisions I'm thinking about.

For my personal workflow, it's kind of chaotic at times, which can be stressful. I try to be as organized as possible, but it gets tricky sometimes when you have so many things you have to do all at once. I try to reserve time when we're in pre-production—I have to do a lot more design then. For example, last fall, when we were finishing our previous game, I tried to reserve two days a week for design only. The reality is that a lot of my time goes to processing email.

Right now, because we're looking for an investor, my time is spent discussing investment opportunities with people. So, to answer your question, I think my workflow depends on what stage of production we're in. During some stages, I don't have to be that involved in the day-to-day making of the game. But at other times, as a designer I have to be very involved with the process. During those times, I don't have as much room to be the CEO and manage the team.

How would you describe the workflow in your company?

Sometimes well organized, sometimes not. As a default, we use our own light version of Agile/Scrum. Sometimes we forgo that and go into kind of an ad hoc mode. That means not making extensive lists of tasks to be completed and then organizing them for weekly and monthly sprints, but rather just diving right into whatever it is that needs to get done first. Things get done faster this way, but if it continues for too long then negative effects start to surface (e.g., people not knowing what others are doing, testing being overlooked, etc.). That's why we try to stick with a more organized model, which still is very light compared to models used by many other companies.

How does the workflow differ when working on different types of games (e.g., different genres, AAA versus casual games, etc.)?

Not that much, actually. I think the workflow stems from the scope of the project. Our games have always been large for mobile games and have up to fourteen months of development time. In this way, they're more akin to the average PC title rather than a mobile game. At the same time, as a small company, we're able to quickly change direction or check our estimations if need be. I don't have experience with real AAA titles that have teams with hundreds of people in them, though. I can only imagine that; what I've heard is that at that level, organizing and project management is very important.

Your games are available through a variety of distribution services (e.g., Steam, App Store, Google Play, etc.). What role do these services play in your business model?

To be frank, Steam hasn't been all that successful for us. We wanted to try it out when we made our first game for iOS and Android. We use the *Unity 3D* engine for our games, which is what most people in mobile use. *Unity* makes it relatively easy to port mobile games to PC. We partnered with a Dutch publisher—Iceberg Interactive—for the PC version of our first game. I think one of the main reasons it didn't go that well was pricing. When the PC version of the game came out on Steam, the mobile game was already free, and the price tag for the PC version was $9.99. The PC gamers were outraged: "Hey, they're trying to rip us off! This game is free on iOS and they're trying to charge us ten bucks!" This kind of thing isn't unique to us; it happens all the time with mobile and PC games because mobile games are so cheap and often even free to play. People don't really like to pay for them on consoles or PC. We actually have a PlayStation version of that game as well, and its sales have been better.

It should be noted that the PC version of the game was basically the same as the mobile version, but we were able to improve the graphics a lot because PCs have greater CPU power. Unfortunately, people tend to think of PC versions as just mobile game ports, and they already have their attitude set when they know it's a mobile game coming to PC. I think consumers didn't realize that we'd done a lot of work to upgrade the game's graphics because we knew we'd get complaints that we didn't do anything for the PC version and just slammed it onto Steam.

How do you deal with issues of community development and management?

Previously, our marketing manager—who I mentioned was with us for only a year and half—handled those tasks for us. Now it's mostly done by our art director. For *Tiny Troopers: Alliance*—which is a much more socially oriented game than its predecessors—we have an active forum that we manage. We also arranged to have the publisher take care of the Facebook page and handle the conversations and user posts on that side. But that community development and management is also something that really needs a dedicated person. If we're going to grow and hire a second development team, a community manager would be one of the support roles I'd like to see be part of that expansion.

What are some of your notable quality of life issues, both routine and exceptional?

In my current position and company, the big thing is stress. The stress comes mainly from two sources: time management and responsibility. In a small company, working as both CEO and lead designer can often create time issues where normal hours are not nearly enough to do everything I need to do. This, in turn, can lead to me neglecting my family, which in turn leads to feelings of guilt. None of this is good for things like sleep, eating well, having free time, exercising, and so on.

Even though Kukouri has a flat organizational structure, as CEO I'm the one ultimately responsible for everything. My decisions affect the company's future, our employees and their families, and my own family's future.

The same issues apply to the exceptional category as well—time management and responsibility—especially when the stress they cause peaks near the launch of a new game.

What are some of your notable career progression issues?

Getting promoted isn't really an issue: I'm not only CEO and lead designer, I'm also a shareholder and member of the board. The time issues I mentioned above mean that I have no time to study to improve my skills. Granted, one learns a lot from doing, but on a personal level it would be nice to be able to learn by taking time to study as well.

What are the industrial issues driving your business decisions?

I think the mobile games market is really polarized. You have companies making millions of dollars every day, and developers releasing games that make no money at all. For most developers, it's not a sustainable business. One problem is that there are no middle-tier developers. There's not room for them. Either you make it really big or you don't make it at all. As a result, there are lots of companies struggling or dying out. You don't read about those in the press. You only hear about the Cinderella stories: the few companies that are making tons of money. That's not the reality for 99% of the developers in mobile.

We've been really lucky so far with the success we've had and somehow we've found success in the middle tier that hardly exists. You can't build a long-term strategy in mobile focused around being a small developer. If you do, you risk your next game not making any money—and then you're in big trouble. A few misses in a row and you're quickly out of business. I see that many times a year in Finland.

What is your survival strategy?

To hire a second team and also make bigger games. We need to become a medium-sized fish at least, before all the little fishes become extinct. That's the survival strategy in mobile.

How does that strategy square with the collaborative nature of the Finnish game industry?

If I help someone out, that doesn't necessarily mean that I hurt myself as a result. Their success doesn't take away from our success (unless, of course, they poach my employees). Also, game development is a small industry in Finland, and a small community. If we help each other out, then when you're in need (e.g., if your company goes under) and if you've been nice to others, you're going to land a job with another company. But if you're not a nice person or don't help others, then they're not going to help you out when you need it.

For example—and this is a big company we're talking about here—Rovio laid off more than a hundred people last year, including a twenty-person studio in Tampere. When the director of the Tampere studio heard about the impending layoffs, he immediately started planning his own company. The directors at Rovio gave him permission to start planning the company during the time he was still a Rovio employee. He also hired everybody from the Rovio Tampere team. Rovio let them stay in the office and gave them all of the office furniture, going above and beyond what they would have needed to do for the employees.

As someone who grew up at the same pace as gaming culture through the 1970s, '80s, and '90s, I have a dream job. I consider myself very fortunate in that sense. I know that for many people, their day job is something they loathe more than love—I've been there myself. Game development isn't easy, however. It's serious business. Survival isn't guaranteed for small indie companies; quite the opposite, in fact. It's hard work, but work I love and have the privilege of doing with a great team in a country considered the leader for mobile games.

Cameron Rogers
Legal

Cameron Rogers is the founder and principal attorney at Cam Rogers Legal. Previously he worked as in-house counsel at Guesswork Television (a division of the Token Group) and as an attorney at Marshalls and Dent. He has also worked in the film industry, and served as an executive producer on *The Infinite Man*. He holds a bachelor of laws and legal practice from Flinders University, and was a University of Melbourne Centre for Media and Communication Law "New Voices in Media Law" finalist in 2010. His shipped titles include the *Gamebook Adventures* series, *Automation, Pac-Man 256, Shooty Skies, Crossy Road*, and the *Train Conductor* series.

* * * * *

How did you come to work in games?

I've had a varied career since I graduated from university. I studied film and always figured that I'd work in the industry as a producer. The first job I got was with an organization called the South Australian Film Corporation (SAFC), which is designed to fund the local film and television industries. The SAFC runs all kinds of programs related to film development: programs for writers and emerging directors, short and feature film programs, and so forth. They also did a bit of digital media stuff back when I worked for them in 2004, but I worked as a project coordinator and their digital media support was still in its infancy.

Once I got into my career a bit more, I was offered a job at Marshalls and Dent, which is a mid-tier law firm in Melbourne with a longstanding media practice. One of the people I worked for was Bryce Menzies, whose reputation looms large in the Australian film industry. He's been the executive producer on dozens of films.

At Marshalls and Dent, I quickly realized that if I was going to bring any new clients into the firm it wasn't going to be in the area of film, because everybody already knew Bryce. So I started turning my attention to other areas of entertainment. I'd had an interest in games growing up, and they were an area in which the firm didn't practice, despite having a large entertainment division. It seemed like an area of growth, and an obvious step for me to explore professionally. The timing was quite good because a lot of independent game studios were starting to pop up in Australia. I just sort of followed people on Twitter, walked around, introduced myself, and wound up acting as independent legal counsel for quite a large number of them.

It wasn't enough to sustain me at the beginning, though, so I got a job at a television production company and worked there for two years until my law practice was at a point where I felt that I could do it exclusively. I've been going strong ever since, and I'm pretty happy with the way my practice operates. I see the law as fundamentally a service industry. It's not about me or my firm at all, really; it's about how we can help the client. To that end, I see flexibility, timing, and transparency as key issues. I'm interested in anything that'll destigmatize the law and lawyers.

I also find that as a principal in my own law practice, I'm able to balance work life and home life pretty well. With a young family, that's important. The industry itself is a lot of fun, too. It's the right combination of art, technology, and commerce for me, and my clients don't take themselves too seriously, which seems to be a global thing. Certainly my professional colleagues in the US and Europe have a similar outlook.

At present, I'm the only law practice in Australia that manages games clients as a priority. With the growth of games internationally and e-sports taking off, though, I don't think it'll remain that way for long.

Was the work you did in film and television similar to what you do now in games?

I was the legal business affairs manager at Token. It's quite a large company by Australian standards, and handles talent management, television production, and event management, with a strong emphasis on comedy. I was pretty much working exclusively in television production. As the business affairs manager, my role was to work with and advise the television producers. It was something of a mini executive producer role, I suppose, and I'd work out the contracts. The producers would come to me and say they needed to engage person X for a specific role, and I'd put the contract

together, get it all happening, and manage the process. I was also responsible for negotiating with the network on behalf of the producers in relation
to rights management and that kind of thing. While I was doing that, I was
also building my games practice on the side, so it was a very busy period.

I have an entrepreneurial streak, and I was never going to be happy working
in a firm where the work was just handed to me. In a sense, I like to own the
relationships I have, and games were a place where I felt that I could do that.
As a result, I've become the professional I am because of the way I actively
pursued these new clients. There was no mandate from Marshalls and Dent,
but they were certainly happy for me to do it. I still have a good relationship
with them, and especially with Bryce, the senior partner there. I speak to
him all the time, and in fact there's a strange parallel between his career and
mine: when he was starting out in the late 1970s, the film industry was a lot
like what the games industry is now; there had been a few hits but it wasn't
really considered a proper industry.

I learned a lot from Bryce about practicing as a lawyer. In essence, he taught
me that you don't have to pretend to be anyone you're not to develop and
maintain professional relationships in the law. I don't generally wear a suit—
I think my clients would freak out if they saw me wearing one. The things
I look for in clients who inspire me are professionalism, lateral thinking,
and honesty. They're the values I learned from Bryce, and what I now pride
myself on. There are a lot of game companies with similar values, and therefore the game industry is a good fit for me.

To return to the question about the similarities among film, television, and
games for someone like me, I'll note that I'm a qualified solicitor, and I practice accordingly. That said, the way I tend to market myself is as someone
who handles business affairs and legal services, not unlike what I did for
Token. Of course, it's a bit different with games because my clients are often
a little green when it comes to matters of the law. The game industry is
on the young side generally, and as a result, its people are pretty inexperienced (though the lack of experience is generally made up for by boundless
enthusiasm). I often have to do a lot of things other lawyers wouldn't, such
as explain the difference between a lawyer and an accountant. I tend to be
presented with problems that aren't strictly legal problems; people come to
me wanting business advice, and since I have experience in both business
affairs and legal services, I can help clients more broadly than many other
solicitors. The business affairs side of things speaks to a more strategic role,

whereas the legal services aspect speaks to the purely legal role. One important thing I took from my time at Token is the ability to help people make strategic decisions. You have to think through the implications of a given solution in order to future-proof the client, and this is particularly true in games, where new platforms emerge regularly.

The good thing about my time at both the SAFC and Token was that I got a deep understanding of how the entertainment industry operates generally, in terms of what makes a good film proposal and what funding bodies look for. You know the old adage: "Fund the team, not the project." It was a good way for me to see how the industry operated, and I was working closely with many different producers. Most of the people who worked at the SAFC were very qualified and had produced feature films—I was rubbing shoulders with some interesting people. In that sense, I learned a lot about how to make a creative project go. I find the professional skills I learned there are directly transferable to the games industry.

I've not only worked with funding bodies and on the in-house legal side, I've also spent time as a production lawyer and I've produced films myself. I've had something of a 360-degree experience in film, and I think my game expertise stems in part from that. Games started as an area of interest, and somewhere along the line it all clicked into place. Now I'm in a position where I understand the business side of game development and distribution as much as the legal side.

How do the film and video game industries in Australia compare?

It's interesting because film has a long and fairly celebrated tradition in Australia going back to the growth period of the 1970s, when a lot of Australian films were highly regarded internationally. There's still quite a strong industry here, albeit one that's largely propped up by the federal government and the various state-based funding bodies (e.g., the SAFC). The government wants to support film as part of the nation's cultural output. They see it as important that we have Australian stories on screen. Also, when you invest in a film, a lot of the money ends up being spent on people on the ground. Feature films typically employ thirty to forty people for ten to twelve weeks, and thus the money the government invests is a cash injection into the economy.

When you look at games, the federal government currently believes that they don't have the same type of "cultural" impact as film. In Australia, games are seen as a lesser art form or industry, and that's reflected in the way they're funded. This is extremely shortsighted and unfortunate. I'd like to see some federal support for games in the form of grants, location-based offsets, and tax benefits so that Australia could again get a work-for-hire industry happening. Work-for-hire creates opportunities for developers to learn and hone skills. Unfortunately, there's a chronic lack of such opportunities for international studios looking to get work made here, as well as a lack of funding opportunities for local game developers looking to develop their own IP. Film Victoria is now the only funding organization in the country that supports game development and distribution.

This hasn't always been the case. The federal government set up a twenty million dollar game development fund through Screen Australia in 2012. Everybody around Australia was excited—it's what we'd been wanting for a long time, a meaningful infusion of cash into the game industry. It was going to set up all of these indie studios that had been operating with two or three people and give them a leg up so that they could grow. Unfortunately, a new government came in and pulled the rug out. The whole funding mechanism disappeared. I think this indicates how games are perceived in this county, as more of a hobby or a pastime rather than an industry to be supported as part of the national identity. The crazy thing is that the games they did invest in during that short window actually made money and were well received.

Of course, I don't want to see work-for-hire for non-Australian companies develop at the expense of developing our own IP here at home, but I think it's a good space for people to perfect their skills and get used to working in a team environment. It is easy to learn and get better when you work at a big studio because there are more clearly defined roles and you know the hierarchy. It helps if you like work-for-hire or the structure of the company is set up in such a way that you know it's built for success and can scale up.

Indie companies, on the other hand, tend to be just small groups of people (often friends) working together. They're not all that well-equipped when the game goes big to be able to manage that success, so some experience in a larger company doing work-for-hire stuff would be helpful. It'd give these kinds of developers experience in running a games business, like reporting to senior management, or knowledge of what a delivery manager does. They could learn how a project moves from concept through to delivery, as well as the different roles employees can have. I think these are really important and useful things to learn in the game industry. But again, I certainly wouldn't want to see it happen at the expense of people's original ideas. That's why if you've got a twenty-year-old kid just emerging out of university who has the talent to be a developer, then it'd probably be a good idea for her to work at a larger company just to get some time under her belt, plying her trade and learning the ropes.

The US is buying about $1.36 Australian at the moment, so I think we're not far off from seeing work-for-hire happen in Australia again. It'll soon become a much more attractive proposition to American publishers. Prior to 2007, the Australian industry went too far in the wrong direction. You had a handful of large studios with 150–200 workers or more. Blue Tongue Entertainment maybe had even 300 people working for it, and Krome Studios had even more. That, in my opinion, was probably too big; it has to be a happy medium. There have to be the indies, and there have to be some larger developers who are doing the bigger titles as well. Ideally, it would be a mix.

What is the full range of services you provide as a game lawyer?

Because I'm based in Melbourne, I work with a government funding body called Film Victoria, which supports the game industry as well as the film industry. Film Victoria prides itself on its involvement in games. That's part of the reason Melbourne is a bit of a hotspot for games—there's a funding mechanism there to help people with their projects. The money is typically provided as a grant, but in order to be able to apply for it, Film Victoria requires what's known as a "solicitor's opinion letter," which is where I come in. The solicitor is responsible for making sure that the copyright is in order. For me to be able to issue that opinion, I have to have looked through all the underlying rights and make sure the applicant—the game developer—has the rights they need to make the game. Obviously, Film Victoria is a government body; it's not in the business of funding projects that can't make it to market. And so, they basically put the legal obligation on game developers to prove they have the rights they say they have.

One of the main services I perform for developers, therefore, is to look at the underlying rights and make sure everything is in place. That's what's known as reviewing "the chain of title." If there are gaps, I need to work out the best way to fix them. As a solicitor, you're looking at all of the people who've contributed to the game up until the Film Victoria application is submitted, even if those contributions are only on paper. The game might just be an idea at the point of completing the funding application, or it could be in alpha and the developers are looking for finishing money. In the latter case, you have to make sure the music agreements are in place, the coders' agreements are in place, the artists' agreements are in place—essentially, you need an agreement for everyone who has contributed or is going to contribute to the game. In that respect, I'm fundamentally a contract lawyer and an intellectual property lawyer.

That said, I also help set up game companies as corporate entities, which I do in collaboration with Luke Henry from LDB Accountants. Essentially, when clients want to establish a company, Luke will set up the structure and I'll draft the shareholders' agreement, which governs the relationship between the shareholders and our client.

Beyond corporate setup and copyright, I also provide services related to the day-to-day management of companies. These services might include drafting independent contractor or employee agreements, or they might be something else that the developers need as part of what they do. In this case, I'm acting as an industry lawyer, meaning that anything that winds up in front of the client I can assist with (e.g., publisher and merchandising agreements, joint venture agreements, product placement deals, non-disclosure agreements, and even retail leases occasionally). In addition, sometimes my clients decide they want to invest part of their revenue in other game companies, so I handle the due process side of things there.

If I feel I don't have the capacity or understanding to address a particular problem, I've got a professional network of people I can draw on to assist me. For example, if a client comes to me with an unusual question about corporation law, I'll manage that problem for them by finding the person best able to answer it, engage that expert, obtain the advice, and then transmit it to the client in lay terms. In cases like this, I'm functioning in a legal management capacity.

I offer plenty of services for more established developers, as well. For example, when you're dealing with a large company that's notoriously protective of its intellectual property (e.g., Namco, Sony, or Disney), it can turn into a David and Goliath type of scenario. In situations like these, I try to retain rights on behalf of my client and to not throw the proverbial baby out with the bathwater. This means a lot of mining the contract details to make sure the contracts are as balanced as they can be. Clients are often so thrilled to be working with such well-known brands that they'll sign anything. I'm there to explain the implications of what they're agreeing to, and to get them to think carefully.

In terms of big Australian studios, they don't really exist anymore. Before 2006–7, pretty much every established studio here had 100+ employees, and there was much more work-for-hire for American publishers. That's no longer the case. It's a very fragmented scene here now, and the majority of my clients are small studios who run things pretty lean. A lot of the time my work is just about helping them get their games to market.

Things are starting to change a bit, though, because there have been quite a few recent successes here (e.g., *Crossy Road*, *Shooty Skies*, *Land Sliders*). The types of questions I'm being asked now are less about the production side of things and have more to do with either the distribution side or with the secondary monetization of intellectual property.

How does the international nature of video games impact your job?

I've got a network of lawyers that I can draw on internationally should the need arise. There's Ryan P. Morrison in New York, for example, and Jas Purewal in the UK. I've actually got a client at the moment who's based in Australia but his business partner is located in Florida, which made setting up their company a bit challenging. The immediate question for them involved deciding where to set up the company. One guy is in America, one guy is in Australia, so where's the IP held? If you aren't careful with something like this, you can run into double taxation issues.

When there's cross-jurisdiction on issues, things get problematic, but that's not exclusive to the games industry. There's strong precedent in other areas of law, which I can draw from. Energy construction, for example, has a lot of cross-jurisdictional things that happen, such as an Indian company setting up in Australia, or an American company setting up in South Africa. In terms of resolving cross-jurisdictional problems, I don't always have to look to games for the answers.

How often are you required to go to court on behalf of your clients?

Hardly ever—once in 2015, for example—and it's usually in relation to things like a bad debt where someone hasn't paid what they owe for services rendered.

This isn't to say that there aren't disputes. There are plenty, but they generally always get settled, because nobody really takes intellectual property matters to court here unless it's a really big issue. IP matters are expensive to resolve and notoriously difficult to win, and people typically opt to settle.

One of my clients is Hipster Whale, and their *Crossy Road* game has been extremely successful and spawned hundreds of clones and copies. Early on, that bothered my client, but they quickly realized that in games the climate shifts so rapidly that you're better off focusing your attention on being first to market with a cool idea and really doing it well rather than looking over your shoulder to see who's copying you. I think the whole idea of chasing down people who are copying what you're doing is a bit of a red herring, and it distracts you from the real name of the game: being innovative, interesting, and accessible. Early on in a company, you often see concern about copyright infringement, but as more people get into the industry and become senior practitioners, that's not something that bothers them very much.

Of course, by all means protect your rights. If somebody is infringing on your copyright, then close them down. Where that seems to come up more is in the area of merchandising. If somebody starts selling fake *Crossy Road* T-shirts or something, we'll definitely close that down because that's a violation and a misrepresentation. The people who are buying that merchandise might actually believe they're buying authentic Hipster Whale *Crossy Road* stuff. But in terms of the actual gameplay, all games borrow from the games that came before them. You look at a game that's been successful, and you might borrow the style or technique, and there's no copyright on those elements.

As an attorney, do you get caught up in the experience of crunch time?

Yes, and I think it's the same in the film industry. For a lawyer, it's really busy right at the beginning of a project and then the people go away and do the creative stuff. They make their game or their film and just before it gets distributed there's a mad flurry on the legal side again. Generally, the first flurry is around the financing side, so you provide the client with the documents they need, be they independent contractor's agreements, composer agreements, or whatever's necessary to get the game made. And then the client gets into game development mode and that's where they're the happiest. That's the business they know: getting the game made. Just before the game is released, there's another flurry when the client tries to make sure that everything is in place. That might be when people start thinking, "Maybe we should get a trademark in relation to this stuff." Or they might want to get a better understanding of the scope of the game, some idea of how successful it might be, how much money they've got, and what's next.

What does your service process look like for new clients?

Well, that depends on who they are and where they're at. If it's someone who's coming with a game idea, the first thing I ask is who did (or is doing) the programming and the art. Then I ask how the idea came about. A client might say, "We were at a game jam and we all worked on it together." So then I have to ask who ran the game jam, and I'll want to look at the contract in relation to the jam. Some jams take a rights interest in any games that are created as a part of the event. Basically, I begin by cross-examining the client to get the nuts and bolts of who actually contributed to the game. I need to find out what documents might be in place that would affect the rights position. For example, if you're a university student in Australia, the copyright of what you create as part of your studies is owned by the university. So if a client comes to me with that kind of game, I have to get a rights assignment from the university from the very beginning in order for the rights to be handed over to the client.

Asking after issues that might impact the rights positions generally takes some time because the client thinks they have the answers: They say, "It's just so and so, so and so, and me." But you have to leave it for a little while, then revisit it. Eventually, it suddenly emerges: "Oh, that's right, so and so contributed to the game three months ago, when it was just an idea." That's a problem, of course, as I then need to get some sort of rights assignment from that person.

After working through the rights assignment, I try to sort out what kind of structure the client is looking to set up. I also need to know how serious the client is on a practical level, because it's all well and good for three guys fresh out of university to say they want to start a company together and start working on games. But once you set up a company and you're a shareholder, it can be difficult to extricate yourself from that situation. So, I need to gauge how committed clients are, and I generally put some hard questions to them about their intentions. Again, this isn't really law, but I think good lawyers always try to think about what the client is trying to achieve, rather than simply answering their questions. You have to try to preempt problems.

Once we're all on the same page, we just start moving through the establishment of the company, working with the accountant and getting things set up. Sometimes the platform the client intends to develop for changes the questions I ask, but not necessarily at the very beginning. Further down the track is when it'd be more likely to come up. If you're creating a game for mobile and you're just going to be publishing on iOS, that's different than if you're going to be releasing the game on Xbox or PlayStation. Obviously, if you're dealing with the PlayStation, you've got to have the Sony PlayStation agreement in place, and you need to talk through that document and what it means.

Depending on how things are funded—for example, if a game has gone through the development process with Sony—there are different obligations and hold backs, but the rights issue is always the most important. The more you deal with the way a game is going to be released and distributed, the more the peculiarities associated with those actions emerge.

I have clients who make car-racing games, for example, and some who make digital books. The types of questions I ask just in relation to the nature of each of these projects are different. On the one hand, you've got writers agreements and book options, and on the other hand you've got 3D artists agreements and even real-world racetrack licensing arrangements. There's a very broad scope in terms of what's expected of me to be able to advise on, and so the nature of the game and how it's distributed will always impact the types of questions I ask.

Where do intellectual property protection mechanisms (e.g., non-disclosure agreements) come into play?

It depends on the nature of the property you're trying to protect. If you've got one company that's looking to sell and another company looking to buy, there's obviously certain financial business affairs information that's going to come into possession by the purchaser. That's critical information and needs to be protected. In that circumstance, I'm all for NDAs flying in all directions, as long as they're mutual and both parties are on the same page and aware of the obligations.

However, if every time you're looking to hire somebody into your company and you produce an NDA just to find out their skill set, that's a bit more of a paranoid position to take. I know that in the US you guys are big on

NDAs, probably more so than we are in Australia. There's definitely a place for them, but the timing and nature of the work would dictate whether or not they're useful. I wouldn't advise my clients to issue an NDA unless they knew they were going to be divulging something critical (e.g., technology, an idea, etc.). If two companies are thinking of working together on a joint venture, where one is going to buy another one, for example, then confidentiality provisions are critical. But anything short of that would have to be determined on a case-by-case basis.

The other thing about NDAs is that you've got to be careful to make sure the terms are substantially similar across the company, or you can find yourself in a situation where it's too difficult to keep track of what your obligations are with respect to any kind of knowledge that might come into your possession. For example, if your NDA always says that the confidentiality period is two years, then as long as you're always working within that time frame there's little danger of forgetting, because it's always a two-year deal. But if you start signing other people's NDAs and the terms are slightly different, then you're in a position where you've got to manage those documents. Knowledge has to be compartmentalized so that you know when and how it can be released. You can run into problems from a business management point of view. If you have four or five people working for you with NDAs in relation to ten different companies and the time frames don't match up, then it's hard to know when and how you can disclose information to anyone. Add third-party contractors to the mix, and who knows what information anyone has and what they're supposed to do with it. On top of this, you can paint yourself into a corner if you start issuing too many NDAs and worrying too much about what's being said.

If you're talking about indie developers just working on their own titles and doing no work-for-hire, then NDAs don't really come into the equation because the developers own the company and they keep their information to themselves. They're not dealing with any third parties, and therefore there's no need to issue that kind of agreement. Now having said that, in all of the independent contractors' agreements I draw up, there are always confidentiality provisions contained therein. These cover the non-disclosure requirements without necessarily being part of a stand-alone NDA. But, it also depends on who the client is working for. I've got a number of clients who've done work for Disney, and Disney's NDA is pages long. The different types and means of disclosure are covered in a number of different ways, and they really try to lock that stuff down. So, it really depends on who you're contracting with.

One issue I face in relation to individual developers is when an artist is engaged by a games company as an artist. Under Australian and American law, if you're an employee, the copyright of what you create is automatically owned by your employer. But if you're an artist, you might be working on art at home for yourself. You've got to be really careful in that situation about what work is considered work for your boss, and what work is considered your own. And that's often an area where I've got to try to introduce that idea into the contract so that the client doesn't wind up inadvertently having all of the work they've created outside of their job being assigned to their employer. In this industry, work outside of the workplace is quite common because it's an industry of passion. You often see artists, in particular, who make things on their own time, and then their employer tries to claim it.

This type of stuff comes up quite often because game companies often have events on Friday afternoons where everyone's drinking beers and shooting the breeze about game ideas and such. I know that some of the more successful games in Australia have benefited from this sort of thing: developers just literally sitting around having a conversation on a Friday afternoon. I believe *Fruit Ninja* came up that way. As long as it's being done in the context of what the company is asking you to do, then it's fine that those ideas then become the property of the company. But if it's not your intention, and it's something that's happening after-hours among your friends, you've got to be careful that those ideas don't get used when you go back to work or get lost to you when you're done working at that company. It's about everybody being clear, and my hope is that it's helpful just for me to explain to my clients that under Australian law you're an employee and you've got to be careful about where and when you do your own work. Don't bring work materials home and start using them to create your own stuff, and don't start doing your own things at work and expect that to be okay. You've got to be smarter about the way you operate.

I try to protect my clients by putting an acknowledgment in the agreement from the employer saying that the client is an artist by trade and that any art created by that person doesn't automatically mean that work will be owned by the employer. You have to specify if it's done between the hours of 9:00 a.m. and 5:00 p.m. with company materials in relation to the project the employee has been hired to work on—that kind of work will automatically be owned. But if it's done independently, on the artist's own time and without any kind of reference to their paid work as an employee, then that creative output should remain their own.

▶ DISCUSSION

There are a number of different themes in this set of interviews, but notably they are united in how they reveal the extent to which the game industry is fueled by (if not founded on) stress. Every job has its anxieties and fatigue, of course: challenging colleagues, anxiety-producing financial decisions, and so on. Judging by these interviews with business insiders, however— people who understand in the most practical terms how the game industry operates—to be in games is to submit to workplace practices predicated on constant elevated professional and personal torque and tension.

As Clinnick notes, for example, the game industry has developed such that there is now considerable pressure on independent developers to be multi-skilled. They must not only have a primary area of expertise (e.g., programming), but also secondary and tertiary areas in which they can operate competently (e.g., business, sound). As educators, we wonder where such polymathic abilities are to be developed beyond the crucible of the job itself. As industry scholars, we are obliged to inquire after the implications of this pressure on an industry that has long been structured on highly specialized job classes. Not coincidentally, the workplace stress caused by the necessity of multiskilling has also contributed to the rise of what media scholar John C. Caldwell terms "para-industries." Differentiated from meta-texts (texts that refer to other texts) and para-texts (texts that supplement other texts), para-industries are "the ubiquitous industrial, cultural and corporate fields that surround, buffer and complicate any access to what we traditionally regard as our primary objects of media research" (721).

In the case of the video game industry, one broad para-industry that has emerged is comprised of service providers like Clinnick and Rogers, who offer training, legal assistance, and contract services to developers of all types. What makes these para-industries is not simply that their primary functions are the completion of labor invented elsewhere (e.g., texture generation, platform porting, chain of title reviews, etc.), but that this extended labor exists in a simultaneously symbiotic and critical relationship to the central industry. Whether in law, finance, or public relations, para-industrial laborers work both in and outside the industry, often framing themselves as having left the industry's caustic environs for kinder, gentler locales that ultimately prove to be absolutely interwoven with (and subject to) the pleasures and acerbities of the industry they serve.

Video game para-industries, in other words, share with their core industry many of the same endemic problems. Clinnick, for instance, discusses the connection between crunch time and gender diversity in the workplace, suggesting that if the game workforce were more diverse in terms of gender and family unit construction—and less driven by what she describes as "affluent, educated, single men" who consider working long hours a badge of honor—crunch might not be so common. Yet, in many cases, gender diversity is as problematic in the para-industries as in the core industry, which suggests that despite the separation of extended services from core work, phenomena like crunch remain not only exhausting in terms of human potential and attitude, but also continue to yield products, experiences, and workplaces that are as fraught with problematic gender, race, and labor issues as the embattled core industry itself.

While it is unsurprising in certain ways that para-industries ideologically mirror the game industry they support, in other ways para-industries seem poised to become the thin end of a transformational wedge. Of particular relevance here is the unavoidable result of the organizational dissociation (i.e., outsourcing/contract work) now common in the game industry, namely that efforts to keep lines of communication open and clear throughout the far-flung development process must be redoubled if the quality of work is to be high. When work that was once in-house is outsourced, the challenge of keeping projects moving forward consistently and with mutually understood objectives, timings, and aesthetics suddenly requires a heightened level of clear communication among teams and individuals. The interviews here reveal this new emphasis on communication in the many ways that the specter of ignorance—and its elimination—are addressed by various stakeholders.

For example, several of our interviewees discuss the challenge of educating developers about key aspects of their own industry, from the importance and methods of marketing, to the deleterious communication breakdowns that can occur when (for instance) the technical and artistic development teams within a studio are allowed to coexist in a culture of mutually grudging acceptance. Similarly, there seems to be a perpetually unhealthy relationship between marketing/PR and the development side of the industry, wherein marketing is often viewed on a continuum that ranges from "necessary evil" to "the dark side." All too frequently, our interviewees suggest, the service para-industry becomes responsible for promoting its own value to the core industry, despite the fact that part of the reason various elements of the industry are spun off is because the core industry cannot consistently support these vital services internally. A strange dynamic emerges in such cases: as game development studios pare down to become leaner and more agile, much of the institutional knowledge about the areas that were cut is lost. When studios later contract for these outside services (e.g., marketing and legal), the consultants necessarily end up educating developers about the work they do and justifying their fee structures and recommendations— an inefficient and frustrating business model to be sure. As Clinnick puts it: "Agencies make money off . . . people not knowing what they don't know."

It is perhaps just such frustrations—as well as the potential for cost savings— that drives many developers to skip over outsourcing altogether, choosing instead to do the work themselves. As our interviewees suggest, however, this often leads to a host of poor decisions that ultimately negatively impact the success of the product and studio alike. While consultants in the service para-industry generally recognize that their expertise does not guarantee success in the marketplace, they acknowledge that game developers are increasingly challenged to be expert in a multitude of business disciplines in order to turn a profit in the game industry. The response of para-industries is, it seems to us, reasonable; they encourage clients to recognize the risk they are already taking by being in an industry that is increasingly driven by business models that somehow must create value out of products that are expensive to produce and yet cheap (or free) in the marketplace. Video game para-industries also aim to "future-proof" clients by teaching them how to think about game development systemically as well as technically and creatively. There seems to be traction in this approach, particularly as developers begin to see the products they are creating not just as ends in and of themselves, but also as ends to the next game to be produced, to good work/life balance for all employees, and to overall job satisfaction.

Arguably, this drive to create and embed community support within the industry is a sign that the industry generally is becoming aware of the problems created by disconnected and intensely competitive environments. In fact, several of the interviews highlight the generous and cooperative aspects of the game industry, particularly on the independent side of the equation.

This is echoed by other interviews in the book, and appears to partly con-travene the prevalence of legal mechanisms designed to protect intellectual property and maintain market competitiveness (e.g., non-disclosure agree-ments). A sizable portion of the industry clearly aims to create and foster collaboration and equity, not only within individual studios but even across rival companies. This creates an interesting dynamic of competition and community that not only shapes labor practices (e.g., hiring and firing as noticeably network-based) but also the products of this labor (i.e., games).

This situation echoes a number of related observations made by the inter-viewees about why good development teams go bad. Soares, for example, suggests that most crunch events are avoidable, emerging not out of an endemic quality of game development but out of "bad management and project planning." Similarly, Rogers discusses how the industry, in its zeal to protect (and capitalize) its intellectual property, has created an impossible labor situation in which artists are unable to produce work that is entirely their own—no matter when or where they created it. This is one of several important problems created by non-disclosure agreements and their ilk: they protect property often at the expense of the people who create it.

Legal issues also influence games through public policy—a fact underscored by Rogers, who discusses the legal profession as a service industry—which, in turn, shapes the business of game development in a number of tangible ways. For example, Frisch recounts that it was precisely the German legal and social sentiment about privacy protection that dissuaded his company from incor-porating a third-party data collection application in its most recent game, despite the fact that the data from such an application would be invaluable to business operations.[1] The granularity of this effect—the conscious and specific design decision shaped by domestic public policy—surprises us, particularly in light of the globalized nature of the game market in which commercial suc-cess is often determined by transnational consumption. Here is a moment in which local policy is intruding on a business model that is anything but local.

On the fiscal side, in addition to the usual financial challenges companies of all sizes face, developers who receive state-derived funding encumber addi-tional and idiosyncratic obligations that can directly impact their business operations. According to Frisch, projects supported by the German govern-ment, for example, make international partnerships difficult if not impos-sible, essentially ensuring that companies receiving such funding cannot grow beyond the national border. Pursuing state support thus represents a significant decision for game companies, not only in terms of corporate growth but also of the labor involved in this growth.

In response to such idiosyncratic financing factors, the industry is awash in strategies—we are tempted to say schemes—for optimizing the development, rollout, and support of games, from banking a small reserve of cash to ensure that new projects can be supported while revenues from earlier projects are fading, to running Kickstarter campaigns, to quantifying everything about a game's development, distribution, and consumption processes. Examples of this last strategy include calculating the LTV of the average player, the cost of acquiring a single new user, and the return on investment for game development on virtually every conceivable game platform: computers, dedicated consoles, and mobile devices, of course, but also cash registers, wearables, car dashboards, airplane screens, hotel cable systems, and dozens of other unique and unexpected locations for game content. So common are these and related assessments that game companies are increasingly hiring (or contracting with) data analysts who specialize in quantifying the smallest details of the industry in hopes that in aggregate their analyses will reveal possible leverage points in the market. Perhaps the most interesting facet of the drive to measure one's way to wealth is that it is often attended by language (and sometimes actual milestones) that reveals a kind of mystified faith in win-states in the game industry itself: selling a million units, striking up the perfect collaboration with a colleague after work, or opening one's own studio, for example. According to our interviews, these and other calculations or calculated risks suggest just how data driven the industry has become: even its fantasies are numerically rationalized.

The epitome of this phenomenon is the treadmill sometimes created among contract companies. Many of the interviews in this book, but especially those in the business discipline, describe the importance, dynamism, and implications of contract labor. Contingency is not the exception but the rule in games today, which piqued our curiosity about the short- and long-term implications of this labor model. What the interviews revealed is that it is now common for independent studios founded on the dream of creating innovative new games to turn to the provision of contract services for other entities in order pay the bills during lean times. With rare exceptions, however, the game industry largely exists in a constant state of scarcity, which means that ambitious and visionary studios frequently get caught in the grind of doing nothing but (not infrequently poorly paid) contract work, a kind of digital-age wage slavery. Despite some indicators that the game industry is becoming self-aware about the ubiquity of its exploitative practices, at least as many trends (including the fact that the interviewees in this chapter refer to the necessity of "good luck" for professional success) indicate that game development may well reach a point in the not-too-distant future in which the majority of its labor will be contingent, and this contingency will be inescapable.

Also striking is how the effects of the free-to-play model of development and distribution are impacting game design and business broadly. Not only are developers having to design to that model in order to stay afloat (see Soares), but the model is also causing consolidation in the market because only the largest companies have the resources for the user acquisition and promotion essential to success in the free-to-play sphere. Developers are thus being squeezed from both ends, despite the general democratization of the development process accompanying the emergence of new technologies and distribution platforms. In other words, developers are being forced to design games around microtransactions and advertising, and yet cannot afford to operate in such an environment—even though many of the technical and financial barriers associated with game development have dropped dramatically in recent years.

The gradual—or perhaps occasional—industry-level self-reflection that our interviewees repeatedly suggest is taking place seems to be leading to a variety of positive changes for the industry in terms of work/life balance, intercorporate collaboration, fairer contracts for artists and other creative talent, an increasingly diverse workforce, and more opportunities to experiment with a range of positions and levels of personal and financial investment. At the same time, competition everywhere in the industry—including Scandinavia, where an esprit de corps exists alongside an industry as precarious there as it is anywhere else in the world—suggests that, from a global perspective, the game industry and its para-industries are likely to get worse in terms of labor before they get better. Avoiding such a stifling set of working conditions may well prove to be the most important "business" for the game industry to address today.

▶ NOTE

1   Soares recounts a similar friction between European developers and US publishers, with legal/cultural differences manifesting themselves in the business realm.

▶ WORKS CITED

Bibliography

Caldwell, John C. "Para-Industry, Shadow Academy." *Cultural Studies* 28.4 (2014): 720–40. Print.

Covey, Stephen R. *The 7 Habits of Highly Effective People: Powerful Lessons in Personal Change.* New York: Simon & Schuster, 2013. Print.

"Transitions: Gamasutra Salary Survey 2014." *Gamasutra: The Art & Business of Making Games.* UBM Tech. 22 Jul. 2014. 1–8. Web. 10 Oct. 2015. <http://www.gamesetwatch.com/2014/09/05/GAMA14_ACG_SalarySurvey_F.pdf>

Filmography

The Infinite Man. Dir. Hugh Sullivan. Hedone Productions, 2014. Film.

Gameography

Assassin's Creed. Ubisoft Montreal. Ubisoft, 2007. Multiple platforms.

Automation. Camshaft Software. 2015. Personal computer.

Bonza National Geographic. Minimega. Minimega, 2015. Multiple platforms.

Commander: Conquest of the Americas. Nitro Games. Nitro Games, 2010. Personal computer.

Crossy Road. Hipster Whale. Hipster Whale, 2014. Multiple platforms.

East India Company. Nitro Games. Nitro Games, 2009. Personal computer.

Fruit Ninja. Halfbrick Studios. Halfbrick Studios, 2010. Multiple platforms.

Game of Peace. State Museum for Art and Culture of Muenster/Studio Fizbin. Studio Fizbin, 2014. Museum installation.

Gamebook Adventures (franchise). Tin Man Games. Tin Man Games, 2010–present. Multiple platforms.

The Inner World. Studio Fizbin/Headup Games. Studio Fizbin, 2013. Multiple platforms.

L.A. Noire. Team Bondi. Rockstar Games/Take-Two Interactive, 2011. Multiple platforms.

Land Sliders. Prettygreat. Prettygreat, 2015. Multiple platforms.

Monsterrific. Kukouri Mobile Entertainment. Kukouri Mobile Entertainment, 2015. iOS.

Mori. Element 105. Element 105, 2015. iOS.

Opera Maker. Filmtank/Studio Fizbin. Studio Fizbin, 2015. Multiple platforms.

Pac-Man 256. Hipster-Sprockets. Bandai Namco, 2015. Multiple platforms.

Read Only Memories. MidBoss. MidBoss, 2015. Multiple platforms.

Rogue Singularity. Considerable Content. Considerable Content, 2016. Personal computer.

The Secret of Monkey Island. LucasArts. LucasArts, 1990. Multiple platforms.

Shooty Skies. Mighty Games. Mighty Games, 2015. Multiple platforms.

Tiny Troopers. Kukouri Mobile Entertainment. Kukouri Mobile Entertainment, 2012. Multiple platforms.

Tiny Troopers 2: Special Ops. Kukouri Mobile Entertainment. Chillingo, 2013. iOS.

Tiny Troopers: Alliance. Kukouri Mobile Entertainment. Chillingo, 2014. iOS.

Tiny Troopers: Joint Ops. Kukouri Mobile Entertainment/Wired Productions. Sony, 2014. Multiple platforms.

Train Conductor (franchise). Voxel Agents. Voxel Agents, 2009–2014. Multiple platforms.

The Walking Dead. Telltale Games. Telltale Games, 2012. Multiple platforms.

Woody Two-Legs: Attack of the Zombie Pirates. Nitro Games. Nitro Games, 2010. Personal computer.

Softography

App Annie (https://www.appannie.com)

Google Calendar (https://www.google.com/calendar)

Google Docs (https://www.google.com/docs)

Trello (https://trello.com)

Conclusion

We began this book with the tongue-in-cheek comparison of the video game industry to a hot dog factory, its clockworks concealed to keep consumers from seeing its nonpareils and grotesqueries alike. The unseen beauties of the game industry, of course, are readily imaginable: sweeping creative license, a laid-back workplace culture, and the potential for independent wealth. From the outside, the game industry seems as if it is literally playing at work.

The game industry can indeed be delectable. Consider the pleasure with which music supervisor Jared Emerson-Johnson characterizes his work in Chapter Six, and the ease with which he brushes off invoicing, debt collection, and other unpleasant tasks: "I don't especially love it, but I also don't mind it much—it's expected, part of the job." Or recall the pervasive "passion" that marketing and public relations consultant Lauren Clinnick invokes, a descriptor that perfuses many of the interviews in this book. The video game industry is overfull with employees enamored with and fulfilled by the creativity and collaboration of the development process.

That said, the interviews here also suggest that such workplace libertarianism is hardly the rule. Interviewees celebrate their flexible arrival and departure times, modest parental leave allowances, and the occasional boss-made meal, to be sure. Far more common and strongly voiced themes include, however, the sickening "death march" of crunch time (John Alvarado), the industry's nauseating chauvinism (Carolyn VanEseltine), and the objectionably low pay scale (Jacek Tuschewski). Game development can be a nasty business, truly, grinding up even the most talented and committed people and their ideals.

Of course, game industry work is defined by more than just delectation and disgust. More important—and ultimately the central clarification of this book—is that the game industry is largely defined by paradoxes and contradictions. There is the paradox of meticulous planning in the face of inevitable unpredictability that designer Andrew Rubino describes, the peripatetic nature of game careers that artist Victoria Sarkissian discusses, the pain/pleasure nexus of interdisciplinary communication outlined by Charles Babb, and more—all of which point to the same thing: working in the video game industry is at least as challenging as any other hybrid corporate/manufacturing job (e.g., software engineering or the academy) where capitalism's imperative to do more with less yields all manner of strange stick/carrot configurations.

On its own, the fact that a twenty-first-century industry is, at the global scale, highly motivated to cut costs in order to maximize profits is hardly surprising. What is remarkable is that the unconscionably mundane manifestations of this globalized context—exploited labor here and (far worse) abroad, union-busting tactics, minimal health and retirement benefits, discrimination of every stripe—are so well hidden. We talk to people nearly every day who want advice about how to break into the game industry, and as we noted in the Introduction, bookstore shelves are lined with volumes aimed at providing just such assistance; the occasional unfavorable story about video game violence or misogyny barely makes a dent in the protective shell that surrounds the industry.

Such resilience, it seems to us, is largely bolstered by two key factors, both of which operate in their own paradoxical ways to shield the industry from significant industrial transformation. The first factor is the industry's deep association with youth culture. On the one hand, the industry's connection to game playing—and thus to children and youth—suggests that oversight of the industry must be robust; children, after all, are a vulnerable and precious population. And indeed, industry oversight is pervasive and calculated, largely through the ESRB rating system and its various international equivalents. A conspicuous absence from almost all of the interviews, however, is any mention of children and youth as a key demographic of games, even by employees working at studios that primarily produce games for young people. Carolyn VanEseltine (quality assurance) and Tobias Frisch (sales/finance) are the sole exceptions, the former discussing the role of QA in meeting ESRB review criteria and the latter noting that government funding is more easily obtained if a studio's games are child-friendly. These are hardly commanding concerns about the well-being of youth, speaking more to the industry's highest priority: efficiently navigating the legal and financial channels that will get products to market as quickly and painlessly as possible.

This paradox—the youth-oriented game industry is only tangentially interested in young people per se—suggests to us that the video game industry actually benefits when the public focus stays on its products rather than its process. When journalists and watchdog groups concentrate on monitoring what games depict instead of how games are made, the industry's shadowy labor practices are tacitly accepted while industrially controlled game content is placed in the attention-absorbing media spotlight. In other words, every time the public is served up a story about the latest malignancy in a particular game, it is simultaneously being distracted from an array of far more real and consequential operations being deployed in real life.

The second factor that contributes to the industry's slowness to enact meaningful improvement in working conditions has to do with the various legal protections—non-disclosure, non-compete, and non-defamation agreements, among others—executed in most of the major global game development hubs. On the surface, such contracts protect a studio's intellectual property, effectively ensuring that the corporate owner—and presumably that company's employees—can continue to prosper as a result of the resources (including human labor) that have been invested in that IP. Paradoxically, however, it is precisely these agreements that make it exceedingly risky for an employee—present or past—to divulge unseemly workplace practices. In many instances, we suspect, it would be short work for a corporate attorney to quell with extreme prejudice the divulgence of such company secrets. Even if it were not, it became clear to us as we negotiated approvals for the interviews in this book that all but the most cavalier (or legally trained) employees feared the worst that could come from violating an NDA or other such employment contract. In this way, the legal documents that nominally protect studios of all sizes from IP theft simultaneously and collectively protect the industry itself from having its labor practices revealed, critiqued, and changed.

These two factors are among many that account for how the video game industry has slowed the pace of improved labor relations within itself. This book is merely one pass at these questions of game industry work, a pass made, moreover, largely from a single (if transdisciplinary) perspective. True, the critical analyses herein draw on approaches from political economy, critical/cultural media theory, rhetorics of technology, and insider experience, but there are many other ways of seeing and doing industry inquiry. We hope that readers will be inspired to conduct additional and more sustained studies of the game industry's infrastructures, cultures, and ideologies. We can easily imagine, for instance, that ethnographies, critical discourse analyses, systematic literature reviews, and other approaches that are, by definition, well suited to unpacking the human condition are already under way, and we look forward to becoming familiar with them. If games themselves are to be deeply understood, so too must the industrial and corporeal processes that produce them.

The same can be said for the market structures governing these processes. Again, the macro-level picture is well drawn. The game market is organized geographically, with most software production and consumption headquartered in a handful of regions—North America, Europe, Australia, and Japan—and most hardware production is located elsewhere (Nichols; Brookey). Accordingly, a smattering of companies earns the majority of the available revenue, and these companies are principally involved in software publishing and hardware manufacture. Despite developments in specialized national markets and localized play practices—thanks in part to new distribution platforms, increased high-speed Internet penetration, and various economic incentives and disincentives—the global game industry remains largely as it has been for many years: undiffused.

It is here where ground-level studies of game labor can be especially helpful, delineating as they do the agents and processes that give shape to industry structures. Macro-level schemata of game development typically describe a monadic model of production consisting of dedicated pre-production, production, and publication periods spread out over the course of a year or more and done by teams ranging in size from a single designer working on a passion project to hundreds of specialists collaborating on a AAA title. When seen through the eyes of developers, though, game production appears considerably more heterogeneous and dynamic. For one thing, a game's intended distribution platform can radically change a studio's development time frame, division of labor, and production process. Games produced for mobile operating systems or social networks, for example, often require relatively short production times but demand continued attention and updating long after release. In contrast, console projects tend to carry fairly fixed schedules geared toward getting a game to market in time for major shopping events or theatrical releases. This type of game development also requires approved access to specialized (and expensive) hardware and software development kits, all but relegating small and independent game makers to the mobile, social, and PC platforms rather than the big-money consoles.

Second, company size impacts development style, labor practices, and overall budget. Smaller companies often rely on workers to provide a range of skills, while larger companies tend to emphasize job specialization. Similarly, because smaller companies have smaller gross profit potential and concomitant profit margins, their production models often center on rapid release schedules and lithe development practices. Larger companies can opt to effect similar systems, though this is far from a given because such companies are better able to withstand market fluctuations. Larger companies are also better positioned to take advantage of globalized production conditions, such as the availability of high-quality work-for-hire contractors and contract houses. Moreover, the legal demands for employees at larger companies tend to be more substantial than in other development sectors. Employees at these companies are often required to agree to a range of legal restrictions such as non-compete agreements and non-disclosure contracts upon both hiring and firing, the subtle but industrially substantial side effects of which we note above.

Third, while macro-level diagrams of the game industry would seem to point to a sharp dividing line between mainstream and independent development, the interviews in this book portray a remarkably interconnected world where professional networks cut across production style and size. These networks are important for finding contract labor for tasks throughout the entire game development process—as well as for rallying support in times of crisis—and are formed and maintained through game jams, professional interest groups, and the cultivation of clustered areas of production within a particular city or region. They are also vital for the "permanent" labor force, which nearly all of our interviewees pointed out is only as permanent as the last paid project milestone. In an industry where changing workplaces happens almost annually, it is virtually unavoidable that developers in all disciplines will work in studios of various sizes throughout their careers, and in no particular order of size: small-medium-large, large-small-medium, medium-medium-small, and so on. Consequently, workers who remain in the industry for a decade or more tend to have an exceptionally wide range of employment experiences to draw from, as well as an equally diverse Rolodex to consult when necessary. The point is not that there are real labor and methodological differences between mainstream and independent development, but rather that these differences do not necessarily prevent workers within the industry from crossing back and forth between them in order to stay employed.

Finally, the ties between games and other creative industries constellate around specific types of labor as much as around the cross-pollination of intellectual property and visual effects. While a number of these ties have been detailed elsewhere—programming, visual effects, and intellectual property are the chief articulations between film and games, for example (Brookey)—the interviews in this book depict a number of other crucial overlaps, including legal, marketing, and sound/music design. Because of these overlaps, there has been an emergence of specialist contractors geared toward working with the gamut of present-day creative industries (including video games), as well as of new possibilities for industrial convergence. As of this writing, such innovations are materializing particularly strongly in the virtual and augmented reality sectors, with both new and ported games appearing on virtual reality and augmented reality platforms ranging from the cheapest cardboard contraptions to the priciest immersive theaters. Regardless of platform, however, specialist skill sets different from those necessary to create 2D presentational experiences are increasingly required to enter and compete in these new and growing markets. Time will tell if new labor practices will attend—or merely be attenuated by—the evolving hard and soft development skills of such so-called presence-based gaming innovations.

Clearly for us, studying labor is an essential part of coming to understand the video game medium and its cultures, including its scholarly cultures. Labor—more than technology and desire—is where games originate. And labor—more than play at times—is the gravity well of game meaning. To borrow and pervert Ian Bogost's famous adaptation of a chemical engineering term, labor is *the* unit operation, *the* site of action within the video game industry. Studying labor has a wonderfully practical side as well, namely helping the game industry to imagine alternatives to its seemingly intractable human resource problems (e.g., diversity, crunch, sustainable workforce management, and so on).

We conclude this book, then, with an invitation to our colleagues in the academy, in the industry, and in the journalistic arts. Help us continue to build connections among our spheres of influence so that the people who play games may be better understood by the craftspeople who create them, and—more pressingly—so that these craftspeople may be better understood and cared for by those of us who are captivated—personally or professionally—by the products of their labor.

▶ WORKS CITED

Bogost, Ian. *Unit Operations: An Approach to Videogame Criticism.* Cambridge: MIT Press, 2008. Print.

Brookey, Robert Alan. *Hollywood Gamers: Digital Convergence in the Film and Video Game Industries.* Bloomington: Indiana University Press, 2010. Print.

Nichols, Randy. "Who Plays, Who Pays? Mapping Video Game Production and Consumption Globally." *Gaming Globally: Production, Play, and Place.* Ed. Nina B. Huntemann and Ben Aslinger. New York: Palgrave Macmillan, 2013. 19–39. Print.

Index